FOUNDATIONS OF ECONOMETRICS

ADVANCED TEXTBOOKS IN ECONOMICS

VOLUME 7

Editors:

C. J. BLISS

M. D. INTRILIGATOR

1976

NORTH-HOLLAND PUBLISHING COMPANY
AMSTERDAM · OXFORD

AMERICAN ELSEVIER PUBLISHING CO., INC.
NEW YORK

FOUNDATIONS OF ECONOMETRICS

ALBERT MADANSKY

Graduate School of Business
University of Chicago

1976

NORTH-HOLLAND PUBLISHING COMPANY
AMSTERDAM · OXFORD

AMERICAN ELSEVIER PUBLISHING CO., INC.
NEW YORK

North-Holland ISBN for this series: 0 7204 3600 1
North-Holland ISBN for this volume: 0 7204 3607 9 (cloth-bound)
North-Holland ISBN for this volume: 0 7204 3806 3 (paperback)
American Elsevier ISBN: 0 444 10906 4 (cloth-bound)
American Elsevier ISBN: 0 444 10943 9 (paperback)

Library of Congress Cataloging in Publication Data

Madansky, Albert, 1934–
Foundations of econometrics.

(Advanced textbooks in economics; v. 7)
An outgrowth of a one-year graduate course in econometrics that the author taught at UCLA in 1962–65 and at Yale in 1972–73.
Includes bibliographies.
1. Econometrics. I. Title.
HB139.M33 330'.01'82 75-25610
ISBN 0-444-10906-4 (Elsevier)

PUBLISHERS:
NORTH-HOLLAND PUBLISHING COMPANY–AMSTERDAM
NORTH-HOLLAND PUBLISHING COMPANY, LTD.–OXFORD

SOLE DISTRIBUTORS FOR THE U.S.A. AND CANADA:
AMERICAN ELSEVIER PUBLISHING COMPANY, INC.
52 VANDERBILT AVENUE, NEW YORK, N.Y. 10017

PRINTED IN THE NETHERLANDS

Preface

This book is an outgrowth of a one-year graduate course in econometrics that I taught at UCLA in 1962–65 and again at Yale in 1972–73. Though in principle it is designed for students with no substantial background in linear algebra, statistics, or econometrics, in practice the book should be used as a second course in econometrics, for those students who are not content with learning econometric practice and wish to understand the underlying basis for the techniques taught in a modern first course in econometrics.

Much of the material in this book was at the frontier of research in econometrics in 1962. Today this material is more commonplace among econometricians, though scattered through the book are some insights and unifying themes which I have not yet seen in the econometric literature. There are many more topics in econometrics which could have been covered, e.g., spectral analysis, exact sampling distributions of simultaneous equations estimates, and Bayesian econometrics, but the topics and level of treatment in this book will amply fill a one-year graduate course.

The reader should be forewarned that I am a bit idiosyncratic in my notation. In chapter IV, I invent a new notation for simultaneous equation models which, though imperfect, is of greater mnemonic value than that of the two current sets of notation for such models. I also use lower case letters to denote scalar variables, upper case letters to denote matrix variables, regular type to denote non-random variables, and bold-face type to denote random variables. Thus we can look at a symbol and know whether or not it is a matrix and whether or not it is random. (No longer need we write X for a random variable and x for its value, equations like $X = x$, and no longer will we be confused about what symbols to use for a random matrix and its value.) At the blackboard one can easily denote randomness by using the printer's symbol ~ under the letter to indicate randomness, e.g., what appears in this book as $\boldsymbol{u}$ would be written at the blackboard as $\underset{\sim}{u}$.

Finally, I would like to acknowledge my debts to my teachers and my students. The influence especially of courses taught by Ingram Olkin and William H. Kruskal on the material in this book will be apparent to them. My students, especially those of my 1972–73 Yale class, helped greatly by finding errors, rooting out the unteachable, and asking stimulating questions. I also gratefully acknowledge the encouragement of my UCLA colleagues Karl Brunner, Jack Hirshleifer, and Michael Intriligator to write up my lectures as a text and the stimulating influence of the Cowles Foundation which gave me the impetus to complete this book.

December, 1974 ALBERT MADANSKY

Contents

I

Matrix theory

The presentation of the small portion of matrix theory to which you will be exposed in this chapter begins (section 1) with an admittedly unmotivated presentation of the elementary formal operations with matrices. Our aim in the beginning is merely to acquaint you with matrices, and get you as used to manipulating them as you are to manipulating real numbers arithmetically. We follow this introduction with the theory of linear transformations in n-dimensional Euclidean vector spaces (section 2) and then (section 3) motivate the elementary operations with matrices by interpreting a matrix as a representation of a linear transformation on such a space.

Next (section 4), we examine a special linear transformation, the projection transformation, which will be used many times over in our description of econometric methods. In section 5, we introduce in a motivated fashion that object familiar to you from college algebra days (though never motivated for you then), the determinant. We get back to matrices in section 6, in which we study properties of a special type of matrix, the symmetric matrix. In section 7, we introduce the generalized inverse, a concept which will be found quite useful in expediting our presentation of some aspects of both parameter estimation and hypothesis testing in econometric models. Finally, in section 8, we present the Dwyer–MacPhail notation so helpful in computing derivatives of functions of matrices.

If you have already studied matrix theory, you would still be well advised not to ignore this chapter. You may still find novel things in this chapter, derivations if not facts. If you insist on ignoring this chapter, let me at least warn you now of an idiosyncracy of this book. *All vectors are row vectors.* I do this for two reasons, ease of typography and consistency with the standard practice of describing points of the plane (i.e., vectors in Euclidean 2-space) by their Cartesian coordinates as (x, y).

The price I will pay for this in later chapters is that standard econometric models will at a superficial glance look a bit different from the way they appear elsewhere. Be assured that this is only superficial. (And besides, the hope is that, having read this book, you will have minimal need to look elsewhere.)

1. Matrix operations

The rectangular m by n array of real numbers,

$$A = \begin{bmatrix} a_{11} & a_{12} \cdots a_{1n} \\ a_{21} & a_{22} \cdots a_{2n} \\ & \vdots \\ a_{m1} & a_{m2} \quad a_{mn} \end{bmatrix},$$

will be called an $m \times n$ (read "m by n") *matrix*. The *order* of the matrix is the pair of numbers (m, n), where m, the first member of the pair, is the number of rows and n, the second member of the pair, is the number of columns of the matrix. The number a_{ij}, the element in the ith row and the jth column of the matrix A, will be called the (i, j)th *coordinate* of A. A description of all the a_{ij}, for $i = 1, \ldots, m$, $j = 1, \ldots, n$, is thus a description of the matrix A, and vice versa. We will sometimes, for ease of expression, say "A is the $m \times n$ matrix of a_{ij}'s"; what we mean by this is that A is the $m \times n$ matrix whose (i, j)th coordinate is a_{ij}, for $i = 1, \ldots, m$, $j = 1, \ldots, n$. All matrices will be denoted by upper case Latin letters, and their coordinates by the corresponding lower case Latin letters.

Two matrices A and B of the same order are said to be *equal* if $a_{ij} = b_{ij}$ for all i and j. Equality of matrices is defined only for matrices of like order.

Given an $m \times n$ matrix A, we denote by A' the $n \times m$ matrix obtained from A by defining its (i, j)th coordinate a'_{ij} as a_{ji}. The matrix A' is called *A-transpose.* Note that the rows of A are now the columns of A'.

Exercise: Show that $(A')' = A$.

If A is an $m \times n$ matrix with (i, j)th coordinate a_{ij} and B is an $m \times n$

matrix with (i, j)th coordinate b_{ij}, then we define the *matrix sum of* A and B, $A + B$, as the $m \times n$ matrix with (i, j)th coordinate $a_{ij} + b_{ij}$. Notice that the matrix sum is defined only for matrices of the same order.

Exercise: Check that the following hold if A, B, and C are $m \times n$ matrices:

$$A + B = B + A,$$
$$(A + B) + C = A + (B + C),$$
$$(A + B)' = A' + B'.$$

Suppose A is an $m \times n$ matrix and B is a $p \times q$ matrix. We define the *Kronecker product* of A and B, $A \otimes B$, as the $mp \times nq$ matrix,

$$\begin{bmatrix}
a_{11}b_{11} & a_{11}b_{12} \cdots a_{11}b_{1q} & a_{12}b_{11} & a_{12}b_{12} \cdots a_{12}b_{1q} & \cdots a_{1n}b_{1q} \\
a_{11}b_{21} & a_{11}b_{22} \cdots a_{11}b_{2q} & a_{12}b_{21} & a_{12}b_{22} \cdots a_{12}b_{2q} & \cdots a_{1n}b_{2q} \\
\cdot & & & & \\
\cdot & & & & \\
\cdot & & & & \\
a_{11}b_{p1} & a_{11}b_{p2} \cdots a_{11}b_{pq} & a_{12}b_{p1} & a_{12}b_{p2} \cdots a_{12}b_{pq} & \cdots a_{1n}b_{pq} \\
a_{21}b_{11} & a_{21}b_{12} \cdots a_{21}b_{1q} & a_{22}b_{11} & a_{22}b_{12} \cdots a_{22}b_{1q} & \cdots a_{2n}b_{1q} \\
\cdot & & & & \\
\cdot & & & & \\
\cdot & & & & \\
a_{21}b_{p1} & a_{21}b_{p2} \cdots a_{21}b_{pq} & a_{22}b_{p1} & a_{22}b_{p2} \cdots a_{22}b_{pq} & \cdots a_{2n}b_{pq} \\
\cdot & & & & \\
\cdot & & & & \\
\cdot & & & & \\
a_{m1}b_{11} & a_{m1}b_{12} \cdots a_{m1}b_{1q} & a_{m2}b_{11} & a_{m2}b_{12} \cdots a_{m2}b_{1q} & \cdots a_{mn}b_{1q} \\
\cdot & & & & \\
\cdot & & & & \\
\cdot & & & & \\
a_{m1}b_{p1} & a_{m1}b_{pq} \cdots a_{mn}b_{pq} & a_{m2}b_{p1} & a_{m2}b_{p2} \cdots a_{m2}b_{pq} & \cdots a_{mn}b_{pq}
\end{bmatrix}.$$

Notice that even when $mp = nq$, $A \otimes B$ need not equal $B \otimes A$.

When A is a 1×1 matrix (i.e., $A = a$, a being a real number) it is usual to suppress the symbol "$\otimes$" in $A \otimes B$ and write the Kronecker product of A and B as aB. We call this the *scalar multiple* of a and B.

Exercise: Check that the following hold if c and d are real numbers and A and B are $m \times n$ matrices:

$$\begin{aligned}(c+d)A &= cA + dA,\\ c(dA) &= (cd)A,\\ (cA)' &= cA',\\ c(A+B) &= cA + cB.\end{aligned}$$

With the operation of scalar multiple defined, the Kronecker product of A and B described above can be expressed more succinctly as

$$A \otimes B = \begin{bmatrix} a_{11}B & a_{12}B & \cdots & a_{1n}B \\ a_{21}B & a_{22}B & \cdots & a_{2n}B \\ \cdot & & & \\ \cdot & & & \\ \cdot & & & \\ a_{m1}B & a_{m2}B & \cdots & a_{mn}B \end{bmatrix}.$$

Aided by the scalar multiple operation, the definition of *matrix difference* of A and B, $A - B$ is quite easy. Like the matrix sum, the matrix difference is only defined for matrices of the same order, and is given by $A - B = A + (-1)B$.

If A is an $m \times n$ matrix and B is an $n \times p$ matrix, then we define the *matrix product* of A and B, AB, as the $m \times p$ matrix whose (i, j)th coordinate is given by

$$\sum_{k=1}^{n} a_{ik} b_{kj}.$$

Notice that the matrix product is defined only for matrices such that the first member of the product has as many columns as the second member has rows. Thus, though AB is defined, BA is not defined except when $m = p$.

Exercise: (1) Check that, provided that the matrix products given below are defined, the following hold:

$$\begin{aligned}(AB)C &= A(BC),\\ A(cB) &= c(AB), \qquad \text{where } c \text{ is a real number},\\ A(B+C) &= AB + AC,\\ (A+B)C &= AC + BC,\\ (AB)' &= B'A'.\end{aligned}$$

(2) Let

$$A = \begin{bmatrix} 1 & 6 & -2 \\ 4 & 0 & 4 \\ 7 & 2 & 0 \\ -6 & 3 & 3 \end{bmatrix}, \qquad B = \begin{bmatrix} 2 & -1 & 3 \\ 0 & 2 & 1 \\ 4 & -2 & 3 \\ 2 & -3 & 4 \end{bmatrix}.$$

Compute AB' and $A'B$.

The motivation behind this at-first-glance strange definition of the product of two matrices will be given in the next section. To assure you now that this strange definition of matrix multiplication is helpful, consider the m simultaneous linear equations

$$\begin{aligned} a_{11}x_1 + a_{12}x_2 + \cdots + a_{1n}x_n &= b_1, \\ a_{21}x_1 + a_{22}x_2 + \cdots + a_{2n}x_n &= b_2, \\ &\vdots \\ a_{m1}x_1 + a_{m2}x_2 + \cdots + a_{mn}x_n &= b_m, \end{aligned}$$

in the n unknowns $x_1, x_2, \ldots, x_n$. The equations can be rewritten quite succinctly in matricial form as the matrix equation

$$AX' = B',$$

where A is the $m \times n$ matrix of a_{ij}'s, X is the n-vector of x_i's, and B is the m-vector of b_i's.

Exercise: Show that, in general, there is no unique solution to m simultaneous linear equations in n unknowns if $n > m$.

An $n \times m$ matrix A can be partitioned into blocks of submatrices A_1, A_2, A_3, A_4 of order $p \times q$, $p \times m - q$, $n - p \times q$, and $n - p \times m - q$, respectively, as follows:

$$A = \begin{bmatrix} A_1 & A_2 \\ A_3 & A_4 \end{bmatrix}.$$

Let

$$C = \begin{bmatrix} C_1 & C_2 \\ C_3 & C_4 \end{bmatrix}.$$

Exercise: Check that

$$AC = \begin{bmatrix} A_1C_1 + A_2C_3 & A_1C_2 + A_2C_4 \\ A_3C_1 + A_4C_3 & A_3C_2 + A_4C_4 \end{bmatrix}.$$

Note the analogy to matrix multiplication. This generalizes in an obvious fashion for matrices partitioned into more blocks. This fact can be used to solve the following exercise.

Exercise: Show that, provided the matrix products given below are defined, the following holds:

$$(A \otimes B)(C \otimes D) = AC \otimes BD.$$

We shall need a special symbol for an $m \times n$ matrix all of whose elements are 0. We call such a matrix the $m \times n$ *zero matrix* and denote it by the symbol 0 as well. It will be clear from context whether the symbol 0 means the number "zero" or the zero matrix, and, in case it is the latter, what is the order of the matrix. The $m \times n$ zero matrix has the property that, for any $m \times n$ matrix A, $A + 0 = A$. Thus the matrix 0 behaves in matrix addition like the number 0 behaves in addition of real numbers.

We shall need a special symbol for the $n \times n$ matrix whose (i, i)th coordinate is 1, $i = 1, \ldots, n$, and whose (i, j)th coordinate is 0, $i \neq j$, $i, j = 1, \ldots, n$. This matrix, called the $n \times n$ *identity matrix*, will be denoted by the symbol I. Thus I has the form

$$I = \begin{bmatrix} 1 & 0 & 0 \cdots 0 \\ 0 & 1 & 0 \cdots 0 \\ 0 & 0 & 1 \cdots 0 \\ \cdot & & \\ \cdot & & \\ \cdot & & \\ 0 & 0 & 0 \cdots 1 \end{bmatrix},$$

and it will be clear from context what the order of I will be. The identity matrices have the property that, for any $m \times n$ matrix A, $AI = A$ and $IA = A$. (Query: What are the orders of the identity matrices in these equations?) Thus I behaves in matrix multiplication like 1 behaves in multiplication of real numbers.

We have already defined matrix sum, matrix difference, and matrix product. In analogy with the arithmetic operations on the real numbers, one might also ask to define matrix quotient. The definition of "matrix quotient" is much more complicated, however. To see what the problems are in constructing a definition of such an operation as matrix division, let us first look at division in the real numbers. We must remember that every real number a (except $a = 0$) has a reciprocal, sometimes written $1/a$ but more suggestively for us written as a^{-1}, with the property that $aa^{-1} = a^{-1}a = 1$. Thus, for $b \neq 0$, the quotient $a \div b$ is obtained as the product $ab^{-1} = b^{-1}a$.

Analogously, given an $n \times p$ matrix B, we should first define what we mean by its "reciprocal", B^{-1}. We can attempt a definition of B^{-1} as the matrix which satisfies $B^{-1}B = BB^{-1} = I$, and immediately note that this is fruitless except when $n = p$, for otherwise at least one of the products $B^{-1}B$ and BB^{-1} is undefined.

We next might seek to have B^{-1} be a $p \times n$ matrix satisfying both $B^{-1}B = I$ and $BB^{-1} = I$, where the two identity matrices are $p \times p$ and $n \times n$ in size, respectively. But then we are confronted with a contradiction. For, if $p < n$, say, the np coordinates of B^{-1} are the unique solution of the p^2 simultaneous linear equations given by $B^{-1}B = I$, an impossibility.

So we restrict ourselves to *square matrices*, i.e., those which are square arrays of real numbers. Let B be an $n \times n$ matrix, and define B^{-1} (called *B-inverse*) as the $n \times n$ matrix satisfying $B^{-1}B = BB^{-1} = I$. The matrix B^{-1}, when it exists, is unique. For suppose there exists another $n \times n$ matrix C satisfying $BC = I$ (or $CB = I$), then $B^{-1}BC = B^{-1}$ (or $CBB^{-1} = B^{-1}$) and so we see that $C = B^{-1}$. Thus there exists only one $n \times n$ matrix satisfying $BB^{-1} = I$ (or $B^{-1}B = I$). When B^{-1} exists, we will call B *invertible* or *non-singular*.

Exercise: Show that $(AB)^{-1} = B^{-1}A^{-1}$.

Now let A be an $m \times n$ matrix. We define the "quotient" A "divided by" B by the matrix product AB^{-1}, provided B^{-1} exists. It is clear that, unlike the case in the real numbers where $ab^{-1} = b^{-1}a$, AB^{-1} may be defined but $B^{-1}A$ need not be, unless $m = n$, and even then AB^{-1} need not equal $B^{-1}A$.

Once you are familiar with the theory of determinants, to be covered in section 5 of the chapter, you will have at your disposal the concepts necessary to understand a standard method of computing a matrix inverse, namely Cramer's rule. At this juncture, though, we can provide you with a "bootstrapping" method of computing a matrix inverse by relying on properties of products of partitioned matrices.

Suppose

$$A = \begin{bmatrix} A_1 & A_2 \\ A_3 & A_4 \end{bmatrix},$$

with A an $n \times n$ matrix and A_1 a $p \times p$ matrix. Let both A and A_1 be non-singular. Write

$$A^{-1} = C = \begin{bmatrix} C_1 & C_2 \\ C_3 & C_4 \end{bmatrix},$$

where C_1 is a $p \times p$ matrix (and you can easily figure out the orders of the other submatrices in C). Then

$$C_4 = (A_4 - A_3 A_1^{-1} A_2)^{-1},$$
$$C_3 = -C_4 A_3 A_1^{-1},$$
$$C_2 = -A_1^{-1} A_2 C_4,$$
$$C_1 = A_1^{-1}(I - A_2 C_3).$$

Exercise: Check this. Also show that if A_4 is non-singular then

$$C_4 = A_4^{-1}(I - A_3 C_2),$$
$$C_3 = -A_4^{-1} A_3 C_1,$$
$$C_2 = -C_1 A_2 A_4^{-1},$$
$$C_1 = (A_1 - A_2 A_4^{-1} A_3)^{-1}.$$

The "bootstrapping" procedure alluded to earlier associated with these relations is the following. For simplicity, take $p = n - 1$. Then given A_1^{-1}, the computation of C is trivial, as C_4 is the inverse of the 1×1 matrix $A_4 - A_3 A_1^{-1} A_2$. What remains is to find A_1^{-1}, the inverse of an $(n-1) \times (n-1)$ matrix. Well, just repeat the argument, $n - 1$ times, until the A_1 whose inverse is to be found is a 1×1 matrix. Knowing that inverse, work your way up again to your ultimate goal, the inverse of the $n \times n$ matrix A. As a bit of practice, try the following exercise.

Exercise: Find A^{-1} when A is

(a) $$\begin{bmatrix} 3 & 0 \\ -1 & 2 \end{bmatrix},$$

(b) $$\begin{bmatrix} 3 & 0 & -1 \\ -1 & 2 & 7 \\ 4 & 6 & 5 \end{bmatrix},$$

(c) $$\begin{bmatrix} 3 & 0 & -1 & 4 \\ -1 & 2 & 7 & 3 \\ 4 & 6 & 5 & 2 \\ 2 & 1 & 8 & 7 \end{bmatrix}.$$

In addition to finding inverses of partitioned matrices, we will also have occasion to find the inverse of a matrix of the form $A + U'SV$, where A is a non-singular $p \times p$ matrix, U is a $q \times p$ matrix, S is a $q \times q$ matrix, and V is a $q \times p$ matrix. If $A + U'SV$ is non-singular, its inverse is given by

$$(A + U'SV)^{-1} = A^{-1} - A^{-1}U'S(S + SVA^{-1}U'S)^{-1}SVA^{-1}.$$

In particular, if $S = I$ and $q = 1$, then

$$(A + U'V)^{-1} = A^{-1} - \frac{A^{-1}U'VA^{-1}}{(1 + VA^{-1}U')}.$$

Exercise: Check this.

2. Euclidean spaces and linear transformations

Let $X = (x_1, x_2, \ldots, x_n)$ be an array of n real numbers. We shall call such an array a *Euclidean n-vector*, or, for brevity, an n-vector. We sometimes also use the term n-vector to denote an $n \times 1$ matrix. When describing the (i, j)th coordinate of an n-vector, we shall delete the superfluous subscript "1". As a notational convention, all unprimed n-vectors will be $1 \times n$ matrices, or row vectors. All primed n-vectors will be $n \times 1$ matrices, or column vectors. Thus knowledge that a given matrix is an n-vector and noticing whether the matrix is primed or unprimed will suffice to tell you whether the n-vector is a row vector or a column vector.

We shall call the set of all Euclidean n-vectors *Euclidean n-space*, or simply n-space. This is the generalization of the characterization of a point in the plane, i.e., in Euclidean two-space, by a pair of numbers (x, y), or of a point in three-dimensional space by a triplet of numbers (x, y, z).

Specializing some of the elementary matrix operations of section 1, we see that we can perform only two kinds of matrix operations on n-vectors which will still result in n-vectors: we can add two vectors together and we can multiply a vector by a real number.

The m n-vectors, $X_1, \ldots, X_m$, are *linearly dependent* if there exist m real numbers, $c_1, \ldots, c_m$, with some c_i not equal to zero, such that

$$c_i X_1 + \cdots + c_m X_m = 0,$$

the zero n-vector. If $c_1 X_1 + \cdots + c_m X_m = 0$ holds only for $c_1 = \cdots = c_m = 0$, then $X_1, \ldots, X_m$ are *linearly independent.*

Exercise: Show that n m-vectors must be linearly dependent if $n > m$.

A vector Y is said to be a *linear combination* of vectors $X_1, \ldots, X_m$ if there are real numbers $a_1, \ldots, a_m$ such that

$$Y = a_1 X_1 + \cdots + a_m X_m.$$

If the non-zero n-vectors $X_1, \ldots, X_m$ are linearly dependent, then of the coefficients $a_1, \ldots, a_m$ such that $a_1 X_1 + \cdots + a_m X_m = 0$, there is one, a_i, say, such that $a_i \neq 0$ and $a_{i+1} = a_{i+2} = \cdots = a_m = 0$. Then X_i is a linear combination of its predecessors, $X_1, \ldots, X_{i-1}$.

A set of n-vectors $X_1, \ldots, X_m$ is a *basis* for Euclidean n-space if (1) $X_1, \ldots, X_m$ are linearly independent and (2) all n-vectors are expressible as linear combinations of $X_1, \ldots, X_m$.

Let $E_1 = (1, 0, 0, \ldots, 0)$, $E_2 = (0, 1, 0, \ldots, 0), \ldots, E_n = (0, 0, \ldots, 0, 1)$, so that E_i has a 1 as the ith element of the vector and zeros elsewhere. Since $\sum_{i=1}^{n} c_i E_i = 0$ implies that $c_i = 0$, $i = 1, \ldots, n$, the vectors $E_1, \ldots, E_n$ are linearly independent. Let $Y = (y_1, \ldots, y_n)$ be an arbitrary n-vector. Then Y is expressible as $Y = y_1 E_1 + y_2 E_2 + \cdots + y_n E_n$, a linear combination of $E_1, \ldots, E_n$. Thus $E_1, \ldots, E_n$ is a basis for Euclidean n-space. We call this the *elementary basis*, and all n-vectors which we consider will, unless otherwise stated, be understood to be expressed as linear combinations of these basis vectors.

The elementary basis plays the same role in the theory of Euclidean vector spaces as the number 10 does in arithmetic. Just as when I write the number 11 you implicitly assume that it is "eleven", i.e., $1 \times 10^1 + 1 \times 10^0$ and not "three", i.e., $1 \times 2^1 + 1 \times 2^0$, so too when I write a vector $Y = (y_1, \ldots, y_n)$, you should implicitly assume that $Y =$

$y_1E_1 + \cdots + y_nE_n$ and not $Y = y_1X_1 + \cdots + y_nX_n$, where $X_1, \ldots, X_n$ is another basis. Just as a number, to whatever base, is a description of how many items are in a set, so too is a vector, expressed as a linear combination of whatever basis vectors, a description of where a point lies in Euclidean space. The basis vectors are merely a reference system by which to locate points in n-space. Though $E_1, \ldots, E_n$ is a convenient reference system, it is by no means the only reference system for Euclidean n-space. Any basis will do.

Exercise: What would be the coordinates of the vector $Y = (3, 5)$ if our reference system were the basis $X_1 = (1, 1)$, $X_2 = (1, -1)$?

We will soon see a relatively simple geometric way of determining the coordinates of a vector relative to some types of basis other than the elementary basis. But before we do this, let us prove the following theorem, which is fundamental to the theory of Euclidean spaces.

Theorem 1: *Every basis of Euclidean n-space is composed of n vectors.*

Proof: Let $X_1, \ldots, X_m$ be a basis for Euclidean n-space. Since X_1 is a linear combination of the E's, the vectors $X_1, E_1, \ldots, E_n$ are linearly dependent. Thus, one of the E's, say E_i, is a linear combination of the preceding vectors $X_1, E_1, \ldots, E_{i-1}$. Delete this vector from the set, leaving us with $X_1, E_1, \ldots, E_{i-1}, E_{i+1}, \ldots, E_n$. These vectors are linearly independent, for if not then the ith coordinate of X_1 would be 0, thereby contradicting that E_i is a linear combination of $X_1, E_1, \ldots, E_{i-1}$, all of which have 0 as ith coordinate.

All the vectors in Euclidean n-space are linear combinations of these n vectors as well, as they were linear combinations of the $n+1$ vectors $X_1, E_1, \ldots, E_n$, and all we deleted was a linearly dependent member of this set. Thus X_2 is a linear combination of $X_1, E_1, \ldots, E_{i-1}, E_{i+1}, \ldots, E_n$, and so the vectors $X_2, X_1, E_1, \ldots, E_{i-1}, E_{i+1}, \ldots, E_n$ are linearly dependent. Since X_2 and X_1 are linearly independent, it must be one of the E's, say E_j, which is also a linear combination of its predecessors in the set $X_2, X_1, E_1, \ldots, E_{i-1}, E_{i+1}, \ldots, E_n$. Delete this vector, leaving us once again with n linearly independent vectors such that all the vectors of Euclidean n-space are linear combinations of these.

We must be able to continue this argument m times, until we have included $X_1, \ldots, X_m$, that is, we must have $n \geqslant m$. For if not, we will have a subset $X_1, \ldots, X_n$ of $X_1, \ldots, X_m$ such that all the vectors of Euclidean n-space are linear combinations of these. But X_{n+1} is linearly independent of $X_1, \ldots, X_n$, as $X_1, \ldots, X_m$ is a basis, which contradicts this conclusion.

Now we can go through the entire argument once again reversing the roles played by the E's and the X's and conclude that $m \geqslant n$. Thus we see that $m = n$.

Theorem 1 tells us a very important fact, that any set $X_1, \ldots, X_n$ of n linearly independent n-vectors are a basis for n-space. For if some other vector X_{n+1} is not a linear combination of $X_1, \ldots, X_n$ then $X_1, \ldots, X_{n+1}$ would be a basis, contradicting Theorem 1.

By the *inner product* of two n-vectors X and Y we mean the real number XY'. The vectors X and Y are said to be *orthogonal* if their inner product is zero. A basis is said to be an *orthogonal basis* if all pairs of vectors in the basis are orthogonal. Thus, for example, the elementary basis is an orthogonal basis. Let us see how to find the coordinates of a vector relative to an arbitrary orthogonal basis.

Let X be the vector of interest and $U_1, \ldots, U_n$ be an orthogonal basis for n-space. If X is to be expressed as $X = a_1U_1 + \cdots + a_nU_n$, then $XU_i' = a_iU_iU_i'$, since $U_iU_j' = 0$ for all $j \neq i$. We see that the ith coordinate of X relative to the orthogonal basis $U_1, \ldots, U_n$ is $a_i = XU_i'/U_iU_i'$.

Exercise: Check your solution to the previous exercise using this result.

Let $\mathscr{X}$ and $\mathscr{Y}$ be n- and m-dimensional Euclidean vector spaces, respectively. A *transformation* T from $\mathscr{X}$ into $\mathscr{Y}$ is a way of associating with each X in $\mathscr{X}$ a vector $Y = T(X)$ in $\mathscr{Y}$. Transformations T_1 and T_2 are equal if $T_1(X) = T_2(X)$ for all X in $\mathscr{X}$. A transformation T is *linear* if it satisfies the following conditions.

(1) $T(aX) = aT(X)$, where a is a real number.

(2) $T(X_1 + X_2) = T(X_1) + T(X_2)$.

Thus $T(0) = T(0 \cdot X) = 0T(X) = 0$ for all linear transformations T, so that the origin stays put under linear transformations. This is at variance with terminology used in analytic geometry, in which $T(X) = T((x_1, x_2, x_3)) = (x_1 + a, x_2 + b, x_3 + c)$, i.e., a shift of the origin, is called a "linear" transformation.

As an example of a linear transformation, let $\mathscr{X}$ be 2-space and $\mathscr{Y}$ be

3-space, and let $T(X) = (x_1 + x_2, x_1 - x_2, x_1 + 2x_2)$, where $X = (x_1, x_2)$. The linear transformation T is portrayed graphically in figure 1. It can be further seen that T transforms points (x_1, x_2) into points on the plane in $\mathcal{Y}$ defined by $y_3 = (3y_1 - y_2)/2$.

Let's look more closely at the set of vectors $T(X)$ for all X in $\mathcal{X}$. As in the above example, this set of vectors may not comprise all of $\mathcal{Y}$. This is why I stress the word "into" in the definition of a transformation given above. Thus the set of vectors $T(X)$ is not Euclidean m-space but only a subset of it.

A *subspace* $\mathcal{S}$ of Euclidean n-space $\mathcal{X}$ is a subset of $\mathcal{X}$ satisfying the following:

(1) If X and Y are in $\mathcal{S}$, then $X + Y$ is in $\mathcal{S}$,

(2) If X is in $\mathcal{S}$, then cX is in $\mathcal{S}$ for all real c.

Exercise: Let T be a linear transformation from $\mathcal{X}$ into $\mathcal{Y}$. Show that the set of vectors $T(X)$, for X in $\mathcal{X}$, is a subspace of $\mathcal{Y}$.

We can extend the definition of the term "basis" to apply to subspaces as well. Suppose we found the largest possible collection of vectors of $\mathcal{S}$ which were linearly independent. There is of course no unique such collection. However, the number of members of such a collection, call it p, is unique, by the same argument as used to prove Theorem 1. A basis for a subspace $\mathcal{S}$ of Euclidean n-space is any set of p linear independent vectors of $\mathcal{S}$.

Exercise: It might be instructive for you to go through for yourself the details of the argument of the proof of Theorem 1, applied to a new situation. Prove the following: Let $\mathcal{S}$ be a subspace of n-space. Let

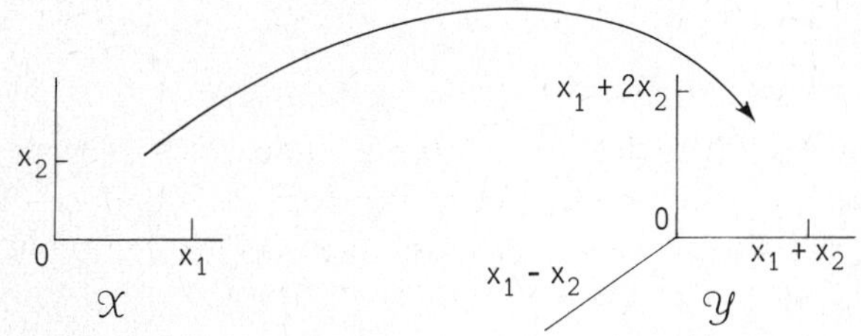

FIGURE 1

$X_1, \ldots, X_p$ and $X_1^*, \ldots, X_q^*$ be two sets of linearly independent vectors of $\mathcal{S}$, each set having the property that all other vectors of $\mathcal{S}$ are linear combinations of members of the set. Then $p = q$.

Thus the number of vectors in the basis of the subspace defined by the set of vectors $T(X)$ may be less than m. Many texts use the word "dimension" of a vector space to mean the number of members of a basis for the vector space. Thus, though T is a transformation from n-space into m-space, according to this definition of dimension the space of $T(X)$'s may be of lower dimension than m, the number of elements of the vector $T(X)$.

Let T_1 and T_2 be two linear transformations from Euclidean n-space into Euclidean n-space. We can define $T = T_1 + T_2$, the *sum* of T_1 and T_2, as the transformation T which associates with each vector X the vector $T(X) = T_1(X) + T_2(X)$.

We can define $T = T_2T_1$, the *product* of T_1 and T_2, as the transformation T which associates with each vector X the vector $T(X) = T_2(T_1(X))$. Thus the product of T_2 and T_1 associates with X the vector $T_1(T_2(X))$ which may be different from the vector $T_2(T_1(X))$. For brevity, we write $T = T_1 + T_2$ and $T = T_2T_1$ when we mean sum of T_1 and T_2 and product of T_1 and T_2, respectively. Note the inversion of the order of the transformations in the notation for the product.

Exercise: Check that the transformations $T_1 + T_2$ and T_2T_1 are linear transformations.

Let T be a linear transformation from n-space $\mathcal{X}$ into m-space $\mathcal{Y}$. A linear transformation is said to be *one–one* if, for any two distinct vectors X_1 and X_2 of $\mathcal{X}$, we have $T(X_1) \neq T(X_2)$. A linear transformation is said to be *onto* if, for every vector Y in $\mathcal{Y}$ there corresponds at least one X in $\mathcal{X}$, such that $T(X) = Y$. If T is both one–one and onto we shall say that T is *invertible* or *non-singular*. When T is invertible, for each Y in $\mathcal{Y}$ there corresponds a unique X in $\mathcal{X}$ such that $T(X) = Y$.

If T is onto, then $n \geq m$. For let $Y_1, \ldots, Y_m$ be a basis for $\mathcal{Y}$ and let $T(X_i) = Y_i$, $i = 1, \ldots, m$. Let $m > n$. Then $X_1, \ldots, X_m$ are linearly dependent, i.e., there are c_i not all zero such that $\sum_{i=1}^m c_iX_i = 0$. But

$$T\left(\sum_{i=1}^{m} c_iX_i\right) = \sum_{i=1}^{m} c_iY_i = 0,$$

if and only if $c_i = 0$, $i = 1, \ldots, m$, which contradicts the above.

If T is one–one, then $n \leqslant m$. For let $X_1, \ldots, X_n$ be a basis for $\mathscr{X}$. Let $X = \sum_{i=1}^{n} c_i X_i$. Suppose the vectors $T(X_i)$, $i = 1, \ldots, n$, are not linearly independent. Then $0 = \sum_{i=1}^{n} c_i T(X_i) = T\left(\sum_{i=1}^{n} c_i X_i\right)$, with not all the $c_i = 0$. But $T(0) = 0$ and, as T is one–one, $\sum_{i=1}^{n} c_i X_i = 0$. Since the X's are a basis, this contradicts the above. Thus the $T(X_i)$ are linearly independent, and so $n \leqslant m$.

The following theorem gives a necessary and sufficient condition for a linear transformation to be invertible.

Theorem 2: *Let $X_1, \ldots, X_n$ be a basis for $\mathscr{X}$. A linear transformation T from $\mathscr{X}$ into $\mathscr{X}$ is invertible if and only if the vectors $T(X_1), \ldots, T(X_n)$ are linearly independent.*

Proof: Let T be invertible, and suppose that $T(X_1), \ldots, T(X_n)$ are not linearly independent. Then there are real numbers $c_1, \ldots, c_n$, not all zero, such that $\sum_{i=1}^{n} c_i T(X_i) = 0$, which implies that $T\left(\sum_{i=1}^{n} c_i X_i\right) = 0$. Since T is invertible and $T(0) = 0$, we see that $\sum_{i=1}^{n} c_i X_i = 0$, which contradicts our hypothesis that $X_1, \ldots, X_n$ is a basis.

Conversely, suppose $T(X_1), \ldots, T(X_n)$ are linearly independent. Then they are a basis for $\mathscr{X}$. Now consider the linear transformation S defined by $S(T(X)) = X$ for all X in $\mathscr{X}$.

Now let $T(\tilde{X}_1) = T(\tilde{X}_2)$ for some $\tilde{X}_1$ and $\tilde{X}_2$ in $\mathscr{X}$. Then $\tilde{X}_1 = S(T(\tilde{X}_1)) = S(T(\tilde{X}_2)) = \tilde{X}_2$. Thus $\tilde{X}_1 \neq \tilde{X}_2$ implies that $T(\tilde{X}_1) \neq T(\tilde{X}_2)$, so that T is one–one.

Let $X_i^* = T(X_i)$, $i = 1, \ldots, n$. Then $S(X_i^*) = S(T(X_i)) = X_i$, so that $T(S(X_i^*)) = X_i^*$, $i = 1, \ldots, n$. As corresponding to each basis element X_i^* in $\mathscr{X}$ there is a vector $X_i = S(X_i^*)$ in $\mathscr{X}$ such that $T(X_i) = X_i^*$, T is onto. Since T is one–one and onto, it is invertible.

When T is invertible we denote by T^{-1} (read "T inverse") the transformation satisfying $T^{-1}T = I$.

Let $X_1, \ldots, X_n$ be a basis for $\mathscr{X}$. We define the *rank* of the linear transformation T from $\mathscr{X}$ into m-space $\mathscr{Y}$ as the largest number of vectors selected from $T(X_1), \ldots, T(X_n)$ which are linearly independent. Obviously the rank of T is at most n. Also, the rank of T is at most m, the dimension of $\mathscr{Y}$. Finally, by Theorem 2 a transformation from n-space into n-space is invertible if and only if its rank is n.

3. Matricial representations of linear transformations

Let $X_1, \ldots, X_n$ be a basis for Euclidean n-space, and let T be a linear transformation from Euclidean n-space into Euclidean n-space. Then $T(X_j)$ is a vector in Euclidean n-space and so can be expressed as a linear combination of the vectors of the basis $X_1, \ldots, X_n$ as

$$T(X_j) = \sum_{i=1}^{n} a_{ij} X_i.$$

We can do this for all $j = 1, \ldots, n$, and can display the coefficients a_{ij} in the array

$$A = \begin{bmatrix} a_{11} & a_{12} \cdots a_{1n} \\ a_{21} & a_{22} \cdots a_{2n} \\ & \cdot \\ & \cdot \\ & \cdot \\ a_{n1} & a_{n2} \cdots a_{nn} \end{bmatrix}.$$

This square array of numbers is the matrix associated with the linear transformation T from Euclidean n-space into Euclidean n-space, *relative to the fixed basis* $X_1, \ldots, X_n$. It is clear that, relative to a different basis $Y_1, \ldots, Y_n$, the transformation T would have a different matrix associated with it, as $T(Y_j) = \sum_{i=1}^{n} b_{ij} Y_i$, where b_{ij} is not necessarily equal to a_{ij}.

In a similar fashion, let $X_1, \ldots, X_n$ be a basis for Euclidean n-space, $Y_1, \ldots, Y_m$ be a basis for Euclidean m-space, and T be a linear transformation from n-space to m-space. Then $T(X_j) = \sum_{i=1}^{m} a_{ij} Y_i$, $j = 1, \ldots, n$, and so the matrix associated with T, *relative to the bases* $X_1, \ldots, X_n$ *in n-space and* $Y_1, \ldots, Y_m$ *in m-space*, is the $m \times n$ matrix

$$A = \begin{bmatrix} a_{11} \cdots a_{1n} \\ a_{21} \cdots a_{2n} \\ \cdot \\ \cdot \\ \cdot \\ a_{m1} \qquad a_{mn} \end{bmatrix}.$$

Unless otherwise specified, we shall present the matrix associated with linear transformations relative to the elementary bases of the relevant spaces.

Exercise: Let T be a transformation from 2-space $\mathscr{X}$ into 2-space $\mathscr{Y}$. Relative to the bases E_1, E_2 in $\mathscr{X}$ and $\mathscr{Y}$, the matrix of T is

$$\begin{bmatrix} 3 & 0 \\ -1 & 2 \end{bmatrix}.$$

Let $X_1 = (1, 1)$, $X_2 = (1, -1)$. What is the matrix of T relative to the basis X_1, X_2 in $\mathscr{X}$ and $\mathscr{Y}$? Relative to the basis X_1, X_2 in $\mathscr{X}$ and E_1, E_2 in $\mathscr{Y}$? Relative to the basis E_1, E_2 in $\mathscr{X}$, X_1, X_2 in $\mathscr{Y}$?

Given the matrix associated with T relative to one basis, how does one in general determine the matrix relative to another basis? I will only consider the problem for linear transformations from n-space to n-space and bases $E_1, \ldots, E_n$ and $X_1, \ldots, X_n$. (The result to follow is not important to the main developments in this chapter. In fact, it will be used only once, in section 5, and again in chapter V. And it is not an error that the previous exercise was placed before this paragraph. It is intended to be handled from first principles, not by rote application of the formula to follow.)

Let A be the matrix of T relative to the elementary basis and B be the matrix of T relative to the basis $X_1, \ldots, X_n$ in both $\mathscr{X}$ and $\mathscr{Y}$. Thus $T(E_j) = \sum_{i=1}^n a_{ij}E_i$ and $T(X_j) = \sum_{i=1}^n b_{ij}X_i$. But $X_i = (x_{i1}, \ldots, x_{in}) = \sum_{j=1}^n x_{ij}E_j$, so that

$$T(X_i) = T\Big(\sum_{j=1}^n x_{ij}E_j\Big) = \sum_{j=1}^n x_{ij}T(E_j)$$

$$= \sum_{j=1}^n x_{ij} \sum_{k=1}^n a_{kj}E_k = \sum_{j=1}^n b_{ji}X_j = \sum_{j=1}^n b_{ji} \sum_{k=1}^n x_{jk}E_k.$$

Therefore $\sum_{j=1}^n b_{ji}x_{jk} = \sum_{j=1}^n x_{ij}a_{kj}$. Let X be the $n \times n$ matrix with jth row the vector X_j. Then $\sum_{j=1}^n b_{ji}x_{jk}$ is the (i, k)th element of $B'X$. Similarly, $\sum_{j=1}^n x_{ij}a_{kj}$ is the (i, k)th element of XA'. Therefore $B'X = XA'$, or $B' = XA'X^{-1}$. We call this the *change of basis formula.*

Let $X_j = E_j^n$, $j = 1, \ldots, n$, $Y_i = E_i^m$, $i = 1, \ldots, m$, where the superscript denotes the order of the vector E_i. Let A be the matrix associated with T relative to these bases. Let X be a vector in n-space. Then the vector $T(X)$ of m-space is expressed, relative to the basis $E_1^m, \ldots, E_m^m$, as XA', for

$$X = \sum_{j=1}^n x_jE_j^n,$$

and

$$\begin{aligned}T(X) &= \sum_{j=1}^{n} x_j T(E_j^n)\\ &= \sum_{j=1}^{n} x_j \sum_{i=1}^{m} a_{ij} E_i^m\\ &= \sum_{i=1}^{m} \left(\sum_{j=1}^{n} x_j a_{ij} \right) E_i^m.\end{aligned}$$

Since $\sum_{j=1}^{n} x_j a_{ij}$ is the ith element of the m-vector XA', we see that $T(X) = XA'$, relative to the basis $E_1^m, \ldots, E_m^m$.

Only if T_1 and T_2 are transformations from n-space to m-space is the sum $T_1 + T_2$ defined. Let A be the $m \times n$ matrix associated with T_1 and B be the $m \times n$ matrix associated with T_2. What is the matrix associated with $T_1 + T_2$? Since

$$\begin{aligned}(T_1 + T_2)(E_j^n) = T_1(E_j^n) + T_2(E_j^n) &= \sum_{k=1}^{m} a_{kj} E_k^m + \sum_{k=1}^{m} b_{kj} E_k^m\\ &= \sum_{k=1}^{m} (a_{kj} + b_{kj}) E_k^m, \qquad j = 1, \ldots, n,\end{aligned}$$

we see that the matrix associated with $T_1 + T_2$ is the matrix $C = A + B$ with typical element $c_{ij} = a_{ij} + b_{ij}$.

Only if T_1 is a transformation from n-space to m-space, and T_2 is a transformation from m-space to p-space is the product $T_2 T_1$ defined. Let A be the matrix associated with T_1 and B be the matrix associated with T_2. What is the matrix associated with $T = T_2 T_1$? Since

$$T_1(E_j^n) = \sum_{k=1}^{m} a_{kj} E_k^m, \qquad j = 1, \ldots, n,$$

and

$$\begin{aligned}T_2(T_1(E_j^n)) &= T_2\left(\sum_{k=1}^{m} a_{kj} E_k^m \right)\\ &= \sum_{k=1}^{m} a_{kj} T_2(E_k^m)\\ &= \sum_{i=1}^{p} \left(\sum_{k=1}^{m} b_{ik} a_{kj} \right) E_i^p, \qquad j = 1, \ldots, n,\end{aligned}$$

we see that the matrix associated with $T = T_2 T_1$ is the matrix $C = BA$ with typical element

$$c_{ij} = \sum_{k=1}^{m} b_{ik} a_{kj}.$$

This indicates why matrix multiplication was defined in such a seemingly extraordinary way in section 1.

Suppose T is an invertible linear transformation, with A the matrix associated with T. What is the matrix associated with T^{-1}? Since the matrix associated with TT^{-1} is I, the $n \times n$ identity matrix, the matrix associated with T^{-1} is A^{-1}.

We defined the rank of a linear transformation earlier essentially as the largest number of vectors selected from $T(E_1^n), \ldots, T(E_n^n)$ which are linearly independent. In terms of the matrix A associated with T, the rank of T is the number of columns of the matrix which, viewed as vectors, are linearly independent. This is apparent, as

$$\begin{aligned} T(E_j^n) &= \sum_{i=1}^{m} a_{ij} E_i^m \\ &= (a_{1j}, \ldots, a_{mj}), \end{aligned}$$

the elements of the jth column of A. Thus if A is an $n \times n$ matrix, it is non-singular if and only if its columns, viewed as vectors, are linearly independent.

Also, since A' is non-singular if and only if A is, we see that A is non-singular if and only if its rows are linearly independent vectors.

This observation leads us to another necessary and sufficient condition for A to be non-singular, given in the following theorem.

Theorem 3: Let A be an $n \times n$ matrix. A is invertible if and only if the only solution of the equation $XA' = 0$ is $X = 0$.

Proof: If X is not the zero vector and $XA' = 0$, then A is not invertible, as the linear transformation associated with A associates 0 with both X and 0.

Also, if A is not invertible, then its columns are not linearly independent, so that there exist n numbers $x_1, \ldots, x_n$, not all zero, such that

$$\sum_{i=1}^{n} x_i A_i = 0,$$

where A_i is the ith column of A. Thus $XA' = 0$ with $X = (x_1, \ldots, x_n) \neq 0$.

Returning briefly to the notion of rank of a matrix, if A is an $m \times n$ matrix, its rank is at most $\min(m, n)$. Now suppose B is an $n \times p$ matrix.

Then, since AB is the matrix of a linear transformation from p-space to n-space to m-space, its rank is at most $\min(m, n, p)$. In fact, we can say something even stronger about the rank of AB, namely that rank $(AB) \leq \min(\text{rank}(A), \text{rank}(B))$. This is so because the number of linearly independent vectors in m-space after the transformation corresponding to A is at most rank A and also at most the number of linearly independent vectors available in n-space to be transformed by A after the transformation corresponding to B, i.e., at most rank B.

Exercise: Let B be a non-singular matrix. Show that rank $(AB) =$ rank (A). *Hint*: $\text{rank}(A) = \text{rank}(ABB^{-1}) \leq \min(\text{rank}(AB), \text{rank}(B^{-1})) = \min(\text{rank}(AB), \text{rank}(B)) \leq \text{rank}(AB)$.

4. Projection transformations

A subspace of Euclidean n-space $\mathscr{X}$ (which may be n-space itself) is said to be the *direct sum* of subspaces $\mathscr{Y}$ and $\mathscr{Z}$ if $\mathscr{Y}$ and $\mathscr{Z}$ are subspaces of $\mathscr{X}$ having only 0 in common and if any X in $\mathscr{X}$ can be expressed as $X = Y + Z$, with Y in $\mathscr{Y}$ and Z in $\mathscr{Z}$.

For example, Euclidean 3-space is the direct sum of the two-dimensional subspace $\mathscr{Y}$ defined as those vectors X satisfying $x_1 + x_2 = 3x_3$ and the one-dimensional subspace $\mathscr{Z}$ defined as those vectors X satisfying $x_3 = 0$ and $3x_1 = 2x_2$. To check this we first must determine what vectors X are in both $\mathscr{Y}$ and $\mathscr{Z}$. But the only vector $X = (x_1, x_2, x_3)$ satisfying both $x_1 + x_2 = 3x_3$ and $3x_1 = 2x_2$, $x_3 = 0$, is the zero vector. To show that any vector X in $\mathscr{X}$ can be expressed as $X = Y + Z$, with Y in $\mathscr{Y}$ and Z in $\mathscr{Z}$, let

$$Y = (x_1 - \tfrac{2}{5}(x_1 + x_2 - 3x_3), x_2 - \tfrac{3}{5}(x_1 + x_2 - 3x_3), x_3),$$

and

$$Z = (\tfrac{2}{5}(x_1 + x_2 - 3x_3), \tfrac{3}{5}(x_1 + x_2 - 3x_3), 0).$$

Then $X = (x_1, x_2, x_3) = Y + Z$. Since $x_1 - \frac{2}{5}(x_1 + x_2 - 3x_3) + x_2 - \frac{3}{5}(x_1 + x_2 - 3x_3) = 3x_3$, and $3[\frac{2}{5}(x_1 + x_2 - 3x_3)] = 2[\frac{3}{5}(x_1 + x_2 - 3x_3)]$, we see that Y and Z so defined are in $\mathscr{Y}$ and $\mathscr{Z}$, respectively.

Let $\mathscr{X}$ be the direct sum of $\mathscr{Y}$ and $\mathscr{Z}$ and let P be the linear transformation defined by $P(X) = Y$. The transformation P is called the *projection transformation of* $\mathscr{X}$ *along* $\mathscr{Y}$ and the subspace $\mathscr{Y}$ is called the *projection* of $\mathscr{X}$ by P. In the above example, the projection transformation of 3-space along $\mathscr{Y}$ takes the vector $X = (x_1, x_2, x_3)$ into the vector $Y = (\frac{3}{5}x_1 - \frac{2}{5}x_2 + \frac{6}{5}x_3, -\frac{3}{5}x_1 + \frac{2}{5}x_2 + \frac{9}{5}x_3, x_3)$, and so has associated matrix

$$A = \begin{bmatrix} \frac{3}{5} & -\frac{2}{5} & \frac{6}{5} \\ -\frac{3}{5} & \frac{2}{5} & \frac{9}{5} \\ 0 & 0 & 1 \end{bmatrix},$$

so that $XA' = Y$.

A pictorial representation of the projection transformation, at least in this example, may be insightful. We see from figure 2 that Y, the projection of X along $\mathscr{Y}$, is obtained by drawing an oblique (not perpendicular) line, the dashed line in the figure, parallel to Z, from X to $\mathscr{Y}$.

It is easy to determine whether a linear transformation is a projection transformation, by using the following theorem.

Theorem 4: P is a projection transformation if, and only if, it is idempotent, i.e., if $PP = P$.

Proof: If P is a projection transformation, then $P(X) = Y$, viewed as a vector in $\mathscr{X}$, can be written as $Y + 0$, Y in $\mathscr{Y}$, 0 in $\mathscr{Z}$. Then $P(P(X)) = P(Y) = Y = P(X)$, or $PP = P$.

If $PP = P$, let $\mathscr{Z}$ be the set of X such that $P(X) = 0$ and $\mathscr{Y}$ be the set of

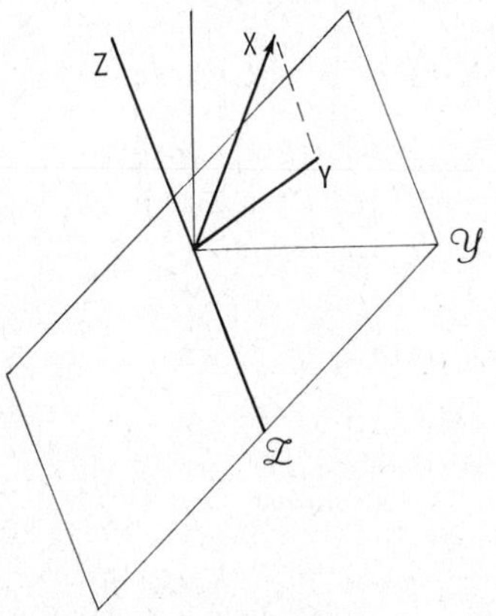

FIGURE 2

X such that $P(X) = X$. Let $Y = P(X)$ and $Z = (I - P)(X)$, where $I(X) = X$. Then $X = P(X) + (I - P)(X) = Y + Z$. Since $P(Y) = P(P(X)) = P(X) = Y$ and $P(Z) = P((I - P)(X)) = P(X) - P(P(X)) = 0$, we see that Y is in $\mathscr{Y}$ and Z is in $\mathscr{Z}$. As the zero vector is the only vector $\mathscr{Y}$ and $\mathscr{Z}$ have in common, we conclude that P is a projection transformation of $\mathscr{X}$ along $\mathscr{Y}$.

Similarly, a matrix A is the matrix of a projection transformation if and only if A is *idempotent*, i.e., $AA = A$. As an example of the matrix of a projection transformation, let B by an $n \times m$ matrix with $B'B$ non-singular. Let $A = B(B'B)^{-1}B'$. Then $AA = A$.

Exercise: Show that if A is the matrix of a projection transformation, then so is $I - A$.

Let $\mathscr{X}$ be the direct sum of $\mathscr{Y}$ and $\mathscr{Z}$, and let $\mathscr{Y}$ and $\mathscr{Z}$ be *orthogonal subspaces*, i.e., any basis vector of $\mathscr{Y}$ is orthogonal to any basis vector of $\mathscr{Z}$. Then the projection transformation P of $\mathscr{X}$ along $\mathscr{Y}$ is called an orthogonal projection transformation. The subspace $\mathscr{Y}$ is called the *orthogonal projection* of $\mathscr{X}$ by P.

Exercise: Let $\mathscr{X}$ be Euclidean n-space, $\mathscr{Y}$ and $\mathscr{Z}$ be orthogonal subspaces, and suppose $\mathscr{Y}$ has an orthogonal basis $X_1, \ldots, X_{n-1}$.

Let P be the projection transformation of $\mathscr{X}$ along $\mathscr{Y}$. Show that the orthogonal projection of a vector X of $\mathscr{X}$ by P is the sum of the orthogonal projections of X on the X_i, $i = 1, \ldots, n-1$. (In section 7 you will learn how to find the orthogonal projection of $\mathscr{X}$ by P when you do not have an orthogonal basis for $\mathscr{Y}$.)

An $n \times n$ matrix A is called *symmetric* if $A = A'$. Symmetric matrices have important general properties which will be explored in great detail in section 6. However, we cannot leave the subject of projection transformations without demonstrating that a projection transformation P is orthogonal if and only if its matrix A is symmetric.

First suppose A is symmetric. Let $X = Y + Z$, with X in $\mathscr{X}$, Y in $\mathscr{Y}$, Z in $\mathscr{Z}$, and where $\mathscr{X}$ is the direct sum of $\mathscr{Y}$ and $\mathscr{Z}$. Let $P(X) = Y = XA$. Then $YZ' = (YA)Z' = ZAY' = 0Y' = 0$, since $ZA = 0$. Thus Y and Z are orthogonal.

Now suppose $\mathscr{Y}$ and $\mathscr{Z}$ are orthogonal subspaces. Let $X_1 = Y_1 + Z_1$, $X_2 = Y_2 + Z_2$, where Y_i is in $\mathscr{Y}$ and Z_i is in $\mathscr{Z}$, $i = 1, 2$. Then

$$X_1AX_2' = Y_1X_2' = Y_1(Y_2+Z_2)' = Y_1Y_2' = (Y_1+Z_1)Y_2'$$
$$= X_1(X_2A)' = X_1A'X_2',$$

for any X_1, X_2. Thus $A = A'$.

Let X and Y be n-vectors. Let $\mathscr{X}$ be a two-dimensional subspace of n-space containing X and Y, and $\mathscr{Y}$ be the one-dimensional subspace of n-space whose basis is Y. What is a basis Z of a one-dimensional subspace $\mathscr{Z}$ of n-space such that (a) $\mathscr{X}$ is the direct sum of $\mathscr{Y}$ and $\mathscr{Z}$, and (b) Y and Z are orthogonal? We require that $\tilde{X} = a_1Y + a_2Z$, for all $\tilde{X}$ in $\mathscr{X}$. Then $\tilde{X}Y' = a_1YY'$, $\tilde{X}Z' = a_2ZZ'$, so that Z satisfies

$$Z = \frac{\tilde{X} - a_1Y}{a_2} = \frac{1}{a_2}\left[\tilde{X} - \left(\frac{\tilde{X}Y'}{YY'}\right)Y\right].$$

Thus, taking $a_2 = 1$ and $\tilde{X} = X$, we see that $Z = X - [(XY')/(YY')]Y$ is a basis for $\mathscr{Z}$, with $ZY' = 0$, and that $\tilde{X}$ is expressible as $a_1Y + Z$.

The projection of $\mathscr{X}$ along $\mathscr{Y}$ is in this case called the *orthogonal projection* of X on Y and is the vector $(XY')/(YY')Y$. The matrix of the projection transformation of $\mathscr{X}$ along $\mathscr{Y}$ is the $n \times n$ matrix $A = Y'Y/YY'$.

Exercise: Check that A is idempotent.

5. Determinants

This section is really an overlong digression from the mainstream in which we are headed, namely to acquaint you with the matrix theory necessary to study econometric theory felicitiously. This is not to say that the notion of a determinant is not useful for us, but only to say that, unlike matrix theory proper, it is only the operational aspects of the determinant which are useful and not the underlying theory of the determinant. So let me tell you why this section is overlong, so as to guide you in the reading of it.

Usually, the determinant is defined without any whys or wherefores, most often in an inelegant manner. Since I begin this section by motivating the definition of the determinant in terms of what desirable properties we might like a real-valued function of a matrix to have, I feel impelled, for completeness sake, to include a proof of the existence and uniqueness of the function having these desirable properties. If you are not that interested in the details of this proof, by all means skim it. It is not essential to the rest of the book. Let me warn you, however, that I did not mean for you to *skip* it, because I do slip in some of the standard algebraic properties of a determinant as I go along.

The final topic treated in this section, the determinant viewed as a volume, is included after all the algebraic properties are detailed not so much for any geometric insight it gives into the determinant but because it will be useful (and used) in chapter II to motivate the Jacobian of a transformation of n variables. Now let us begin.

It would be nice to have a handy way of recognizing that a matrix is invertible. One parsimonious way might be to find a real-valued function D of a matrix which would equal zero if and only if the matrix is not invertible. We know that a matrix is invertible if and only if its rows are linearly independent. Let us see what are the implications of this condition on the desired function D.

Let A be an $n \times n$ matrix, with rows $A_1, \ldots, A_n$. If the rows are linearly dependent, then there exist real numbers $c_1, \ldots, c_n$, with $c_1 \neq 0$, say, such that $c_1A_1 + \cdots + c_nA_n = 0$. Then $A_1 = b_2A_2 + \cdots + b_nA_n$, with $b_i = -c_i/c_1$, $i = 1, 2, \ldots, n$. The function $D(A)$, expressed in terms of the rows of A, is $D(A) = D(A_1, \ldots, A_n) \equiv D(b_2A_2 + \cdots + b_nA_n, A_2, \ldots, A_n)$. We would like $D(A)$ to equal zero in this case. Now let's state some conditions on the function D which will yield the desired result.

Suppose D satisfies the following:

(1) $$D(A_1, \ldots, A_{j-1}, A_j + B_j, A_{j+1}, \ldots, A_n) = D(A_1, \ldots, A_{j-1}, A_j, A_{j+1}, \ldots, A_n) + D(A_1, \ldots, A_{j-1}, B_j, A_{j+1}, \ldots, A_n),$$

(2) $$D(A_1, \ldots, A_{j-1}, cA_j, A_{j+1}, \ldots, A_n) = cD(A_1, \ldots, A_{j-1}, A_j, A_{j+1}, \ldots, A_n).$$

(3) If $A_j = A_k$ for some j, k, $j \neq k$, then $D(A_1, \ldots, A_n) = 0$.

Then we apply (1) to $D(b_2A_2 + \cdots + b_nA_n, A_2, \ldots, A_n)$ $n-1$ times to obtain

$$D(A) = D(b_2A_2, A_2, \ldots, A_n) + \cdots + D(b_nA_n, A_2, \ldots, A_n).$$

Next we apply (2) to each of the above $n-1$ terms, to obtain

$$D(A) = b_2 D(A_2, A_2, \ldots, A_n) + \cdots + b_n D(A_n, A_2, \ldots, A_n).$$

Finally we note that each of the above $n-1$ functions D have as arguments matrices with two identical columns. By applying (3), we see that $D(A) = 0$.

Let us now see if one can find a unique function D which will satisfy conditions (1), (2), and (3). Actually, we will only impose the following condition (3′):

(3′) If $A_j = A_{j+1}$, then $D(A_1, \ldots, A_n) = 0$.

This is because (1) and (3′) imply (3), as we shall now show.

Note first that (1) and (3′) imply

$$D(A_1, \ldots, A_{j-1}, A_j, A_{j+1}, A_{j+2}, \ldots, A_n) =$$
$$-D(A_1, \ldots, A_{j-1}, A_{j+1}, A_j, A_{j+2}, \ldots, A_n)$$

since

$$\begin{aligned}
&D(A_1, \ldots, A_{j-1}, A_j, A_{j+1}, A_{j+2}, \ldots, A_n) \\
&+D(A_1, \ldots, A_{j-1}, A_{j+1}, A_j, A_{j+2}, \ldots, A_n) = \\
&D(A_1, \ldots, A_{j-1}, A_j + A_{j+1}, A_{j+1}, A_{j+2}, \ldots, A_n) \\
&-D(A_1, \ldots, A_{j-1}, A_{j+1}, A_{j+1}, A_{j+2}, \ldots, A_n) \\
&+D(A_1, \ldots, A_{j-1}, A_{j+1} + A_j, A_j, A_{j+2}, \ldots, A_n) \\
&-D(A_1, \ldots, A_{j-1}, A_j, A_j, A_{j+2}, \ldots, A_n) = \\
&D(A_1, \ldots, A_{j-1}, A_j + A_{j+1}, A_{j+1} + A_j, A_{j+2}, \ldots, A_n) = \\
&0.
\end{aligned}$$

Generalizing this result, let $\sigma(1), \ldots, \sigma(n)$ be a permutation of the integers $1, 2, \ldots, n$. Let us count for each $i = 1, \ldots, n$ the number of integers $j = i+1, \ldots, n$ which precede i in the permutation $\sigma(1), \ldots, \sigma(n)$. [For example, if $n = 6$ and $\sigma(1) = 4$, $\sigma(2) = 1$, $\sigma(3) = 5$, $\sigma(4) = 3$, $\sigma(5) = 2$, $\sigma(6) = 6$, so that $1, 2, 3, 4, 5, 6$ is permuted to $4, 1, 5, 3, 2, 6$, then

for $i = 1$, $j = 4$ precedes i,
for $i = 2$, $j = 3, 4, 5$ precede i,
for $i = 3$, $j = 4, 5$ precede i,
for $i = 4$, no $j > i$ precedes i,
for $i = 5$, no $j > i$ precedes i,
for $i = 6$, no $j > i$ precedes i.]

Now take the total of these counts (for the example, the total is $1+3+2=6$). This total represents the minimum number of interchanges of successive integers by which one can go from $1, 2, \ldots, n$ to $\sigma(1), \ldots, \sigma(n)$. [In the example, we go from 1, 2, 3, 4, 5, 6 to 4, 1, 5, 3, 2, 6 in the following six interchanges:

1, 2, 3, 4, 5, 6	
1, 2, 4, 3, 5, 6	1
1, 4, 2, 3, 5, 6	2
4, 1, 2, 3, 5, 6	3
4, 1, 2, 5, 3, 6	4
4, 1, 5, 2, 3, 6	5
4, 1, 5, 3, 2, 5	6.]

We call a permutation σ *even* if the total of these counts is even, *odd* if the total of these counts is odd. Let $\epsilon(\sigma) = +1$ if σ is even, -1 if σ is odd. Then, since D of a matrix with two adjacent rows interchanged is the negative of D of the original matrix, we see that $D(A_{\sigma(1)}, \ldots, A_{\sigma(n)}) = \epsilon(\sigma) D(A_1, \ldots, A_n)$. Each successive interchange from $1, \ldots, n$ to $\sigma(1), \ldots, \sigma(n)$ provides $a - 1$ as a multiplier of $D(A_1, \ldots, A_n)$.

Now if $A_j = A_k$ for $j \neq k$, then let σ be the permutation which interchanges $j+1$ and k and leaves the rest of the integers in their natural order. Then $(A_{\sigma(1)}, \ldots, A_{\sigma(n)})$ is a matrix with adjacent rows equal. By (3′), $D(A_{\sigma(1)}, \ldots, A_{\sigma(n)}) = 0$. Therefore, $D(A_1, \ldots, A_n) = 0$. Thus (3′) and (1) imply (3).

The existence of a function D satisfying (1), (2), and (3′) is provided by defining it recursively in n and checking that this function satisfies (1), (2), and (3′) by an induction on n.

For $n = 1$, define $D(A_1) = a_{11}$. For $n \geqslant 2$, for any choice of i, define

$$D(A) = \sum_{k=1}^{n} (-1)^{i+k} a_{ik} D_{ik}(A),$$

where $D_{ij}(A)$ is D of the $(n-1) \times (n-1)$ matrix formed from A by deleting the ith and jth column. $D_{ij}(A)$ is called the (i, j)th *minor* of A.

Exercise: (1) Show that if

$$A = \begin{bmatrix} a_{11} & a_{12} \\ a_{21} & a_{22} \end{bmatrix},$$

then $D(A)$ so defined reduces to $D(A) = a_{11}a_{22} - a_{12}a_{21}$, for any choice of i. (2) Check that if $n = 2$ then $D(A) = a_{11}a_{22} - a_{12}a_{21}$ satisfies (1), (2), and (3′).

Now assume that the function D so defined satisfies (1), (2), and (3′) for all matrices of order $n - 1$. We will first show that $D(A)$ thus satisfies (1), (2), and (3′) for A an $n \times n$ matrix, deferring for later the problem of proving that $D(A)$ so defined has the same value regardless of the choice of i in the definition.

Let $A = (A_1, \ldots, A_{j-1}, A_j + B_j, A_{j+1}, \ldots, A_n)$. For $k \neq j$, by the induction hypothesis, $D_{ik}(A)$ satisfies (1). Also a_{ik} doesn't depend on the jth row of A. For $k = j$, $D_{ik}(A)$ doesn't depend on the jth row of A and the jth term of $D(A)$ is $(a_{ij} + b_{ij})D_{ij}(A) = a_{ij}D_{ij}(A) + b_{ij}D_{ij}(A)$. Thus $D(A)$ satisfies (1).

A similar argument shows that $D(A)$ satisfies (2).

Let $A = (A_1, \ldots, A_{j-1}, A_j, A_j, A_{j+1}, \ldots, A_n)$. For $k \neq j, j+1$, $D_{ik}(A) = 0$ by the induction hypothesis.

Thus,

$$\begin{aligned} D(A) &= (-1)^{i+j}a_{ij}D_{ij}(A) + (-1)^{i+j+1}a_{i,j+1}D_{i,j+1}(A) \\ &= (-1)^{i+j}a_{ij}(D_{ij}(A) - D_{i,j+1}(A)) \\ &= 0, \end{aligned}$$

and $D(A)$ satisfies (3′).

Note that $D(A)$ so defined is not unique, in that $D(A) = c\sum_{k=1}^{n}(-1)^{i+k}a_{ik}D_{ik}(A)$ also satisfies (1), (2), and (3′), for c an arbitrary real number. To eliminate this, we impose a scaling condition on the function D, namely:

(4) $\quad D(I) = D(E_1, \ldots, E_n) = 1.$

Then if $c = 1$, $D(I) = (-1)^{2i}D_{ii}(I)$, and, since $D_{ii}(I)$ satisfies (4) by the induction hypothesis, i.e., $D_{ii}(I) = 1$, $D(I)$ also satisfies (4).

Exercise: Show that only if $c = 1$, does $D(I) = 1$.

The preceding proof that $D(A)$ satisfies (1)–(4) did not depend on the choice of i in the definition. Thus all we have shown so far is that the n functions $D_i(A) = \sum_{k=1}^{n}(-1)^{i+k}a_{ik}D_{ik}(A)$, $i = 1, \ldots, n$, each satisfy (1)–(4). To see that $D_i(A) = D_j(A)$ for $i < j$, consider the matrix A^*

formed from A with rows $A_1, \ldots, A_{i-1}, A_j, A_i, \ldots, A_{j-1}, A_{j+1}, \ldots, A_n$. For this permutation, $\epsilon(\sigma) = (-1)^{j-i}$. Also, $D_{ik}(A^*) = D_{jk}(A)$. Then,

$$D_i(A^*) = \sum_{k=1}^{n} (-1)^{i+k} a_{ik}^* D_{ik}(A^*)$$

$$= \sum_{k=1}^{n} (-1)^{i+k} a_{jk} D_{jk}(A).$$

But $D_i(A) = \epsilon(\sigma) D_i(A^*) = \sum_{k=1}^{n} (-1)^{j-i}(-1)^{i+k} a_{jk} D_{jk}(A) = D_j(A)$. So we see that this definition of $D(A)$ doesn't depend on choice of i.

A more general question is whether conditions (1)–(4) determine a unique function, i.e., whether $D(A)$ so defined is the only function satisfying (1)–(4). We prove this by induction on n.

Exercise: Show that for $n = 2$ conditions (1)–(4) imply that $D(A) = a_{11}a_{22} - a_{12}a_{21}$.

Suppose that $D(A)$ so defined is the only function satisfying (1)–(4) for $(n-1) \times (n-1)$ matrices. Now let $B_i^1 = A_i - a_{in}E_n$ and $B_i^2 = a_{in}E_n$. Then $A_i = B_i^1 + B_i^2$. Then, using condition (1) n successive times, we see that

$$D(A) = D(B_1^1 + B_1^2, \ldots, B_n^1 + B_n^2)$$

$$= \sum_{i_1=1}^{2} \cdots \sum_{i_n=1}^{2} D(B_1^{i_1}, \ldots, B_n^{i_n}).$$

Now suppose $i_1 = \cdots = i_n = 1$. Since $B_1^1, \ldots, B_n^1$ are all n-vectors with nth coordinate equal to 0, they must be linearly dependent. But we have already seen that (1)–(3) imply that D of a set of linearly dependent vectors is zero. Thus $D(B_1^1, \ldots, B_n^1) = 0$.

Similarly, if i_j and i_k both equal 2, then, since B_j^2 and B_k^2 are linearly dependent (since they both have first $n-1$ coordinates equal to 0), D of any n B's where more than one of the i_j's is a 2 will equal 0. Therefore,

$$\begin{aligned} D(A) &= D(B_1^2, B_2^1, \ldots, B_n^1) + D(B_1^1, B_2^2, B_3^1, \ldots, B_n^1) \\ &\quad + \cdots + D(B_1^1, \ldots, B_{n-1}^1, B_n^2) \\ &= D(B_1^2, B_2^1, \ldots, B_n^1) - D(B_2^2, B_1^1, B_3^1, \ldots, B_n^1) \\ &\quad + D(B_3^2, B_1^1, B_2^1, B_4^1, \ldots, B_n^1) \\ &\quad + \cdots + (-1)^{n+1} D(B_n^2, B_1^1, \ldots, B_{n-1}^1) \end{aligned}$$

by successively interchanging adjacent rows until B_i^2 is brought to the first row. But, for example,

$$\begin{aligned} D(B_1^2, B_2^1, \ldots, B_n^1) &= D(a_{1n}E_n, A_2 - a_{2n}E_n, \ldots, A_n - a_{2n}E_n) \\ &= a_{1n}D(E_n, A_2 - a_{2n}E_n, \ldots, A_n - a_{2n}E_n). \end{aligned}$$

The matrix with rows $E_n, A_2 - a_{2n}E_n, \ldots, A_n - a_{2n}E_n$ looks like

$$C = \begin{bmatrix} 0 & 0 & \cdots 0 & 1 \\ a_{21} & a_{22} & \cdots a_{2,n-1} & 0 \\ \cdot & & & \\ \cdot & & & \\ \cdot & & & \\ a_{n1} & a_{n2} & \cdots a_{n,n-1} & 0 \end{bmatrix} = \begin{bmatrix} 0 & 1 \\ A_{1n} & 0 \end{bmatrix}.$$

Now consider the $(n-1) \times (n-1)$ matrix

$$A_{1n} = \begin{bmatrix} a_{21} & a_{22} & \cdots a_{2,n-1} \\ \cdot & & \\ \cdot & & \\ \cdot & & \\ a_{n1} & a_{n2} & \cdots a_{n,n-1} \end{bmatrix},$$

and define a new function $D^*(A_{1n})$ by $D^*(A_{1n}) = D(C)$, for whatever function D satisfies (1)–(4) for $n \times n$ matrices. By our induction hypothesis, the function D defined above is the only function which satisfies (1)–(4) for $(n-1) \times (n-1)$ matrices. Therefore, $D^*(A_{1n}) = D(A_{1n})$, and this quantity equals what we have called $D_{1n}(A)$.

If we go through this argument for all $i = 1, \ldots, n$, and put the pieces together, we find that

$$\begin{aligned} D(A) &= a_{1n}D_{1n}(A) - a_{2n}D_{2n}(A) + a_{3n}D_{3n}(A) \\ &\quad + \cdots + (-1)^{n-1}a_{nn}D_{nn}(A) \\ &= \sum_{i=1}^{n} (-1)^{n-i}a_{in}D_{in}(A). \end{aligned}$$

The argument did not depend on choice of the nth row of A for defining the B's, and so we see that, for all $k = 1, \ldots, n$, since $(-1)^{k-i} = (-1)^{k+i}$, the function

$$D(A) = \sum_{i=1}^{n} (-1)^{i+k}a_{ik}D_{ik}(A)$$

is the unique function satisfying (1)–(4).

We call $D(A)$ the *determinant* of A, and sometimes write it as $|A|$.

Exercise: Compute $|A|$ for the following matrices:

$$\begin{bmatrix} 3 & 0 & -1 \\ -1 & 2 & 7 \\ 4 & 6 & 5 \end{bmatrix},$$

$$\begin{bmatrix} 3 & 0 & -1 & 4 \\ -1 & 2 & 7 & 3 \\ 4 & 6 & 5 & 2 \\ 2 & 1 & 8 & 7 \end{bmatrix}.$$

Note though that the function

$$D^*(A)=\sum_{k=1}^{n}(-1)^{i+k}a_{ik}D^*_{ik}(A)$$

also satisfies (1)–(4), as the structure of the proof that $D(A)$ satisfies (1)–(4) did not depend on the fact that the summation was over i or over k. Since conditions (1)–(4) determine a unique function, it follows that $D(A)=D^*(A)$. A consequence of this is that $D(A)=D(A')$. This follows from the fact that $D_{ik}(A')=D^*_{ki}(A)$ and $a'_{ik}=a_{ki}$, so that $D(A')=\sum_{k=1}^{n}(-1)^{i+k}a_{ki}D^*_{ki}(A)=D^*(A)=D(A)$.

Now let $C=AB$, where A, B, and C are $n\times n$ matrices, so that $C'_j=b_{1j}A'_1+\cdots+b_{nj}A'_n$, where C'_j is the jth column of C and A'_j is the jth column of A. Then

$$\begin{aligned} D(C)&=D(C'_1,\ldots,C'_n)\\ &=D(b_{11}A'_1+\cdots+b_{n1}A'_n,\ldots,b_{1n}A'_1+\cdots+b_{nn}A'_n)\\ &=\sum_{i_1=1}^{n}\cdots\sum_{i_n=1}^{n}D(b_{i_11}A'_{i_1},\ldots,b_{i_nn}A'_{i_n}), \end{aligned}$$

using (1) n^n times. Now, using (2) we obtain

$$D(C)=\sum_{i_1=1}^{n}\cdots\sum_{i_n=1}^{n}b_{i_11}\cdots b_{i_nn}D(A'_{i_1},\ldots,A'_{i_n}).$$

But the only terms in the summand which are non-zero are, as a consequence of (3), those terms for which $i_1,\ldots,i_n$ are distinct, i.e., are permutations of $1,\ldots,n$. Thus,

$$\begin{aligned} D(C)&=\sum_{\sigma}b_{\sigma(1)1}\cdots b_{\sigma(n)n}D(A'_{\sigma(1)},\ldots,A'_{\sigma(n)}),\\ &=\sum_{\sigma}b_{\sigma(1)1}\cdots b_{\sigma(n)n}\epsilon(\sigma)D(A'_1,\ldots,A'_n), \end{aligned}$$

a sum of $n!$ terms. Now suppose $A = I$. Then $C = B$, and we have the result that

$$D(B) = \sum_{\sigma} \epsilon(\sigma) b_{\sigma(1)1} \cdots b_{\sigma(n)n}.$$

From this it follows that $D(C) = D(B)D(A)$, or, as it is usually expressed, $|AB| = |A| \cdot |B|$.

The following theorem has been anticipated by our heuristic discussion of the properties of the function $|A|$ and formally shows that A is invertible if and only if $|A| \neq 0$.

Theorem 5: Let $A_1, \ldots, A_n$ be n vectors in n-space. Then $D(A_1, \ldots, A_n) = 0$ if and only if the vectors are linearly dependent.

Proof: If $c_1A_1 + \cdots + c_nA_n = 0$ with $c_1 \neq 0$, say, then $A_1 = b_2A_2 + \cdots + b_nA_n$, and

$$\begin{aligned} D(A) &= D(b_2A_2 + \cdots + b_nA_n, A_2, \ldots, A_n) \\ &= b_2D(A_2, A_2, \ldots, A_n) + \cdots + b_nD(A_n, A_2, \ldots, A_n) \\ &= 0. \end{aligned}$$

Conversely, if $A_1, \ldots, A_n$ are linearly independent, then A is invertible. Then, since $I = AA^{-1}$,

$$1 = |I| = |AA^{-1}| = |A| \cdot |A^{-1}|,$$

so that $|A| \neq 0$, and $|A^{-1}| = |A|^{-1}$.

Thus the following are equivalent: (1) A is invertible, (2) $|A| \neq 0$, (3) columns of A are linearly independent, as are the rows of A, (4) rank $A = n$, (5) $XA' = 0$ implies $X = 0$. This summarizes all we know about invertibility.

In addition to the inductive computational description of A^{-1} given in section 1 in terms of a partitioning of A, we can present a formula for A^{-1} in terms of determinants as follows. Recall that $D_{ij}(A)$ is the determinant of the $(n-1) \times (n-1)$ submatrix of a matrix A whose ith row and jth column are deleted. Let a^{ij} denote the (i, j)th element of A^{-1}.

Theorem 6: $a^{ij} = (-1)^{i+j} D_{ji}(A)/|A|, \quad i, j = 1, \ldots, n.$

Proof: We must show that

$$\sum_{j=1}^{n} a_{ij} D_{kj}(A)(-1)^{j+k} = \begin{cases} |A| & \text{if } k = i, \\ 0 & \text{if } k \neq i. \end{cases}$$

For $k = i$, we note that $\sum_{j=1}^{n} a_{ij}D_{ij}(A)(-1)^{i+j}$ is just the definition of $|A|$.

For $k \neq i$, replace the kth row of A by the ith row, and call this new matrix A^*. We know that $|A^*| = 0$. But

$$0 = |A^*| = \sum_{j=1}^{n} a_{kj}^* D_{kj}(A^*)(-1)^{j+k} = \sum_{j=1}^{n} a_{ij}D_{kj}(A)(-1)^{j+k},$$

because $D_{kj}(A^*) = D_{kj}(A)$.

Exercise: Using Theorem 6, find A^{-1} when A is

(a) $\begin{bmatrix} 3 & 0 \\ -1 & 2 \end{bmatrix}$,

(b) $\begin{bmatrix} 3 & 0 & -1 \\ -1 & 2 & 7 \\ 4 & 6 & 5 \end{bmatrix}$,

(c) $\begin{bmatrix} 3 & 0 & -1 & 4 \\ -1 & 2 & 7 & 3 \\ 4 & 6 & 5 & 2 \\ 2 & 1 & 8 & 7 \end{bmatrix}$.

(This is the same exercise as given in section 1. Compare for yourself the work involved here with that using the method of section 1.)

A matrix A is said to be *lower triangular* if $a_{ij} = 0$ for all i, j with $i < j$. A matrix A is said to be *upper triangular* if $a_{ij} = 0$ for all i, j with $i > j$. A matrix A is said to be *diagonal* if $a_{ij} = 0$ for all i, j with $i \neq j$.

Exercise: Let A be triangular (either lower, upper, or both, i.e., diagonal). Show that $|A| = a_{11}a_{22} \cdots a_{nn}$.

Suppose A can be partitioned as

$$A = \begin{bmatrix} A_1 & A_2 \\ A_3 & A_4 \end{bmatrix},$$

where A_1 is $m \times m$ and $|A_4| \neq 0$. Then $|A| = |A_4||A_1 - A_2A_4^{-1}A_3|$. This result is useful as an alternative (to the definition) "bootstrapping" way of computing a determinant, taking A_4 as a 1×1 matrix.

Exercise: (1) Prove this. *Hint*: Let

$$B = \begin{bmatrix} I & 0 \\ -A_4^{-1}A_3 & I \end{bmatrix}.$$

What is $|AB|$?

(2) Use this to find the determinants of the following matrices:

$$\begin{bmatrix} 3 & 0 & -1 \\ -1 & 2 & 7 \\ 4 & 6 & 5 \end{bmatrix},$$

$$\begin{bmatrix} 3 & 0 & -1 & 4 \\ -1 & 2 & 7 & 3 \\ 4 & 6 & 5 & 2 \\ 2 & 1 & 8 & 7 \end{bmatrix}.$$

This concludes our discussion of algebraic properties of determinants. We now turn our attention to a geometric interpretation of the determinant.

Consider a parallelotope (a generalization of the parallelopiped of 3-space) in n-space formed by lines from 0 to each of the m linearly independent n-vectors $A_1, \ldots, A_m$ ($m \leqslant n$) and from 0 and each vector A_i to all vectors $A_i + A_j$, $j \neq i$. For example, when $n = 3$ and $m = 2$, with $A_1 = (1, 1, 1)$, $A_2 = (2, 1, 0)$, then the parallelotope is the shaded area of figure 3, i.e., the parallelogram formed by $(0, 0, 0)$, $(1, 1, 1)$, $(2, 1, 0)$, and $(3, 2, 1)$.

How shall we define the "volume" of a parallelotope in n-space? We do this in analogy with the definition of the "volume" (i.e., area) of a parallelogram or of a parallelopiped, as the product of the "volume" of the base (i.e., the length of the base for parallelograms and the area of the base for parallelopipeds) and the length of the altitude. A parallelotope formed from $m \leqslant n$ linearly independent n-vectors lies on some m-

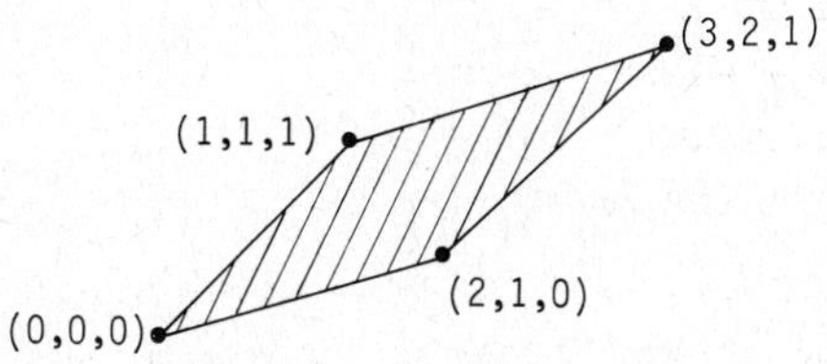

FIGURE 3

dimensional subspace of n-space. We can define the *base* of a parallelotope as the parallelotope formed from any $m-1$ of these m n-vectors. Now consider the vector excluded in the formation of the base, say A_1, and let B be its orthogonal projection along the base. We call the vector $A_1 - B$ the *altitude* of the parallelotope, as it is orthogonal to the base and extends from the base to the excluded point A_1. Finally, we define the *length* of a vector X as the square root of XX'. The *volume of a parallelotope* is defined as the product of the length of the altitude and the volume of the base.

Let A be the $m \times n$ matrix,

$$A = \begin{bmatrix} A_1 \\ \cdot \\ \cdot \\ \cdot \\ A_m \end{bmatrix},$$

of rank m. We shall prove the following theorem.

Theorem 7: The square of the volume of the parallelotope formed from $A_1, \ldots, A_m$ is $|AA'|$.

Proof: Let $A_1 = B + C$, where C is a linear combination of $A_2, \ldots, A_m$ and $BA_i' = 0$, $i = 2, \ldots, m$. Vectors B and C satisfying this can be found, because one can always project A_1 orthogonally along the subspace for which $A_2, \ldots, A_m$ is a basis and then take B to be A_1 minus the projection. Then,

$$A = \begin{bmatrix} B \\ A_2 \\ \cdot \\ \cdot \\ \cdot \\ A_m \end{bmatrix} + \begin{bmatrix} C \\ 0 \\ \cdot \\ \cdot \\ \cdot \\ 0 \end{bmatrix}.$$

Let $C = \sum_{i=2}^{m} c_i A_i$, and let

$$A^* = A - \sum_{i=2}^{m} \begin{bmatrix} c_i A_i \\ 0 \end{bmatrix},$$

where 0 denotes an $(m-1) \times n$ zero matrix. Then $A^* = \left[\begin{smallmatrix} B \\ D \end{smallmatrix}\right]$ where D is the lower $(m-1)\times n$ submatrix of A. Now

$$A^*A^{*\prime}=\binom{B}{D}(B'D')=\begin{pmatrix}BB' & BD'\\ DB' & DD'\end{pmatrix}=\begin{pmatrix}BB' & 0\\ 0 & DD'\end{pmatrix},$$

since D is composed of the last $m-1$ rows of A and $BA_i'=0$ for these rows. Therefore,

$$|A^*A^{*\prime}|=(BB')|DD'|.$$

Let J_{ij} be the $m\times m$ matrix with a 1 in row i, column j, and 0 elsewhere. Then,

$$A^*=A-\sum_{j=2}^{m}J_{1j}c_jA=\Big(I-\sum_{j=2}^{m}c_jJ_{1j}\Big)A=TA,$$

where T is the triangular matrix

$$T=\begin{bmatrix}1 & -c_2\cdots-c_m\\ & 1 & & 0\\ & & \cdot\\ & & & \cdot\\ & & & & \cdot\\ & 0\\ & & & & & 1\end{bmatrix}.$$

Therefore $|A^*A^{*\prime}|=|TAA'T'|=|AA'|$, as $|T|=1$.

Now D is the matrix whose rows are a basis for an $(m-1)$-dimensional subspace of n-space. Let our induction hypothesis be that $|DD'|$ is the square of the volume of the parallelotope with edges the vectors $A_2,\dots,A_m$, i.e., the square of the volume of the base of the parallelotope formed from $A_2,\dots,A_m$. Then we see that $|AA'|=(BB')|DD'|$ is the square of the volume of the parallelotope formed from $A_1,\dots,A_m$, as B is the altitude of this parallelotope and BB' is the square of the altitude's length.

Note that the above argument did not depend on the choice of vectors forming the base, and so is complete.

When $m=n$, $|AA'|=|A|^2$, so that the absolute value of $|A|$, say $|A|^+$, is the volume of the parallelotope formed by $A_1,\dots,A_n$.

Let $Y=XA'$, where X is an n-vector and A' is the $n\times n$ matrix of a linear transformation of the n-space $\mathscr{X}$ of X's to the n-space $\mathscr{Y}$ of Y's. If $X_1,\dots,X_n$ form a parallelotope in $\mathscr{X}$, then $Y_1=X_1A',\dots,Y_n=X_nA'$

form the image parallelotope in $\mathscr{Y}$. But

$$\begin{vmatrix} Y_1 \\ \cdot \\ \cdot \\ \cdot \\ Y_n \end{vmatrix}^+ = \begin{vmatrix} X_1 \\ \cdot \\ \cdot \\ \cdot \\ X_n \end{vmatrix}^+ |A|^+.$$

Then the volume of a parallelotope in $\mathscr{Y}$ is $|A|^+$ times the volume of the antecedent parallelotope in $\mathscr{X}$.

6. Orthogonal transformations and symmetric matrices

Let A be an $n \times n$ matrix. The vector $X \neq 0$ is called a *characteristic vector of* A and the scalar λ is its associated *characteristic root* if X and λ satisfy the equation $XA = \lambda X$. Clearly if X is a characteristic vector of A, then, as $X(A - \lambda I) = 0$ with $X \neq 0$, the matrix $A - \lambda I$ is not invertible. Therefore, λ is a solution of the equation $|A - \lambda I| = 0$, sometimes called the *characteristic equation.*

Exercise: Let λ be a characteristic root of A and $\mathscr{X}$ be the set of vectors X such that $XA = \lambda X$. Show that $\mathscr{X}$ is a subspace.

Let $C = A - \lambda I$. Since $|C| = \sum_\sigma \epsilon(\sigma) c_{\sigma(1)1} \cdots c_{\sigma(n)n}$ and $c_{ii} = a_{ii} - \lambda$, $c_{ij} = a_{ij}$, $j \neq i$, we see that $|A - \lambda I|$ is an nth degree polynomial in λ, and thus, by the fundamental theorem of algebra, the polynomial equation $|A - \lambda I| = 0$ has n roots (not all distinct or real, of course). If λ is a real root of the characteristic equation, since $A - \lambda I$ is singular, there exists a vector $X \neq 0$ such that $X(A - \lambda I) = 0$, or $XA = \lambda X$. But if λ is an imaginary root of $|A - \lambda I| = 0$, we cannot find a Euclidean n-vector X satisfying $XA = \lambda X$ for that λ, as XA is a vector of real numbers.

Exercise: Find the characteristic roots of the following matrices:

(a) $\begin{bmatrix} 3 & 1 \\ 1 & 4 \end{bmatrix}$,

(b) $\begin{bmatrix} 3 & -1 & 0 \\ 3 & 4 & 0 \\ 0 & 0 & 5 \end{bmatrix}$.

Find corresponding characteristic vectors for matrix (a).

An $n \times n$ matrix B is called *orthogonal* when $BB' = I$. Thus $B^{-1} = B'$ for orthogonal matrices. If B is orthogonal, then the characteristic roots of BAB' are the same as those of A, for $|BAB' - \lambda I| = |BAB' - \lambda BB'| = |B||A - \lambda I||B'| = 0$ if and only if $|A - \lambda I| = 0$.

An $n \times n$ matrix A is called *symmetric* when $A = A'$.

Theorem 8: *If A is symmetric, then all its characteristic roots are real numbers.*

Proof: Suppose $\lambda = a + bi$ is a characteristic root of A, where $i = \sqrt{-1}$. Let $Z = X + iY$ be the vector satisfying $ZA = \lambda Z$, where X and Y are Euclidean vectors. Let $\bar{Z} = X - iY$ and $\bar{\lambda} = a - bi$. Then $ZA\bar{Z}' = XAX' - iXAY' + iYAX' + YAY'$ (recalling that $i^2 = -1$). But $ZA\bar{Z}' = \lambda Z\bar{Z}' = \lambda XX' - i\lambda XY' + i\lambda YX' + \lambda YY'$. Since $XAY' = YAX'$ and $XY' = YX'$, we see that

$$XAX' + YAY' = \lambda(XX' + YY').$$

But both $XAX' + YAY'$ and $XX' + YY'$ are real numbers. Therefore $b = 0$ and λ is real.

The n real characteristic roots of a symmetric matrix A need not be distinct. We call the *multiplicity* of a characteristic root λ_i the number of times the factor $(\lambda - \lambda_i)$ occurs in the factorization of the polynomial $|A - \lambda I|$.

What is the rank of the matrix $A - \lambda_i I$, when A is symmetric? Let $\mathscr{X}_i$ be the subspace of all vectors X satisfying $XA = \lambda_i X$. Let m_i be the dimension of $\mathscr{X}_i$. Now express n-space as a direct sum of $\mathscr{X}_i$ and $\mathscr{Y}_i$, where $\mathscr{Y}_i$ is a subspace orthogonal to $\mathscr{X}_i$. Let us first find the matrix of the linear transformation T corresponding to A when our basis consists of $X_1, \ldots, X_{m_i}$ in $\mathscr{X}_i$ and $X_{m_i+1}, \ldots, X_n$ in $\mathscr{Y}_i$. Since $T(X) = XA$, $T(X_j) = X_jA = \lambda_i X_j$ if $j = 1, \ldots, m_i$. Also, when $j = m_i + 1, \ldots, n$, X_j is orthogonal to any vector of $\mathscr{X}_i$ so that $T(X_j)X'_k = X_jAX'_k = \lambda_i X_j X'_k = 0$ for $k = 1, \ldots, m_i$. Therefore $T(X_j)$ is orthogonal to any vector of $\mathscr{X}_i$. From this we see that the matrix of T relative to the basis $X_1, \ldots, X_n$ is

$$B = \begin{bmatrix} \lambda_i I & 0 \\ 0 & C \end{bmatrix}.$$

Since, as seen in section 3, $B = XAX^{-1}$, where X is the matrix whose jth row is the vector X_j, we note that $|A - \lambda I| = |A - \lambda X^{-1}X| = |X^{-1}||XAX^{-1} - \lambda I||X| = |B - \lambda I| = (\lambda_i - \lambda)^{m_i}|C - \lambda I|$. But λ_i is not a root of $|C - \lambda I| = 0$, by construction of $\mathcal{Y}_i$. Therefore m_i, the dimension of $\mathcal{X}_i$, must equal the multiplicity of λ_i.

The main theorem relating symmetric and orthogonal matrices is the following.

Theorem 9: *Let A be a symmetric* $n \times n$ *matrix. Then there exists an orthogonal matrix B such that* $BAB' = D$, *where D is a diagonal matrix.*

Before proving this theorem, let us see what it tells us about the relationship between A, B, and D. If $BAB' = D$, then $|BAB' - \lambda I| = |D - \lambda I| = 0$ if and only if the roots of the characteristic equation of BAB' are the diagonal elements of D. But since B is orthogonal these roots are the characteristic roots of A as well. Also, if $BA = DB$, then, letting B_i be the ith row of B, we have $B_iA = d_{ii}B_i$. Thus B_i is the characteristic vector corresponding to the characteristic root d_{ii} of A. The rows of B are then characteristic vectors of A.

Now consider the linear transformation T for which A is the matrix relative to the elementary basis. Consider now a new orthogonal basis for n-space, consisting of the n rows of B. What would be the matrix of T relative to this basis?

By the change of basis formula, the matrix is given by $BAB^{-1} = BAB'$. But since $BAB' = D$, we see that relative to the basis $B_1, \ldots, B_n$, the matrix of T is D.

The essence of our proof, then, is to show that given A we can construct an orthogonal basis B from its characteristic vectors and a diagonal matrix D from its characteristic roots such that, relative to the basis of characteristic vectors, the matrix of the linear transformation corresponding to A is the diagonal matrix D. The proof follows.

Proof: Let $\lambda_1, \ldots, \lambda_p$ be the different characteristic roots of A. (*Query*: Why must $p \leqslant n$?) Let $\mathcal{X}_j$ be the subspace of all vectors X satisfying $XA = \lambda_j X$.

Let P_j be the orthogonal projection transformation of n-space along $\mathcal{X}_j$, and define $X_j = P_j(X)$ for any vector X.

[To follow this construction concretely, I interpolate an example along with the proof of the theorem. Let

$$A = \begin{bmatrix} 1 & 0 & 0 \\ 0 & 2 & 1 \\ 0 & 1 & 2 \end{bmatrix}.$$

Check that $\lambda_1 = 1$, $\lambda_2 = 3$ are the only characteristic roots of A. The subspace $\mathscr{X}_1$ is the set of vectors with $x_2 + x_3 = 0$. The subspace $\mathscr{X}_2$ is the set of scalar multiples of the vector (0, 1, 1). Thus the matrix corresponding to P_1 is

$$\begin{bmatrix} 1 & 0 & 0 \\ 0 & \frac{1}{2} & -\frac{1}{2} \\ 0 & -\frac{1}{2} & \frac{1}{2} \end{bmatrix},$$

and the matrix corresponding to P_2 is

$$\begin{bmatrix} 0 & 0 & 0 \\ 0 & \frac{1}{2} & \frac{1}{2} \\ 0 & \frac{1}{2} & \frac{1}{2} \end{bmatrix}.$$

Exercise: Check this. *Hint*: First find the matrix of the projection transformation of $X = (x_1, x_2, x_3)$ on the subspace with basis (0, 1, 1).]

Since $\lambda_i X_i X_j' = X_i A X_j' = X_j A X_i' = \lambda_j X_j X_i'$ and $\lambda_i \neq \lambda_j$, we see that $X_i X_j' = 0$ for all $i \neq j$. Since for all X the vectors $X_i = P_i(X)$ and $X_j = P_j(X)$ are orthogonal, the orthogonal projection of X_j along $\mathscr{X}_i$ and of X_i along $\mathscr{X}_j$ are the zero vector. That is $P_i(P_j(X)) = P_j(P_i(X)) = 0$. Therefore the P_i are orthogonal in the sense that $P_i P_j = 0$, the transformation which associates the zero vector with each vector.

Let $P = P_1 + \cdots + P_p$. Then P is a projection transformation.

Since the dimension of $\mathscr{X}_j$ is m_j, the multiplicity of λ_j, the dimension of the space which is the direct sum of the $\mathscr{X}_j$'s is $\sum_{j=1}^{p} m_j = n$. Thus $P = I$.

Then

$$XA = P(X)A = \sum_{i=1}^{p} P_i(X)A = \sum_{i=1}^{p} X_i A$$
$$= \sum_{i=1}^{p} \lambda_i X_i = \sum_{i=1}^{p} \lambda_i P_i(X) = Q(X),$$

where Q is the linear transformation given by

$$Q = \sum_{i=1}^{p} \lambda_i P_i.$$

Choose as basis in each of the $\mathscr{X}_j$'s the ranges of each of the P_j's, a set of orthogonal vectors of length equal to 1. Since $\sum_{j=1}^{p} P_j = I$, the totality of the vectors of these bases is a basis for n-space. Recall that the matrix A is the matrix of the linear transformation Q relative to the elementary basis. We know that P_i of any basis element is either 0 or the basis element, and that $XA = \sum_{i=1}^{p} \lambda_i R_i(X)$. Therefore, relative to this newly constructed basis, the matrix corresponding to the linear transformation Q is diagonal, with elements λ_i on the diagonal. Take B to be the matrix of orthogonal basis vectors of length equal to 1. Then $BA = DB$, where D is the matrix of λ_i's, with each λ_i repeated m_i times.

[In our above example, take $X_1 = (0, 1/\sqrt{2}, -1/\sqrt{2})$ and $X_2 = (1, 0, 0)$ as an orthogonal basis of length 1 in $\mathscr{X}_1$, and $X_3 = (0, 1/\sqrt{2}, 1/\sqrt{2})$ as a basis of length 1 in $\mathscr{X}_2$. Take

$$B = \begin{bmatrix} 0 & 1/\sqrt{2} & -1/\sqrt{2} \\ 1 & 0 & 0 \\ 0 & 1/\sqrt{2} & 1/\sqrt{2} \end{bmatrix}.$$

Then

$$BA = \begin{bmatrix} 0 & 1/\sqrt{2} & -1/\sqrt{2} \\ 1 & 0 & 0 \\ 0 & 1/\sqrt{2} & 1/\sqrt{2} \end{bmatrix} \begin{bmatrix} 1 & 0 & 0 \\ 0 & 2 & 1 \\ 0 & 1 & 2 \end{bmatrix} =$$

$$DB = \begin{bmatrix} 1 & 0 & 0 \\ 0 & 1 & 0 \\ 0 & 0 & 3 \end{bmatrix} \begin{bmatrix} 0 & 1/\sqrt{2} & -1/\sqrt{2} \\ 1 & 0 & 0 \\ 0 & 1/\sqrt{2} & 1/\sqrt{2} \end{bmatrix} = \begin{bmatrix} 0 & 1/\sqrt{2} & -1/\sqrt{2} \\ 1 & 0 & 0 \\ 0 & 3/\sqrt{2} & 3/\sqrt{2} \end{bmatrix}.]$$

The characteristic equation $|A - \lambda I| = 0$ is a polynomial in λ, expressible as $\sum_{i=0}^{n} \alpha_i \lambda^i = 0$. There is a celebrated theorem of matrix theory, the Cayley–Hamilton theorem, which says that every matrix A "satisfies" its characteristic equation. That is, defining A^i as A multiplied by itself i times and A^0 as I, the theorem says that the matrix $\sum_{i=0}^{n} \alpha_i A^i$ is the zero matrix. This is difficult to prove in general, but as we only need the result (in section 7) for symmetric matrices, let us prove it, easily, in that special case.

Let $p(x)$ be a polynomial. Let A be a symmetric matrix, B an orthogonal matrix, and

$$BAB' = \begin{bmatrix} \lambda_1 & & 0 \\ & \ddots & \\ 0 & & \lambda_n \end{bmatrix} = D.$$

Define the matrix $C_p(A)$ as

$$C_p(A) = B' \begin{bmatrix} p(\lambda_1) & & & 0 \\ & \cdot & & \\ & & \cdot & \\ & & & \cdot \\ 0 & & & p(\lambda_n) \end{bmatrix} B.$$

Let $q(x)$ be the polynomial $q(x) = |A - xI| = \sum_{i=0}^{n} \alpha_i x^i$. Then $C_q(A) = 0$, the zero matrix, as $q(\lambda_i) = 0$ for $i = 1, \ldots, n$. But

$$C_q(A) = B' \begin{bmatrix} q(\lambda_1) & & & 0 \\ & \cdot & & \\ & & \cdot & \\ & & & \cdot \\ 0 & & & q(\lambda_n) \end{bmatrix} B$$

$$= \sum_{i=0}^{n} \alpha_i B' \begin{bmatrix} \lambda_1^i & & 0 \\ & \cdot & \\ & & \cdot \quad \cdot \\ & & \cdot \\ 0 & & \lambda_n^i \end{bmatrix} B$$

$$= \sum_{i=0}^{n} \alpha_i B' D^i B$$

$$= \sum_{i=0}^{n} \alpha_i A^i.$$

Therefore every symmetric matrix satisfies its characteristic equation.

Let A be a symmetric matrix with all its characteristic roots nonnegative. Such a symmetric matrix is called *positive semidefinite.* Define $D^{\frac{1}{2}}$ as the diagonal matrix with diagonal elements the square roots of the characteristic roots of A. Then $A = B'DB = B'D^{\frac{1}{2}}D^{\frac{1}{2}}B = C'C$, where $C = D^{\frac{1}{2}}B$. This matrix C is not unique, for if F is orthogonal, then A can be expressed as $A = C'F'FC = G'G$, where $G = FC$.

Exercise: (Vinograd's Theorem) Let A be a non-singular symmetric matrix, with $A = BB' = CC'$, where B and C are non-singular. Show that $B = CQ$, where Q is an orthogonal matrix.

When A is *positive definite*, however, that is when all its characteristic roots are positive, we can find a unique lower triangular matrix T, with $t_{ii} > 0$ for all i, such that $A = TT'$. To obtain T, we first define matrices D_{ij} with $D_{00} = 1$, $D_{1j} = a_{1j}$, and

$$D_{ij} = \begin{bmatrix} & & a_{1j} \\ & & \cdot \\ A_{i-1,i-1} & & \cdot \\ & & \cdot \\ & & a_{i-1,j} \\ a_{i1} \cdots & a_{i,i-1} & a_{ij} \end{bmatrix},$$

for $i = 2, \ldots, n$, $j = i, \ldots, n$, where $A_{i-1,i-1}$ is the upper left-hand $(i-1)\times(i-1)$ submatrix of A. If $A = TT'$, then D_{ij} can also be written as

$$D_{ij} = \begin{bmatrix} T_{i-1} & 0 \\ & \\ & \\ t_{i1} \cdots & t_{ii} \end{bmatrix} \begin{matrix} T'_{i-1} \\ \\ \\ 0 \end{matrix} \begin{bmatrix} t_{j1} \\ \cdot \\ \cdot \\ \cdot \\ t_{ji} \end{bmatrix},$$

where T_{i-1} is the upper left-hand $(i-1)\times(i-1)$ submatrix of T. Thus,

$$|D_{ij}| = t_{11}^2 \cdots t_{i-1,i-1}^2 t_{ii} t_{ji},$$

as the determinant of a triangular matrix is the product of its diagonal elements.

When A is positive definite, the decomposition of A into a product of a lower triangular matrix and its transpose is unique, for if B is orthogonal and TB is to be triangular, then B must have $+1$ or -1 on the diagonal and zeros elsewhere. Then the only triangular decomposition with $t_{ii} > 0$ for all i is the one where $B = I$.

From the formula for $|D_{ij}|$, we see that

$$t_{ii} = \sqrt{\left(\frac{|D_{ii}|}{|D_{i-1,i-1}|}\right)},$$

and

$$t_{ji} = \frac{|D_{ij}|}{\sqrt{(|D_{ii}||D_{i-1,i-1}|)}}.$$

Exercise: (1) Obtain similar formulae for an upper triangular matrix T (one with all zeros below the diagonal) such that $A = TT'$.

(2) Find a triangular decomposition of

(a) $\begin{bmatrix} 3 & 1 \\ 1 & 3 \end{bmatrix}$

(b) $\begin{bmatrix} 3 & 1 & 0 \\ 1 & 3 & 2 \\ 0 & 2 & 3 \end{bmatrix}$.

Earlier we defined a symmetric matrix as positive definite (semidefinite) if all its characteristic roots were positive (non-negative). The following theorem gives another definition of positive definiteness (semidefiniteness).

Theorem 10: *A is positive definite (semidefinite) if and only if, for any vector* $X \neq 0$, $XAX' > 0$ $(XAX' \geqslant 0)$.

Proof: Let $A = BDB'$, B orthogonal and D diagonal with the characteristic roots of A as diagonal elements. Suppose A is positive definite (semidefinite). Then $XAX' = XBDB'X' = YDY'$, say, where $Y = XB$. But $YDY' = \sum_{i=1}^{n} d_{ii} y_i^2 > 0$ $(\geqslant 0)$ unless $Y = 0$. Since X was arbitrary, we see that $XAX' > 0$ $(XAX' \geqslant 0)$.

Suppose now that $XAX' > 0$ $(XAX' \geqslant 0)$ for all $X \neq 0$. Since $A = BDB'$, $XBDB'X' > 0$ $(XBDB'X' \geqslant 0)$ for all X. Take $X = E_i B'$. Then $E_i D E_i' > 0$ $(E_i D E_i' \geqslant 0)$, or $d_{ii} > 0$ $(d_{ii} \geqslant 0)$. As this can be done for all i, we see that A is positive definite (semidefinite).

Exercise: Let A be a positive definite and B be a non-singular matrix. Show that BAB' is positive definite.

We will need the following theorem for the proof of the corollary of Theorem 12.

Theorem 11: *Let A, B, and* $A - B$ *be positive definite. Then* $B^{-1} - A^{-1}$ *is positive definite.*

Proof: Let $A = TT'$ and $C = T^{-1}BT'^{-1}$. Let $QCQ' = D$, where Q is an orthogonal and D is a diagonal matrix. Then, since $A - B$ is positive definite, so is $QT^{-1}(A - B)T'^{-1}Q' = I - D$.

Now $B^{-1}-A^{-1}=T'^{-1}(C^{-1}-I)T^{-1}=T'^{-1}Q'(D^{-1}-I)QT^{-1}$. Since $I-D$ is positive definite, so is $D^{-1}-I$ and consequently so is $B^{-1}-A^{-1}$.

Let A be an $n\times m$ matrix with AA' invertible, and B be an $n\times m$ matrix.

Theorem 12: *$BB'-BA'(AA')^{-1}AB'$ is positive semidefinite.*

Proof: For any n-vectors X and Y we have

$$\begin{aligned}0&\leqslant (XA+YB)(XA+YB)'\\&=XAA'X'+YBB'Y'+YBA'X'+XAB'Y'\\&=(XC+YBA'C'^{-1})(XC+YBA'C'^{-1})'\\&\quad+Y(BB'-(BA')(AA')^{-1}AB')Y',\end{aligned}$$

where C is a triangular matrix satisfying $AA'=CC'$. Let $X=-YBA'(CC')^{-1}$. Then the above inequality reduces to

$$0\leqslant Y(BB'-BA'(AA')^{-1}AB')Y',$$

for all Y.

Corollary: *If BA' and BB' are invertible and $B\neq BA'(AA')^{-1}A$, then $(AB')^{-1}(AA')(BA')^{-1}-(BB')^{-1}$ is positive semidefinite.*

Proof: If $B\neq BA'(AA')^{-1}A$, then $XA+YB$ in the proof of Theorem 12 is zero if and only if Y is zero. Thus $BB'-BA'(AA')^{-1}AB'$ is positive definite. Now, an application of Theorem 11 proves the corollary.

7. Generalized inverse

Let us find a matrix X which satisfies

(1) $AXA=A$,

(2) $(XA)'=XA$,

(3) $(AX)'=AX$,

(4) $XAX=X$,

where A is an $m\times n$ matrix. Note that if X satisfies (1)–(4), then X'

satisfies (1)–(4) when A is replaced by A'. It is clear that $X = A^{-1}$ is the only matrix which satisfies (1)–(4) when $m = n$ and A is invertible. In general, a matrix X which satisfies (1)–(4) is called a *generalized inverse* (sometimes *pseudo-inverse*) of A.

Conditions (3) and (4) imply $XAX = X(AX)' = XX'A' = X$. Conversely, $XX'A' = X$ implies $(AX)(AX)' = AX$, and since $(AX)(AX)'$ is symmetric, AX must be also, i.e., $AX = (AX)'$. Thus $X(AX)' = X = XAX$. We can therefore replace (3) and (4) by $XX'A' = X$.

Exercise: Show that (1) and (2) are equivalent to $XAA' = A'$.

Suppose we can find a matrix B, which is symmetric and satisfies $BA'AA' = A'$. Let $X = BA'$. Then $B(BA'AA') = BBA'AA' = BBA'(AA'AB)A' = B(BA'AA')ABA'$, or, replacing $BA'AA'$ by A' in the extreme expressions of this set of equations, we have $BA' = BA'ABA'$, so that $X = XX'A'$. Consequently $X = BA'$ satisfies (1)–(4).

Now let us find B satisfying this condition. Consider the matrix $A'A$. As it is symmetric, it satisfies its characteristic equation,

$$p(A'A) = \sum_{i=0}^{n} c_i (A'A)^i = 0.$$

Take $B = -c_r^{-1}\{c_{r+1}I + \cdots + c_n(A'A)^{n-r-1}\}$, where c_r is the first non-zero coefficient of the polynomial p. Then,

$$B(A'A)^{r+1} = -c_r^{-1}\{c_{r+1}(A'A)^{r+1} + \cdots + c_n(A'A)^n\}.$$

Since

$$0 = \sum_{i=r}^{n} c_i (A'A)^i$$

implies

$$-c_r^{-1}\{c_{r+1}(A'A)^{r+1} + \cdots + c_n(A'A)^n\} = (A'A)^r,$$

we see that

$$\begin{aligned} B(A'A)^{r+1} &= -c_r^{-1}\{c_{r+1}(A'A)^{r+1} + \cdots + c_n(A'A)^n\} \\ &= (A'A)^r. \end{aligned}$$

We would like to be able to conclude from this that B so defined satisfies $BA'AA' = A'$. However, $A'A$ need not be invertible.

To help continue the argument, let us introduce a "peeling off" lemma.

Lemma: *Let C, D, and E be matrices such that $CE'E = DE'E$. Then $CE' = DE'$.*

Proof: Since

$$0 = (CE'E - DE'E)(C - D)' = (CE' - DE')(CE' - DE')',$$

and the diagonal elements of $(CE' - DE')(CE' - DE')'$ are the sums of squares of the rows of $CE' - DE'$, we see that $CE' = DE'$.

Applying this lemma to the equation $B(A'A)^{r+1} = (A'A)^r$, making the correspondence $B(A'A)^r \leftrightarrow C, (A'A)^{r-1} \leftrightarrow D, A \leftrightarrow E$, we can "peel off" an A, leaving us with $BA'(AA')^r = A'(AA')^{r-1}$. Now make the correspondence $BA'(AA')^{r-1} \leftrightarrow C, A'(AA')^{r-2} \leftrightarrow D, A' \leftrightarrow E$, and we can "peel off" an A', leaving us with $B(A'A)^r = (A'A)^{r-1}$. Continue this successively until finally we have the desired result, $BA'AA' = A'$.

We generally dub BA' as the matrix A^+, the generalized inverse of A.

Exercise: (1) Check that when $A'A$ is invertible, so that $m \geqslant n$, $B = (A'A)^{-1}$ and $X = (A'A)^{-1}A'$.

(2) Show that AA^+, A^+A, $I - AA^+$, and $I - A^+A$ are matrices of projection transformations.

(3) Show that $(A^+)' = (A')^+$.

(4) Let D be a diagonal matrix. Show that D^+ is a diagonal matrix whose (i, i)th element is given by

$$d_{ii}^+ = \begin{cases} 1/d_{ii} & \text{if} \quad d_{ii} \neq 0, \\ 0 & \text{if} \quad d_{ii} = 0. \end{cases}$$

The result of exercise (4) is extremely useful in providing a computational procedure for finding the generalized inverse of a matrix. First consider the case of a symmetric matrix S. Since S can be written as $S = BDB'$, where B is an orthogonal and D is a diagonal matrix, we see that $S^+ = BD^+B'$. Now consider an arbitrary matrix A. Since AA' is symmetric, $(AA')^+$ is of the form BD^+B', where the non-zero elements of D^+ are the reciprocals of the non-zero characteristic roots of AA' and where B is orthogonal. Using Vinograd's theorem, we see that $A = BD^{\frac{1}{2}}Q'$, where Q is orthogonal and $D^{\frac{1}{2}}$ is the diagonal matrix with diagonal elements, the square roots of those of D. Then $A^+ = Q(D^{\frac{1}{2}})^+B'$. But $(AA')^+ = BD^+B'$ and $A' = QD^{\frac{1}{2}}B'$, so that $A'(AA')^+ = QD^{\frac{1}{2}}D^+B'$. Since $D^{\frac{1}{2}}D^+ = (D^{\frac{1}{2}})^+$, we see that $A'(AA')^+ = Q(D^{\frac{1}{2}})^+B' = A^+$. We have then in $A^+ = A'BD^+B'$ a handy computational formula for A^+.

One important property of the generalized inverse is that it enables us to describe succinctly the matrix of the orthogonal projection transformation of p-space onto a subspace without knowing an orthogonal basis for the subspace. Let $Y_1, \ldots, Y_q$ be q linearly independent p-vectors, and let $\mathscr{Y}$ be the subspace of p-space with $Y_1, \ldots, Y_q$ as basis. Let Y be the $q \times p$ matrix whose rows are $Y_1, \ldots, Y_q$. Then YY' is non-singular, so that, making the correspondence $Y \leftrightarrow A'$, $q \leftrightarrow n$, $p \leftrightarrow m$, between the notation used in developing the generalized inverse and that of this problem, we know that $(Y')^+ = (YY')^{-1}Y$, or $Y^+ = Y'(YY')^{-1}$.

Consequently, $Y^+Y = Y'(YY')^{-1}Y$ is the matrix of a projection transformation. Also, by property (1), $YY^+Y = Y$, so that for each $i = 1, \ldots, q$, $Y_iY^+Y = Y_i$. Thus the linear transformation whose matrix is Y^+Y leaves all basis vectors of $\mathscr{Y}$ unchanged.

Now, since $I - Y^+Y$ is also a projection transformation, and is orthogonal to Y^+Y, it must project vectors onto a subspace $\mathscr{X}$ which is orthogonal to $\mathscr{Y}$. Then p-space is a direct sum of $\mathscr{Y}$ and $\mathscr{X}$, and $Y'(YY')^{-1}Y$ is the matrix of the orthogonal projection of p-space onto the q-dimensional subspace with basis $Y_1, \ldots, Y_q$.

Exercise: Check that when $Y_1, \ldots, Y_q$ are orthogonal, then $Y'(YY')^{-1}Y$ reduces to the matrix obtained in section 4, namely $Y'Y/YY'$.

The generalized inverse is a useful concept in characterizing the solution of linear equations, as seen from the following theorem. We consider in this theorem a quite general setting, wherein A, B, C, and X are matrices of appropriate order.

Theorem 13: *The equation $AXB = C$ has a solution X if and only if $AA^+CB^+B = C$, in which case the solution is*

$$X = A^+CB^+ + Y - A^+AYBB^+,$$

where Y is an arbitrary matrix.

Proof: If X satisfies $AXB = C$, then $C = AXB = AA^+AXBB^+B = AA^+CB^+B$. If $C = A(A^+CB^+)B$, then A^+CB^+ is a solution of $AXB = C$.

The general solution is this particular solution plus any matrix X which satisfies $AXB = 0$. If X is of the form $Y - A^+AYBB^+$, then $AXB = AYB - AA^+AYBB^+B = AYB - AYB = 0$. Also, if $AXB = 0$, then $X = Y - A^+AYBB^+$ and so is of this form. Therefore all X's satisfying $AXB = 0$ are of the form $Y - A^+AYBB^+$, where Y is an arbitrary matrix.

In chapter III we will primarily be dealing with an equation of the form $AX = I$. By Theorem 13, this equation has a solution if and only if $AA^+ = I$. In that case, X must be of the form

$$X = A^+ + Y - A^+AY,$$

where Y is an arbitrary matrix. If A is an $n \times m$ matrix of full rank n, then $A^+ = A'(AA')^{-1}$, so that

$$X = A'(AA')^{-1} + Y - A'(AA')^{-1}AY.$$

We shall show that this representation of X is equivalent to the representation of X as

$$X = MA'(AMA')^{-1},$$

where M is a symmetric $m \times m$ matrix of rank at least n such that AMA' is non-singular. Since $X = MA'(AMA')^{-1}$ is obviously a solution of $AX = I$, we see that for any M there is at least one Y such that the two representations are identical. Thus, to show the equivalence, it suffices to prove that for any Y there corresponds an M such that the two representations of X are identical.

We must, then, solve the equation

$$A'(AA')^{-1} + Y - A'(AA')^{-1}AY = MA'(AMA')^{-1}$$

for M. This is equivalent to the equation

$$\begin{aligned} 0 &= A'(AA')^{-1}(AMA') + YAMA' - A'(AA')^{-1}AYAMA' - MA' \\ &= (A'(AA')^{-1}A + YA - A'(AA')^{-1}AYA - I)MA'. \end{aligned}$$

Let $G = A'(AA')^{-1}A + YA - A'(AA')^{-1}AYA - I$. Then $GMA' = 0$. By Theorem 13, this has a solution M (since $GG^+0A'^+A' = 0$) satisfying $M = W - G^+GWA'A'^+$, where W is arbitrary. Thus for any Y there are many matrices M such that $X = MA'(AMA')^{-1}$ is a solution of $AX = I$.

But is there a W such that $M = W - G^+GWA'A'^+$ is symmetric? Yes, for the matrix $I - G^+G$ is symmetric, so if $W = I - G^+G$, then

$$\begin{aligned} M &= I - G^+G - G^+G(I - G^+G)A'A'^+ \\ &= I - G^+G = W, \end{aligned}$$

which is symmetric.

Finally, can a symmetric M have rank n or greater? Let us once again look at $M = I - G^+G$.

Since G^+G is the matrix of a projection transformation into the subspace $\mathcal{G}$ whose basis is composed of some $m - n$ linearly independent rows of G, the rank of G^+G is at most $m - n$. Since $I - G^+G$ is the matrix of a projection into the subspace of m-space orthogonal to $\mathcal{G}$, the rank of $M = I - G^+G$ is at least $m - (m - n) = n$.

We summarize this development in the following theorem.

Theorem 14: *Let A be an $n \times m$ matrix of rank n. All solutions of the equation $AX = I$ are of the form $X = MA'(AMA')^{-1}$, where M is a symmetric $m \times m$ matrix of rank at least n.*

We define the *trace* of an $n \times n$ matrix C, $\operatorname{tr} C$, as the sum of its diagonal elements. Let A be an $m \times n$ matrix. Define $\|A\| = \operatorname{tr} AA' = \sum_{i=1}^{m} \sum_{j=1}^{n} a_{ij}^2$.

Exercise: Show that $\operatorname{tr} AB = \operatorname{tr} BA$, $\operatorname{tr} ABC = \operatorname{tr} BCA = \operatorname{tr} CAB \neq \operatorname{tr} CBA$.

Let X be a $p \times n$ matrix and B be a $p \times m$ matrix. We say that $\hat{X}$ is the *ordinary least squares solution* of the equation $XA' = B$ if $\|XA' - B\| \geqslant \|\hat{X}A' - B\|$, i.e., the matrix $\hat{X}$ minimizes $\sum_{i=1}^{p} \sum_{j=1}^{m} \left(\sum_{k=1}^{n} x_{ik}a_{jk} - b_{ij}\right)^2 = \operatorname{tr}(XA' - B)(XA' - B)'$. The following theorem characterizes the ordinary least squares solution of the system of p sets of m simultaneous linear equations in n unknowns.

Theorem 15: *The ordinary least squares solution $\hat{X}$ of $XA' = B$ is $\hat{X} = BA^{+\prime}$.*

Proof:

$$
\begin{aligned}
\|XA' - B\| &= \|AX' - B'\| \\
&= \|A(X' - A^+B') + (I - AA^+)(-B')\| \\
&= \operatorname{tr}\{A(X' - A^+B')(X - BA^{+\prime})A' \\
&\quad + (I - AA^+)B'B(I - AA^+)' \\
&\quad - A(X' - A^+B')B(I - AA^+)' \\
&\quad - (I - AA^+)B'(X - BA^{+\prime})A'\} \\
&= \|AX - AA^+B'\| + \|(I - AA^+)B'\|,
\end{aligned}
$$

since $\operatorname{tr} AA^+B'B(I - AA^+)' = \operatorname{tr} B'B(I - AA^+)'AA^+ = 0$ and $\operatorname{tr} AX'B \times (I - AA^+)' = \operatorname{tr} X'B(A - AA^+A) = 0$. Therefore,

$$\|XA' - B\| \geqslant \|A(A^+B') - B'\| = \|(BA^{+\prime})A' - B\|,$$

with equality only if $XA' = (BA^{+\prime})A'$.

8. Derivatives of functions of matrices

Let X be an $m \times n$ matrix, and Y be a $p \times q$ matrix whose elements y_{ij} are functions f_{ij} of the elements of X (e.g., $Y = AXB$, where A is a $p \times m$ and B is an $n \times q$ matrix). In many circumstances we will be interested in the derivatives of the y's with respect to the x's. To discuss this felicitously, let us adopt the following notation. We call the matrix $\partial Y/\partial x_{ij}$ the $p \times q$ matrix whose (r, s)th element is $\partial y_{rs}/\partial x_{ij}$. We call the matrix $\partial y_{rs}/\partial X$ the $m \times n$ matrix whose (i, j)th element is $\partial y_{rs}/\partial x_{ij}$.

Let J_{ij} denote a matrix with a one as (i, j)th element and zeros elsewhere. The order of J_{ij} will be clear from context. Trivial consequences of the use of this notation are the following:

(1) If $Y = A$ is not a function of X, then

$$\frac{\partial Y}{\partial x_{ij}} = 0, \qquad \frac{\partial y_{rs}}{\partial X} = 0.$$

(2) If $Y = X$, then

$$\frac{\partial Y}{\partial x_{ij}} = J_{ij}, \qquad \frac{\partial y_{rs}}{\partial X} = J_{rs}.$$

(3) If $Y = X'$, then

$$\frac{\partial Y}{\partial x_{ij}} = J_{ji}, \qquad \frac{\partial y_{rs}}{\partial X} = J_{sr}.$$

(4) If $Y = U(X) + V(X)$, where U and V are matrices which are functions of X, then

$$\frac{\partial Y}{\partial x_{ij}} = \frac{\partial U}{\partial x_{ij}} + \frac{\partial V}{\partial x_{ij}},$$

$$\frac{\partial y_{rs}}{\partial X} = \frac{\partial u_{rs}}{\partial X} + \frac{\partial v_{rs}}{\partial X}.$$

Now let's crack the hard nut.

(5) Let $Y = UV$, where U is a $p \times t$ and V is a $t \times q$ matrix, and both U and V are functions of X. Since

$$y_{rs} = \sum_{\alpha=1}^{t} u_{r\alpha} v_{\alpha s},$$

we see that

$$\frac{\partial y_{rs}}{\partial x_{ij}} = \sum_{\alpha=1}^{t} \left\{ \frac{\partial u_{r\alpha}}{\partial x_{ij}} v_{\alpha s} + u_{r\alpha} \frac{\partial v_{\alpha s}}{\partial x_{ij}} \right\},$$

so that

$$\frac{\partial Y}{\partial x_{ij}} = \left[\frac{\partial U}{\partial x_{ij}}\right] V + U \left[\frac{\partial V}{\partial x_{ij}}\right],$$

and

$$\frac{\partial y_{rs}}{\partial X} = \sum_{\alpha=1}^{t} \frac{\partial u_{r\alpha}}{\partial X} v_{\alpha s} + \sum_{\alpha=1}^{t} u_{r\alpha} \frac{\partial v_{\alpha s}}{\partial X}.$$

Corollaries of this are the following.

(5a) If $U = A$, independent of X, and $V = X$, so that $Y = AX$, then

$$\frac{\partial Y}{\partial x_{ij}} = AJ_{ij},$$

$$\frac{\partial y_{rs}}{\partial X} = \sum_{\alpha=1}^{m} a_{r\alpha} J_{\alpha s} = A' J_{rs}.$$

(5b) If $U = X$ and $V = B$, independent of X, so that $Y = XB$, then

$$\frac{\partial Y}{\partial x_{ij}} = J_{ij} B,$$

$$\frac{\partial y_{rs}}{\partial X} = J_{rs} B'.$$

Now let $Y = X^{-1}$, where X and Y are $n \times n$ matrices. What is $\partial y_{rs} / \partial X$ and $\partial Y / \partial x_{ij}$? We can solve this problem using the following trick. Write $XY = I$. Then, differentiating both sides of this equation with respect to x_{ij}, we obtain

$$\frac{\partial X}{\partial x_{ij}} Y + X \frac{\partial Y}{\partial x_{ij}} = 0,$$

or

$$J_{ij} X^{-1} + X \frac{\partial X^{-1}}{\partial x_{ij}} = 0,$$

$$\frac{\partial Y}{\partial x_{ij}} = \frac{\partial X^{-1}}{\partial x_{ij}} = -X^{-1}J_{ij}X^{-1}.$$

Also taking $U = X$, $V = Y$, $Y = I$ in (5), we see that

$$\begin{aligned} 0 &= \sum_{\alpha=1}^{n} \frac{\partial x_{r\alpha}}{\partial X} y_{\alpha s} + \sum_{\alpha=1}^{n} x_{r\alpha} \frac{\partial y_{\alpha s}}{\partial X} \\ &= \sum_{\alpha=1}^{n} J_{r\alpha} y_{\alpha s} + \sum_{\alpha=1}^{n} x_{r\alpha} \frac{\partial y_{\alpha s}}{\partial X}. \end{aligned}$$

From the previous result, we know that $\partial y_{\alpha s}/\partial x_{ij} = -y_{\alpha i}y_{js}$. Thus the (i, j)th element of $\sum_{\alpha=1}^{n} x_{r\alpha}\, \partial y_{\alpha s}/\partial X$ is

$$\sum_{\alpha=1}^{n} x_{r\alpha} \frac{\partial y_{\alpha s}}{\partial x_{ij}} = -\sum_{\alpha=1}^{n} x_{r\alpha} y_{\alpha i} y_{js} = -\delta_{ri} y_{js},$$

where $\delta_{ri} = 0$ if $r \neq i$, 1 if $r = i$. Note also that the (i, j)th element of $X'\, \partial y_{rs}/\partial X$ is

$$\begin{aligned} \sum_{k=1}^{n} x_{ki} \frac{\partial y_{rs}}{\partial x_{ij}} &= -\sum_{k=1}^{n} x_{ki} y_{rk} y_{js} \\ &= -\delta_{ri} y_{js}. \end{aligned}$$

Finally, noting that $\sum_{\alpha=1}^{n} J_{r\alpha} y_{\alpha s} = J_{rs} Y'$, we see that

$$0 = J_{rs} Y' + X' \frac{\partial y_{rs}}{\partial X},$$

or

$$\frac{\partial y_{rs}}{\partial X} = -(X')^{-1} J_{rs} Y' = -(X^{-1})' J_{rs} (X^{-1})'.$$

As evidenced by this example, it is easier to compute $\partial Y/\partial x_{ij}$ than to compute $\partial y_{rs}/\partial X$. It is possible to derive the latter matrix from the former by applying the following rules:

(i) Change any pre- or post-multiplier of J to its transpose.

(ii) Change any pre-multiplier of J' to a post-multiplier of J' and any post-multiplier of J' to a pre-multiplier of J'.

Thus, from

$$\frac{\partial Y}{\partial x_{ij}} = -X^{-1}J_{ij}X^{-1},$$

we obtain immediately that

$$\frac{\partial y_{rs}}{\partial X} = -(X^{-1})' J_{rs} (X^{-1})',$$

which checks with the above result.

As a more complex example of these rules, suppose $Y = XAX'$. Then,

$$\frac{\partial Y}{\partial x_{ij}} = J_{ij}AX' + XAJ_{ji}.$$

To find $\partial y_{rs}/\partial X$, we use rules (i) and (ii) in succession and obtain the following:

$$J_{ij}AX' + XAJ_{ji} \rightarrow J_{rs}XA' + XAJ_{sr} \rightarrow J_{rs}XA' + J_{sr}XA = \partial y_{rs}/\partial X.$$

Exercise: Find $\partial Y/\partial x_{ij}$ and $\partial y_{rs}/\partial X$ where $Y = AXX'$.

Many times we will be interested in the derivative with respect to each of the x's of a scalar function f of a matrix function Y of X. Using the chain rule, we see that

$$\frac{\partial f}{\partial X} = \sum_{r=1}^{p} \sum_{s=1}^{q} \frac{\partial f}{\partial y_{rs}} \frac{\partial y_{rs}}{\partial X}.$$

Let A be an $n \times n$ matrix, with $f(A) = |A|$. Then $\partial |A| / \partial a_{ij} = (-1)^{i+j} D_{ij}(A)$, i.e., $(-1)^{i+j}$ times the (i, j)th minor of A. As we use this so often, let us define the (i, j)th *cofactor* of A as $A_{ij} = (-1)^{i+j} D_{ij}(A)$. If A is symmetric, then $\partial |A| / \partial a_{ii} = A_{ii}$ and $\partial |A| / \partial a_{ij} = 2A_{ij}$ for $i \neq j$.

9. References

For a better presentation of the geometric point of view toward matrix theory (especially in sections 2, 3, and 5) see:

Halmos, P. R., 1942, Finite dimensional vector spaces (Princeton University Press, Princeton).

A good textbook treatment of the material in sections 1 and 2, along with analternative treatment of the material in sections 4 and 5, is:

Birkhoff, G. and S. MacLane, 1953, A survey of modern algebra (MacMillan, New York).

Our presentation of section 4 is modeled after that of:

Schreier, O. and E. Sperner, 1952, Introduction to modern algebra and matrix theory (Chelsea, New York).

A lucid presentation of the theory of the generalized inverse is given in the following papers:

Penrose, R., 1955, A generalized inverse for matrices, Proceedings of the Cambridge Philosophical Society 1, pp. 406–413.

Penrose, R., 1956, On best approximate solution to linear matrix equations, Proceedings of the Cambridge Philosophical Society 52, pp. 17–19.

The material of section 8 is taken from:

Dwyer, P. S. and M. S. MacPhail, 1948, Symbolic matrix derivatives, Annals of Mathematical Statistics 19, pp. 517–534.

II

Multivariate statistical analysis

Distribution and point estimation theory

Though the multivariate normal distribution is the probability distribution of paramount importance in econometrics, we begin this chapter (section 1) with a rapid overview of modern probability theory. This is partly for your edification and to dislodge from you some misconceptions you may have, due to poor pedagogy or poor elementary statistics texts, about continuous probability distributions, partly for general background for what is to follow, and partly to enable us to develop in a motivated fashion some useful results in probability distribution theory typically considered "advanced". You are not expected to understand all the allusions in section 1; but do ponder them. In section 2, we specialize the general discussion of section 1 rapidly to the consideration of the multivariate normal distribution and related probability distribution.

The two main problems of statistical inference are that of point estimation and hypothesis testing. The usual econometric textbook is organized somewhat along the following lines: for each econometric model-type presented, both the estimation procedures and test procedures are given. Though such books are useful for references, as all material on a given model-type is in one place, I feel that they do not represent good pedagogy, as the reader must flit back and forth from estimation theory to hypothesis testing theory as the model-types parade by. This book completely separates estimation theory for a given model from testing theory for the same model, treating first estimation theory for the standard econometric models and then in turn tests of hypotheses about those models. Thus, though section 3 describes point estimation theory, section 4 describes a particular method of point estimation, the method of maximum likelihood, and section 5 describes the application of this method to the multivariate normal distribution, it is not followed by a section on the theory of testing hypothesis and a section on the application of this theory to the multivariate normal distribution. Look for that material in chapter V. Instead, expect in chapters III–IV a presentation of estimation theory for various econometric models.

1. Multivariate probability distributions

Though the subject matter of plane geometry, points, line segments and circles, is an idealization of real-life constructs, it is not necessary to understand the nature of these real-life constructs to understand plane geometry. All one needs are the formal definitions of the terms "point", "line segment", and "circle". So too is it unnecessary to understand the nature of the real-life construct corresponding to the term "probability" to understand the mathematical theory of probability.

The basic terms of probability theory are "sample space", "event", and "probability". To help make matters concrete, you might think of the sample space as a set whose elements, the "events", are all the possible results or outcomes of an idealized experiment in which chance plays a role. The *sample space* $\mathscr{S}$ is a set, with elements s, called *events*. We call a sample space *discrete* if it has a finite or denumerably infinite number of elements (i.e., as many elements as there are integers). We call a sample space *continuous* if the number of elements of the sample space is the cardinality of the continuum, i.e., it has as many elements as there are real numbers. We shall not consider sample spaces with cardinality (roughly speaking, number of elements) greater than that of the continuum (e.g., the set of all bounded continuous functions $f(x)$ defined on the interval $[0, 1]$).

You are certainly familiar with the theory of probability for discrete sample spaces. In this theory, we can label the elements of $\mathscr{S}$ as $s_1, s_2, \ldots$. There is a function p which associates with each event s_i a number $p(s_i)$, called the *probability of the event* s_i. The $p(s_i)$'s satisfy the conditions $p(s_i) > 0$ and $\sum_{i=1}^{\infty} p(s_i) = 1$.

From this function p we can define another function P which associates a real number with each subset of $\mathscr{S}$. If S is a subset of $\mathscr{S}$, then $P(S)$ is defined as $P(S) = \sum_{s_i \in S} p(s_i)$. The function P is called a *probability measure*. Denoting by $\{s_i\}$ the subset of $\mathscr{S}$ consisting of only the event s_i, we see that $P(\{s_i\}) = p(s_i)$. If 0 is the null set, then $P(0) = 0$. Finally, $P(\mathscr{S}) = 1$.

A simple example of a discrete sample space along with the values of the associated function p is the following description of the outcome of the tossing of an unfair coin three times, where H denotes "heads" and T "tails".

$$
\begin{array}{ll}
s_1 = \{\text{HHH}\}, & p(s_1) = 1/27; \\
s_2 = \{\text{HHT}\}, & p(s_2) = 2/27; \\
s_3 = \{\text{HTH}\}, & p(s_3) = 2/27; \\
s_4 = \{\text{THH}\}, & p(s_4) = 2/27; \\
s_5 = \{\text{HTT}\}, & p(s_5) = 4/27; \\
s_6 = \{\text{THT}\}, & p(s_6) = 4/27; \\
s_7 = \{\text{TTH}\}, & p(s_7) = 4/27; \\
s_8 = \{\text{TTT}\}, & p(s_8) = 8/27.
\end{array}
$$

We will have more to say about this example shortly. But first, let us summarize important properties of the probability measure P in the discrete case. They are

(1) $P(\mathcal{S}) = 1$.

(2) $P(S) > 0$ for all subsets S of $\mathcal{S}$.

(3) If $\{S_i\}$ is a sequence of disjoint subsets of $\mathcal{S}$, then

$$P\left(\bigcup_{i=1}^{\infty} S_i\right) = \sum_{i=1}^{\infty} P(S_i).$$

Now consider as a simple example of a continuous sample space the surface of a billiard table for the "experiment" in which a billiard ball stops at random on the table. The events are the points of the table, and it is natural to deem the probability that the ball stops in a given subset S of the table as proportional to the area of S. Then, though the ball will land on some point, the probability associated with any point (in fact, with any line or denumerable set of lines) on the table is 0. Possible events have zero probabilities; property 2 above is violated. And if we wanted to have our cake, we couldn't eat it, as if we required properties 2 and 3 to hold for *all* subsets of $\mathcal{S}$, including events, then $P(\mathcal{S})$ would be infinite and property 1 wouldn't hold.

It is also a fact that property 3 itself cannot hold for *all* subsets of the billiard table if $P(S)$ is taken to be the area of S. The proof of this is beyond the scope of this introductory essay. The essence of this statement, though, is that unlike events whose area is 0 and so whose probability measure is definable and defined to be 0, there are subsets S

for which $P(S)$ cannot be meaningfully defined at all without the function P violating property 3. In fact, the cardinality of the set of all subsets of the set of all real numbers (or of $\mathcal{S}$ in this case) is greater than that of the continuum, so by our ground rules we cannot consider the sample space of subsets of $\mathcal{S}$.

So modern probability theory rules out such subsets from consideration, and takes as the only subsets of $\mathcal{S}$ worthy of consideration the *Borel sets*. These sets are the smallest class $\mathcal{B}$ of sets in $\mathcal{S}$ with the properties:

(1) $\mathcal{S}$ is contained in $\mathcal{B}$.

(2) If S is in $\mathcal{B}$, then so is its complement.

(3) If $\{S_i\}$ is a sequence of subsets of $\mathcal{S}$, each in $\mathcal{B}$, then $\bigcup_{i=1}^{\infty} S_i$ is in $\mathcal{B}$.

When $\mathcal{S}$ is the real line, rather than an arbitrary set, then $\mathcal{B}$ is the class of sets generated by (possibly a denumerable number of) unions, intersections, and complements of half-open, half-closed intervals $(a, b]$. Even in this down-to-earth situation, it is impossible to point to a definite example of a set which is not a Borel set. All that is known is that such sets exist. (It is analogous to a situation which might have been in the beginning of the creation of mathematics, where one could prove abstractly that irrational numbers exist without yet being able to point to one.) But we choose to ignore them and not assign probability measure to them.

More generally, if $\mathcal{S}$ is Euclidean n-space, we define a half-open, half-closed hyperrectangle as the set of n-vectors U such that $a_i < u_i \leqslant b_i$, $i = 1, \ldots, n$. The Borel sets are all sets generated from such sets by (possibly denumerable) set-theoretic operations. Only these are assigned probability measure. It can also be shown for this example that the probability measure of any n-vector, i.e., any event in $\mathcal{S}$, is 0.

Because abstract spaces like $\mathcal{S}$ and $\mathcal{B}$ are difficult to work with mathematically, whereas we have lots of tools (e.g., calculus) with which to go to work on Euclidean n-space, it is quite convenient to forsake $\mathcal{S}$ and instead introduce substitute real-valued or vector-valued descriptions of our idealized experiment.

A *random variable* is a function $\boldsymbol{x}$ which associates a real number $\boldsymbol{x}(s)$ with every event s in the sample space $\mathcal{S}$. An *n-vector-valued random variable* is a function $\boldsymbol{X}$ which associates a Euclidean n-vector $\boldsymbol{X}(s)$ with every event s in the sample space $\mathcal{S}$. Let $\boldsymbol{X}$ be an n-vector-valued random variable, i.e., $\boldsymbol{X}(s) = (\boldsymbol{x}_1(s), \ldots, \boldsymbol{x}_n(s))$. We usually delete the argument s of the random variable and so write it as $\boldsymbol{X} = (\boldsymbol{x}_1, \ldots, \boldsymbol{x}_n)$. This deletion, though, leads us into some notational anomalies like the equation $\boldsymbol{X} = X = (x_1, \ldots, x_n)$, by which we shall mean that the random variable (or function) $\boldsymbol{X}(s)$ takes on the value X (a vector, in this case). [Note the notational convention of denoting random vectors by boldface upper case letters and the vector-value of the random vector by the same upper case letter, though not bold-faced. Random variables, i.e., one-dimensional random vectors, are denoted by boldface lower case letters, and their values by the same lower case letter, though not bold-faced. This is consistent with the convention of chapter I in which scalars, i.e., 1-vectors, were lower case letters, as were coordinates of vectors. Thus, also, the coordinates of a random vector are boldface lower case letters.]

Getting back to our example of a non-numeric discrete sample space involving coin tossing, we might define the following random variables:

	$\boldsymbol{W}(s)$	$\boldsymbol{X}(s)$	$\boldsymbol{y}(s)$	$\boldsymbol{z}(s)$
$s_1 = \{HHH\}$	$(1, 1, 1)$	$(15, 21, 7)$	π	3
$s_2 = \{HHT\}$	$(1, 1, 0)$	$(32, -1, 2)$	e	2
$s_3 = \{HTH\}$	$(1, 0, 1)$	$(1, 0, 1)$	17	2
$s_4 = \{THH\}$	$(0, 1, 1)$	$(5, 9, 25)$	-22	2
$s_5 = \{HTT\}$	$(1, 0, 0)$	$(-1, -3, -5)$	$\sqrt{2}$	1
$s_6 = \{THT\}$	$(0, 1, 0)$	$(4, 6, 14)$	10^{24}	1
$s_7 = \{TTH\}$	$(0, 0, 1)$	$(11, 12, -20)$	11	1
$s_8 = \{TTT\}$	$(0, 0, 0)$	$(21, 0, 22)$	-3	0

The point to this is that *any* real or vector-valued function of s is a random variable. Some (like $\boldsymbol{z}$ and $\boldsymbol{W}$) are more interesting than others, either because they summarize information about the experiment (like $\boldsymbol{z}$, which is the number of heads in s) or because of aesthetics (like $\boldsymbol{W}$, from which s is mnemonically easier to reconstruct than from $\boldsymbol{X}$).

Corresponding to the probability measure P on the Borel sets of $\mathcal{S}$, there is a probability measure $P_{\boldsymbol{X}}$, sometimes called a *probability law*, induced on the Borel sets of Euclidean n-space, given by

$$P_{\boldsymbol{X}}(B) = P(\boldsymbol{X}^{-1}(B)),$$

i.e., the probability measure $P_{\boldsymbol{X}}$ of a Borel set B of n-space is the same as the probability measure, under P, of the Borel set of $\mathcal{S}$ which is mapped into B by the function $\boldsymbol{X}$. (Implicit in this, of course, is the fact, not to be proved here, that the inverse image of a Borel set is a Borel set.)

We now suppress $\mathcal{S}$, the sample space for our experiment, and its probability measure P, completely from our mind and only deal with Euclidean n-space and the probability measure $P_{\mathbf{X}}$. Or, if you would rather, pretend that $\mathcal{S}$ is Euclidean n-space. As the Borel sets of n-space are generated by set operations on the half-open, half-closed hyperrectangles of n-space, it suffices to know the probability measure on these sets. From this, the measure on other Borel sets is calculable using property 3 of probability measures.

The probability measure $P_{\mathbf{X}}$ for all Borel sets is determinable, for example, once we know the probability measure on semi-infinite intervals of the form $(-\infty, \ldots, -\infty) < (\boldsymbol{x}_1, \ldots, \boldsymbol{x}_n) \leqslant (x_1, \ldots, x_n)$, where the inequality sign between vectors is to be read as n inequality signs, one between each pair of ith coordinates, $i = 1, \ldots, n$. We give the probability measure on this Borel set s special name, the *cumulative distribution function*, and reserve for it a special symbol, $F_{\mathbf{X}}(X)$. This function is, formally,

$$\begin{aligned} F_{\mathbf{X}}(X) &= P_{\mathbf{X}}(\{\boldsymbol{X} \mid -\infty < \boldsymbol{X} \leqslant X\}) \\ &= P_{\mathbf{X}}(\{\boldsymbol{X} \mid \boldsymbol{x}_1 \leqslant x_1, \ldots, \boldsymbol{x}_n \leqslant x_n\}), \end{aligned}$$

where $\{\boldsymbol{X} \mid -\infty < \boldsymbol{X} \leqslant X\}$ is read as "the set of random vectors $\boldsymbol{X}$ satisfying $-\infty < \boldsymbol{X} \leqslant X$".

Exercise: In our discrete example above, plot $F_{\mathbf{W}}(W)$ and $F_z(z)$.

Note that $F_{\mathbf{X}}(\infty) = P_{\mathbf{X}}(\{\boldsymbol{X} \mid -\infty < \boldsymbol{X} \leqslant \infty\}) = P_{\mathbf{X}}(\mathcal{S}) = 1$, that $F_{\mathbf{X}}(-\infty) = P_{\mathbf{X}}(\{\boldsymbol{X} \mid -\infty < \boldsymbol{X} \leqslant -\infty\}) = 0$, and that $F_{\mathbf{X}}(X) \geqslant 0$ for all X.

Often $F_{\mathbf{X}}(X)$ will depend not only on X but on the values of a set of variables $\theta_1, \ldots, \theta_k$, say. In such a case, we call these quantities *parameters* of the distribution $F_{\mathbf{X}}(X)$. All parameters of distribution will be denoted by Greek letters to distinguish them from the argument of the distribution function, the values of the random variables.

We will only be interested in continuous multivariate distributions in which the partial derivative

$$\frac{\partial^n F_{\mathbf{X}}(X)}{\partial x_1 \cdots \partial x_n} = f_{\mathbf{X}}(x_1, \ldots, x_n) = f_{\mathbf{X}}(X)$$

exists except perhaps at a denumerable number of points. This function $f_{\mathbf{X}}(X)$ is called the *probability density function* of $\boldsymbol{X}$. This function need not exist, even though $F_{\mathbf{X}}(X)$ exists and is a continuous function of X. So you see that the probability density function is not at all central in the development of probability theory, as you may have been led to believe from some elementary texts. (And it is not its continuity or lack of continuity as a function of X that distinguishes discrete and continuous probability distributions. Continuity or lack of continuity of the probability density function is a symptom, not a cause.)

One final word on notation is in order here. The symbols F and f will be used throughout as generic symbols denoting cumulative distribution function and probability density function. The subscript to these symbols will be the name of the random vector whose cumulative distribution function and probability density function is being described. The argument of F and f is an arbitrary vector name, usually, though not necessarily, the same letter name as that of the random vector.

The probability density function of $\boldsymbol{X}$ has the following useful interpretation. Suppose we want to determine

$$P_{\mathbf{X}}(\{\boldsymbol{X}|X \leqslant \boldsymbol{X} \leqslant X + \Delta X\}) =$$
$$P_{\mathbf{X}}(\{\boldsymbol{X}|x_1 \leqslant \boldsymbol{x}_1 \leqslant x_1 + \Delta x_1, \dots, x_n \leqslant \boldsymbol{x}_n \leqslant x_n + \Delta x_n\}).$$

This is given by

$$\int_{x_1}^{x_1+\Delta x} \cdots \int_{x_n}^{x_n+\Delta x_n} f_{\mathbf{X}}(u_1, \dots, u_n)\, \mathrm{d}u_n \cdots \mathrm{d}u_1$$

which, by the mean value theorem of the integral calculus, is equal to

$$f_{\mathbf{X}}(x_1^0, \dots, x_n^0)\Delta x_1 \cdots \Delta x_n,$$

where $x_i \leqslant x_i^0 \leqslant x_i + \Delta x_i$, $i = 1, \dots, n$, when $f_{\mathbf{X}}(X)$ is a continuous function of X. Now write $x_i^0 = x_i + \theta_i \Delta x_i$, where $0 \leqslant \theta_i \leqslant 1$, for $i = 1, \dots, n$. Then $f_{\mathbf{X}}(X^0) = f_{\mathbf{X}}(X) + \sum_{i=1}^{n} \theta_i \Delta x_i\, \partial f_{\mathbf{X}}(X)/\partial x_i + o(\Delta x_1)$, where the symbol $o(y)$ is shorthand for a function $g(y)$ with the property that $\lim_{y\to 0} g(y)/y = 0$.

Then

$$f_{\mathbf{X}}(X^0)\Delta x_1 \cdots \Delta x_n = f_{\mathbf{X}}(X)\Delta x_1 \cdots \Delta x_n + o(\Delta x_1),$$

so that, replacing Δx_i by $\mathrm{d}x_i$, we have that, to first-order terms, $P_{\mathbf{X}}(\{\boldsymbol{X}|X \leqslant \boldsymbol{X} \leqslant X + \Delta X\}) = f_{\mathbf{X}}(X)\, \mathrm{d}x_1 \cdots \mathrm{d}x_n$.

Now suppose that instead of the random variables $\boldsymbol{x}_1, \dots, \boldsymbol{x}_n$ we were interested in a related set of random variables $\boldsymbol{y}_1, \ldots, \boldsymbol{y}_n$ given by $\boldsymbol{y}_1 = h_1(\boldsymbol{x}_1, \ldots, \boldsymbol{x}_n), \ldots, \boldsymbol{y}_n = h_n(\boldsymbol{x}_1, \ldots, \boldsymbol{x}_n)$, where $h_1, \ldots, h_n$ are n continuous real-valued functions possessing continuous derivatives. Let $k_1, \ldots, k_n$ denote the inverse transformations to $h_1, \ldots, h_n$, i.e., $\boldsymbol{x}_i = k_i(\boldsymbol{y}_1, \ldots, \boldsymbol{y}_n)$, $i = 1, \ldots, n$, which we assume to exist and to also be continuously differentiable. Given the probability density function of $\boldsymbol{X}$, how does one determine the probability density function of $\boldsymbol{Y} = (\boldsymbol{y}_1, \ldots, \boldsymbol{y}_n)$?

Before developing a general method for determining the probability density function of $\boldsymbol{Y}$, let us consider a simple example to illustrate the principle involved. Let $\boldsymbol{y}_1 = h_1(\boldsymbol{x}_1, \boldsymbol{x}_2) = \boldsymbol{x}_1/(\boldsymbol{x}_1^2 + \boldsymbol{x}_2^2)$, $\boldsymbol{y}_2 = h_2(\boldsymbol{x}_1, \boldsymbol{x}_2) = \boldsymbol{x}_2/(\boldsymbol{x}_1^2 + \boldsymbol{x}_2^2)$, so that $\boldsymbol{x}_1 = \boldsymbol{y}_1/(\boldsymbol{y}_1^2 + \boldsymbol{y}_2^2)$, $\boldsymbol{x}_2 = \boldsymbol{y}_2/(\boldsymbol{y}_1^2 + \boldsymbol{y}_2^2)$. This transformation takes the rectangle $x_1 \leqslant \boldsymbol{x}_1 \leqslant x_1 + \mathrm{d}x_1$, $x_2 \leqslant \boldsymbol{x}_2 \leqslant x_2 + \mathrm{d}x_2$ into the region R given in figure 4. Then $P_{\boldsymbol{X}}\{(x_1, x_2) \leqslant (\boldsymbol{x}_1, \boldsymbol{x}_2) \leqslant (x_1, x_2) + (\mathrm{d}x_1, \mathrm{d}x_2)\} = f_{\boldsymbol{X}}(x_1, x_2)\, \mathrm{d}x_1\, \mathrm{d}x_2 = P_{\boldsymbol{Y}}\{(\boldsymbol{y}_1, \boldsymbol{y}_2) \in R\}$.

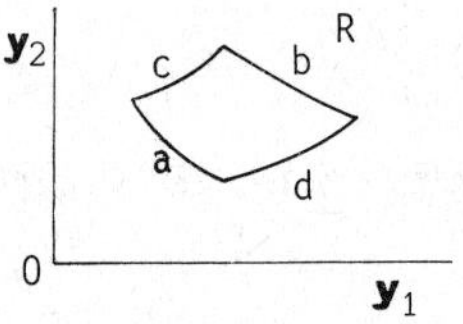

FIGURE 4

The curves defining R are given by the following:

(a) $\quad y_1/(y_1^2 + y_2^2) = x_1,$

(b) $\quad y_1/(y_1^2 + y_2^2) = x_1 + \mathrm{d}x_1,$

(c) $\quad y_2/(y_1^2 + y_2^2) = x_2,$

(d) $\quad y_2/(y_1^2 + y_2^2) = x_2 + \mathrm{d}x_2.$

Let us record the following derivatives:

$$\frac{\partial}{\partial y_1}\left(\frac{y_1}{y_1^2 + y_2^2}\right) = \frac{y_2^2 - y_1^2}{(y_1^2 + y_2^2)^2} = -\frac{\partial}{\partial y_2}\left(\frac{y_2}{y_1^2 + y_2^2}\right)$$

$$\frac{\partial}{\partial y_2}\left(\frac{y_1}{y_1^2 + y_2^2}\right) = -\frac{2y_1 y_2}{(y_1^2 + y_2^2)^2} = \frac{\partial}{\partial y_1}\left(\frac{y_2}{y_1^2 + y_2^2}\right).$$

Now, approximating each of the curves defining R by a first-order Taylor series around $(y_1, y_2) = (x_1/(x_1^2 + x_2^2),\ x_2/(x_1^2 + x_2^2))$, we have the approximations

$$\text{(a*)} \qquad x_1 = \frac{y_1}{y_1^2+y_2^2} + \frac{y_2^2-y_1^2}{(y_1^2+y_2^2)^2}(\mathbf{y}_1 - y_1) - \frac{2y_1y_2}{(y_1^2+y_2^2)^2}(\mathbf{y}_2 - y_2),$$

$$\text{(b*)} \qquad x_1 + dx_1 = \frac{y_1}{y_1^2+y_2^2} + \frac{y_2^2-y_1^2}{(y_1^2+y_2^2)^2}(\mathbf{y}_1 - y_1) - \frac{2y_1y_2}{(y_1^2+y_2^2)^2}(\mathbf{y}_2 - y_2);$$

$$\text{(c*)} \qquad x_2 = \frac{y_2}{y_1^2+y_2^2} - \frac{2y_1y_2}{(y_1^2+y_2^2)^2}(\mathbf{y}_1 - y_1) - \frac{y_2^2-y_1^2}{(y_1^2+y_2^2)^2}(\mathbf{y}_2 - y_2),$$

$$\text{(d*)} \qquad x_2 + dx_2 = \frac{y_2}{y_1^2+y_2^2} - \frac{2y_1y_2}{(y_1^2+y_2^2)^2}(\mathbf{y}_1 - y_1) - \frac{y_2^2-y_1^2}{(y_1^2+y_2^2)^2}(\mathbf{y}_2 - y_2).$$

For dx_1 and dx_2 sufficiently small, (b*) is approximately parallel to (a*), as is (d*) to (c*). Let

$$J = \begin{bmatrix} j_{11} & j_{12} \\ j_{21} & j_{22} \end{bmatrix} = \begin{bmatrix} \dfrac{y_2^2-y_1^2}{(y_1^2+y_2^2)^2} & \dfrac{-2y_1y_2}{(y_1^2+y_2^2)^2} \\ \dfrac{-2y_1y_2}{(y_1^2+y_2^2)^2} & -\dfrac{y_2^2-y_1^2}{(y_1^2+y_2^2)^2} \end{bmatrix}^{-1}.$$

Thus the area of R is approximately the area of the parallelogram given in figure 5.

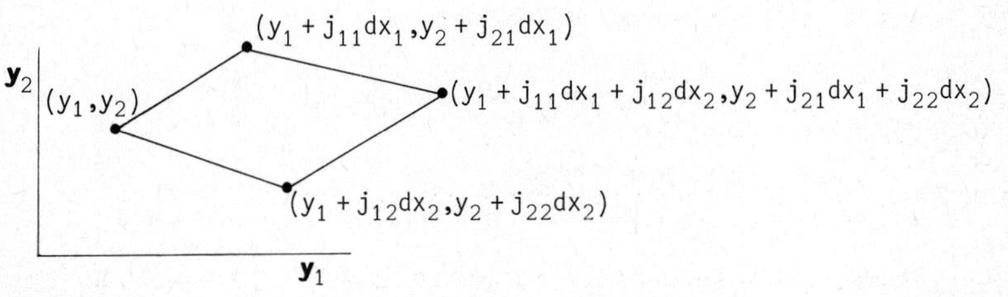

FIGURE 5

Taking $(y_1, y_2) = 0$ will not alter the area of the parallelogram. In this case we see that the area of this parallelogram is that of the parallelogram formed from the vectors $(\mathrm{d}x_1, 0)J$ and $(0, \mathrm{d}x_2)J$. Thus, its area is $|J|^+ \, \mathrm{d}x_1 \, \mathrm{d}x_2$, using a result of section 5 of chapter I.

Now let $f_{\mathbf{Y}}(y_1, y_2)$ be the probability density function of $\mathbf{Y}$. For R small enough, the probability that $\mathbf{Y}$ is in R should be, to first-order terms, the area of R times $f_{\mathbf{Y}}(y_1, y_2)$. On the other hand, it must also equal $f_{\mathbf{X}}(x_1, x_2)\,\mathrm{d}x_1\,\mathrm{d}x_2$. Therefore for every (x_1, x_2) and concomitant (y_1, y_2) we have

$$f_{\mathbf{X}}(x_1, x_2)\,\mathrm{d}x_1\,\mathrm{d}x_2 = f_{\mathbf{Y}}(y_1, y_2)|J|\,\mathrm{d}x_1\,\mathrm{d}x_2,$$

or, more precisely,

$$f_{\mathbf{Y}}(y_1, y_2) = f_{\mathbf{X}}(k_1(y_1, y_2), k_2(y_1, y_2))|J^{-1}|^+.$$

That is, the probability density function of $\mathbf{Y}$ is obtained by multiplying the probability density function of $\mathbf{X}$, when evaluated at $X = (k_1(Y), k_2(Y))$, by the absolute value of the determinant of the matrix

$$J^{-1} = \begin{bmatrix} \dfrac{\partial k_1(y_1, y_2)}{\partial y_1} & \dfrac{\partial k_2(y_1, y_2)}{\partial y_1} \\ \dfrac{\partial k_1(y_1, y_2)}{\partial y_2} & \dfrac{\partial k_2(y_1, y_2)}{\partial y_2} \end{bmatrix}.$$

More generally, let $x_i = k_i(y_1, \ldots, y_n)$, $i = 1, \ldots, n$. We can approximate x_i by

$$x_i = \sum_{j=1}^{n} (y_j - y_j)\frac{\partial k_i(y_1, \ldots, y_n)}{\partial y_j}.$$

Let

$$J^{-1} = \begin{bmatrix} \dfrac{\partial k_1(y_1, \ldots, y_n)}{\partial y_1} & \cdots & \dfrac{\partial k_n(y_1, \ldots, y_n)}{\partial y_1} \\ \cdot & & \\ \cdot & & \\ \cdot & & \\ \dfrac{\partial k_1(y_1, \ldots, y_n)}{\partial y_n} & \cdots & \dfrac{\partial k_n(y_1, \ldots, y_n)}{\partial y_n} \end{bmatrix}.$$

Then, to first-order terms, $X = (\mathbf{Y} - Y)J^{-1}$, or $\mathbf{Y} = Y + XJ$.

We would like to use this approximation to obtain the volume of the image, under $h_1, \ldots, h_n$, of a rectangular parallelotope in n-space whose volume is $dx_1 \cdots dx_n$. Consider then the parallelotope formed from the vectors $dx_1E_1, \ldots, dx_nE_n$. Its image under the transformation $h_1, \ldots, h_n$ is approximately the parallelotope formed from the n vectors $Y_1 = dx_1E_1J, \ldots, Y_n = dx_nE_nJ$. The volume of this parallelotope is

$$\begin{vmatrix} dx_1 & & 0 \\ & \ddots & \\ 0 & & dx_n \end{vmatrix} |J|^+.$$

If the rectangular parallelotope is rigidly shifted so that the zero vector vertex is replaced by the vector X as a vertex, then the image parallelotope would also be rigidly shifted so that instead of the zero vector as vertex it now has as vertex the vector $Y = (h_1(X), \ldots, h_n(X))$. At any rate, the volumes would remain unchanged. Thus for every X and concomitant Y, we have

$$\begin{aligned} P_{\mathbf{X}}(\{X \leqslant \mathbf{X} \leqslant X + dx\}) &= f_{\mathbf{X}}(X)\, dx_1 \cdots dx_n \\ &= f_{\mathbf{Y}}(Y)|J|^+\, dx_1 \cdots dx_n, \end{aligned}$$

so that

$$f_{\mathbf{Y}}(Y) = f_{\mathbf{X}}(k_1(Y), \ldots, k_n(Y))|J^{-1}|^+.$$

Since $h_i(k_1(Y), \ldots, k_n(Y)) = y_i$ for $i = 1, \ldots, n$, we see that

$$\begin{aligned} \frac{\partial h_i(k_1(Y), \ldots, k_n(Y))}{\partial y_j} &= \begin{cases} 1, & \text{if } j = i, \\ 0, & \text{if } j \neq i, \end{cases} \\ &= \sum_{l=1}^{n} \frac{\partial h_i(X)}{\partial x_l} \frac{\partial k_l(Y)}{\partial y_j}. \end{aligned}$$

Thus the matrix whose (i, j)th element is $\partial h_j(X)/\partial x_i$ is the inverse of the matrix whose (i, j)th element is $\partial k_i(Y)/\partial y_j$, i.e.,

$$J = \begin{bmatrix} \dfrac{\partial h_1(x_1, \ldots, x_n)}{\partial x_1} & \cdots & \dfrac{\partial h_n(x_1, \ldots, x_n)}{\partial x_1} \\ \vdots & & \\ \dfrac{\partial h_1(x_1, \ldots, x_n)}{\partial x_n} & \cdots & \dfrac{\partial h_n(x_1, \ldots, x_n)}{\partial x_n} \end{bmatrix}.$$

This matrix J is called the *Jacobian matrix* of the transformations

$h_1, \ldots, h_n$, and $|J|^+$, sometimes denoted by $J(X \to Y)$, is called the *Jacobian* of the transformations $h_1, \ldots, h_n$. Then $|J^{-1}|^+ = J(Y \to X)$, the Jacobian of the transformation $k_1, \ldots, k_n$. We summarize the result of the determination of $f_Y(Y)$ by the relation

$$f_Y(Y) = f_X(k_1(Y), \ldots, k_n(Y))J(Y \to X).$$

Exercise: (1) Let $Y = (y_1, \ldots, y_n) = (x_1, \ldots, x_n)A'$, where A is an invertible $n \times n$ matrix. Show that $J(Y \to X) = 1/|A|^+$.

(2) Let $f_X(X) = (1/2\pi)\exp\{-(x_1^2 + x_2^2)/2\}$. Let $\boldsymbol{Y} = (\sqrt{(\boldsymbol{x}_1^2 + \boldsymbol{x}_2^2)}, \tan^{-1}(\boldsymbol{x}_1/\boldsymbol{x}_2))$. What is the probability density function of $\boldsymbol{Y}$? What is the sample space of $\boldsymbol{X}$? What is the sample space of $\boldsymbol{Y}$?

The *marginal cumulative distribution function* of the subvector $\dot{\boldsymbol{X}} = (\boldsymbol{x}_1, \ldots, \boldsymbol{x}_p)$ of $\boldsymbol{X}$ is given by

$$\begin{aligned}
&F_{\dot{X}}(x_1, \ldots, x_p) = \\
&P\{\boldsymbol{x}_1 \leqslant x_1, \ldots, \boldsymbol{x}_p \leqslant x_p, \boldsymbol{x}_{p+1} \leqslant \infty, \ldots, \boldsymbol{x}_n \leqslant \infty\} = \\
&F_X(x_1, \ldots, x_p, \infty, \ldots, \infty) = \\
&\int_{-\infty}^{x_1} \cdots \int_{-\infty}^{x_p} \int_{-\infty}^{\infty} \cdots \int_{-\infty}^{\infty} f_X(u_1, \ldots, u_n)\,\mathrm{d}u_n \cdots \mathrm{d}u_1,
\end{aligned}$$

and the *marginal probability density function* of $\dot{\boldsymbol{X}} = (\boldsymbol{x}_1, \ldots, \boldsymbol{x}_p)$ is given by

$$f_X(x_1, \ldots, x_p) = \frac{\partial^p F_X(x_1, \ldots, x_p, \infty, \ldots, \infty)}{\partial x_1 \cdots \partial x_p},$$

or equivalently by

$$f_{\dot{X}}(x_1, \ldots, x_p) = \int_{-\infty}^{\infty} \cdots \int_{-\infty}^{\infty} f_X(x_1, \ldots, x_n)\,\mathrm{d}x_{p+1} \cdots \mathrm{d}x_n.$$

Exercise: (1) Let $\boldsymbol{y}_1 = h(\boldsymbol{X})$, where h is a continuous differentiable function from n-space to the real line. What is the probability density function of $\boldsymbol{y}_1$? *Hint*: Consider the transformation $\boldsymbol{y}_1 = h(\boldsymbol{X})$, $\boldsymbol{y}_2 = \boldsymbol{x}_2, \ldots, \boldsymbol{y}_n = \boldsymbol{x}_n$. Let $\boldsymbol{x}_1 = k(\boldsymbol{Y})$. Then,

$$f_{y_1}(y_1) = \int_{-\infty}^{\infty} \cdots \int_{-\infty}^{\infty} \frac{\partial k(Y)}{\partial y_1} f_X(k(Y), y_2, \ldots, y_n)\,\mathrm{d}y_2 \cdots \mathrm{d}y_n.$$

(2) Suppose $f_X(X)$ is expressible as $f_X(X) = \prod_{i=1}^n g_i(x_i)$. Show that

$f_{x_i}(x_i)$, the marginal probability density function of x_i, is proportional to $g_i(x_i)$.

The $(h_1, \ldots, h_n)$th *moment* of a multivariate distribution function is defined as

$$\mathscr{E}x_1^{h_1} \cdots x_n^{h_n} = \int_{-\infty}^{\infty} \cdots \int_{-\infty}^{\infty} x_1^{h_1} \cdots x_n^{h_n} f_X(x_1, \ldots, x_n)\, dx_1 \cdots dx_n.$$

The special moment where $h_i = 1$ and $h_j = 0$, $j \neq i$, is called the first moment or *mean* of the marginal distribution of x_i, or the *expected value* of x_i, $\mathscr{E}x_i$. The n-vector whose ith coordinate is $\mathscr{E}x_i$ is called the *mean vector of* X.

The $(h_1, \ldots, h_n)$th *moment about the mean* (or *central moment*) of a multivariate distribution is defined as

$$\mathscr{E}[(x_1 - \mathscr{E}x_1)^{h_1} \cdots (x_n - \mathscr{E}x_n)^{h_n}] =$$
$$\int_{-\infty}^{\infty} \cdots \int_{-\infty}^{\infty} (x_1 - \mathscr{E}x_1)^{h_1} \cdots (x_n - \mathscr{E}x_n)^{h_n} f_X(x_1 \cdots x_n)\, dx_1 \cdots dx_n.$$

The special central moment where $h_i = 2$ and $h_j = 0$, $j \neq i$, is called the *variance* of the marginal distribution of x_i, sometimes written $\mathscr{V}x_i$. The special central moment where $h_i = h_j = 1$ for a pair of distinct subscripts i, j, and $h_k = 0$, $k \neq i, j$, is called the *covariance* of x_i and x_j, sometimes written $\mathscr{C}(x_i, x_j)$. The $n \times n$ matrix whose (i, j)th coordinate is $\mathscr{C}(x_i, x_j)$ and (i, i)th coordinate is $\mathscr{V}(x_i)$ is called the *variance–covariance matrix*, or, for brevity, the *covariance matrix* of X.

Exercise: (1) Show that $\mathscr{E}(ax_1 + bx_2 + c) = a\mathscr{E}x_1 + b\mathscr{E}x_2 + c$.

(2) Show that $\mathscr{V}(ax_1 + bx_2 + c) = a^2\mathscr{V}x_1 + b^2\mathscr{V}x_2 + 2ab\mathscr{C}(x_1, x_2)$.

(3) Show that $\mathscr{C}(ax_1 + bx_2 + c, dx_3 + ex_4 + f) = ad\mathscr{C}(x_1, x_3) + bd\mathscr{C}(x_2, x_3) + ae\mathscr{C}(x_1, x_4) + be\mathscr{C}(x_2, x_4)$.

Hint: Let $y_1 = ax_1 + bx_2 + c$, $y_2 = x_2, \ldots, y_n = x_n$. Then, for example,

$$\begin{aligned}\mathscr{E}y_1 &= \int_{-\infty}^{\infty} y_1 f_{y_1}(y_1)\, dy_1 \\ &= \int_{-\infty}^{\infty} \cdots \int_{-\infty}^{\infty} y_1 f_Y(Y)\, dy_1 \cdots dy_n \\ &= \int_{-\infty}^{\infty} \cdots \int_{-\infty}^{\infty} (ax_1 + bx_2 + c) f_X(X)\, dx_1 \cdots dx_n.\end{aligned}$$

(4) Let Y be a matrix of random variables. Define $\mathscr{E}Y$ as the matrix

with (i, j)th coordinate $\mathscr{E}y_{ij}$. Let μ be the mean vector and Σ be the covariance matrix of the n-vector $\boldsymbol{X}$. Show that $\Sigma = \mathscr{E}(\boldsymbol{X} - \mu)'(\boldsymbol{X} - \mu)$.

Let C be the covariance matrix of $\boldsymbol{X}$. One can generalize exercises 2 and 3 to conclude that if $\boldsymbol{Y} = \boldsymbol{X}A$, where A is an $n \times n$ matrix, then the covariance matrix of $\boldsymbol{Y}$ is $A'CA$. Since C is a symmetric matrix, it can be written as $C = QDQ'$, where Q is an orthogonal and D is a diagonal matrix. Take $A = Q$. Then $A'CA = D$. But $d_{ii} = \mathscr{E}(y_i - \mathscr{E}y_i)^2 \geq 0$. Therefore we conclude that all covariance matrices are positive semidefinite.

The *correlation* between x_i and x_j, sometimes written $\rho(x_i, x_j)$, is defined by $\rho(x_i, x_j) = \mathscr{C}(x_i, x_j)/\sqrt{(\mathscr{V}(x_i)\mathscr{V}(x_j))}$. Since the matrix

$$\begin{bmatrix} \mathscr{V}(x_i) & \mathscr{C}(x_i, x_j) \\ \mathscr{C}(x_i, x_j) & \mathscr{V}(x_j) \end{bmatrix}$$

is positive semidefinite, its determinant is non-negative. From this we see that $\rho^2(x_i, x_j) \leq 1$.

Let y be a random variable with $\mathscr{E}y = \mu$, $\mathscr{V}y = \sigma^2$. Let x be a random variable with

$$f_x(x) = \begin{cases} k, & \text{if } (x - \mu)^2/\sigma^2 \leq 3, \\ 0, & \text{otherwise.} \end{cases}$$

Then $\mathscr{E}x = \mu$, $\mathscr{V}x = \sigma^2$. This density corresponds to the situation in which any value of x in the interval $[\mu - \sqrt{3}\,\sigma, \mu + \sqrt{3}\,\sigma]$ is equally probable, and all other values have zero probability. The interval $[\mu - \sqrt{3}\,\sigma, \mu + \sqrt{3}\,\sigma]$ is a geometric measure of the concentration of the distribution of any random variable y with finite variance around its mean μ.

The generalization of this measure of concentration to multivariate probability distributions is an ellipsoid centered at the mean of the distribution. Let μ be the mean vector and Σ the covariance matrix of a random vector $\boldsymbol{Y}$. Define $g(\boldsymbol{X}) = (\boldsymbol{X} - \mu)\Sigma^{-1}(\boldsymbol{X} - \mu)'$. Let

$$f_X(X) = \begin{cases} k, & \text{if } g(\boldsymbol{X}) \leq n + 2, \\ 0, & \text{otherwise.} \end{cases}$$

Then $\boldsymbol{X}$ has the same mean vector and covariance matrix as does $\boldsymbol{Y}$.

The set of X's such that $(X - \mu)\Sigma^{-1}(X - \mu)' = n + 2$ is called the *ellipsoid of concentration* corresponding to all distributions with mean μ and covariance matrix Σ.

Exercise: Let $\mathbf{Y}$ and $\mathbf{Z}$ be random n-vectors with $\mathscr{E}\mathbf{Y} = \mathscr{E}\mathbf{Z} = \mu$. Let Σ_1 be the covariance matrix of $\mathbf{Y}$, Σ_2 be the covariance matrix of $\mathbf{Z}$, with $\Sigma_1 - \Sigma_2$ positive definite. Show that the ellipsoid of concentration corresponding to the distribution of $\mathbf{Z}$ is contained in the ellipsoid of concentration corresponding to the distribution of $\mathbf{Y}$. (This result will be of use in our consideration of efficiency of estimators in section 3.)

We now come to the type of distribution derived from a multivariate distribution which will be most useful to us, the conditional distribution. For any Borel sets A and B, the *conditional probability of A given B*, $P(A|B)$, is defined by $P(A|B) = P(A \cap B)/P(B)$. In particular, thus, taking $A = \{\mathbf{X}|x_1 \leqslant \mathbf{x}_1 \leqslant x_1 + \Delta x_1, \ldots, x_p \leqslant \mathbf{x}_p \leqslant x_p + \Delta x_p\}$ and $B = \{\mathbf{X}|x_{p+1} \leqslant \mathbf{x}_{p+1} \leqslant x_{p+1} + \Delta x_{p+1}, \ldots, x_n \leqslant \mathbf{x}_n \leqslant x_n + \Delta x_n\}$,

$$P(A|B) = \frac{\int_{x_1}^{x_1+\Delta x_1} \cdots \int_{x_n}^{x_n+\Delta x_n} f_{\mathbf{X}}(u_1, \ldots, u_n)\, du_n \cdots du_1}{\int_{-\infty}^{\infty} \cdots \int_{-\infty}^{\infty} \int_{x_{p+1}}^{x_{p+1}+\Delta x_{p+1}} \cdots \int_{x_n}^{x_n+\Delta x_n} f_{\mathbf{X}}(u_1, \ldots, u_n)\, du_n \cdots du_{p+1}\, du_p \cdots du_1}.$$

Let $\dot{U} = (u_1, \ldots, u_p)$ and $\ddot{U} = (u_{p+1}, \ldots, u_n)$. By the mean value theorem, there exist $u^o_{p+1}(\dot{U}), \ldots, u^o_n(\dot{U})$, $n-p$ functions of $\dot{U}$, satisfying $x_i \leqslant u^o_i(\dot{U}) \leqslant x_i + \Delta x_i$, $i = p+1, \ldots, n$, such that

$$P(A|B) = \frac{\int_{x_1}^{x_1+\Delta x_1} \cdots \int_{x_p}^{x_p+\Delta x_p} f_{\mathbf{X}}(u_1, \ldots, u_p, u^o_{p+1}(\dot{U}), \ldots, u^o_n(\dot{U}))\Delta x_{p+1} \cdots \Delta x_n\, du_p \cdots du_1}{\int_{-\infty}^{\infty} \cdots \int_{-\infty}^{\infty} f_{\mathbf{X}}(u_1, \ldots, u_p, u^o_{p+1}(\dot{U}), \ldots, u^o_n(\dot{U}))\Delta x_{p+1} \cdots \Delta x_n\, du_1 \cdots du_p} =$$

$$\frac{\int_{x_1}^{x_1+\Delta x_1} \cdots \int_{x_p}^{x_p+\Delta x_p} f_{\mathbf{X}}(\dot{U}, \ddot{U}^o(\dot{U}))\, du_p \cdots du_1}{\int_{-\infty}^{\infty} \cdots \int_{-\infty}^{\infty} f_{\mathbf{X}}(\dot{U}, \ddot{U}^o(\dot{U}))\, du_1 \cdots du_p}.$$

Let $\Delta x_{p+1}, \ldots, \Delta x_n$ approach zero. Then $\ddot{U}^o(\dot{U})$ approaches $\ddot{X} = (x_{p+1}, \ldots, x_n)$ and $P(A|B) = P_{\mathbf{X}}\{x_1 \leqslant \mathbf{x}_1 \leqslant x_1 + \Delta x_1, \ldots, x_p \leqslant \mathbf{x}_p \leqslant x_p + \Delta x_p | \mathbf{x}_{p+1} = x_{p+1}, \ldots, \mathbf{x}_n = x_n\}$. Replacing $\Delta x_1, \ldots, \Delta x_n$ by $dx_1, \ldots, dx_n$, we have, to first-order terms,

$$P(A|B) = \frac{f_{\mathbf{X}}(x_1, \ldots, x_p, x_{p+1}, \ldots, x_n)\, dx_1 \cdots dx_p}{\int_{-\infty}^{\infty} \cdots \int_{-\infty}^{\infty} f_{\mathbf{X}}(\dot{U}, \ddot{X})\, du_1 \cdots du_p} = \frac{f_{\mathbf{X}}(X)\, dx_1 \cdots dx_p}{f_{\ddot{\mathbf{X}}}(\ddot{X})}.$$

Thus if $\mathbf{X}$ is the n-vector $\mathbf{X} = (\dot{\mathbf{X}}, \ddot{\mathbf{X}})$, we define the *conditional probability density function of* $\mathbf{X}$, *given* $\ddot{\mathbf{X}} = \ddot{X}$, as

$$f_{\dot{\mathbf{X}}|\ddot{\mathbf{X}}}(\dot{X}) = \frac{f_{\mathbf{X}}(X)}{f_{\ddot{\mathbf{X}}}(\ddot{X})}.$$

We say that $\dot{\mathbf{X}}$ and $\ddot{\mathbf{X}}$ are independent if $f_{\dot{\mathbf{X}}|\ddot{\mathbf{X}}}(\dot{X}) = f_{\dot{\mathbf{X}}}(\dot{X})$, i.e., if the conditional probability density function of $\dot{\mathbf{X}}$ given $\ddot{\mathbf{X}} = \ddot{X}$ does not depend on $\ddot{X}$ (and consequently is the marginal probability density function of $\dot{\mathbf{X}}$). In that case, $f_{\mathbf{X}}(X) = f_{\dot{\mathbf{X}}}(\dot{X}) f_{\ddot{\mathbf{X}}}(\ddot{X})$.

Exercise: (1) Show that if $\dot{\mathbf{X}}$ and $\ddot{\mathbf{X}}$ are independent, then $C(\mathbf{x}_i, \mathbf{x}_j) = 0$ for any element $\mathbf{x}_i$ of $\dot{\mathbf{X}}$, $\mathbf{x}_j$ of $\ddot{\mathbf{X}}$.

(2) Let $\mathbf{X} = (\mathbf{x}_1, \mathbf{x}_2)$, with $\mathbf{x}_2 = \mathbf{x}_1^2$, and $f_{\mathbf{x}_1}(x_1)$ given by the following table:

x_1	-2	-1	1	2
$f_{\mathbf{x}_1}(x_1)$	$\frac{1}{4}$	$\frac{1}{4}$	$\frac{1}{4}$	$\frac{1}{4}$

What is $f_{\mathbf{X}}(x_1, x_2)$? What is $f_{\mathbf{x}_2}(x_2)$? Are $\mathbf{x}_1$ and $\mathbf{x}_2$ independent? Compute $C(\mathbf{x}_1, \mathbf{x}_2)$.

As a final topic in this section, we define some types of limits which will be useful to us in our treatment of point estimation.

Limit of a sequence of numbers: Given a sequence $\{x_n, n = 1, 2, \ldots\}$ of real numbers, we say that the sequence has a *limit a* if for any choice of $\epsilon > 0$ there corresponds an integer $N = N(\epsilon)$ such that for all $n > N$ we have $|x_n - a| < \epsilon$. We write this as $\lim_{n\to\infty} x_n = a$.

Limit in probability of a sequence of random variables: Given a sequence $\{x_n, n = 1, 2, \ldots\}$ of random variables, we say that the sequence has a *limit in probability a* if for any choice of $\epsilon > 0$ the sequence of numbers

$$p_n = P_{\mathbf{x}_n}\{a - \epsilon \leqslant \mathbf{x}_n \leqslant a + \epsilon\} = F_{\mathbf{x}_n}(a + \epsilon) - F_{\mathbf{x}_n}(a - \epsilon)$$

has 1 as its limit. That is, for any choice of $\epsilon > 0$ and any choice of $\delta > 0$ there corresponds an integer $N = N(\epsilon, \delta)$ such that, for all $n > N$, we have $p_n = P_{\mathbf{x}_n}\{a - \epsilon \leqslant \mathbf{x}_n \leqslant a + \epsilon\} > 1 - \delta$. When $\mathbf{x}_n$ has a limit in probability a we write this as $\operatorname{plim}_{n\to\infty} \mathbf{x}_n = a$.

If $\{\boldsymbol{X}_n, n = 1, 2, \ldots\}$ is a sequence of random p-vectors, then we say $\operatorname{plim}_{n\to\infty} \boldsymbol{X}_n = A$ if $\operatorname{plim}_{n\to\infty} \boldsymbol{x}_{ni} = a_i$ for $i = 1, \ldots, p$.

The celebrated *weak law of large numbers* is an example of a limit in probability of a sequence of random variables. In this example, there is an underlying sequence of independent identically distributed random variables $\boldsymbol{y}_n$, with $\mathscr{E}\boldsymbol{y}_n = \pi < \infty$. Taking $\boldsymbol{x}_n = \sum_{i=1}^{n} \boldsymbol{y}_i/n$, the weak law of large numbers says that $\operatorname{plim}_{n\to\infty} \boldsymbol{x}_n = \pi$.

A standard mathematical shorthand notation useful in describing limiting behavior of sequences of numbers is the order notation embodied in the symbols O and o. We say that $a_n = O(b_n)$ if the sequences $\{a_n, n = 1, 2, \ldots\}$ and $\{b_n, n = 1, 2, \ldots\}$ satisfy the condition that the derived sequence $\{c_n, n = 1, 2, \ldots\}$, where $c_n = a_n/b_n$, is bounded, i.e., there exists a finite number m and some N such that, for all $n > N$, $|c_n| < m$. We say that $a_n = o(b_n)$ if, when $c_n = a_n/b_n$, $\lim_{n\to\infty} c_n = 0$. Thus, if $\lim_{n\to\infty} a_n = 0$, we write $a_n = o(1)$, and if $\{a_n, n = 1, 2, \ldots\}$ is a bounded sequence, then we write $a_n = O(1)$.

An analogous notation for describing limiting behavior of sequences of random variables is the order notation embodied in the symbols O_p and o_p. We say that $\boldsymbol{x}_n = O_p(a_n)$ if for any choice of $\epsilon > 0$ there exists a finite number $m = m(\epsilon)$ and some $N = N(\epsilon)$ such that, for all $n > N$, $p_n = P_{\boldsymbol{x}_n}\{|\boldsymbol{x}_n| < ma_n\}$ has 1 as its limit. (Note that the sequence $\{\boldsymbol{y}_n, n = 1, 2, \ldots\}$, where $\boldsymbol{y}_n = \boldsymbol{x}_n/a_n$, need not have a probability limit. Only if m is independent of ϵ can one say that $\operatorname{plim}_{n\to\infty} \boldsymbol{y}_n = m$.) We say that $\boldsymbol{x}_n = o_p(a_n)$ if $\operatorname{plim}_{n\to\infty} \boldsymbol{x}_n/a_n = 0$.

We will say that a sequence of [random] matrices is $O(a_n)$ or $o(a_n)[O_p(a_n)$ or $o_p(a_n)]$ if each of its elements has that property.

Let $\boldsymbol{X}$ be a random vector and $g(\boldsymbol{X})$ be a non-negative function of $\boldsymbol{X}$. Consider the set $S = \{X : g(X) \geq k\}$. Then,

$$\mathscr{E}g(\boldsymbol{X}) \geq k \int_S f_{\boldsymbol{X}}(X)\, \mathrm{d}X = kP_{\boldsymbol{X}}(X \in S).$$

This generalized version of Tchebychef's theorem has great application in determining the stochastic order of various random variables. For example, if $\boldsymbol{Y} = (\boldsymbol{y}_1, \ldots, \boldsymbol{y}_n)$, where the $\boldsymbol{y}_i$ are independent and identically distributed, and $g(\boldsymbol{Y}) = \left|\sum_{i=1}^{n} (\boldsymbol{y}_i/n - \mathscr{E}\boldsymbol{y}_i)\right|^2$, then

$$P_{\boldsymbol{Y}}(g(Y) < k^2) > \left|-\frac{\mathscr{E}g(\boldsymbol{Y})}{k^2}\right| = -\frac{\sigma^2}{nk^2},$$

where

$$\sigma^2 = \mathscr{V}\mathbf{Y}_i = \mathscr{E}(y_i - \mathscr{E}y_i)^2.$$

Therefore, for any choice of ϵ, there is an $m(\epsilon) = \sigma\epsilon$ such that for all n,

$$P_Y\left(\left|\sum_{i=1}^{n} y_i/n - \mathscr{E}y_i\right| < m/\sqrt{n}\right) \geq 1 - 1/\epsilon^2,$$

so that, if $x_n = \sum_{i=1}^{n} y_i/n$ and $\pi = \mathscr{E}y_i$, we see that $x_n - \pi = O_p(1/\sqrt{n})$.

Exercise: Show that if $x_n = \sum_{i=1}^{n} y_i^p/n$ and $\mu_p = \mathscr{E}y_i^p$, then $x_n - \mu_p = O_p(1/\sqrt{n})$.

A theorem that has great usefulness in determining limiting behavior of sequences of random variables in econometrics is the following:

Theorem 16: *Suppose that*

$$f_{jn}(\mathbf{X}_n) = O_p(a_{jn}), \qquad j = 1, \ldots, J,$$

and

$$g_{kn}(\mathbf{X}_n) = o_p(b_{kn}), \qquad k = 1, \ldots, K.$$

Further, suppose that if

$$f_{jn}(X_n) = O(a_{jn}), \qquad j = 1, \ldots, J,$$
$$g_{kn}(X_n) = o(b_{kn}), \qquad k = 1, \ldots, K.$$

then $h_n(X_n) = O(c_n)$. *It follows that* $h_n(\mathbf{X}_n) = O_p(c_n)$.

As a simple example of the use of this theorem, let

$$\mathbf{X}_n = (y_n, z_n, y, z), \qquad g_{1n}(\mathbf{X}_n) = y_n - y,$$
$$g_2(\mathbf{X}_n) = z_n - z, \qquad h_n(\mathbf{X}_n) = y_n z_n - yz,$$
$$a_n = b_n = c_n = 1/\sqrt{n}.$$

That is, suppose $y_n - y = O_p(1/\sqrt{n})$ and $z_n - z = O_p(1/\sqrt{n})$. Since $y_n - y = O(1/\sqrt{n})$, and $z_n - z = O(1/\sqrt{n})$ implies that $h_n(X_n) = y_n z_n - yz = O(1/\sqrt{n})$, it follows that $h_n(\mathbf{X}_n) = O_p(1/\sqrt{n})$, i.e., $y_n z_n - yz = O_p(1/\sqrt{n})$.

More generally let $\operatorname{plim}_{n\to\infty} y_n - y'_n = 0$, $\operatorname{plim}_{n\to\infty} z_n - z'_n = 0$, $y'_n = O_p(1)$, $z'_n = O_p(1)$, and $f(y, z)$ be a function jointly continuous in y and z. Then, $\operatorname{plim}_{n\to\infty} f(y_n, z_n) - f(y'_n, z'_n) = 0$.

The workhorse result in deriving limiting behavior of random variables which is corollary to Theorem 16 is the following. Suppose $x_n = a + o_p(r_n)$ and let $\lim_{n\to\infty} r_n = 0$. If $f(x)$ is a continuously differentiable function, then

$$f(x_n) = f(a) + (x_n - a)f'(a) + \cdots + (x_n - a)^s \frac{f^{(s)}(a)}{s!} + o_p(r_n^s),$$

where $f^{(s)}(a)$ is the sth derivative of $f(x)$ evaluated at $x = a$.

One should note that in deriving asymptotic results one must not fall into the trap of determining that some random quantity is $o_p(1)$ and thus that its asymptotic expected value is $o(1)$. It is not necessarily true that if $x_n = o_p(1)$ then $\mathscr{E}x_n = o(1)$.

Limit in distribution of a sequence of random vectors: Given a sequence $\{\boldsymbol{X}_n, n = 1, 2, \ldots\}$ of random p-vectors, we say that the sequence has a *limit in distribution* $\boldsymbol{X}$ if there exists a random p-vector $\boldsymbol{X}$ such that, for all values X at which $F_{\boldsymbol{X}}(X)$ is a continuous function, we have $\lim_{n\to\infty} F_{\boldsymbol{X}_n}(X) = F_{\boldsymbol{X}}(X)$. We sometimes abbreviate this concept by writing $\mathscr{L}(\boldsymbol{X}_n) \to \mathscr{L}(\boldsymbol{X})$, mnemonically meaning that the probability law of $\boldsymbol{X}_n$ has as limit the probability law of $\boldsymbol{X}$.

Note that if $\mathscr{L}(\boldsymbol{X}_n) \to \mathscr{L}(\boldsymbol{X})$ and $\boldsymbol{X}$ is a degenerate random vector, i.e., $\boldsymbol{X} \equiv X$, a given vector, then $\operatorname{plim}_{n\to\infty} \boldsymbol{X}_n = X$, that is, each of the elements of $\boldsymbol{X}_n$ have a limit in probability, namely the corresponding element of X.

A theorem which is fundamental to the study of asymptotic properties of parameter estimates is the following important convergence theorem.

Theorem 16a: *If* $\mathscr{L}(\boldsymbol{X}_n) \to \mathscr{L}(\boldsymbol{X})$, *where* $\boldsymbol{X}$ *is a p-vector, then*

$$\mathscr{L}(\phi(\boldsymbol{X}_n)) \to \mathscr{L}(\phi(\boldsymbol{X})),$$

where ϕ *is any continuous function from p-space to r-space.*

The corollary to this theorem when $\boldsymbol{X} = A$ is a degenerate random p-vector, namely that $\operatorname{plim}_{n\to\infty} \boldsymbol{X}_n = A$ and ϕ is a continuous function from p-space to n-space implies $\operatorname{plim}_{n\to\infty} \phi(\boldsymbol{X}_n) = \phi(A)$ when $\phi(A)$ exists, is sometimes called *Slutsky's theorem.*

2. Multivariate normal distribution

The random n-vector $\boldsymbol{X}$ is *multivariate normally distributed with parameters* μ *and* Σ if its probability density function is

$$f_X(x_1, \ldots, x_n) = (2\pi)^{-n/2}|\Sigma|^{\frac{1}{2}} \exp\{-\tfrac{1}{2}(X-\mu)\Sigma^{-1}(X-\mu)'\},$$

where μ is an n-vector $(\mu_1, \ldots, \mu_n)$ and Σ is an $n \times n$ positive definite matrix with (i, j)th coordinate σ_{ij}. [Contrary to our earlier declaration, we dub the vector $(\mu_1, \ldots, \mu_n)$ by the lower case Greek letter μ, rather than by the upper case Greek letter M, in keeping with traditional notation and in order to avoid your confusing upper case "mu", a vector of parameters, with upper case "em".] For brevity, when X is multivariate normally distributed with parameters μ and Σ, we say that X is distributed as $N(\mu, \Sigma)$.

The multivariate normal distribution is central to work in econometrics not because people have shown empirically that random vectors which arise from economic phenomena are distributed in this way. Rather, it is because of the *central limit theorem*. This theorem says that if $\boldsymbol{X}_1, \boldsymbol{X}_2, \ldots$ is a sequence of random vectors which are independent and identically distributed with mean vector μ and covariance matrix Σ, then $\mathcal{L}\left((1/\sqrt{n})\sum_{i=1}^{n}(\boldsymbol{X}_i-\mu)\right) \to \mathcal{L}(\boldsymbol{Y})$ as $n \to \infty$, where $\boldsymbol{Y}$ is distributed on $N(0, \Sigma)$. Thus a multivariate normal random vector is the limit in distribution of an average of arbitrarily (but commonly) distributed independent random variables.

There are three standard transformations of the multivariate normal distribution with which one should be familiar, the shift transformation, the linear transformation, and a special linear transformation, the standardizing transformation.

(1) *Shift transformation*: Let $\boldsymbol{X}$ be distributed as $N(\mu, \Sigma)$, and let $\boldsymbol{Y} = \boldsymbol{X} - \mu$. Then $J(Y \to X) = |I| = 1$, and so

$$f_Y(y_1, \ldots, y_n) = (2\pi)^{-n/2}|\Sigma|^{-\frac{1}{2}} \exp\{-\tfrac{1}{2}Y\Sigma^{-1}Y'\}.$$

Thus $\boldsymbol{Y}$ is distributed as $N(0, \Sigma)$.

(2) *Linear transformation*: Let $\boldsymbol{X}$ be distributed as $N(\mu, \Sigma)$ and let $\boldsymbol{Y} = \boldsymbol{X}A$, where A is invertible. Then $J(Y \to X) = 1/|A|^+$, and

$$\begin{aligned} f_Y(y_1, \ldots, y_n) &= (2\pi)^{-n/2}|\Sigma|^{-\frac{1}{2}}(|A|^+)^{-1} \exp\{-(yA^{-1}-\mu)\Sigma^{-1}(yA^{-1}-\mu)'/2\} \\ &= (2\pi)^{-n/2}|A'\Sigma A|^{-\frac{1}{2}} \exp\{-(y-\mu A)(A'\Sigma A)^{-1}(y-\mu A)'/2\}. \end{aligned}$$

From this we conclude that $\boldsymbol{Y}$ is distributed as $N(\mu A, A'\Sigma A)$.

(3) *Standardizing transformation*: Let $\boldsymbol{X}$ be distributed as $N(\mu, \Sigma)$. Since Σ is positive definite, let $\Sigma^{-1} = TT'$, where T is an upper triangular matrix. Let $\boldsymbol{Y} = \boldsymbol{X}T$. Then $\boldsymbol{Y}$ is distributed as $N(\mu T, T'\Sigma T)$. Since $T'\Sigma T = T'(TT')^{-1}T = I$, we see that $\boldsymbol{Y}$ is distributed as $N(\mu T, I)$. Note that $f_Y(Y) = \prod_{i=1}^{n} f_{y_i}(y_i)$, where y_i is distributed as $N\left(\sum_{j=1}^{i} \mu_j t_{ji}, 1\right)$. Thus the y_i's are independent.

Exercise: Let Δ be a given diagonal matrix and $\boldsymbol{X}$ be distributed as $N(\mu, \Sigma)$. What is the matrix A of the linear transformation such that $\boldsymbol{Y} = \boldsymbol{X}A$ is distributed as $N(\mu A, \Delta)$? Check that the y_i's are independent. Note that when $\Delta = I$, $A = T$, where $\Sigma^{-1} = TT'$.

Let us now determine the marginal distribution of $\dot{\boldsymbol{X}} = (\boldsymbol{x}_1, \ldots, \boldsymbol{x}_p)$ when $\boldsymbol{X}$ is distributed as $N(\mu, \Sigma)$. Let $\boldsymbol{Z} = (\boldsymbol{X} - \mu)T$, where $\Sigma^{-1} = TT'$, and T is an upper triangular matrix. Then $\boldsymbol{Z}$ is distributed as $N(0, I)$.

Let $\dot{\boldsymbol{Z}} = (z_1, \ldots, z_p)$ and $\dot{\boldsymbol{Y}} = (y_1, \ldots, y_p)$, where $\boldsymbol{Y} = \boldsymbol{X} - \mu$. Then $\dot{\boldsymbol{Y}} = \dot{\boldsymbol{Z}}T_1^{-1}$, where T_1 is the upper left-hand $p \times p$ submatrix of T, so that $\dot{\boldsymbol{Y}}$ is distributed as $N(0, T_1^{-1\prime} I T_1^{-1})$. But

$$\Sigma^{-1} = \begin{pmatrix} T_1 & T_2 \\ 0 & T_3 \end{pmatrix} \begin{pmatrix} T_1' & 0 \\ T_2' & T_3' \end{pmatrix}$$

implies that

$$\Sigma = \begin{pmatrix} T_1'^{-1} & 0 \\ U_2' & U_3' \end{pmatrix} \begin{pmatrix} T_1^{-1} & U_2 \\ 0 & U_3 \end{pmatrix} = \begin{pmatrix} \Sigma_{11} & \Sigma_{12} \\ \Sigma_{21} & \Sigma_{22} \end{pmatrix}.$$

Therefore $T_1'^{-1}T_1^{-1} = \Sigma_{11}$ and $\dot{\boldsymbol{Y}}$ is distributed as $N(0, \Sigma_{11})$. Since $\dot{\boldsymbol{X}} = \dot{\boldsymbol{Y}} + \dot{\mu}$, we see that $\dot{\boldsymbol{X}} = (\boldsymbol{x}_1, \ldots, \boldsymbol{x}_p)$ is distributed as $N(\dot{\mu}, \Sigma_{11})$, where $\dot{\mu} = (\mu_1, \ldots, \mu_p)$.

In particular, the marginal probability density function of $\boldsymbol{x}_i$ is given by

$$f_{x_i}(x_i) = (2\pi)^{-\frac{1}{2}} \sigma_{ii}^{-\frac{1}{2}} \exp\{-(x_i - \mu_i)^2/2\sigma_{ii}\}.$$

To compute $\mathscr{E}\boldsymbol{x}_i$, we note that

$$\begin{aligned} \mathscr{E}\boldsymbol{x}_i &= \int_{-\infty}^{\infty} x_i f_{x_i}(x_i)\,\mathrm{d}x_i \\ &= \int_{-\infty}^{\infty} (x_i - \mu_i) f_{x_i}(x_i)\,\mathrm{d}x_i + \mu_i \\ &= \frac{1}{\sqrt{(2\pi)}} \int_{-\infty}^{\infty} \left(\frac{x_i - \mu_i}{\sqrt{\sigma_{ii}}}\right) \exp\{-(x_i - \mu_i)^2/2\sigma_{ii}\}\,\mathrm{d}x_i + \mu_i \end{aligned}$$

$$= \frac{1}{\sqrt{(2\pi)}} \int_{-\infty}^{\infty} \exp\{-(x_i - \mu_i)^2/2\sigma_{ii}\}\, d(-\exp\{-(x_i - \mu_i)^2/2\sigma_{ii}\}) + \mu_i$$

$$= \frac{-1}{\sqrt{(2\pi)}} \exp\{-(x_i - \mu_i)^2/2\sigma_{ii}\}\Big|_{-\infty}^{\infty} + \mu_i = \mu_i.$$

Thus the vector μ is the mean vector of $\boldsymbol{X}$.

Exercise: Show that $\mathscr{E}\boldsymbol{x}_i^2 = \sigma_{ii} + \mu_i^2$, so that $\mathscr{V}\boldsymbol{x}_i = \sigma_{ii}$.

Let $\phi = (\phi(1), \ldots, \phi(n))$ be a permutation of the integers $1, \ldots, n$. Let A be a matrix with $a_{i\phi(i)} = 1$ and $a_{ij} = 0$ for $j \neq \phi(i)$, $i = 1, \ldots, n$. Now suppose we are interested in the marginal distribution of $\dot{\boldsymbol{X}}_\phi = (\boldsymbol{x}_{\phi(1)}, \ldots, \boldsymbol{x}_{\phi(p)})$. But if $\boldsymbol{X} = (\boldsymbol{x}_1, \ldots, \boldsymbol{x}_n)$ is distributed as $N(\mu, \Sigma)$, $\boldsymbol{X}_\phi = (\boldsymbol{x}_{\phi(1)}, \ldots, \boldsymbol{x}_{\phi(n)})$ is distributed as $N(\mu A, A'\Sigma A)$. Thus $\dot{\boldsymbol{X}}_\phi$ is multivariate normally distributed with parameters $\dot{\mu}_\phi = (\mu_{\phi(1)}, \ldots, \mu_{\phi(p)})$ and Σ_ϕ, the upper left-hand $p \times p$ submatrix of $A'\Sigma A$.

Exercise: (1) Check that the (i, j)th element of Σ_ϕ is $\sigma_{\phi(i)\phi(j)}$.
(2) What is the marginal probability density function of $(\boldsymbol{x}_i, \boldsymbol{x}_j)$ when $\boldsymbol{X}$ is distributed as $N(\mu, \Sigma)$? Show that $C(\boldsymbol{x}_i, \boldsymbol{x}_j) = \sigma_{ij}$.

Since the diagonal elements of Σ are the variance of the marginal distributions of the $\boldsymbol{x}_i$ and the off-diagonal elements are the covariances of pairs $\boldsymbol{x}_i$, $\boldsymbol{x}_j$, the matrix Σ is the covariance matrix of $\boldsymbol{X}$.

Let $\boldsymbol{X}$ be distributed as $N(\mu, \Sigma)$. Then the conditional probability density function of $\dot{\boldsymbol{X}}$ given $\ddot{\boldsymbol{X}} = \ddot{X}$ is

$$f_{\dot{X}|\ddot{X}}(\dot{X}) = \frac{|\Sigma|^{-\frac{1}{2}} \exp\{-(X-\mu)\Sigma^{-1}(X-\mu)'/2\}}{(2\pi)^{(n-p)/2}|\Sigma_{22}|^{-\frac{1}{2}} \exp\{-(\ddot{X}-\ddot{\mu})\Sigma_{22}^{-1}(\ddot{X}-\ddot{\mu})'/2\}}$$

where

$$\Sigma = \begin{pmatrix} \Sigma_{11} & \Sigma_{12} \\ \Sigma_{21} & \Sigma_{22} \end{pmatrix},$$

and Σ_{11} is a $p \times p$ submatrix of Σ. Let $\Sigma^{-1} = \Lambda$ be likewise partitioned as

$$\Lambda = \begin{pmatrix} \Lambda_{11} & \Lambda_{12} \\ \Lambda_{21} & \Lambda_{22} \end{pmatrix}.$$

Then,

$$(X-\mu)\Sigma^{-1}(X-\mu)' = (\dot{X}-\dot{\mu})\Lambda_{11}(\dot{X}-\dot{\mu})' + (\ddot{X}-\ddot{\mu})\Lambda_{22}(\ddot{X}-\ddot{\mu})' + 2(\dot{X}-\dot{\mu})\Lambda_{12}(\ddot{X}-\ddot{\mu})'.$$

Noting that $\Sigma_{22}^{-1} = \Lambda_{22} - \Lambda_{21}\Lambda_{11}^{-1}\Lambda_{12}$, we see that

$$(X-\mu)\Sigma^{-1}(X-\mu)' - (\ddot{X}-\ddot{\mu})\Sigma_{22}^{-1}(\ddot{X}-\ddot{\mu})' =$$
$$[(\dot{X}-\dot{\mu})+(\ddot{X}-\ddot{\mu})\Lambda_{21}\Lambda_{11}^{-1}]\Lambda_{11}[(\dot{X}-\dot{\mu})+(\ddot{X}-\ddot{\mu})\Lambda_{21}\Lambda_{11}^{-1}]'.$$

Also, since $|\Sigma| = |\Sigma_{22}||\Sigma_{11} - \Sigma_{12}\Sigma_{22}^{-1}\Sigma_{21}|$, we see that $|\Sigma|^{-\frac{1}{2}}/|\Sigma_{22}|^{-\frac{1}{2}} = |\Sigma_{11} - \Sigma_{12}\Sigma_{22}^{-1}\Sigma_{21}|^{-\frac{1}{2}} = |\Lambda_{11}|^{\frac{1}{2}}$. Thus,

$$f_{\dot{X}|\ddot{X}}(\dot{X}) = (2\pi)^{-(n-p)/2}|\Lambda_{11}|^{\frac{1}{2}}$$
$$\times \exp\{-\tfrac{1}{2}[\dot{X}-\dot{\mu}+(\ddot{X}-\ddot{\mu})\Lambda_{21}\Lambda_{11}^{-1}]\Lambda_{11}$$
$$\times[\dot{X}-\dot{\mu}+(\ddot{X}-\ddot{\mu})\Lambda_{21}\Lambda_{11}^{-1}]'\},$$

so that $\dot{\boldsymbol{X}}$ given $\ddot{\boldsymbol{X}} = \ddot{X}$ is distributed as $N(\dot{\mu} - (\ddot{X}-\ddot{\mu})\Lambda_{21}\Lambda_{11}^{-1}, \Lambda_{11}^{-1})$ or, in terms of Σ rather than Λ, as $N(\dot{\mu} + (\ddot{X}-\ddot{\mu})\Sigma_{22}^{-1}\Sigma_{21}, \Sigma_{11} - \Sigma_{12}\Sigma_{22}^{-1}\Sigma_{21})$.

Exercise: (1) What is $\mathscr{E}(\dot{\boldsymbol{X}}|\ddot{X})$, $\mathscr{V}(\dot{\boldsymbol{X}}|\ddot{X})$ when $p=1$ and $n=2$? When $p=1$ and $n=3$?

(2) What is the covariance matrix of $\dot{\boldsymbol{X}}|\ddot{X}$ when $p=2$ and $n=3$? Under what conditions is it a diagonal matrix?

The vector $(\dot{\mu} - \ddot{\mu}\Sigma_{22}^{-1}\Sigma_{11}) + \ddot{X}\Sigma_{22}^{-1}\Sigma_{21}$ is often called the *regression* of $\dot{\boldsymbol{X}}$ on $\ddot{X}$, the matrix $\Sigma_{22}^{-1}\Sigma_{21}$ is often called the *matrix of regression coefficients of* $\dot{\boldsymbol{X}}$ *on* $\ddot{X}$, and the elements of the covariance matrix $\Sigma_{11} - \Sigma_{12}\Sigma_{22}^{-1}\Sigma_{21}$ are called the *partial covariances of* $\dot{\boldsymbol{X}}$ *given* $\ddot{X}$. The *partial correlations* of $\dot{\boldsymbol{X}}$ given $\ddot{X}$ are obtained from the partial covariance matrix $\Sigma_{11} - \Sigma_{12}\Sigma_{22}^{-1}\Sigma_{21}$ in the same manner as ordinary correlations are obtained from a covariance matrix.

Quite often, we will be concerned with the regression of a random variable $\boldsymbol{x}_1$ on $\ddot{X}$. One useful property of the regression of $\boldsymbol{x}_1$ on $\ddot{X}$ is embodied in the following theorem.

Theorem 17: $\mathscr{V}(\boldsymbol{x}_1 - \mu_1 + \ddot{\mu}\Sigma_{22}^{-1}\Sigma_{21} - \ddot{\boldsymbol{X}}\Sigma_{22}^{-1}\Sigma_{21}) \leq \mathscr{V}(\boldsymbol{x}_1 - a - \ddot{\boldsymbol{X}}B')$ *for all* $n-1$ *vectors* B *and scalars* a.

Proof: Since the constants a and $\mu_1 - \ddot{\mu}\Sigma_{22}^{-1}\Sigma_{21}$ do not affect the variance calculation, we need only compare $\mathscr{V}(\boldsymbol{x}_1 - \ddot{\boldsymbol{X}}\Sigma_{22}^{-1}\Sigma_{11})$ with $\mathscr{V}(\boldsymbol{x}_1 - \ddot{\boldsymbol{X}}B')$. But

$$\mathscr{V}(\boldsymbol{x}_1 - \ddot{\boldsymbol{X}}B') = \sigma_{11} + B\Sigma_{22}B' - \Sigma_{21}'B' - B\Sigma_{21},$$

and

$$\mathcal{V}(\boldsymbol{x}_1 - \ddot{\boldsymbol{X}}\Sigma_{22}^{-1}\Sigma_{21}) = \sigma_{11} - \Sigma_{21}'\Sigma_{22}^{-1}\Sigma_{21}.$$

Differentiating $\mathcal{V}(\boldsymbol{x}_1 - \ddot{\boldsymbol{X}}B')$ with respect to B and setting the derivative equal to zero yields the matrix equation

$$2B\Sigma_{22} - 2\Sigma_{21}' = 0,$$

so that $B = \Sigma_{21}'\Sigma_{22}^{-1}$ satisfies this equation. The $(n-1)\times(n-1)$ matrix of second derivatives of $\mathcal{V}(\boldsymbol{x}_1 - \ddot{\boldsymbol{X}}B')$ with respect to B can be partitioned in such a way that its ith $1\times(n-1)$ block is $2\partial B\Sigma_{22}/\partial b_i = 2E_i\Sigma_{22}$ so that the full matrix is $2\Sigma_{22}$ which is positive definite. Therefore, $B = \Sigma_{21}'\Sigma_{22}^{-1}$ minimizes $\mathcal{V}(\boldsymbol{x}_1 - \ddot{\boldsymbol{X}}B')$.

Another property of the regression of $\boldsymbol{x}_1$ on $\ddot{X}$ is that it maximizes $\rho^2(\boldsymbol{x}_1, a + \ddot{\boldsymbol{X}}B')$. This can be seen by noting that

$$\rho^2(\boldsymbol{x}_1, a + \ddot{\boldsymbol{X}}B') = \frac{(\Sigma_{12}B')^2}{\sigma_{11}B\Sigma_{22}B'},$$

and

$$\partial\rho^2(\boldsymbol{x}_1, a + \ddot{\boldsymbol{X}}B')/\partial B = \frac{2[(\Sigma_{12}B')B\Sigma_{22}B' - (\Sigma_{12}B')^2B\Sigma_{22}]}{\sigma_{11}(B\Sigma_{22}B')} = 0,$$

when $B = \Sigma_{12}\Sigma_{22}^{-1}$.

Exercise: Show that the matrix of second derivatives of $\rho^2(\boldsymbol{x}_1, a + \ddot{\boldsymbol{X}}B')$ with respect to B is negative definite.

The quantity $\rho(\boldsymbol{x}_1, \mu_1 - \ddot{\mu}\Sigma_{22}^{-1}\Sigma_{21} - \ddot{\boldsymbol{X}}\Sigma_{22}^{-1}\Sigma_{21})$ is called the *multiple correlation coefficient* between $\boldsymbol{x}_1$ and $\ddot{\boldsymbol{X}}$. A useful formula is

$$\begin{aligned} 1 - \rho^2(\boldsymbol{x}_1, \mu_1 - \ddot{\mu}\Sigma_{22}^{-1}\Sigma_{21} - \ddot{\boldsymbol{X}}\Sigma_{22}^{-1}\Sigma_{21}) &= \frac{\sigma_{11} - \Sigma_{12}\Sigma_{22}^{-1}\Sigma_{21}}{\sigma_{11}} \\ &= \frac{|\Sigma|}{\sigma_{11}|\Sigma_{22}|}. \end{aligned}$$

Exercise: Check this by first determining the maximum value of ρ^2 and then using our result about the determinant of a partitioned matrix.

The multiple correlation coefficient has the following interpretation. Since $\mathcal{V}(\boldsymbol{x}_1|\ddot{X}) = \sigma_{11} - \Sigma_{12}\Sigma_{22}^{-1}\Sigma_{21}$, $1 - \rho^2(\boldsymbol{x}_1, \mu_1 - \ddot{\mu}\Sigma_{22}^{-1}\Sigma_{21} - \ddot{\boldsymbol{X}}\Sigma_{22}^{-1}\Sigma_{21})$ is the proportionate reduction in the variance of $\boldsymbol{x}_1$ due to knowledge of a value of $\ddot{\boldsymbol{X}}$.

3. Point estimation theory

Suppose $\boldsymbol{X}$ is an n-vector valued random variable and that we know the form of the distribution (e.g., that it is a multivariate normal distribution) but not the parameters. Let $\Theta = (\theta_1, \ldots, \theta_k)$ be the unknown parameters, and think of Θ as a vector in a subset Ω (not necessarily a subspace) of k-space. [For example, Θ may be the $k = n(n+1)/2$ distinct elements σ_{ij}, $j \geq i$, of the covariance matrix Σ of a multivariate normal distribution with known mean vector. Then Θ is not a subspace of k-space, but only a subset, consisting of those σ_{ij} such that the matrix Σ is positive definite. For $k = 1$, this would be the positive real line, which is not a subspace of one-dimensional space.]

We would like to determine a vector-valued function of $\boldsymbol{X}$, $\hat{\Theta}(\boldsymbol{X})$, which associates with each value of $\boldsymbol{X}$ a point in Ω. Such a function will be called a *point estimator* or *estimator*, for short, of Θ. The value $\hat{\Theta}(X)$ of $\hat{\Theta}(\boldsymbol{X})$ for a given value X of $\boldsymbol{X}$ will be called an *estimate* of Θ.

Of course, one can choose any old function $\hat{\Theta}$ to be an estimator of Θ. But we would like to restrict ourselves to "good" estimators. What do we mean by "good" estimators? Well, first of all we need a yardstick with which to assess estimators. Given a disutility function $w(\hat{\Theta}(X), \Theta)$, reflecting the economic loss to us due to having used $\hat{\Theta}(X)$ as an estimate of Θ – not a trivial "given", at that – the principle of expected utility maximization tells us that a good estimator $\hat{\Theta}$ of Θ is one which minimizes $\mathscr{E}w(\hat{\Theta}(\boldsymbol{X}), \Theta)$, i.e., minimizes the expected disutility of having used the estimator $\hat{\Theta}$ to estimate Θ.

It would be especially nice if the estimator $\hat{\Theta}$ minimizes $\mathscr{E}w(\hat{\Theta}(\boldsymbol{X}), \Theta)$ for each Θ in Ω. But this is impossible if w is a reasonable disutility function, for a reasonable disutility function w would have the property that if $\hat{\Theta}(X) = \Theta$ then $w(\Theta, \Theta) = 0$. But we can always find an estimator $\hat{\Theta}(\boldsymbol{X})$ which has $\mathscr{E}w(\hat{\Theta}(\boldsymbol{X}), \Theta) = 0$ for some vector Θ. For we can take $\hat{\Theta}(\boldsymbol{X}) = \Theta^o$ for all $\boldsymbol{X}$, where Θ^o is some vector in Ω; then $\mathscr{E}w(\hat{\Theta}(\boldsymbol{X}), \Theta) = w(\Theta^o, \Theta)$ which equals 0 for $\Theta = \Theta^o$. For an estimator $\hat{\Theta}$ to minimize $\mathscr{E}w(\hat{\Theta}(\boldsymbol{X}), \Theta)$ for each Θ in Ω, $\hat{\Theta}$ would have to give a perfect estimate for all Θ. Such an estimator hardly ever exists. So, given a disutility function, or, as it is usually called, a loss function, one narrows one's search for uniformly (in Θ) best estimators (i.e., ones which minimize expected loss) from the class of all estimators $\hat{\Theta}$ to the class of all estimators $\hat{\Theta}$ which have some other "nice" property as well.

What shall be our choice of loss function? For mathematical convenience, the usual choice when $k = 1$ is $w(\hat{\theta}(X), \theta) = (\hat{\theta}(X) - \theta)^2$, so that $\mathscr{E}(\hat{\theta}(\boldsymbol{X}) - \theta)^2$ is the *mean-squared-error* of the estimator $\hat{\theta}$. When $k = 1$ and $\mathscr{E}\hat{\theta}(\boldsymbol{X}) = \theta$, then $\mathscr{E}(\hat{\theta}(\boldsymbol{X}) - \theta)^2 = \mathscr{V}\hat{\theta}(\boldsymbol{X})$, so that the expected loss of the estimator $\hat{\theta}$ is measured by its variance in this case. This is seen from the following exercise.

Exercise: Show that $\mathscr{E}(\hat{\theta}(\boldsymbol{X}) - \theta)^2 = \mathscr{V}\hat{\theta}(\boldsymbol{X}) + (\theta - \mathscr{E}\hat{\theta}(\boldsymbol{X}))^2$ when $k = 1$.

In order to construct a real-valued loss function when $k > 1$, however, we are confronted with a greater degree of arbitrariness. One loss function, a simple generalization of mean-squared-error when $k = 1$, is $\sum_{i=1}^{k} \mathscr{E}(\hat{\theta}_i(\boldsymbol{X}) - \theta_i)^2$, the sum of the mean-squared-errors for each of the coordinates of Θ. But this loss function does not take into account the fact that $\hat{\theta}_i(\boldsymbol{X})$ and $\hat{\theta}_j(\boldsymbol{X})$ are not independent random variables, so that the error in $\hat{\theta}_i$ and in $\hat{\theta}_j$ are "double-counted".

To eliminate this difficulty, one might consider the $k \times k$ matrix $C(\hat{\Theta})$ with (i, j)th element

$$c_{ij}(\hat{\Theta}) = \mathscr{E}[(\hat{\theta}_i(\boldsymbol{X}) - \theta_i)(\hat{\theta}_j(\boldsymbol{X}) - \theta_j)],$$

and take as our loss function $|C(\hat{\Theta})|$. The matrix $C(\hat{\Theta})$ is called the *co-mean-squared-error* matrix (CMSE matrix, for short) of $\hat{\Theta}$.

Exercise: Show that $C(\hat{\Theta})$ is positive semidefinite.

If $\mathscr{E}\hat{\theta}_i(\boldsymbol{X}) = \theta_i$ for all $i = 1, \ldots, k$, then $C(\hat{\Theta})$ is the covariance matrix of $\hat{\Theta}$. In this case, $|C(\hat{\Theta})|$ is called the *generalized variance* of $\hat{\Theta}$.

We prefer not to define a loss function for the case $k > 1$, but instead make the following definition. We say that $\hat{\Theta}$ is *efficient* if, for all other estimators $\hat{\Theta}^*$, $C(\hat{\Theta}^*) - C(\hat{\Theta})$ is positive semidefinite.

Exercise: Let $\hat{\Theta}^*$ be efficient. Show that $\hat{\Theta}^*$ minimizes both $|C(\hat{\Theta})|$ and $\sum_{i=1}^{k} \mathscr{E}(\hat{\theta}_i(\boldsymbol{X}) - \theta_i)^2$.

We say $\hat{\Theta}_1$ is *relatively as efficient* as $\hat{\Theta}_2$ if $C(\hat{\Theta}_2) - C(\hat{\Theta}_1)$ is positive semidefinite. Unlike other comparisons of $\hat{\Theta}_1$ and $\hat{\Theta}_2$ on the basis of the generalized variance or the sum of the mean-squared-errors for each of the coordinates of Θ, in which one or the other of these estimators is "more efficient", i.e., has small expected loss function, this definition of efficiency may lead to non-comparability of these estimators. Neither the matrix $C(\hat{\Theta}_1) - C(\hat{\Theta}_2)$ nor the matrix $C(\hat{\Theta}_2) - C(\hat{\Theta}_1)$ may be positive semidefinite. But perhaps it is better to have a definition of relative efficiency which sometimes leads to non-comparability of estimators. For then one will hopefully think hard about one's actual loss function for the problem at hand and the tradeoffs between good estimation of θ_i and good estimation of θ_j. This is much better than dodging the problem of specifying one's loss function by adopting one of the *ad hoc* functions described above just because it can compare all estimators.

Actually, our reason for this definition of relative efficiency is that, for a large class of problems with which we will deal in chapter III, we will find estimators which are efficient by our definition (and consequently minimize generalized variance and sum of mean-squared-errors as well). Thus these estimators are efficient in a stronger sense than usually cited.

A geometric interpretation of this criterion may be helpful here. The matrix $C(\hat{\Theta}_2) - C(\hat{\Theta}_1)$ being positive semidefinite implies that $C^{-1}(\hat{\Theta}_1) - C^{-1}(\hat{\Theta}_2)$ is positive definite. Thus, for any k-vector Y, we have $Y(C^{-1}(\hat{\Theta}_1) - C^{-1}(\hat{\Theta}_2))Y' = 0$, or $YC^{-1}(\hat{\Theta}_1)Y' = YC^{-1}(\hat{\Theta}_2)Y'$. Viewed as functions of Y, the quantities $YC^{-1}(\hat{\Theta}_1)Y'$ and $YC^{-1}(\hat{\Theta}_2)Y'$ describe ellipsoids in k-space, each centered at Θ. The inequality has the interpretation that the ellipsoid corresponding to $\hat{\Theta}_2(\boldsymbol{X})$ is contained in the ellipsoid corresponding to $\hat{\Theta}_1(\boldsymbol{X})$. Heuristically, the variation of $\hat{\Theta}_1(\boldsymbol{X})$ around Θ in k-space is smaller than that of $\hat{\Theta}_2(\boldsymbol{X})$ around Θ.

When $\hat{\Theta}_1(\boldsymbol{X})$ and $\hat{\Theta}_2(\boldsymbol{X})$ are unbiased estimators of Θ, $YC(\hat{\Theta}_i)Y'$ is the variance of $Y\hat{\Theta}'_i(\boldsymbol{X})$, so that this criterion says that $\hat{\Theta}_2(\boldsymbol{X})$ is relatively as efficient as $\hat{\Theta}_1(\boldsymbol{X})$ if the variance of any linear function of $\hat{\Theta}_2(\boldsymbol{X})$ is at most equal to the variance of the same linear function of $\hat{\Theta}_1(\boldsymbol{X})$. This criterion in this case also says that the ellipsoid of concentration of the distribution of $\hat{\Theta}_1(\boldsymbol{X})$ contains that of the distribution of $\hat{\Theta}_2(\boldsymbol{X})$.

Though we would like to find an estimator $\hat{\Theta}$ which is efficient, unfortunately such an estimator cannot be found in general. So we sometimes confine ourselves to a more restricted class of estimators, *unbiased* estimators, i.e., estimators $\hat{\Theta}$ such that $\mathscr{E}\hat{\Theta}(\boldsymbol{X}) = \Theta$ for all Θ. Or even to a more restrictive class of estimators, *linear unbiased* estimators, i.e., unbiased estimators $\hat{\Theta}$ which are affine transformations of X, $XA + B$ (i.e., a linear transformation plus a shift), where A is an $n \times k$ matrix and B is a k-vector. Efficient estimators in these classes of estimators are called *best unbiased* and *best linear unbiased* estimators, respectively. (Note that the usage of "linear" in this definition conforms with the analytic geometry usage of "linear", rather than the usage in chapter I.)

A property that we would like our optimality properties of estimators to have is invariance with respect to transformations of the parameter space. By this we mean that if $\hat{\Theta}(\boldsymbol{X})$ is a "good" estimator of Θ by some criterion and if we reparameterize so that now $\Xi = (\xi_1, \ldots, \xi_k)$ is our new parameter, where $\xi_i = \phi_i(\Theta)$, $i = 1, \ldots, k$, then $\hat{\Xi}(\boldsymbol{X}) = (\phi_1(\hat{\Theta}(\boldsymbol{X})), \ldots, \phi_k(\hat{\Theta}(\boldsymbol{X}))$ should be a "good" estimator of Ξ by the same criterion. A trivial example of invariance of an optimality property is the criterion of best linear unbiasedness when the ϕ_i are linear functions. But the criterion of unbiasedness is not invariant in general, as can be seen from the following exercise.

Exercise: Let $\boldsymbol{x}$ be distributed as $N(\mu, 1)$. Let $\xi = \mathrm{e}^{\mu}$. Show that $\mathscr{E}\mathrm{e}^{x} \neq \xi$.

Neither is the criterion of efficiency invariant in general. However, when $k = 1$ and ϕ is a monotonically increasing function of θ, then $\hat{\theta}(\boldsymbol{X})$ being efficient implies that $\hat{\xi}(\boldsymbol{X}) = \phi(\hat{\theta}(\boldsymbol{X}))$ is efficient.

Exercise: Prove this.

When our interest in the probability distribution of $\boldsymbol{X}$ centers not on its form but on its parameters Θ, we will highlight this interest by writing the cumulative distribution function and the probability density function of $\boldsymbol{X}$ as $F_{\boldsymbol{X}}(X; \Theta)$ and $f_{\boldsymbol{X}}(X; \Theta)$, respectively. Until now we have only given an informal definition of "parameter of a distribution", namely some vector other than X whose value you need to know in order to compute $F_{\boldsymbol{X}}(X)$. Formally, what we really want of a "parameter" is that if $F_{\boldsymbol{X}}(X; \Theta_1) \neq F_{\boldsymbol{X}}(X; \Theta_2)$ for some X, then $\Theta_1 \neq \Theta_2$, i.e., different distributions of the same functional form have different parameters. A parametrization of a class of distributions of the same functional form with this property is called a *sufficient parametrization*, and the parameter Θ is called a *sufficient parameter.* We will only be interested in sufficient parameters of distributions, and with this understanding will omit the adjective "sufficient" henceforth in discussing parameters.

This is a minor quibble, as the following example of an insufficient parametrization will bring out. Suppose $\boldsymbol{x}$ is distributed as $N(\mu, \sigma^2)$, and take $\theta = \mu/\sigma$. Then all normal distributions with $\mu/\sigma = \theta_0$ are distinct but have the same value θ_0 of the insufficient parameter θ. Of course, $\Theta = (\mu, \sigma^2)$ is a sufficient parameter.

The reason we were so finicky in our definition of parameter is to juxtapose this definition of parameter with that of an identifiable parameter. The (sufficient) parameter Θ is called an *identifiable parameter* if $\Theta_1 \neq \Theta_2$ implies that for some X, $F_X(X; \Theta_1) \neq F_X(X; \Theta_2)$. That is, distinct parameters lead to distinct probability distributions. A parametrization of a class of distributions of the same functional form with this property is called an *identifiable parametrization*, and for brevity we shall say that the parameter Θ is identifiable.

As an example of an unidentifiable parametrization, let x be distributed as $N(\mu, 1)$ and take $\Theta = (\theta_1, \theta_2)$, with $\theta_1 + \theta_2 = \mu$. Then all vectors Θ with $\theta_1 + \theta_2 = \mu_0$ are distinct but lead to the same probability distribution.

For purposes of pinning down the probability distribution once we know its parameters, we require that the parameter vector Θ be sufficient and identifiable. Then there is a one-to-one correspondence between Θ and $F_X(X; \Theta)$. But sometimes even sufficient and identifiable parameters are not very nice to deal with, in the sense that it is "impossible" to estimate Θ given an observed value X of $\boldsymbol{X}$. I don't really mean impossible, because one can always "guesstimate" Θ, even without an observed value of $\boldsymbol{X}$. What I really mean is embodied in the following definition. A parameter Θ is *estimable* if there exists an unbiased estimator $\hat{\Theta}(\boldsymbol{X})$ of Θ. A parameter Θ is *inestimable* if there exists no unbiased estimator $\hat{\Theta}(\boldsymbol{X})$ of Θ. So what I meant by "impossible" was merely inestimable. (Note that when I say "there exists no unbiased estimator", I do not mean that one has not been found; rather, I mean that it can be proven that one *cannot* be found.)

To fix ideas, consider the case when $\boldsymbol{x}$ is distributed as $N(\mu, 1)$. Since $\mathscr{E}\boldsymbol{x} = \mu$, $\hat{\theta}(\boldsymbol{x}) = \boldsymbol{x}$ is an unbiased estimator of μ so that μ is estimable. Now suppose $\boldsymbol{x}$ is distributed as $N(0, \sigma^2)$. Since $\mathscr{E}\boldsymbol{x}^2 = \sigma^2$, $\hat{\theta}(\boldsymbol{x}) = \boldsymbol{x}^2$ is an unbiased estimator of σ^2, so that σ^2 is estimable. Finally, suppose $\boldsymbol{x}$ is distributed as $N(\mu, \sigma^2)$. Here $\Theta = (\theta_1, \theta_2) = (\mu, \sigma^2)$, and $\hat{\theta}_1(\boldsymbol{x}) = \boldsymbol{x}$ is an unbiased estimator of μ. But suppose there exists a $\hat{\theta}_2(\boldsymbol{x})$ satisfying

$$\sigma^2 = \int_{-\infty}^{\infty} \frac{\hat{\theta}_2(x)}{\sqrt{(2\pi)}\sigma} \exp\{-(x-\mu)^2/2\sigma^2\}\, dx.$$

Let $v = (x-\mu)^2$, so that $dx = dx/2\sqrt{v}$ and the integral equation is equivalent to

$$\sqrt{(2\pi)}\sigma^3 = \int_0^\infty \hat{\theta}_2(\mu \pm \sqrt{v}) \exp\{-v/2\sigma^2\} \, dv.$$

Now let $\alpha = 1/2\sigma^2$ and $g(\mu, v) = \hat{\theta}_2(\mu \pm \sqrt{v})$. Then we must have

$$\sqrt{\left(\frac{\pi}{4\alpha^3}\right)} = \int_0^\infty g(\mu, v) \exp\{-\alpha v\} \, dv,$$

for all μ, so that $g(\mu, v)$ must not depend on μ. In fact, the integral is the Laplace transform of $g(\mu, v)$, so that $g(\mu, v)$ is the inverse Laplace transform of $\sqrt{\pi}/2\alpha^{\frac{3}{2}}$. By the unicity of the Laplace transform, there is only one function whose Laplace transform is $\sqrt{\pi}/2\alpha^{\frac{3}{2}}$, and those readers familiar with gamma functions can easily determine that this function is $\sqrt{v}$. But taking $\hat{\theta}_2(\mu \pm \sqrt{v}) = \sqrt{v} = |x - \mu|$ is impossible, as μ is unknown. Also, this function is not independent of μ. This contradiction established that no unbiased estimator of σ^2 exists, so that σ^2 is inestimable.

Exercise: Let $\boldsymbol{X} = (\boldsymbol{x}_1, \boldsymbol{x}_2)$, where $\boldsymbol{x}_1, \boldsymbol{x}_2$ are independent random variables distributed as $N(\mu, \sigma^2)$. Show that $\alpha \boldsymbol{x}_1 + (1-\alpha)\boldsymbol{x}_2$ is an unbiased estimator of μ, for all $0 \leq \alpha \leq 1$. Show that $(\boldsymbol{x}_1 - \boldsymbol{x}_2)^2/2$ is an unbiased estimator of σ^2. Thus for a sample size of 2 the parameters $\Theta = (\mu, \sigma^2)$ of the univariate normal distribution are estimable.

Another desirable property of an estimator $\hat{\Theta}$ can be described intuitively as follows. Suppose Θ is identifiable, so that there is a one-to-one correspondence between Θ and $F_{\boldsymbol{X}}(X; \Theta)$. Let $\boldsymbol{X}_1, \ldots, \boldsymbol{X}_N$ be N independent n-vectors, each with the same cumulative distribution function $F_{\boldsymbol{X}}(X; \Theta)$. We call these N n-vectors a *random sample* from $F_{\boldsymbol{X}}$ and call N the *sample size.* Let $\boldsymbol{t}_N(X)$ be the proportion of vectors of $\boldsymbol{X}_1, \ldots, \boldsymbol{X}_N$ which are less than or equal to the vector X. By the weak law of large numbers, as $N \to \infty$, the random variable $\boldsymbol{t}_N(X)$ approaches the number $F_{\boldsymbol{X}}(X; \Theta)$ in probability. This is true for all X, so that as $N \to \infty$, the random function $\boldsymbol{t}_N(X)$, viewed as a function of X, approaches the cumulative distribution function of X, $F_{\boldsymbol{X}}(X; \Theta)$, in probability.

Thus, loosely speaking, when our sample size is large we can estimate $F_{\boldsymbol{X}}(X; \Theta)$ almost perfectly by $\boldsymbol{t}_N(X)$. It would be nice if in such a situation we could devise an estimator $\hat{\Theta}(\boldsymbol{X}_1, \ldots, \boldsymbol{X}_N)$ such that, as $N \to \infty$, $\hat{\Theta}(\boldsymbol{X}_1, \ldots, \boldsymbol{X}_N)$ is an "almost perfect" estimate of Θ for all sequences $\{\boldsymbol{X}_i, i = 1, 2, \ldots\}$. [Of course, if each of the elements of Θ, viewed as a function of $F_{\mathbf{X}}(X)$, $\theta_i(F_{\mathbf{X}}(X))$, $i = 1, \ldots, k$, is a continuous function of $F_{\mathbf{X}}(X)$ for some X, then by Slutsky's theorem, $\hat{\theta}_i(\boldsymbol{X}_1, \ldots, \boldsymbol{X}_N) = \hat{\theta}_i(t_N(X))$ approaches θ_i in probability as $N \to \infty$ for $i = 1, \ldots, k$. But this need not be the case.]

How do we define precisely the desideratum that $\hat{\Theta}(\boldsymbol{X}_1, \ldots, \boldsymbol{X}_N)$ is an "almost perfect" estimator of Θ for large N? First of all, let us drop the condition, made primarily for motivational purposes, that the N n-vectors $\boldsymbol{X}_i$ are independent and identically distributed. As we are really interested only in this case and one other, where $\hat{\Theta}$ depends not on sample size but on n, the order of the vector $\boldsymbol{X}$, let us devise a bit of notation to cover these two cases simultaneously. We suppose that $\boldsymbol{X}$ is an mM-vector and that our estimator is $\hat{\Theta}_M(\boldsymbol{X}) = \hat{\Theta}(\boldsymbol{X}_m, \boldsymbol{X}_{2m}, \ldots, \boldsymbol{X}_{Mm})$. (The two cases of interest are $M = N$, $m = n$, and $M = n$, $m = 1$.) In any given problem, the appropriate value of m will be clear. Thus, given M, the order mM of the vector of random variables used by $\hat{\Theta}$ to estimate Θ will be clear from context. As we shall denote this mM vector by the symbol $\boldsymbol{X}$, with no subscript to remind you of its order, we need only indicate to you the value of M, and will do so only as a subscript on $\hat{\Theta}$. For short, then, our estimator is $\hat{\Theta}_M(\boldsymbol{X})$.

We say that $\hat{\Theta}_M(\boldsymbol{X})$ is a *consistent estimator* of Θ if $\operatorname{plim}_{M\to\infty} \hat{\Theta}_M(\boldsymbol{X}) = \Theta$. That is, given the sequence $\boldsymbol{X}_m, \boldsymbol{X}_{2m}, \ldots$, and the induced sequence of random k-vectors $\{\hat{\Theta}(\boldsymbol{X}_m, \boldsymbol{X}_{2m}, \ldots, \boldsymbol{X}_{Mm}), M = 1, 2, \ldots\}$, we say that $\hat{\Theta}_M(\boldsymbol{X})$ is a consistent estimator of Θ if this sequence of estimators has Θ as its limit in probability.

As a direct consequence of Slutsky's theorem, the criterion of consistency is invariant with respect to continuous transformations of the parameter space. This is one of the reasons that consistency is a more desirable property of an estimator than is unbiasedness.

Suppose $\hat{\Theta}_M$ is not an unbiased estimator of Θ. Define the *bias* of $\hat{\Theta}_M$ as $B(\hat{\Theta}_M, \Theta) = \mathscr{E}\hat{\Theta}_M(\boldsymbol{X}) - \Theta$. Then $\hat{\Theta}_M(\boldsymbol{X}) - \Theta = \hat{\Theta}_M(\boldsymbol{X}) - \mathscr{E}\hat{\Theta}_M(\boldsymbol{X}) + B(\hat{\Theta}_M, \Theta)$. In many cases, by the weak law of large numbers, $\hat{\Theta}_M(\boldsymbol{X})$ is a consistent estimator of its expected value, $\mathscr{E}\hat{\Theta}_M(\boldsymbol{X})$. If such a $\hat{\Theta}_M$ is also a consistent estimator of Θ, then $\lim_{M\to\infty} B(\hat{\Theta}_M, \Theta) = 0$, so that $\hat{\Theta}_M$ is "asymptotically unbiased". This is sometimes given as a heuristic interpretation of the definition of a consistent estimator. Note well, though, that this interpretation depends on $\hat{\Theta}_M$ being a consistent estimator of its mean.

A common situation where this is not the case is one where $\hat{\Theta}_M(\boldsymbol{X})$

converges in distribution to some random k-vector $\boldsymbol{Y}$ with mean $\boldsymbol{\Theta}$ and where $\mathscr{E}\hat{\boldsymbol{\Theta}}_M(\boldsymbol{X})$ converges to $\mathscr{E}\boldsymbol{Y} = \boldsymbol{\Theta}$ but, since $\boldsymbol{Y}$ has a non-degenerate probability distribution, we cannot say that $\operatorname{plim}_{M\to\infty} \hat{\boldsymbol{\Theta}}_M(\boldsymbol{X}) = \boldsymbol{\Theta}$. In this case, we would want to say that $\hat{\boldsymbol{\Theta}}_M(\boldsymbol{X})$ is asymptotically unbiased, since $\lim_{M\to\infty} \mathscr{E}\hat{\boldsymbol{\Theta}}_M(\boldsymbol{X}) = \boldsymbol{\Theta}$, yet would not want to confuse this notion with that of the consistency of an estimator.

Notice one important thing, that the existence of a consistent estimator of a parameter $\boldsymbol{\Theta}$ implies that the parameter is identifiable. This is because if a parameter $\boldsymbol{\Theta}$ is not identifiable, then there is no one-to-one correspondence between $F_{\mathbf{X}}(X; \boldsymbol{\Theta})$ and $\boldsymbol{\Theta}$. Consequently, it is not clear which "parameter" of the pair $\boldsymbol{\Theta}_1$ and $\boldsymbol{\Theta}_2$ satisfying $F_{\mathbf{X}}(X; \boldsymbol{\Theta}_1) = F_{\mathbf{X}}(X; \boldsymbol{\Theta}_2)$ for all X is the limit in probability of $\hat{\boldsymbol{\Theta}}_M(\boldsymbol{X})$, so that we cannot talk of a consistent estimator of an unidentifiable parameter.

Unlike the situation in which a parameter is estimable if and only if an unbiased estimator of it exists, it is not true that a parameter is identifiable if and only if a consistent estimator exists. It is a difficult technical matter to determine necessary and sufficient conditions for the existence of consistent estimators.

The final criterion of goodness of an estimator is quite commonly applied in econometrics, yet is quite strange at first sight. Suppose $\hat{\boldsymbol{\Theta}}_M(\boldsymbol{X})$ is a consistent estimator of $\boldsymbol{\Theta}$. Moreover, suppose that the random k-vector $\boldsymbol{Y}_M = \sqrt{M}(\hat{\boldsymbol{\Theta}}_M(\boldsymbol{X}) - \boldsymbol{\Theta})$ has as limit in distribution the random k-vector $\boldsymbol{Y}$ which is distributed as $N(0, \Sigma)$. We then say, quite loosely, that $\hat{\boldsymbol{\Theta}}_M(\boldsymbol{X})$ is *asymptotically normally distributed* with asymptotic distribution $N(\boldsymbol{\Theta}, M^{-1}\Sigma)$. We call Σ the *asymptotic covariance matrix* of $\hat{\boldsymbol{\Theta}}_M(\boldsymbol{X})$.

A frequently made error is to confuse the mean vector and covariance matrix of the asymptotic distribution of $\boldsymbol{Y}_M$ with the limit, as $M \to \infty$, of the mean vector and covariance matrix of $\boldsymbol{Y}_M$. As an example of the discrepancy, let $k = 1$ and

$$y_M = \begin{cases} y, & \text{with probability} \quad 1 - \dfrac{1}{M}, \\[2ex] y + M, & \text{with probability} \quad \dfrac{1}{M}. \end{cases}$$

Then,

$$F_{y_M}(y) = \left(1 - \frac{1}{M}\right) F_y(y) + \frac{1}{M} F_y(y - M),$$

so that

$$\lim_{M\to\infty} F_{y_M}(y) = F_y(y).$$

Yet,

$$\mathscr{E}y_M = \left(1 - \frac{1}{M}\right)\mathscr{E}y + \left(\frac{1}{M}\right)\mathscr{E}(y + M) = \mathscr{E}y + 1,$$

for all M, so that

$$\lim_{M\to\infty} \mathscr{E}y_M = \mathscr{E}y + 1 \neq \mathscr{E}y.$$

Exercise: Find $\mathscr{V}y_M$ in this example, recalling that $\mathscr{V}y_M = \mathscr{E}y_M^2 - [\mathscr{E}y_M]^2$. The moral of this example is that to find an asymptotic covariance matrix one should find the limiting distribution of $\boldsymbol{Y}_M$ first, not find the covariance matrix of $\boldsymbol{Y}_M$ and compute its limit.

Now let's record the promised final criterion, good only for asymptotically normally distributed estimators. Let $\hat{\Theta}_{1M}(\boldsymbol{X})$ and $\hat{\Theta}_{2M}(\boldsymbol{X})$ be two estimators of Θ, with asymptotic normal distributions $N(\Theta, M^{-1}\Sigma_1)$, $N(\Theta, M^{-1}\Sigma_2)$, respectively. We say $\hat{\Theta}_{1M}$ is *asymptotically relatively as efficient as* $\hat{\Theta}_{2M}$ if $\Sigma_2 - \Sigma_1$ is positive semidefinite. We say that the asymptotically $N(\Theta, M^{-1}\Sigma)$ distributed estimator $\hat{\Theta}_M(\boldsymbol{X})$ is *asymptotically efficient* if for all other estimators $\hat{\Theta}^*_M(\boldsymbol{X})$ with asymptotic normal distributions $N(\Theta, M^{-1}\Sigma^*)$, $\Sigma^* - \Sigma$ is positive semidefinite. A geometric interpretation of this criterion is that for any value T of $\hat{\Theta}_M(\boldsymbol{X})$, the ellipsoid $M(T-\Theta)\Sigma^{-1}(T-\Theta)'$ lies wholly within the ellipsoid of concentration of the asymptotic distribution of $\hat{\Theta}^*_M(\boldsymbol{X})$.

What is strange about this criterion is the slavish devotion to asymptotically normally distributed estimators in the definition of the criterion of asymptotic efficiency. This strangeness, along with another drawback of the definition illustrated by the following example, will be dispelled shortly with the introduction of an alternative non-classical criterion of efficiency.

Consider the following example. Let $\boldsymbol{X}_n = (\boldsymbol{x}_1, \ldots, \boldsymbol{x}_n)$ be a random sample from the $N(\theta, 1)$ distribution. Let $\hat{\theta}(\boldsymbol{X}_n) = \sum_{i=1}^{n} x_i/n$, which is distributed as $N(\theta, 1/n)$. Thus, the asymptotic variance of $\hat{\theta}(\boldsymbol{X}_n)$ is 1. Now define

$$\hat{\theta}_1(\boldsymbol{X}_n) = \begin{cases} \hat{\theta}(\boldsymbol{X}_n), & \text{if } |\hat{\theta}(\boldsymbol{X}_n)| \geq 1/n^{\frac{1}{4}}, \\ \alpha\hat{\theta}(\boldsymbol{X}_n), & \text{if } |\hat{\theta}(\boldsymbol{X}_n)| < 1/n^{\frac{1}{4}}, \end{cases}$$

where $\alpha < 1$. Then,

$$F_{\hat{\theta}_1(\mathbf{x}_n)}(\theta_1) = F_{\hat{\theta}(\mathbf{x}_n)}(\theta_1)[1 - F_{\hat{\theta}(\mathbf{x}_n)}(1/n^{\frac{1}{4}}) + F_{\hat{\theta}(\mathbf{x}_n)}(-1/n^{\frac{1}{4}})] + F_{\hat{\theta}(\mathbf{x}_n)}(\theta_1/\alpha)[F_{\hat{\theta}(\mathbf{x}_n)}(1/n^{\frac{1}{4}}) - F_{\hat{\theta}(\mathbf{x}_n)}(-1/n^{\frac{1}{4}})].$$

As $n \to \infty$, $F_{\hat{\theta}_1(\mathbf{X}_n)}(\theta_1)$ approaches $\lim_{n\to\infty} F_{\hat{\theta}(\mathbf{X}_n)}(\theta_1)$ if θ_0, the true value of θ, is not zero, and it approaches $\lim_{n\to\infty} F_{\hat{\theta}(\mathbf{X}_n)}(\theta_1/\alpha)$ if $\theta_0 = 0$. Thus if $\theta_0 \neq 0$, $\hat{\theta}_1(\mathbf{X}_n)$ has the same asymptotic variance as does $\hat{\theta}(\mathbf{X}_n)$, namely 1. But if $\theta_0 = 0$, $\hat{\theta}_1(\mathbf{X}_n)$ has the asymptotic distribution

$$f_{\hat{\theta}_1}(\theta_1) = \frac{1}{\sqrt{(2\pi)}\alpha} \exp\{-\theta_1^2/2\alpha^2\},$$

and so has asymptotic variance $\alpha^2 < 1$.

The moral of this example is that the asymptotic relative efficiency or inefficiency of an estimator depends on which particular parameter is the true one. This is a fault not of the estimator but of the definition of asymptotic efficiency.

An alternative definition of efficiency and concomitantly of asymptotic efficiency arises from the adoption of an alternative loss function. As we are really interested in the concentration of probability of an estimator around the true parameter, why not measure this by the probability that the ellipsoid of concentration of the estimator is so-and-so large? More precisely, consider the random variable $\mathbf{y}(\hat{\Theta}_M) = (\hat{\Theta}_M(\mathbf{X}) - \Theta)C^{-1}(\hat{\Theta}_M) \times (\hat{\Theta}_M(\mathbf{X}) - \Theta)'$. We might take as our disutility function

$$w_\epsilon(\hat{\Theta}_M(\mathbf{X}), \Theta) = \begin{cases} 1, & \text{if } \mathbf{y}(\hat{\Theta}_M) \geq \epsilon, \\ 0, & \text{if } \mathbf{y}(\hat{\Theta}_M) < \epsilon, \end{cases}$$

penalizing us only if the ellipsoid $(\hat{\Theta}_M(X) - \Theta)C^{-1}(\hat{\Theta}_M).\ (\hat{\Theta}_M(\mathbf{X}) - \Theta)'$ is too large, but not by the magnitude of the estimation error.

Then $\mathscr{E}w_\epsilon(\hat{\Theta}(\mathbf{X}), \Theta) = P_{y(\Theta_M)}(\{\mathbf{y}(\hat{\Theta}_M) \geq \epsilon\})$. We would then say that $\hat{\Theta}_{M1}$ has *relatively as good concentration* as does $\hat{\Theta}_{M2}$ if $P_{y(\hat{\Theta}_{M1})} \times (\{\mathbf{y}(\hat{\Theta}_{M1}) \geq \epsilon\}) \leq P_{y(\hat{\Theta}_{M2})}(\{\mathbf{y}(\hat{\Theta}_{M2}) \geq \epsilon\})$ for all ϵ. Similarly, we can say that $\hat{\Theta}_{M1}$ has *relatively as good asymptotic concentration* as does $\hat{\Theta}_{M2}$ if $\lim_{M\to\infty} P_{y(\hat{\Theta}_{M1})}(\{\mathbf{y}(\hat{\Theta}_{M1}) \geq \epsilon\})/P_{y(\hat{\Theta}_{M2})}(\{\mathbf{y}(\hat{\Theta}_{M2}) > \epsilon\}) \leq 1$ for all ϵ.

It is not true that if $\hat{\Theta}_{M1}$ has relatively as good asymptotic concentration as does $\hat{\Theta}_{M2}$ then $\hat{\Theta}_{M1}$ is asymptotically as efficient as is $\hat{\Theta}_{M2}$. However, one can bridge the two criteria by the following device.

Let $\hat{\Theta}_M$ be a consistent estimator of Θ, not necessarily asymptotically normally distributed. Let $\mathbf{Z}_M$ be a random k-vector distributed as $N(0, C_M^*)$. The matrix $C_M^*(\hat{\Theta}_M, \epsilon)$ is called the *effective CMSE matrix* of $\hat{\Theta}_M$, given ϵ, if

$$P_{y(\hat{\Theta}_M)}(\{\mathbf{y}(\hat{\Theta}_M) \geq \epsilon\}) = P_Z(\{\mathbf{Z}_M C_M^{*-1}(\hat{\Theta}_M, \epsilon)\mathbf{Z}_M' \geq \epsilon\}).$$

Thus we call $\lim_{M\to\infty} C_M^*(\hat{\Theta}_M, \epsilon)$ the effective *asymptotic covariance* *matrix* of $\hat{\Theta}_M$, as it is the asymptotic covariance matrix of the limit in distribution of the sequence of vectors $\{\boldsymbol{Z}_M, M = 1, 2, \ldots\}$.

We can then say that $\hat{\Theta}_{M1}$ has relatively as good asymptotic concentration as does $\hat{\Theta}_{M2}$ if

$$\limsup_{M\to\infty} [C^*_M(\hat{\Theta}_{M2}, \epsilon) - C^*_M(\hat{\Theta}_{M1}, \epsilon)]$$

is positive semidefinite for all ϵ. This looks like the old definition of relative asymptotic efficiency, except that (1) $\hat{\boldsymbol{\Theta}}_M$ is not asymptotically normally distributed, (2) there is this extraneous ϵ in the definition, (3) we are considering not the CMSE matrix of $\hat{\boldsymbol{\Theta}}_M$ but a substitute matrix C^*_M, the covariance matrix of a substitute random vector $\boldsymbol{Z}_M$, and (4) we look at $\lim_{M\to\infty} C^*_M$ rather than the limiting covariance matrix of $\hat{\boldsymbol{\Theta}}_M$ or the covariance matrix of the limiting distribution of $\hat{\boldsymbol{\Theta}}_M$.

We can rid ourselves of the dependence on ϵ by replacing the criterion by the following one. We say that $\hat{\Theta}_{M1}$ has *relatively as good asymptotic effective covariance matrix as* $\hat{\Theta}_{M2}$ if

$$\limsup_{M\to\infty} \limsup_{\epsilon\to 0} [C^*_M(\hat{\Theta}_{M2}, \epsilon) - C^*_M(\hat{\Theta}_{M1}, \epsilon)]$$

is positive semidefinite. We have also rid ourselves of the asymptotic normality assumption for $\hat{\Theta}_M(\boldsymbol{X})$ by bringing in a substitute multivariate normally distributed random vector $\boldsymbol{Z}_M$. The effect of this is not only to eliminate the drawbacks of the classical definition. As will be seen in the next section, maximum likelihood estimators will have relatively as good an asymptotic effective covariance matrix as any other estimator, though they need not be asymptotically efficient by the classical definition. Also, this definition reduces to the classical definition when $\hat{\Theta}_M(\boldsymbol{X})$ is asymptotically normally distributed as

$$N(\Theta, M^{-1} \limsup_{M\to\infty} \limsup_{\epsilon\to 0} C^*_M(\hat{\Theta}_M, \epsilon)).$$

4. Maximum likelihood method of point estimation

Recall our interpretation of the probability density function $f_{\boldsymbol{X}}(X; \Theta)$ times $\prod_{i=1}^n dx_i$ as approximately the probability that $X \leq \boldsymbol{X} \leq X + \Delta X$. For each value X of $\boldsymbol{X}$ we can determine the value of Θ, $\hat{\Theta}(X)$, for which the probability that $\boldsymbol{X}$ roughly equals that X (more precisely, is within ΔX of that X) is maximum. This is accomplished by simply maximizing $f_X(X;\Theta)$ with respect to Θ. The maximizer, $\hat{\Theta}(X)$, viewed as a function of $\mathbf{X}$, is called the *maximum likelihood estimator* $\hat{\Theta}(\mathbf{X})$ of Θ.

Since the log function is a monotonically increasing function of its argument, an equivalent maximization problem, which in most of our work will be much simpler, is that of maximizing $\log f_X(X;\Theta)$ with respect to Θ, where log is understood to mean "logarithm to base e".

For a given value X, the function $f_X(X;\Theta)$, as a function of Θ, is called the *likelihood function of* Θ. In case $\int\int f_X(X;\Theta)\,d\theta_1\cdots d\theta_k$ is finite, then under suitable normalization, i.e., multiplication by some function $g(X)$, the resulting function $g(X)f_X(X;\Theta)$ can be interpreted as $f_{\mathbf{\Theta}}(\Theta;X)$, a "probability density function" of $\mathbf{\Theta}$ with parameter X. Thus maximizing $f_X(X;\Theta)$ with respect to Θ can be interpreted as maximizing the "probability" that $\mathbf{\Theta}$ equals $\hat{\Theta}(X)$, if you wish to accept the notion that a parameter Θ can be treated as a random variable $\mathbf{\Theta}$ and have a probability density function $f_{\mathbf{\Theta}}(\Theta;X)$ proportional to $f_X(X;\Theta)$.

The following theorem shows that the maximum likelihood estimator is invariant with respect to single-valued invertible transformations of the parameter space.

Theorem 18: *Let $f(\Theta)$ be a real valued function of the vector Θ, and let ϕ be a function from the space of Θ's to the space of Ξ's, whose inverse exists and is single-valued. Let $g(\Xi)=f[\phi^{-1}(\Xi)]$. If $f(\Theta)$ is maximum at Θ_0, then $g(\Xi)$ is maximum at $\Xi_0=\phi(\Theta_0)$.*

Proof: Since $f(\Theta_0)\geqslant f(\Theta)$, we see that

$$
\begin{aligned}
g(\Xi) &= f[\phi^{-1}(\Xi)] = f(\Theta) \leqslant f(\Theta_0) \\
&= g[\phi(\Theta_0)] = g(\Xi_0),
\end{aligned}
$$

so that $g(\Xi)$ is maximum at $\Xi=\Xi_0$.

If Θ_0 is the unique maximizer, then the inequality is strict for $\Theta\neq\Theta_0$ and Ξ_0 is the unique maximizer.

Interpreting $f(\Theta)$ as $f_X(X;\Theta)$ and $g(\Xi)$ as $f_X(X;\Xi)$ in the above theorem, one then sees the invariance of maximum likelihood estimators.

We shall compute many maximum likelihood estimators in the course of this book. As drill in computing them, and to show that they need not be unbiased, consider the following exercises.

Exercise: Let $\boldsymbol{X} = (\boldsymbol{x}_1, \boldsymbol{x}_2)$, where $\boldsymbol{x}_1, \boldsymbol{x}_2$ are independent and $N(\mu, \sigma^2)$. Find the maximum likelihood estimators of μ and of σ^2. What is $\mathscr{E}\hat{\mu}(\boldsymbol{X})$, $\mathscr{E}\hat{\sigma}^2(\boldsymbol{X})$? Consider the random variable $(\boldsymbol{x}_1 - \boldsymbol{x}_2)^2/2$. What is its expected value?

For the remainder of this chapter, we shall deal only with the case where $\boldsymbol{X}$ is an nN-vector $\boldsymbol{X} = (\boldsymbol{X}_1, \ldots, \boldsymbol{X}_N)$, and where $f_{\boldsymbol{X}}(X; \Theta) = \prod_{i=1}^N f_{\boldsymbol{X}}(X_i; \Theta)$, that is, where the $\boldsymbol{X}_i$ are independent and identically distributed variables [which is why the subscript i is deleted from $\boldsymbol{X}$ in $f_{\boldsymbol{X}}(X_i; \Theta)$].

The maximum likelihood estimate $\hat{\Theta}(X)$ of Θ is that vector which maximizes $f_{\boldsymbol{X}}(X; \Theta)$. If $f_{\boldsymbol{X}}(X; \Theta)$ has a maximum in the interior of the space of Θ's, and is differentiable with respect to Θ, then the maximizer can be found as a solution of the vector equation

$$0 = \frac{\partial \log f_{\boldsymbol{X}}(X; \Theta)}{\partial \Theta} = \sum_{i=1}^N \frac{\partial \log f_{\boldsymbol{X}}(X_i; \Theta)}{\partial \Theta}.$$

This equation, called the *likelihood equation*, may have many solutions, one of which is the maximizer of $f_{\boldsymbol{X}}(X; \Theta)$.

It has been shown that, except for some poorly behaved families of probability density functions, the maximum likelihood estimator is a consistent estimator of Θ. The sufficient conditions for consistency do not even include the differentiability of $f_{\boldsymbol{X}}(X; \Theta)$ with respect to Θ.

However, to investigate the asymptotic distribution of the maximum likelihood estimator, we will start with the assumption that $\log f_{\boldsymbol{X}}(X; \Theta)$ is in fact three times differentiable with respect to Θ. Other assumptions will be introduced in the development as needed. The derivation of the asymptotic distribution of the maximum likelihood estimator $\hat{\Theta}(\boldsymbol{X})$ is included here, as a paradigm for future asymptotic distribution calculations.

We assume that $f_{\boldsymbol{X}}(X; \Theta)$ has a maximizer in the interior of the space of Θ's, so that the maximum likelihood estimate $\hat{\Theta}(X)$ of Θ is a root of the likelihood equation,

$$\sum_{i=1}^N \left. \frac{\partial \log f_{\boldsymbol{X}}(X_i; \Theta)}{\partial \Theta} \right|_{\Theta = \hat{\Theta}(X)} = 0.$$

Using Taylor's theorem with remainder, we find that the lth equation,

$l = 1, \ldots, k$, of the vector likelihood equation is

$$0 = \sum_{\alpha=1}^{N} \frac{\partial \log f_{\mathbf{X}_\alpha}(X_\alpha; \Theta)}{\partial \theta_l}\Bigg|_{\Theta=\hat{\Theta}(X)}$$

$$= \sum_{\alpha=1}^{N} \frac{\partial \log f_{\mathbf{X}_\alpha}(X_\alpha; \Theta)}{\partial \theta_l}\Bigg|_{\Theta=\Theta^0}$$

$$+ \sum_{\alpha=1}^{N} \sum_{i=1}^{k} (\hat{\theta}_i - \theta_i^0) \frac{\partial^2 \log f_{\mathbf{X}_\alpha}(X_\alpha; \Theta)}{\partial \theta_l \, \partial \theta_i}\Bigg|_{\Theta=\Theta^0}$$

$$+ \frac{1}{2} \sum_{\alpha=1}^{N} \sum_{i,j=1}^{k} (\hat{\theta}_i - \theta_i^0)(\hat{\theta}_j - \theta_j^0) \frac{\partial^3 f_{\mathbf{X}_\alpha}(X_\alpha; \Theta)}{\partial \theta_l \, \partial \theta_i \, \partial \theta_j}\Bigg|_{\Theta=\Theta^*},$$

where Θ^0 is the true value of Θ and Θ^* is between Θ^0 and $\hat{\Theta}$.

Let $G_0(X)$ be the matrix whose (i, j)th element is $-\partial^2 \log f_{\mathbf{X}}(X; \Theta)/\partial \theta_i \, \partial \theta_j$ evaluated at $\Theta = \Theta^0$, and $H_{\Theta l}(X)$ be the matrix whose (i, j)th element is $\partial^3 \log f_{\mathbf{X}}(X; \Theta)/\partial \theta_l \, \partial \theta_i \, \partial \theta_j$. Then,

$$0 = \frac{1}{N} \sum_{\alpha=1}^{N} \frac{\partial \log f_{\mathbf{X}}(X_\alpha; \Theta)}{\partial \Theta}\Bigg|_{\Theta=\Theta^0} - \frac{1}{N} (\hat{\Theta}(X) - \Theta^0) \sum_{\alpha=1}^{N} G_0(X_\alpha)$$

$$+ \frac{1}{2N} \sum_{\alpha=1}^{N} \{(\hat{\Theta} - \Theta^0) H_{\Theta^* 1}(X_\alpha)(\hat{\Theta} - \Theta^0)', \ldots, (\hat{\Theta} - \Theta^0)$$

$$\times H_{\Theta^* k}(X_\alpha)(\hat{\Theta} - \Theta^0)\}$$

$$= \frac{1}{N} \sum_{\alpha=1}^{N} \frac{\partial \log f_{\mathbf{X}}(X_\alpha; \Theta)}{\partial \Theta}\Bigg|_{\Theta=\hat{\Theta}(X)}.$$

Since

$$\mathscr{E}\, \partial \log f_{\mathbf{X}}(\mathbf{X}; \Theta)/\partial \theta_l =$$

$$\int_{-\infty}^{\infty} \cdots \int_{-\infty}^{\infty} \frac{\partial \log f_{\mathbf{X}}(X; \Theta)}{\partial \theta_l}\Bigg|_{\Theta=\Theta^0} f_{\mathbf{X}}(X, \Theta^0)\, \mathrm{d}x_1 \cdots \mathrm{d}x_n =$$

$$\int_{-\infty}^{\infty} \cdots \int_{-\infty}^{\infty} \frac{\partial f_{\mathbf{X}}(X; \Theta)}{\partial \theta_l}\Bigg|_{\Theta=\Theta^0} \mathrm{d}x_1 \cdots \mathrm{d}x_n =$$

$$\frac{\partial}{\partial \theta_l} \int_{-\infty}^{\infty} \cdots \int_{-\infty}^{\infty} f_{\mathbf{X}}(X; \Theta)\, \mathrm{d}x_1 \cdots \mathrm{d}x_n \Big|_{\Theta=\Theta^0} =$$

$$\frac{\partial}{\partial \theta_l}(1) = 0,$$

we see that

$$\operatorname*{plim}_{N\to\infty} \frac{1}{N} \sum_{\alpha=1}^{N} \frac{\partial \log f_{\mathbf{X}}(\mathbf{X}_\alpha; \Theta)}{\partial \theta_l}\Bigg|_{\Theta=\Theta^0} = 0$$

by the weak law of large numbers.

Also

$$\int_{-\infty}^{\infty} \cdots \int_{-\infty}^{\infty} \frac{\partial^2 \log f_X(X;\Theta)}{\partial\theta_i\,\partial\theta_j}\bigg|_{\Theta=\Theta^0} f_X(X;\Theta^0)\,dx_1\cdots dx_n =$$

$$\int_{-\infty}^{\infty} \cdots \int_{-\infty}^{\infty} \frac{\partial^2 f_X(X;\Theta)}{\partial\theta_i\,\partial\theta_j}\bigg|_{\Theta=\Theta^0} dx_1\cdots dx_n$$

$$-\int_{-\infty}^{\infty} \frac{1}{f_X(X;\Theta)}\frac{\partial f_X(X;\Theta)}{\partial\theta_i}\frac{\partial f_X(X;\Theta)}{\partial\theta_j}\bigg|_{\Theta=\Theta^0} dx_1\cdots dx_n =$$

$$-\mathscr{E}\left\{\frac{\partial \log f_X(X;\Theta)}{\partial\theta_i}\frac{\partial \log f_X(X;\Theta)}{\partial\theta_j}\bigg|_{\Theta=\Theta^0}\right\},$$

which we assume is finite for all i, j. Then by the weak law of large numbers,

$$\operatorname*{plim}_{N\to\infty}\frac{1}{N}\sum_{\alpha=1}^{N} G_0(\boldsymbol{X}_\alpha),$$

exists and equals G_0, the matrix whose (i, j)th element is

$$g_{0ij} = -\mathscr{E}\left[\frac{\partial^2 \log f_X(\boldsymbol{X};\Theta)}{\partial\theta_i\,\partial\theta_j}\bigg|_{\Theta=\Theta^0}\right]$$

$$= \mathscr{E}\left[\frac{\partial \log f_X(\boldsymbol{X};\Theta)}{\partial\theta_i}\frac{\partial \log f_X(\boldsymbol{X};\Theta)}{\partial\theta_j}\bigg|_{\Theta=\Theta^0}\right].$$

Let H_Θ be the $k\times k^2$ matrix

$$H_{\Theta^*} = \frac{1}{2N}\sum_{\alpha=1}^{N}(H_{\Theta^*1}(X_\alpha),\dots,H_{\Theta^*k}(X_\alpha)),$$

and I_k be the $k\times k$ identity matrix. Then

$$\hat{\Theta}(\boldsymbol{X}) - \Theta^0 = \left\{\frac{1}{N}\sum_{\alpha=1}^{N}\frac{\partial \log f_X(\boldsymbol{X}_\alpha;\Theta)}{\partial\Theta}\bigg|_{\Theta=\Theta^0}\right\}$$
$$\times\left\{\frac{1}{N}\sum_{\alpha=1}^{N} G_0(\boldsymbol{X}_\alpha) - H_{\Theta^*}[I_k\otimes(\hat{\Theta}(\boldsymbol{X})-\Theta^0)']\right\}^{-1},$$

provided the inverse matrix exists. Then

$$\sqrt{N}(\hat{\Theta}(\boldsymbol{X}) - \Theta^0)G_0^{\frac{1}{2}} = \left\{\frac{1}{\sqrt{N}}\sum_{\alpha=1}^{N}\frac{\partial \log f_X(\boldsymbol{X}_\alpha;\Theta)}{\partial\theta}\bigg|_{\Theta=\Theta^0}\right\}G_0^{-\frac{1}{2}}$$
$$\times G_0^{\frac{1}{2}}\left\{\frac{1}{N}\sum_{\alpha=1}^{N} G_0(\boldsymbol{X}_\alpha) - H_{\Theta^*}[I_k\otimes(\hat{\Theta}(\boldsymbol{X})-\Theta^0)']\right\}^{-1} G_0^{\frac{1}{2}},$$

where $G_0^{\frac{1}{2}}$ is the triangular decomposition of G_0.

Assume that every element of H_{Θ^*} is bounded and that $\hat{\Theta}(\boldsymbol{X})$ is a consistent estimator of Θ^0. We then see that

$$\operatorname*{plim}_{N\to\infty} \frac{1}{N}\left[\sum_{\alpha=1}^{N} G_0(\boldsymbol{X}_\alpha) - H_{\Theta^*}[I \otimes (\hat{\Theta}(\boldsymbol{X}) - \Theta^0)']\right] = G_0.$$

Thus, the asymptotic distribution of $\sqrt{N}(\hat{\Theta}(\boldsymbol{X}) - \Theta^0)G_0$ is the same as that of

$$\left\{\frac{1}{\sqrt{N}} \sum_{\alpha=1}^{N} \frac{\partial \log f_{\boldsymbol{X}}(\boldsymbol{X}_\alpha;\Theta)}{\partial\Theta}\bigg|_{\Theta=\Theta^0}\right\} G_0^{-\frac{1}{2}}.$$

But the random variable $\partial \log f_{\boldsymbol{X}}(\boldsymbol{X}_\alpha;\Theta)/\partial\Theta|_{\Theta=\Theta^0}$ has mean zero and covariance matrix G_0. By the central limit theorem, then, the asymptotic distribution of

$$\frac{1}{\sqrt{N}} \sum_{\alpha=1}^{N} \frac{\partial \log f_{\boldsymbol{X}}(\boldsymbol{X}_\alpha;\Theta)}{\partial\theta}\bigg|_{\Theta=\Theta^0}$$

is $N(0, G_0)$, so that the asymptotic distribution of

$$\left\{\frac{1}{\sqrt{N}} \sum_{\alpha=1}^{N} \frac{\partial \log f_{\boldsymbol{X}}(\boldsymbol{X}_\alpha;\Theta)}{\partial\Theta}\bigg|_{\Theta=\Theta^0}\right\} G_0^{-\frac{1}{2}},$$

and consequently of $\sqrt{N}(\hat{\Theta}(\boldsymbol{X}) - \Theta^0)G^{\frac{1}{2}}$, is $N(0, I)$. We call the matrix $C_0 = G_0^{-1}$ the asymptotic covariance matrix of $\hat{\Theta}(\boldsymbol{X})$.

We record for future reference that

$$g_{0ij} = -\mathscr{E}\left[\frac{\partial^2 \log f_{\boldsymbol{X}}(\boldsymbol{X};\Theta)}{\partial\theta_i\,\partial\theta_j}\bigg|_{\Theta=\Theta^0}\right]$$

$$= \mathscr{E}\left[\frac{\partial \log f_{\boldsymbol{X}}(\boldsymbol{X};\Theta)}{\partial\theta_i}\frac{\partial \log f_{\boldsymbol{X}}(\boldsymbol{X};\Theta)}{\partial\theta_j}\bigg|_{\Theta=\Theta^0}\right].$$

Reviewing all the assumptions we made in the course of deriving the asymptotic distribution of $\hat{\Theta}(\boldsymbol{X})$, one in particular is noteworthy, namely the assumption that $\hat{\Theta}(\boldsymbol{X})$ is a consistent estimator of Θ^0. The reason for this assumption is that there are situations in which all the other assumptions made in the course of our calculation hold, yet $\hat{\Theta}(\boldsymbol{X})$ is not a consistent estimator of Θ.

Noting that if $\boldsymbol{X}_n = (\boldsymbol{x}_1, \ldots, \boldsymbol{x}_n)$ is a random sample for the $N(\theta, 1)$ distribution, then $\hat{\theta}(\boldsymbol{X}_n) = \sum_{i=1}^{n} \boldsymbol{x}_i/n$ is the maximum likelihood estimator of θ, we see from the example of section 3 that the maximum likelihood estimator is not asymptotically efficient. However, it has been shown that in general the set of parameter values for which one can construct estimators more efficient than the maximum likelihood estimator is a denumerable set.

Further, it has been shown that, under certain regularity conditions, the maximum likelihood estimator has asymptotically smallest effective variance for all values of Θ. This makes it an attractive estimator.

Finally, it should be noted that there are many other estimators with the same asymptotic distribution as that of the maximum likelihood, namely $N(\Theta, N^{-1}C_0)$. These estimators are called regular best asymptotically normal (RBAN) estimators.

5. Maximum likelihood estimation of multivariate normal distribution parameters

Suppose the n-vectors $\boldsymbol{X}_1, \ldots, \boldsymbol{X}_N$ are a random sample, where $\boldsymbol{X}_i$ is distributed as $N(\mu, \Sigma)$. Since

$$f_{\boldsymbol{X}_1,\ldots,\boldsymbol{X}_N}(X_1, \ldots, X_N) = (2\pi)^{-Nn/2}|\Sigma|^{-N/2} \times \exp\left\{-\sum_{i=1}^{N}(X_i - \mu)\Sigma^{-1}(X_i - \mu)'/2\right\},$$

it is this function (or its logarithm) which we must maximize to obtain maximum likelihood estimates of μ and Σ given a random sample from $N(\mu, \Sigma)$.

Since $\sum_{i=1}^{N}(X_i - \mu)\Sigma^{-1}(X_i - \mu)'$ is a 1×1 matrix, it equals its trace, and thus

$$\operatorname{tr}\sum_{i=1}^{N}(X_i - \mu)\Sigma^{-1}(X_i - \mu)' = \operatorname{tr}\sum_{i=1}^{N}(X_i - \mu)'(X_i - \mu)\Sigma^{-1}.$$

Let J be the N-vector of all 1's and X be the $N \times n$ matrix whose ith row is X_i. Then

$$\begin{aligned}\operatorname{tr}\sum_{i=1}^{N}(X_i - \mu)'(X_i - \mu)\Sigma^{-1} &= \operatorname{tr}(X - J'\mu)'(X - J'\mu)\Sigma^{-1} \\ &= \operatorname{tr}(X - J'\mu)\Sigma^{-1}(X - J'\mu)',\end{aligned}$$

and

$$\log f_{\boldsymbol{X}_1,\ldots,\boldsymbol{X}_N}(X_1, \ldots, X_N) = -\left(\frac{Nn}{2}\right)\log 2\pi - \frac{N}{2}\log|\Sigma| - \frac{1}{2}\operatorname{tr}(X - J'\mu)'(X - J'\mu)\Sigma^{-1}.$$

Let $C = (X - J'\mu)'(X - J'\mu)$ and $\Lambda = \Sigma^{-1}$. Then,

$$g(\Lambda) = \log f_{X_1,\ldots,X_N}(X_1, \ldots, X_N)$$
$$= -\left(\frac{Nn}{2}\right)\log 2\pi + \frac{N}{2}\log|\Lambda| - \frac{1}{2}\operatorname{tr} C\Lambda.$$

Theorem 19: If C is positive definite, then $\Lambda = NC^{-1}$ *maximizes* $g(\Lambda)$, *and its maximum value is* $g(NC^{-1}) = -(Nn/2)\log 2\pi + (Nn/2)\log N - (N/2)\log|C| - (Nn/2)$.

Proof: First of all, let us differentiate $g(\Lambda)$ with respect to Λ, set the derivative equal to zero, and see what the solution of these equations is. We see that

$$\frac{\partial g(\Lambda)}{\partial \lambda_{ii}} = \frac{N}{2}\frac{\Lambda_{ii}}{|\Lambda|} - \frac{1}{2}c_{ii} = 0,$$

$$\frac{\partial g(\Lambda)}{\partial \lambda_{ij}} = \frac{N}{2}\frac{2\Lambda_{ij}}{|\Lambda|} - \frac{1}{2}2c_{ij} = 0,$$

so that $\Lambda = NC^{-1}$ solves these equations.

We must next check that this solution maximizes $g(\Lambda)$. As the typical element of the matrix of second derivatives of $g(\Lambda)$ is the $n^2 \times n^2$ matrix which can be partitioned in such a way that its (i, j)th $n \times n$ block is $(N/2)\partial\Lambda^{-1}/\partial\lambda_{ij} = -(N/2)X^{-1}J_{ij}X^{-1}$, and this matrix is negative definite.

We thus conclude that $\hat{\Lambda}(\boldsymbol{X}) = N\{(\boldsymbol{X} - J'\mu)'(\boldsymbol{X} - J'\mu)]^{-1}$. Of course, this estimator depends on a knowledge of μ, which may be unknown. Can we replace μ by its maximum likelihood estimator when it is unknown and have the resulting function be the maximum likelihood estimator of Λ? Also, can we conclude that $\hat{\Lambda}^{-1}(\boldsymbol{X}) = \hat{\Sigma}(\boldsymbol{X})$, the maximum likelihood estimator of Σ? An application of Theorem 18 answers both these questions affirmatively.

When μ is known, then, we have the result that $\hat{\Sigma}(\boldsymbol{X}) = \hat{\Lambda}^{-1}(\boldsymbol{X}) = (1/N)(\boldsymbol{X} - J'\mu)'(\boldsymbol{X} - J'\mu)$.

Now let us find the maximum likelihood estimator of μ. If Λ is known, then we must minimize

$$\sum_{i=1}^{N}(X_i - \mu)\Lambda(X_i - \mu)',$$

with respect to μ. Differentiating with respect to μ and setting the derivative equal to zero gives us the equation

$$-2\sum_{i=1}^{N}(X_i-\mu)\Lambda=0$$

so that

$$\mu=\sum_{i=1}^{N}\frac{X_i}{N}$$

solves this equation. This is the minimizer because the function being minimized is a quadratic function in μ. Therefore $\hat{\mu}(\boldsymbol{X})=\sum_{i=1}^{N}\boldsymbol{X}_i/N$.

When μ is unknown, let us make the correspondence $\Theta\leftrightarrow\mu$, $\phi(\Theta)\leftrightarrow N[(X-J'\mu)'(X-J'\mu)]^{-1}$ and $\Theta_0\leftrightarrow\hat{\mu}(X)$ between the notation of Theorem 18 and that of our problem. We thus see that

$$\Xi_0\leftrightarrow N[(X-J'\hat{\mu}(X))'(X-J'\hat{\mu}(X))]^{-1},$$

so that

$$\hat{\Lambda}(\boldsymbol{X})=N[(\boldsymbol{X}-J'\hat{\mu}(\boldsymbol{X}))'(\boldsymbol{X}-J'\hat{\mu}(\boldsymbol{X}))]^{-1}$$

and

$$\hat{\Sigma}(\boldsymbol{X})=\frac{1}{N}[(\boldsymbol{X}-J'\hat{\mu}(\boldsymbol{X}))'(\boldsymbol{X}-J'\hat{\mu}(\boldsymbol{X}))]$$

are maximum likelihood estimators of Λ and Σ, respectively.

6. References

There exists no book on probability theory that treats the subject rigorously, yet at the intuitive level of this text. The seminal reference for the measure-theoretic approach to probability is, in English translation:

Kolmogorov, A. N., 1950, Foundations of the theory of probability (Chelsea, New York).

The reader might find the treatment in the following reference a bit more fulsome. In addition, it is a good reference for a proof of the weak law of large numbers and the central limit theorem:

Loéve, M., 1960, Probability Theory (Van Nostrand, Princeton).

An attempt at a treatment of measure-theoretic probability at the level of this text, but with little by way of clarifying remarks explain the "whys-and-wherefores" of the definitions and theorems, is made in chapter 1 of:

Wilks, S. S., 1962, Mathematical statistics (Wiley, New York).

For those interested in a discussion of what the term "probability" means, I recommend the early chapters of:

Savage, L. J., 1954, The foundations of statistics (Wiley, New York).

If the notion of "cardinality" alluded to in section 1 is new to you, you would do best by first reading chapter 1 of:

Gamow, G., 1947, One two three . . . infinity (Viking Press, New York).

And then a rigorous treatment, as given, for example, in chapter 13 of:

Graves, L. M., 1956, The theory of functions of real variables (McGraw-Hill, New York).

All the analysis used in this chapter will be found in volume II of:

Courant, R., 1936, Differential and integral calculus (Interscience, New York).

For the rudiments of Laplace transform theory, we find an adequate reference in:

Widder, D. W., 1947, Advanced calculus (Prentice-Hall, New York).

The best reference for multivariate normal distribution theory is:

Anderson, T. W., 1958, An introduction to multivariate statistical analysis (Wiley, New York).

Aside from Wilks' book cited earlier, I recommend Harald Cramer as a fine source for relevant material on point estimation theory. Cramer and Wilks differ in their definition of asymptotically efficient estimators though both define efficient estimators as done in our section 3. Our treatment follows that of Cramer. Wilks' treatment differs in two aspects. First of all, it is based on the limit as $M \to \infty$ of the covariance matrix of $\hat{\Theta}_M$, which, as we saw above, need not exist even though an asymptotic covariance matrix (see section 3) does exist. Secondly, the criterion for asymptotic efficiency is the determinant of the limiting covariance matrix, in contrast with the criterion used by us, which parallels the non-asymptotic criterion.

Cramer, H., 1946, Mathematical methods of statistics (Princeton University Press, Princeton).

A proof of Theorem 16 is given in:

Mann, H. B. and A. Wald, 1943, On stochastic limit and order relationships, Annals of Mathematical Statistics 14, pp. 217–226.

A necessary and sufficient condition for the existence of a consistent estimator is given in:

LeCam, L. and L. Schwartz, 1960, A necessary and sufficient condition for the existence of consistent estimators, Annals of Mathematical Statistics 31, pp. 140–150.

An example of an asymptotically inefficient estimator with greater concentration around the parameter is given in:

Basu, D., 1956, The concept of asymptotic efficiency, Sankhya 17, pp. 193–196.

The criterion of smallest effective variance, proving the efficiency of the maximum likelihood estimator, is introduced in:

Bahadur, R. R., On the asymptotic efficiency of tests and estimates, Sankhya 22, pp. 229–252.

A proof of the consistency of the maximum likelihood estimator is given in:

Wald, A., 1949, Note on the consistency of the maximum likelihood estimate, Annals of Mathematical Statistics 20, pp. 595–601.

An example of a maximum likelihood estimator satisfying all the conditions such that its asymptotic distribution is $N(0, C_0)$, yet is not a consistent estimator, is given in:

Kraft, C. and L. LeCam, 1956, A remark on the roots of the maximum likelihood equation, Annals of Mathematical Statistics 27, pp. 1174–1177.

The example of an estimator with smaller asymptotic variance than that of the maximum likelihood estimator for some parameter value is taken from the following reference, wherein you will find a thorough, but mathematically advanced, treatment of the structure of such examples:

LeCam, L., 1953, On some asymptotic properties of maximum likelihood estimates and related Bayes' estimates, University of California Publications in Statistics 1, pp. 277–329.

A good source to begin reading about RBAN estimates is:

Chiang, C. L., 1956, On regular best asymptotically normal estimates, Annals of Mathematical Statistics 27, pp. 336–351.

III

Linear expected value models

Suppose we are given n numbers $x_1, \ldots, x_n$ and are told that the variable y is related to the x's by

$$y = \beta_1 x_1 + \cdots + \beta_n x_n.$$

Such a relation between non-random variables is called a *linear functional relation.* All that is needed to determine, not estimate, the vector $B = (\beta_1, \ldots, \beta_n)$ is n sets of values $(y_i, x_{1i}, \ldots, x_{ni})$, $i = 1, \ldots, n$. Then, letting X be the $n \times n$ matrix whose (i, j)th element is x_{ij} and Y be the n-vector $Y = (y_1, \ldots, y_n)$, we see that $B = YX'^{-1}$.

Similarly, suppose we are told that the random variable $\boldsymbol{y}$ is related to the random variables $\boldsymbol{x}_1, \ldots, \boldsymbol{x}_n$ by

$$\boldsymbol{y} = \beta_1 \boldsymbol{x}_1 + \cdots + \beta_n \boldsymbol{x}_n.$$

Such a relation between random variables is called a *linear structural relation.* Again, all that is needed to determine, not estimate, the vector $B = (\beta_1, \ldots, \beta_n)$ is n sets of values of the random vector $(\boldsymbol{y}, \boldsymbol{x}_1, \ldots, \boldsymbol{x}_n)$, namely $(y_i, x_{1i}, \ldots, x_{ni})$, $i = 1, \ldots, n$. Then, as before, B is determined by $B = YX'^{-1}$. In both cases, any more than n observations on y and the x's would be superfluous, for we only need n linear equations to determine the n unknown β's, and the additional vectors $(x_{1i}, \ldots, x_{ni})$, $i > n$, are linear combinations of the vectors $(x_{1i}, \ldots, x_{ni})$, $i = 1, \ldots, n$.

A statistically more interesting situation is either of the above where fortunately we can observe the independent variables, the x_i or the $\boldsymbol{x}_i$, without error, but where we do not observe the concomitant dependent variable, y or $\boldsymbol{y}$, but rather the random variable $\boldsymbol{y}^* = y + \boldsymbol{v}$ in the functional relation situation and $\boldsymbol{y}^* = \boldsymbol{y} + \boldsymbol{v}$ in the structural relation situation. Typically, $\mathscr{E}\boldsymbol{v} = 0$, so that in the functional equation situation we have

$$\mathscr{E}\boldsymbol{y}^* = \beta_1 x_1 + \cdots + \beta_n x_n.$$

In addition, in the structural relation situation, it is typically assumed that $\boldsymbol{v}$ is independent of the $\boldsymbol{x}_i$, so that

$$\mathscr{E}(\boldsymbol{y}^*|\boldsymbol{x}_1 = x_1, \ldots, \boldsymbol{x}_n = x_n) = \beta_1 x_1 + \cdots + \beta_n x_n.$$

A major statistical problem is that of estimating $B = (\beta_1, \ldots, \beta_n)$ given N observations on $\boldsymbol{y}^*$ and the independent variables, i.e., $(y_i^*, x_{1i}, \ldots, x_{ni})$, $i = 1, \ldots, N$.

The above situations are univariate examples of the subject of this chapter, namely the variety of situations in which a random n-vector $\boldsymbol{Y}$ (we drop the * from $\boldsymbol{y}^*$ for notational convenience) has expected value $\mathscr{E}\boldsymbol{Y} = XB'$, where B is an $n \times p$ matrix of unknown parameters β_{ij} and X is a known p-vector. Our interest is merely in the estimation of the matrix B. Various models with this common thread, bearing such names as "the general linear hypothesis", "linear regression", "multiple regression", "linear functional relationship", "linear structural relationship", are considered in this chapter. We reserve for chapter IV the treatment of a more detailed estimation problem in a linear expected value model than that of the estimation of B, namely the estimation of the coefficients of an interdependent system of simultaneous linear equations.

One point about this chapter worthy of special note is that there is no explicit introduction of a so-called "error term" into the standard models discussed here, except as given in the introductory paragraphs. Only in section 4, which deals with the "errors-in-variables" model, and in the study of the structural relation when we do not treat it conditionally on X, do we explicitly examine the stochastic nature of the "error term" and its relation to X. Otherwise, the stochastic nature of the error term is directly reflected in the stochastic nature of the primary variable of interest, Y, so that we might as well study Y directly.

The maximum likelihood estimator of B when we have a sample of N independent $\boldsymbol{Y}_i$'s, $\boldsymbol{Y}_i$ distributed as $N(X_iB', \Sigma)$, is given in section 1.1. In section 1.2 various least squares criteria are introduced, and B is estimated for the same model as that of section 1.1 but with the normality assumption dropped.

We treat the more general linear expected value model, where $\boldsymbol{Y} = (\boldsymbol{Y}_1, \ldots, \boldsymbol{Y}_N)$ has covariance matrix Ω and $\mathscr{E}\boldsymbol{Y} = (X_1, \ldots, X_N)(I_N \otimes B')$, where I_N is the $N \times N$ identity matrix from the separate points of view of maximum likelihood estimation and least squares estimation in sections 2.1 and 2.2, respectively. Section 2.3 contains a more detailed analysis of a special model where the errors in the linear relation are an autoregressive sequence. The linear stochastic difference equations model, a more special model than that involving correlated dependent variables discussed in section 2, is treated in section 3. Finally, section 4 contains a detailed discussion of the "errors-in-variables" problem, and includes a detailed characterization of the method of instrumental variables, a procedure for estimating B when there are errors in our observations on the X_i.

1. Independent samples

1.1. Maximum likelihood estimation in normal models

Suppose $\boldsymbol{Y}_1, \ldots, \boldsymbol{Y}_N$ are independent and that $\boldsymbol{Y}_i$ is distributed as $N(X_iB', \Sigma)$, where the X_i are N known p-vectors and B is an $n \times p$ matrix. Thus, aside from the assumption of a linear (in X_i) expected value for $\boldsymbol{Y}_i$, we are making three assumptions, normality, independence, and homoscedasticity (i.e., common covariance matrix), about the $\boldsymbol{Y}_i$. We shall relax these assumptions later. In this section we shall estimate B only in this special case. That this "special" case is quite interesting in itself is readily seen by noting that when $n = 1$ this model is the classical normal multiple regression model. Thus all our work in this section specializes even further to a quite interesting problem in its own right. However, we leave to the reader the details of this and similar specializations.

There are three interesting cases in which such a model arises. One is the functional relation case in which a vector X_i is preselected and we attempt to observe the vector $Z_i = X_iB'$, but, due to measurement error, say, we observe the random vector $\boldsymbol{Y}_i = X_iB' + \boldsymbol{U}_i$, where $\boldsymbol{U}_i$ is distributed as $N(0, \Sigma)$. A second is the regression case where $(\boldsymbol{Y}_i, \boldsymbol{X}_i)$ is distributed as $N(0, \Omega)$, so that the conditional distribution of $\boldsymbol{Y}_i$ given $\boldsymbol{X}_i = X_i$ is $N(X_i\Omega_{22}^{-1}\Omega_{21}, \Omega_{11} - \Omega_{12}\Omega_{22}^{-1}\Omega_{21}) = N(X_iB', \Sigma)$, where

$$\Omega = \begin{bmatrix} \Omega_{11} & \Omega_{12} \\ \Omega_{21} & \Omega_{22} \end{bmatrix},$$

and Ω_{11} is an $n \times n$ matrix. [When $(\boldsymbol{Y}_i, \boldsymbol{X}_i)$ is distributed as $N(\mu, \Omega)$, the distribution of $\boldsymbol{Y}_i$ given $\boldsymbol{X}_i = X_i$ is $N(\mu_1 + (X_i - \mu_2)\Omega_{22}^{-1}\Omega_{21}, \Omega_{11} -$

$\Omega_{12}\Omega_{22}^{-1}\Omega_{21}$), so that we can still write $\mathscr{E}\mathbf{Y}_i = X_i^* B^{*\prime}$, where

$$X_i^* = (1, X_i),$$

$$B^* = \begin{bmatrix} \mu_1 - \mu_2\Omega_{22}^{-1}\Omega_{21} \\ \Omega_{22}^{-1}\Omega_{21} \end{bmatrix} = \begin{bmatrix} \mu_1 - \mu_2\Omega_{22}^{-1}\Omega_{21} \\ B \end{bmatrix}.]$$

The relation $\mathscr{E}\mathbf{Y}|X = XB'$ is, as pointed out in chapter II, the regression of $\mathbf{Y}$ on X.

Lest you come away from this example with the false impression that only if $(\mathbf{Y}_i, \mathbf{X}_i)$ are multivariate normally distributed is $N(X_iB', \Sigma)$, the conditional distribution of $\mathbf{Y}_i$ given $\mathbf{X}_i = X_i$, following is a third example in which such a model arises, the structural relation case. Let $n = p = 1$, and

$$f_{\mathbf{y}_i^*, \mathbf{x}_i}(y^*, x) = f_{\mathbf{x}_i}(x)\frac{1}{\sqrt{(2\pi)}\sigma}\exp\{-(y^* - \beta x)^2/2\sigma^2\}.$$

Then,

$$f_{\mathbf{y}_i^*|\mathbf{x}_i}(y^*) = \frac{1}{\sqrt{(2\pi)}\sigma}\exp\{-(y^* - \beta x_i)^2/2\sigma^2\},$$

so that the expected value of $\mathbf{y}_i$, given $\mathbf{x}_i = x_i$, is βx_i. Yet $f_{\mathbf{x}_i}(x)$, the marginal density function of $\mathbf{x}_i$, is unspecified and need not be a normal density function.

Making the correspondence $v_i \leftrightarrow y_i - \beta x_i$ with the notation in the introduction of this chapter, we see that this is a linear structural relation with error in the dependent variable.

To obtain the maximum likelihood estimator of B and Σ, we consider the logarithm of the likelihood function of the $\mathbf{Y}_i$, viz.,

$$\begin{aligned} \sum_{i=1}^{N} \log f_{\mathbf{Y}_i}(Y_i) &= -\frac{N}{2}\log 2\pi + \frac{N}{2}\log|\Lambda| \\ &\quad - \frac{1}{2}\sum_{i=1}^{N}(Y_i - X_iB')\Lambda(Y_i - X_iB')' \\ &= -\frac{N}{2}\log 2\pi + \frac{N}{2}\log|\Lambda| \\ &\quad - \frac{1}{2}\operatorname{tr}\sum_{i=1}^{N}(Y_i - X_iB')'(Y_i - X_iB')\Lambda, \end{aligned}$$

where $\Lambda = \Sigma^{-1}$. Letting $C = \sum_{i=1}^{N}(Y_i - X_iB')'(Y_i - X_iB')$, we see from

Theorem 19 that, when B is known, $\hat{\Lambda}(\boldsymbol{Y}_1, \ldots, \boldsymbol{Y}_N) = N\boldsymbol{C}^{-1}$, and that, when B is estimated by $\hat{B}(\boldsymbol{Y}_1, \ldots, \boldsymbol{Y}_N) = \hat{\boldsymbol{B}}$,

$$\hat{\Lambda}(\boldsymbol{Y}_1, \ldots, \boldsymbol{Y}_N) = N\left[\sum_{i=1}^{N} (\boldsymbol{Y}_i - X_i\hat{\boldsymbol{B}}')'(\boldsymbol{Y}_i - X_i\hat{\boldsymbol{B}}')\right]^{-1}.$$

There are two paths toward obtaining $\hat{B}(\boldsymbol{Y}_1, \ldots, \boldsymbol{Y}_N)$, both of which are of interest not so much for this problem but for the insight one can gain from this calculation for a later-to-be-treated model. First of all, we might want to substitute $\hat{\Lambda}(Y_1, \ldots, Y_N)$ in place of Λ in the logarithm of the likelihood function from which we see that the maximum likelihood estimate of B is that matrix which minimizes

$$\left|\sum_{i=1}^{N} (Y_i - X_iB')'(Y_i - X_iB')\right|.$$

An alternative path is to begin the estimation process not by estimating Λ, as above, but directly by estimating B. This is achieved by the matrix which minimizes

$$\operatorname{tr} \sum_{i=1}^{N} (Y_i - X_iB')'(Y_i - X_iB')\Lambda.$$

Let X be the $p \times N$ matrix with ith column X_i', Y be the $n \times N$ matrix with ith column Y_i', and let $\Lambda = TT'$. Then,

$$\operatorname{tr} \sum_{i=1}^{N} (Y_i - X_iB')'(Y_i - X_iB')\Lambda = \operatorname{tr} T'(Y - BX)(Y - BX)'T.$$

The usual method for minimizing this function is to set to zero the derivative of this function with respect to B. This yields a set of equations, called the *normal equations*, of the form

$$YX' = BXX',$$

to be solved for B. We take another path, noting that

$$\operatorname{tr} T'(Y - BX)(Y - BX)'T = \|T'Y - T'BX\|,$$

where $\|A\|$ is as defined in section 7 of chapter I. Then, by Theorem 15,

$$\widehat{T'B} = T'YX^{+}.$$

Since T' is non-singular, this implies that

$$\hat{B} = YX^{+}.$$

When X is of full rank p, then $X^+ = X'(XX')^{-1}$, and

$$\hat{B} = YX'(XX')^{-1},$$

the classical result. But the more general result, namely $\hat{B} = YX^+$, is quite important, in that it tells one what to do when one has *multicollinearity*, i.e., when one (or more) of the independent variables $x_1, \ldots, x_p$ are linear functions of the others. Rather than forcing one to discard some of the px's, this form of $\hat{B}$ enables one to use all the data to estimate B. (Of course, one form of X^+ is that obtained by discarding some of the x's and inverting the submatrix of full rank.)

Substituting this value of $\hat{B}$ for B in $\hat{\Lambda}(Y_1, \ldots, Y_N)$, we obtain after a little algebra that

$$\hat{\Sigma}(Y) = [YY' - \hat{B}(XX')\hat{B}']/N.$$

Exercise: Check this.

One could have guessed at this result by considering the case where $(\boldsymbol{Y}_i, \boldsymbol{X}_i)$ is distributed as $N(0, \Omega)$. The conditional distribution of $\boldsymbol{Y}_i$ given $\boldsymbol{X}_i = X_i$ is

$$N(X_i\Omega_{22}^{-1}\Omega_{21}, \Omega_{11} - \Omega_{12}\Omega_{22}^{-1}\Omega_{21}).$$

But the maximum likelihood estimate of Ω_{22} is XX'/N and that of Ω_{21} is XY'/N. Thus, taking $B' = \Omega_{22}^{-1}\Omega_{21}$, we see that the maximum likelihood estimator of B is $\hat{\boldsymbol{B}} = YX'(XX')^{-1}$. Also, taking $\Sigma = \Omega_{11} - \Omega_{12}\Omega_{22}^{-1}\Omega_{21}$, we see that the maximum likelihood estimator of Σ is

$$\begin{aligned} \hat{\boldsymbol{\Sigma}} &= \frac{\boldsymbol{YY}'}{N} - \left(\frac{\boldsymbol{YX}'}{N}\right)(N(XX')^{-1})\left(\frac{\boldsymbol{XY}'}{N}\right) \\ &= [\boldsymbol{YY}' - \hat{\boldsymbol{B}}(XX')\hat{\boldsymbol{B}}']/N. \end{aligned}$$

Of course, this is not a derivation of the maximum likelihood estimates, as we did not need to assume anything about the origin of the X_i's to derive the maximum likelihood estimates.

We shall defer consideration of properties of the estimator $\hat{\boldsymbol{B}} = \boldsymbol{Y}X'(XX')$ for section 1.2, where such a discussion will be more appropriate.

1.2. *Least squares estimation in linear expected value models*

Let us dispense with one of the three assumptions of the model of section 1.1, the normality assumption. Rather than making an alternative distributional assumption, suppose instead that we admit that we do not know the distribution of the $\boldsymbol{Y}_i$, but only that the $\boldsymbol{Y}_i$ are independent with $\mathscr{E}\boldsymbol{Y}_i = X_iB'$ and $\mathscr{C}\boldsymbol{Y}_i = \Sigma$. This specification of the properties of the $\boldsymbol{Y}_i$'s agrees in its mean and covariance matrix with the model for the multivariate normal distribution introduced earlier. We take as our problem the estimation of B; but we cannot use the maximum likelihood method because we have no specified likelihood function. It is obvious that to estimate B in such an incompletely formulated model we must develop another method of estimation.

One that is typically used, called the *method of (ordinary) least squares,* calls for determining $\hat{B}$ which minimizes $U = \sum_{i=1}^{N} (Y_i - X_iB')(Y_i - X_iB')'$, i.e., the sum of squares of deviations of Y_i from its expected value. Since

$$\begin{aligned} U &= \operatorname{tr}(Y - BX)(Y - BX)' \\ &= \|Y - BX\|, \end{aligned}$$

we see that, as in section 1.1, $\hat{\boldsymbol{B}} = \boldsymbol{Y}X^+$. Thus the ordinary least squares estimator of B is identical with the maximum likelihood estimator of B under the normality assumption for this model.

Another method of estimation that is used, generalizing the method of ordinary least squares, is the *method of weighted least squares,* wherein $\hat{B}$ is to minimize

$$V = \sum_{i=1}^{N} (Y_i - X_iB')W_i(Y_i - X_iB')',$$

where the W_i are positive definite $n \times n$ matrices.

In the special case where $W_i = W$, independent of i, we have

$$\begin{aligned} V &= \operatorname{tr}(Y - BX)(Y - BX)'W \\ &= \|YT - BXT\|, \end{aligned}$$

where $W = TT'$. Then again $\hat{\boldsymbol{B}} = \boldsymbol{Y}T(XT)^+ = \boldsymbol{Y}X^+$, and does not depend on W.

In the general case, we differentiate V with respect to B using the rules of section 8 in chapter I. As V is a scalar function of a matrix function of B, we use the chain rule to find that, writing $W_i = T_i T_i'$,

$$\frac{\partial V}{\partial B} = \sum_{i=1}^{N} \sum_{s=1}^{n} \frac{\partial [(Y_i - X_i B')W_i(Y_i - X_i B')']}{\partial [(Y_i - X_i B')]_s} \frac{\partial [(Y_i - X_i B')]_s}{\partial B},$$

where $[(Y_i - X_i B')]_s$ denotes the sth element of the n-vector $(Y_i - X_i B')$. A straightforward calculation yields

$$\frac{\partial [(Y_i - X_i B')W_i(Y_i - X_i B')']}{\partial [(Y_i - X_i B')]_s} = 2[(Y_i - X_i B')W_i]_s,$$

and

$$\begin{aligned} \frac{\partial [(Y_i - X_i B')]_s}{\partial B} &= -\sum_{j=1}^{p} x_{ij} K_{sj} \\ &= -E_s' X_i, \end{aligned}$$

where E_s is the sth elementary n-vector. Therefore

$$\begin{aligned} \frac{\partial V}{\partial B} &= -2 \sum_{i=1}^{N} \sum_{s=1}^{n} [(Y_i - X_i B')W_i]_s E_s' X_i \\ &= -2 \sum_{i=1}^{N} W_i (Y_i - X_i B')' X_i, \end{aligned}$$

since

$$\sum_{s=1}^{n} [(Y_i - X_i B')W_i]_s E_s' = W_i (Y_i - X_i B')'.$$

To obtain the general weighted least squares estimate of B, we solve the equation $\partial V / \partial B = 0$, i.e., find the matrix $\hat{B}$ satisfying

$$\sum_{i=1}^{N} W_i Y_i' X_i = \sum_{i=1}^{N} W_i \hat{B} X_i' X_i.$$

Let $\hat{B}^* = (\hat{\beta}_{11}, \ldots, \hat{\beta}_{1p}, \hat{\beta}_{21}, \ldots, \hat{\beta}_{2p}, \ldots, \hat{\beta}_{n1}, \ldots, \hat{\beta}_{np})$.
Then these equations can be rewritten as

$$\left[\sum_{i=1}^{N} W_i \otimes X_i' X_i\right] \hat{B}^{*\prime} = \sum_{i=1}^{N} W_i Y_i' \otimes X_i,$$

so that when the $np \times np$ matrix $\sum_{i=1}^{N} W_i \otimes X_i' X_i$ is non-singular,

$$\hat{\boldsymbol{B}}^{*\prime} = \left[\sum_{i=1}^{N} W_i \otimes X_i' X_i\right]^{-1} \left[\sum_{i=1}^{N} W_i \boldsymbol{Y}_i' \otimes X_i\right].$$

The covariance matrix of $\hat{\boldsymbol{B}}^*$ is

$$\left[\sum_{i=1}^{N} W_i \otimes X_i'X_i\right]^{-1} \sum_{i=1}^{N} [W_i\Sigma W_i \otimes X_i'X_i]\left[\sum_{i=1}^{N} W_i \otimes X_i'X_i\right]^{-1}.$$

When $W_i = W$ for all i, since $\sum_{i=1}^{N} X_i'X_i = XX'$, we see that

$$\hat{\boldsymbol{B}}^* = \left[\sum_{i=1}^{N} Y_i' \otimes X_i\right](XX')^{-1},$$

and the covariance matrix of $\hat{\boldsymbol{B}}^*$ is

$$\begin{aligned}&[W \otimes XX']^{-1}[W\Sigma W \otimes XX'][W \otimes XX']^{-1}\\&= (W^{-1} \otimes (XX')^{-1})(W\Sigma W \otimes XX')(W^{-1} \otimes (XX')^{-1})\\&= W^{-1}W\Sigma WW^{-1} \otimes (XX')^{-1}XX'(XX')^{-1}\\&= \Sigma \otimes (XX')^{-1}.\end{aligned}$$

Returning to the ordinary least squares estimator of B, we note that it is a solution of the equation $Y = BX$. By Theorem 14, when X is of full rank all solutions of this equation are of the form $B = YMX'(XMX')^{-1}$, where M is a positive definite $N \times N$ matrix. Since $\mathscr{E}\boldsymbol{Y} = BX$, $\mathscr{E}\boldsymbol{B} = \mathscr{E}\boldsymbol{Y}MX'(XMX')^{-1} = BXMX'(XMX')^{-1} = B$, so that all solutions $\boldsymbol{B}$ of the equation $\boldsymbol{Y} = BX$ are unbiased estimators of B.

Thus $\hat{\boldsymbol{B}}^* = (\hat{\beta}_{11}, \ldots, \hat{\beta}_{1p}, \hat{\beta}_{21}, \ldots, \hat{\beta}_{2p}, \ldots, \hat{\beta}_{n1}, \ldots, \hat{\beta}_{np})$ is an unbiased estimator of

$$\hat{B}^* = (\beta_{11}, \ldots, \beta_{1p}, \beta_{21}, \ldots, \beta_{2p}, \ldots, \beta_{n1}, \ldots, \beta_{np}),$$

with covariance matrix $\Sigma \otimes (XX')^{-1}$. Since $\hat{\boldsymbol{B}}^*$ is a linear function of $Y_1, \ldots, Y_N$, when the Y's are normally distributed vectors we see that $\hat{\boldsymbol{B}}^*$ is distributed as $N(B^*, \Sigma \otimes (XX')^{-1})$.

All linear in $\boldsymbol{Y}$ estimators of B are of the form $\hat{\boldsymbol{B}} = \boldsymbol{Y}A + C$. For $\hat{\boldsymbol{B}}$ to be linear and unbiased, A and C must satisfy $B = \mathscr{E}\boldsymbol{Y}A + C = BXA + C$, for all X, or $B(I - XA) = C$. By Theorem 13, this equation has a solution if and only if

$$C(I - XA)^+(I - XA) = C,$$

for all X. This can only hold if $C = 0$.

Then A must satisfy $B = BXA$, for any B. Take $n = p$ and $B = I$. Then, by Theorem 14, this is the case only if $A = MX'(XMX')^{-1}$, where M is a positive definite $N \times N$ matrix. Thus,

$$\hat{\boldsymbol{B}} = \boldsymbol{Y}MX'(XMX')^{-1}$$

characterizes the entire class of linear (in $\boldsymbol{Y}$) unbiased estimators of B.

Let $\hat{\boldsymbol{B}}^* = (\hat{\boldsymbol{B}}_1, \ldots, \hat{\boldsymbol{B}}_n)$, where $\hat{\boldsymbol{B}}_i$ is the ith row of $\hat{\boldsymbol{B}}$. To determine the covariance matrix of $\hat{\boldsymbol{B}}^*$ based on the estimator $\hat{\boldsymbol{B}} = \boldsymbol{Y}A$, consider the following calculation. Since

$$\hat{\boldsymbol{\beta}}_{ij} = \sum_{k=1}^{N} y_{ik} a_{kj},$$

$$\begin{aligned}\mathscr{C}(\hat{\boldsymbol{\beta}}_{ij}, \hat{\boldsymbol{\beta}}_{i'j'}) &= \mathscr{C}\left(\sum_{k=1}^{N} y_{ik} a_{kj}, \sum_{k'=1}^{N} y_{i'k'} a_{k'j'}\right) \\ &= \sum_{k=1}^{N} \sum_{k'=1}^{N} \mathscr{C}(y_{ik} a_{kj}, y_{i'k'} a_{k'j'}) \\ &= \sum_{k=1}^{N} \sum_{k'=1}^{N} a_{kj} a_{k'j'} \mathscr{C}(y_{ik}, y_{i'k'}) \\ &= \sum_{k=1}^{N} a_{kj} a_{kj'} \mathscr{C}(y_{ik}, y_{i'k}),\end{aligned}$$

by independence of $\boldsymbol{Y}_k$ and $\boldsymbol{Y}_{k'}$, $k \neq k'$. Then,

$$\mathscr{C}(\hat{\boldsymbol{\beta}}_{ij}, \hat{\boldsymbol{\beta}}_{i'j'}) = \sum_{k=1}^{N} a_{kj} a_{kj'} \sigma_{ii'},$$

and the covariance matrix of $\hat{\boldsymbol{B}}^*$ is $\Sigma \otimes A'A$.

When $A = X'(XX')^{-1}$, $A'A = (XX')^{-1}$. When $A = MX'(XMX')^{-1}$, $A'A = (XMX')^{-1}XM^2X(XMX')^{-1}$.

Now consider the matrix

$$(XMX')^{-1}(XM^2X')(XMX')^{-1} - (XX')^{-1}.$$

It is of the form $(BA')^{-1}(AA')(AB')^{-1} - (BB')^{-1}$, where $B = ZM$ and $A = Z$, and thus, by the corollary to Theorem 12, is positive semidefinite. Therefore the Kronecker product of Σ with this matrix is positive semidefinite. From this we conclude that among the class of linear unbiased estimators of B, the ordinary least squares estimator is at least as efficient as any other member of the class.

This theorem is a deepened version of the so-called Gauss–Markov theorem, in that it treats the case of general n and proves the best linear unbiasedness property of the ordinary least squares estimator of B in our sense of "best", as defined in chapter II.

Why are we interested in unbiased estimators? Well, suppose we were interested in linear estimators, and dropped the unbiasedness requirement. For simplicity, let $n = 1$. Then, if $\hat{\boldsymbol{B}} = yA + C$, the CMSE matrix of $\hat{\boldsymbol{B}}$ is

$$\sigma^2 A'A + (BXA + C - B)'(BXA + C - B).$$

Suppose that $BXA - B \neq 0$ for some X. Then, for that X,

$$\begin{aligned}(BXA - B + C)'(BXA - B + C) = {} & (BXA - B)'(BXA - B) \\ & + C'(BXA - B) \\ & + (BXA - B)'C + C'C,\end{aligned}$$

which can be arbitrarily large, as B can be made arbitrarily large. This is not very desirable, as we don't want to stand the chance that the CMSE matrix of our estimator of B is very large. Thus, we want $BXA - B = 0$ for all X, in which case we want $\boldsymbol{B}$ to be unbiased. For such estimators the CMSE matrix (really the covariance matrix) is bounded, as a function of B. It is the matrix $\sigma^2 A'A$ which is independent of B.

Before answering the companion question of why we are interested in linear estimators of B, let us note the following interpretation of the least squares estimator. Notice that the matrix $X'(XX')^{-1}X$ (or, more generally, X^+X) is the matrix of an orthogonal projection transformation onto the subspace of N-space whose basis is the p rows of X. Thus $YX'(XX')^{-1}X = \hat{B}X$ is the matrix of orthogonal projections of the n rows of Y onto the subspace of N-space whose basis is the p rows of X, expressed relative to the elementary basis $E_1, \ldots, E_N$.

Since we are interested in estimating $\mathscr{E}Y = BX$, it seems reasonable that the estimator of BX should lie in the subspace of N-space wherein the rows of X are a basis. Now suppose we multiplied each row of Y by an $N \times N$ orthogonal matrix A. The covariance matrix of this new matrix is $\Sigma \otimes A'A = \Sigma \otimes I$, i.e., it is the same as the covariance matrix of Y. Since such a transformation leaves the covariance structure of the problem invariant, and changes the expected value from $\mathscr{E}\boldsymbol{Y} = BX$ to $\mathscr{E}\boldsymbol{Y}A = BXA$, it seems reasonable to require of any estimator $\hat{\Theta}(\boldsymbol{Y})$ of BX that $\hat{\Theta}(\boldsymbol{Y}A) = \hat{\Theta}(\boldsymbol{Y})A$, for A orthogonal.

Now express N-space as the direct sum of two orthogonal subspaces, $\mathscr{X}$ and $\mathscr{Z}$, where $\mathscr{X}$ is the subspace whose basis is the p rows of X. Let $P(Y)$ be the orthogonal projection of the rows of Y onto $\mathscr{X}$ and $Q(Y)$ be the orthogonal projection of the rows of Y onto $\mathscr{Z}$. Since $\mathscr{E}\boldsymbol{Y} = BX$ is in $\mathscr{X}$, we want $\hat{\Theta}(\boldsymbol{Y})$ to also lie in $\mathscr{X}$.

Finally, suppose that instead of Y_i we observe $Y_i + Y_0$, where Y_0 is some fixed vector in $\mathscr{X}$. It is reasonable to require of $\hat{\Theta}(\boldsymbol{Y})$ that $\hat{\Theta}(\boldsymbol{Y} + Y_0'(1, \ldots, 1)) = \hat{\Theta}(\boldsymbol{Y}) + Y_0'(1, \ldots, 1)$ for all $\boldsymbol{Y}$ and all Y_0 in $\mathscr{X}$.

These three reasonable requirements, (1) that $\hat{\Theta}(\boldsymbol{Y})$ lie in $\mathscr{X}$, (2) that

$\hat{\Theta}(Y + Y_0'(1, \ldots, 1)) = \hat{\Theta}(Y) + Y_0'(1, \ldots, 1)$ for Y_0 in $\mathscr{X}$, and (3) that $\hat{\Theta}(YA) = \hat{\Theta}(Y)A$ for A orthogonal, will lead us to conclude that $\hat{\Theta}(\boldsymbol{Y})$ must be the projection of the rows of Y on $\mathscr{X}$. The argument is as follows. Write

$$\hat{\Theta}(\boldsymbol{Y}) = \hat{\Theta}(Q(\boldsymbol{Y}) + P(\boldsymbol{Y})).$$

Then,

$$\hat{\Theta}(\boldsymbol{Y}) = \hat{\Theta}(Q(\boldsymbol{Y})) + P(\boldsymbol{Y})$$

by requirement (2). By requirement (1), $\hat{\Theta}(Q(\boldsymbol{Y}))$ is in $\mathscr{X}$. Suppose $\hat{\Theta}(Q(\boldsymbol{Y})) \neq 0$. But when A is an orthogonal matrix which leaves $\mathscr{X}$ unchanged, so that $Q(\boldsymbol{Y}A) = Q(\boldsymbol{Y})$, we have $\hat{\Theta}(Q(\boldsymbol{Y}A)) = \hat{\Theta}(Q(\boldsymbol{Y}))A = \hat{\Theta}(Q(\boldsymbol{Y}))$ for all $\boldsymbol{Y}$. Since A is non-singular, we must have $\hat{\Theta}(Q(\boldsymbol{Y})) = 0$. Thus $\hat{\Theta}(\boldsymbol{Y})$ must equal $P(\boldsymbol{Y})$, the orthogonal projection of the rows of $\boldsymbol{Y}$ on the subspace of N-space whose basis is the p rows of X. We see, then, that these three requirements not only imply that $\hat{\Theta}(\boldsymbol{Y})$ must be linear in $\boldsymbol{Y}$ but also the precise form of $\hat{\Theta}(\boldsymbol{Y})$, namely $\hat{\Theta}(\boldsymbol{Y}) = P(\boldsymbol{Y})$.

We now turn to a complicating wrinkle of this entire theory, the fact that typically the vector X is not a vector of constants, but is truly a random vector. In that case, all of section 1.1 should be interpreted as a conditional analysis, conditional on $\boldsymbol{X} = X$. The following relationships are useful in computing unconditional expected values and variances from conditional expected values and variances,

$$\mathscr{E}_{\mathbf{X},\mathbf{Y}} g(\boldsymbol{X}, \boldsymbol{Y}) = \mathscr{E}_{\mathbf{X}} \mathscr{E}_{\mathbf{Y}|\mathbf{X}} g(\boldsymbol{X}, \boldsymbol{Y})$$
$$\mathscr{V}_{\mathbf{X},\mathbf{Y}} g(\boldsymbol{X}, \boldsymbol{Y}) = \mathscr{E}_{\mathbf{X}} \mathscr{V}_{\mathbf{Y}|\mathbf{X}} g(\boldsymbol{X}, \boldsymbol{Y}) + \mathscr{V}_{\mathbf{X}} \mathscr{E}_{\mathbf{Y}|\mathbf{X}} g(\boldsymbol{X}, \boldsymbol{Y})$$

Thus,

$$\mathscr{E}_{\mathbf{X},\mathbf{Y}} \hat{\boldsymbol{B}}^* = \mathscr{E}_{\mathbf{X}} \mathscr{E}_{\mathbf{Y}|\mathbf{X}} \hat{\boldsymbol{B}}^* = \mathscr{E}_{\mathbf{X}} B^* = B^*,$$

so that $\hat{\boldsymbol{B}}^*$ is unbiased. Also,

$$\mathscr{V}_{\mathbf{X},\mathbf{Y}} \hat{\boldsymbol{B}}^* = \mathscr{E}_{\mathbf{X}} (\Sigma \otimes (\boldsymbol{X}\boldsymbol{X}')^{-1}) + \mathscr{V}_{\mathbf{X}} \hat{\boldsymbol{B}}^*$$
$$= \Sigma \otimes \mathscr{E}_{\mathbf{X}} (\boldsymbol{X}\boldsymbol{X}')^{-1}.$$

When $\hat{\boldsymbol{B}} = \boldsymbol{Y}\boldsymbol{M}\boldsymbol{X}'(\boldsymbol{X}\boldsymbol{M}\boldsymbol{X}')^{-1}$,

$$\mathscr{V}_{\mathbf{X},\mathbf{Y}} \hat{\boldsymbol{B}}^* = \mathscr{E}_{\mathbf{X}} (\Sigma \otimes (\boldsymbol{X}\boldsymbol{M}\boldsymbol{X}')^{-1}(\boldsymbol{X}\boldsymbol{M}^2\boldsymbol{X}')(\boldsymbol{X}\boldsymbol{M}\boldsymbol{X}')^{-1}) + \mathscr{V}_{\mathbf{X}} \hat{\boldsymbol{B}}^*$$
$$= \Sigma \otimes \mathscr{E}_{\mathbf{X}} (\boldsymbol{X}\boldsymbol{M}\boldsymbol{X}')^{-1}(\boldsymbol{X}\boldsymbol{M}^2\boldsymbol{X}')(\boldsymbol{X}\boldsymbol{M}\boldsymbol{X}')^{-1}.$$

Since for each value X of $\boldsymbol{X}$,

$$(XMX')^{-1}(XM^2X')(XMX')^{-1} - (XX')^{-1}$$

is positive semidefinite, so is

$$\mathscr{E}_{\mathbf{X}}[(\mathbf{XMX}')^{-1}\mathbf{X}M^2\mathbf{X}'(\mathbf{XMX}')^{-1}] - \mathscr{E}_{\mathbf{X}}(\mathbf{XX}')^{-1}.$$

Thus for this model $\hat{\boldsymbol{B}} = \boldsymbol{YX}'(\boldsymbol{XX}')^{-1}$ is the best linear unbiased estimator of B.

Certainly when the $\boldsymbol{X}_i$ are independent and identically distributed, the $\boldsymbol{Y}_i$, conditional on the values of the $\boldsymbol{X}_i$, will be independent. But this is not the only case when this is so. The $\boldsymbol{Y}_i$, conditional on the values of the $\boldsymbol{X}_i$, can be independent and homoscedastic even if the $\boldsymbol{X}_i$ are correlated. For example, let $n = 1$, $N = 2$, and suppose $(\boldsymbol{y}_1, \boldsymbol{y}_2, \boldsymbol{x}_1, \boldsymbol{x}_2)$ is distributed as $N(0, \Omega)$, where

$$\Omega = \begin{bmatrix} \sigma^2 I & T \\ T' & A \end{bmatrix},$$

$\sigma^2 > 1$, and $A = T'T$. Then the conditional distribution of $\boldsymbol{Y} = (\boldsymbol{y}_1, \boldsymbol{y}_2)$ given $(\boldsymbol{x}_1, \boldsymbol{x}_2) = (x_1, x_2) \equiv X$ is

$$N(XA^{-1}T', \sigma^2 I - TA^{-1}T') = N(XT^{-1}, (\sigma^2 - 1)I).$$

Thus the conditional covariance matrix of $\boldsymbol{Y}$ is diagonal so that $\boldsymbol{y}_1$ and $\boldsymbol{y}_2$, conditional on $\boldsymbol{X}$, are independent, even though the x's aren't. And homoscedasticity is preserved, too.

The following more complex model of the nature of the $\boldsymbol{X}_i$, which may be more realistic than that of independence, is that the sample of $\boldsymbol{X}$'s, $\boldsymbol{X}_1, \ldots, \boldsymbol{X}_n$ are neither independent nor identically distributed but that the $p \times n$ matrix $\boldsymbol{X}$, whose ith column is $\boldsymbol{X}'_i$, has the property that

$$\operatorname*{plim}_{N\to\infty} \frac{1}{N} \boldsymbol{XX}' = \Xi,$$

where Ξ is a non-singular $p \times p$ matrix. This matrix is called the *contemporaneous covariance matrix*, though it is not a covariance matrix in the usual sense of the term, i.e., it is not a second central moment. [In case the $\boldsymbol{X}_i$ are independent and identically distributed, Ξ will equal $\mathscr{E}_{\mathbf{X}}(\boldsymbol{XX}')$, by the weak law of large numbers. Thus, $\Sigma \otimes \mathscr{E}_{\mathbf{X}}(\boldsymbol{XX}')^{-1} = \Sigma \otimes \Xi^{-1}$ in that case.]

We cannot say anything in general about the distribution or asymptotic distribution of $\hat{\boldsymbol{B}}^*$ in this case, as these distributions depend critically on the behavior of the $\boldsymbol{X}_i$'s. (A particular model involving an explicit statement about the behavior of the $\boldsymbol{X}_i$'s will be studied in detail in section 3.) However, we can easily compute the limit in probability as $N \to \infty$ of $\mathcal{V}_{Y|X} \sqrt{N} \hat{B}^*$. It is

$$\begin{aligned}\operatorname*{plim}_{N\to\infty} N\mathcal{V}_{Y|X}\hat{B}^* &= \Sigma \otimes \operatorname*{plim}_{N\to\infty} N(XX')^{-1} \\ &= \Sigma \otimes \Xi^{-1}.\end{aligned}$$

This matrix is sometimes called the asymptotic covariance matrix of $\hat{B}^*$, but, as indicated in chapter II, this is a misuse of the term.

This result was computed for all three linear expected value models, the regression, functional, and structural relations in which the Y_i, conditional on the X_i, are independent and homoscedastic. An alternative calculation of this result, for the linear structural relation only [the regression model can, for this purpose, be considered a linear structural relation by making a change of variable from (Y_i, X_i) to $(Y_i - X_iB', X_i) = (V_i, X_i)$ so that $Y_i = X_iB' + V_i$] is instructive and so follows. We suppose that $Y_i = X_iB' + V_i$, where the V_i are assumed independent and homoscedastic, with $\mathscr{E}V_i = 0$ and $\mathscr{E}V'_iV_i = \Sigma$, and, in addition, it is assumed that V_i and X_i are independent. In this case

$$\begin{aligned}\hat{B} = YX'(XX')^{-1} &= (BX + V)X'(XX')^{-1} \\ &= B - VX'(XX')^{-1},\end{aligned}$$

where V is the $n \times N$ matrix whose ith column is V_i. Then, since V is independent of X and $\mathscr{E}V = 0$,

$$\mathscr{E}\hat{B} = B + \mathscr{E}V\mathscr{E}X'(XX')^{-1} = B.$$

Also,

$$\operatorname*{plim}_{N\to\infty} (\hat{B}_i - B_i)'(\hat{B}_j - B_j) = \operatorname*{plim}_{N\to\infty} (XX')^{-1}XV'_iV_jX'(XX')^{-1}.$$

Since V is independent of X, we can compute $\operatorname{plim}_{N\to\infty} N^{-1}V'_iV_j$ first and insert this in the above expression. But $\operatorname{plim}_{N\to\infty} N^{-1}V'_iV_j = \sigma_{ij}I$, by the law of large numbers. Thus,

$$\operatorname*{plim}_{N\to\infty} (\hat{B}_i - B_i)'(\hat{B}_j - B_j) = \sigma_{ij} \operatorname*{plim}_{N\to\infty} (X'X)^{-1}N.$$

As $\hat{B}^* = (\hat{B}_1, \ldots, \hat{B}_n)$, the sample covariance matrix of B^* has as probability limit $\Sigma \otimes \operatorname{plim}_{N\to\infty} N^{-1}(X'X)^{-1} = \Sigma \otimes \Xi^{-1}$. Note the critical role of the independence and homoscedasticity assumptions about the V_i (and thus about the Y_i) in the derivation of this asymptotic result.

2. Correlated samples

2.1. Maximum likelihood estimation in normal models

When the $\boldsymbol{Y}_i$ are correlated, our first instinct is to recast the problem as one where $n \leftrightarrow nN$ and $N \leftrightarrow 1$, so that $\boldsymbol{Y} = (\boldsymbol{Y}_1, \ldots, \boldsymbol{Y}_N)$, which is distributed as $N(X^*(I \otimes B'), \Omega)$, where $X^* = (X_1, \ldots, X_N)$, I is the $N \times N$ identity matrix, and Ω is the covariance matrix of Y. If we do this, we can see immediately that if Ω is unknown then it is inestimable (this is just a generalization of the notion encountered earlier in chapter II, that one cannot estimate a variance unbiasedly from a sample of size 1).

First of all, suppose Ω is known. For this model, the logarithm of the likelihood function is

$$-\frac{nN}{2}\log 2\pi - \frac{1}{2}\log|\Omega| - \frac{1}{2}(Y - X^*(I \otimes B'))\Omega^{-1}(Y - X^*(I \otimes B'))'.$$

Writing Ω^{-1} as

$$\Omega^{-1} = \begin{bmatrix} \Omega^{11} & \cdots & \Omega^{1N} \\ \cdot & & \cdot \\ \cdot & & \cdot \\ \cdot & & \cdot \\ \Omega^{N1} & \cdots & \Omega^{NN} \end{bmatrix},$$

we see that to estimate B we must minimize

$$\begin{aligned}&(Y - X^*(I \otimes B'))\Omega^{-1}(Y - X^*(I \otimes B'))' \\ &= \sum_{i=1}^{N}\sum_{j=1}^{N}(Y_i - X_iB')\Omega^{ij}(Y_i - X_iB')'.\end{aligned}$$

Thus the maximum likelihood estimate of B is the solution of the equation obtained by setting to zero the derivative with respect to B of this quantity, viz.,

$$\sum_{i=1}^{N}\sum_{j=1}^{N}\Omega^{ij}(Y'_i - BX'_i)X_j = 0.$$

Thus,

$$\hat{\boldsymbol{B}} = \left[\sum_{i=1}^{N}\sum_{j=1}^{N}\Omega^{ij}\boldsymbol{Y}'_iX_j\right]\left[\sum_{i=1}^{N}\sum_{j=1}^{N}\Omega^{ij}X'_iX_j\right]^{-1},$$

provided this latter matrix is non-singular.

Now suppose Ω is unknown but that we know something about the structure of Ω. Suppose we put some constraints on Ω. One structure studied earlier is that $\Omega = I \otimes \Sigma$, i.e., the $\boldsymbol{Y}_i$ are independent and have the same covariance matrix. For another, the dependence of the $\boldsymbol{Y}_i$ may sometimes be of the particular simple form that the cross-covariance matrix between $\boldsymbol{Y}_i$ and $\boldsymbol{Y}_j$, i.e., $\mathscr{E}\boldsymbol{Y}_i'\boldsymbol{Y}_j - \mathscr{E}\boldsymbol{Y}_i'\mathscr{E}\boldsymbol{Y}_j$, is of the form $\phi_{ij}(\rho)\Sigma$, where ϕ_{ij} is a known function of a single parameter ρ. Two simple examples, to be considered below, are (1) $\phi_{ij}(\rho) = \rho$ for all i, j, $i \neq j$, $\phi_{ii}(\rho) = 1$, $i = 1, \ldots, N$, and (2) $\phi_{ij}(\rho) = \rho^{|i-j|}$. Let Φ be the matrix of $\phi_{ij}(\rho)$, which we assume to be positive definite. Then $\Omega = \Phi \otimes \Sigma$. The advantage of such a model of dependence is that only one additional parameter, ρ, is introduced into the previous model.

For this model, the logarithm of the likelihood function is

$$-\frac{nN}{2}\log 2\pi - \frac{1}{2}\log|\Phi \otimes \Sigma| - \frac{1}{2}U(\Phi^{-1} \otimes \Sigma^{-1})U',$$

where $U = (U_1, \ldots, U_N) = Y - X^*(I \otimes B')$.

We note that

$$\begin{aligned}\frac{\partial \log|\Phi \otimes \Sigma|}{\partial \rho} &= -\frac{\partial \log|\Phi^{-1} \otimes \Sigma^{-1}|}{\partial \rho} \\ &= -\sum_{i=1}^{N}\sum_{j=1}^{N}\sum_{k=1}^{n}\sum_{l=1}^{n} \phi_{ij}(\rho)\sigma_{kl}\sigma^{kl}\frac{\partial \phi^{ij}(\rho)}{\partial \rho} \\ &= -n\sum_{i=1}^{N}\sum_{j=1}^{N} \phi_{ij}(\rho)\frac{\partial \phi^{ij}(\rho)}{\partial \rho},\end{aligned}$$

where ϕ^{ij} is the (i, j)th element of Φ^{-1} and σ^{kl} is the (k, l)th element of Σ^{-1}.

Also, as

$$U(\Phi^{-1} \otimes \Sigma^{-1})U' = \sum_{i=1}^{N}\sum_{j=1}^{N} \phi^{ij}(\rho)U_i\Sigma^{-1}U_j',$$

we see that the maximum likelihood estimate of ρ is the root $\hat{\rho}$ of the equation

$$n\sum_{i=1}^{N}\sum_{j=1}^{N} \phi_{ij}(\rho)\frac{\partial \phi^{ij}(\rho)}{\partial \rho} = \sum_{i=1}^{N}\sum_{j=1}^{N} U_i\Sigma^{-1}U_j'\frac{\partial \phi^{ij}(\rho)}{\partial \rho},$$

which maximizes the likelihood function.

Since

$$\frac{\partial \log|\Phi \otimes \Sigma|}{\partial \Sigma^{-1}} = -\frac{\partial \log|\Phi^{-1} \otimes \Sigma^{-1}|}{\partial \Sigma^{-1}}$$

$$= -\sum_{i=1}^{N}\sum_{j=1}^{N}\sum_{k=1}^{n}\sum_{l=1}^{n} \phi_{ij}(\rho)\sigma_{kl}\phi^{ij}(\rho)\frac{\partial \sigma^{kl}}{\partial \Sigma^{-1}}$$

$$= -N\sum_{k=1}^{n}\sum_{l=1}^{n} \sigma_{kl}J_{kl}$$

$$= -N\Sigma,$$

and

$$\frac{\partial U(\Phi^{-1} \otimes \Sigma^{-1})U'}{\partial \Sigma^{-1}} = \sum_{i=1}^{N}\sum_{j=1}^{N} \phi^{ij}(\rho)U'_jU_i,$$

we see that the maximum likelihood estimator of Σ is

$$\hat{\Sigma} = \sum_{i=1}^{N}\sum_{j=1}^{N} \frac{\phi^{ij}(\hat{\rho})\hat{U}'_j\hat{U}_i}{N},$$

where $\hat{U} = Y - X^*(I \otimes \hat{B}')$, and $\hat{B}$ is the maximum likelihood estimator of B.

Finally, as an exercise in matrix derivatives, we see that

$$\frac{\partial U(\Phi^{-1} \otimes \Sigma^{-1})U'}{\partial B} = \sum_{i=1}^{N}\sum_{j=1}^{N} \phi^{ij}(\rho)\frac{\partial U_i\Sigma^{-1}U'_j}{\partial B}$$

$$= \sum_{i=1}^{N}\sum_{j=1}^{N} \phi^{ij}(\rho)\sum_{\alpha=1}^{n}\sum_{\beta=1}^{n} \sigma^{\alpha\beta}\left[u_{i\alpha}\frac{\partial u_{j\beta}}{\partial B} + u_{j\beta}\frac{\partial u_{i\alpha}}{\partial B}\right]$$

$$= -\sum_{i=1}^{N}\sum_{j=1}^{N} \phi^{ij}(\rho)\sum_{\alpha=1}^{n}\sum_{\beta=1}^{n} \sigma^{\alpha\beta}$$

$$\times\left[u_{i\alpha}\sum_{k=1}^{p} x_{jk}J_{\beta k} + u_{j\beta}\sum_{k=1}^{p} x_{ik}J_{\alpha k}\right]$$

$$= -2\sum_{i=1}^{N}\sum_{j=1}^{N} \phi^{ij}(\rho)\Sigma^{-1}U'_iX_j$$

$$= -2\sum_{i=1}^{N}\sum_{j=1}^{N} \phi^{ij}(\rho)\Sigma^{-1}(Y'_i - BX'_i)X_j$$

$$= 0,$$

if and only if B satisfies

$$B\sum_{i=1}^{N}\sum_{j=1}^{N} \phi^{ij}(\rho)X'_iX_j = \sum_{i=1}^{N}\sum_{j=1}^{N} \phi^{ij}(\rho)Y'_iX_j,$$

so that the maximum likelihood estimator of B is

$$\hat{\boldsymbol{B}} = \left[\sum_{i=1}^{N}\sum_{j=1}^{N}\phi^{ij}(\hat{\rho})\boldsymbol{Y}_i\boldsymbol{X}_j\right]\left[\sum_{i=1}^{N}\sum_{j=1}^{N}\phi^{ij}(\hat{\rho})\boldsymbol{X}'_i\boldsymbol{X}_j\right]^{-1}.$$

This is obvious when we note that

$$\begin{aligned} U(\Phi^{-1}\otimes\Sigma^{-1})U' &= \sum_{i=1}^{N}\sum_{j=1}^{N}(Y_i - X_iB')\Sigma^{-1}(Y_j - X_jB')'\phi^{ij}(\rho) \\ &= \Sigma^{-1}\sum_{i=1}^{N}\sum_{j=1}^{N}(Y_j - X_jB')'\phi^{ij}(\rho)(Y_i - X_iB'). \end{aligned}$$

An important special case, to be treated more fully in section 2.3, is one where $\phi_{ij}(\rho) = \rho^{|i-j|}$, so that

$$\Phi = \begin{bmatrix} 1 & \rho & \rho^2 & \cdots & \rho^{N-1} \\ \rho & 1 & \rho & \cdots & \rho^{N-2} \\ \cdot & & & & \\ \cdot & & & & \\ \cdot & & & & \\ \rho^{N-1} & \rho^{N-2} & \rho^{N-3} & \cdots & 1 \end{bmatrix},$$

one can easily verify that

$$\Phi^{-1} = (1-\rho^2)^{-1}\begin{bmatrix} 1 & -\rho & 0 & 0 & \cdots & 0 & 0 & 0 \\ -\rho & 1+\rho^2 & -\rho & 0 & \cdots & 0 & 0 & 0 \\ 0 & -\rho & 1+\rho^2 & -\rho & \cdots & 0 & 0 & 0 \\ \cdot & & & & & & & \\ \cdot & & & & & & & \\ \cdot & & & & & & & \\ 0 & 0 & 0 & 0 & \cdots & -\rho & 1+\rho^2 & -\rho \\ 0 & 0 & 0 & 0 & \cdots & 0 & -\rho & 1 \end{bmatrix}.$$

The equation to be solved to obtain the maximum likelihood estimator of ρ is

$$\frac{n}{1-\rho^2}[(N-2)2\rho - 2(N-1)\rho]$$

$$+\frac{2n\rho}{(1-\rho^2)^2}[2+(N-2)(1+\rho^2) - 2(N-1)\rho^2] =$$

$$\frac{1}{1-\rho^2}\left[2\rho\sum_{i=2}^{N-1}U_i\Sigma^{-1}U'_i - 2\sum_{i=1}^{N-1}U_i\Sigma^{-1}U'_{i+1}\right]$$

$$+\frac{2\rho}{(1-\rho^2)^2}\left[U_1\Sigma^{-1}U_1'+U_N\Sigma^{-1}U_N'\right.$$
$$\left.+(1+\rho^2)\sum_{i=2}^{N-1}U_i\Sigma^{-1}U_i'-2\rho\sum_{i=1}^{N-1}U_i\Sigma^{-1}U_{i+1}'\right],$$

or, upon simplification,

$$\rho[U_1\Sigma^{-1}U_1'+U_N\Sigma^{-1}U_N']+2\rho\sum_{i=2}^{N-1}U_i\Sigma^{-1}U_i'-(1+\rho^2)\sum_{i=1}^{N-1}U_i\Sigma^{-1}U_{i+1}'=$$
$$n(N-1)\rho(1-\rho^2).$$

This cubic equation, along with the equations

$$\hat{\Sigma}=\frac{1}{1-\hat{\rho}^2}\left\{U_1'U_1+U_N'U_N+(1+\hat{\rho}^2)\sum_{i=2}^{N-1}U_i'U_i\right.$$
$$\left.-2\sum_{i=1}^{N-1}(U_i'U_{i+1}+U_{i+1}'U_i)\right\},$$

$$\hat{B}=\left[\sum_{i=1}^{N}Y_i'X_i+\hat{\rho}^2\sum_{i=2}^{N-1}[Y_i'X_i+X_i'Y_i]-\hat{\rho}\sum_{i=1}^{N-1}(Y_i'X_{i+1}+X_i'Y_{i+1})\right]$$
$$\times\left[\sum_{i=1}^{N}X_i'X_i+\hat{\rho}^2\sum_{i=2}^{N-1}[X_i'X_i]-\hat{\rho}\sum_{i=1}^{N-1}(X_i'X_{i+1}+X_{i+1}'X_i)\right]^{-1},$$

$$U=Y-X^*(I\otimes\hat{B}'),$$

must be solved for $\hat{B}$, $\hat{\rho}$, and $\hat{\Sigma}$.

When $\Phi=(1-\rho)I+\rho J$, where J is a matrix all of whose elements are 1,

$$\Phi^{-1}=(1-\rho)^{-1}\left[I-\frac{\rho J}{1+\rho(N-1)}\right].$$

Then,

$$\frac{\partial\phi^{ij}(\rho)}{\partial\rho}=\frac{\delta_{ij}}{(1-\rho)^2}-\frac{1+\rho^2(N-1)}{(1-\rho)^2(1+\rho(N-1))^2},$$

where

$$\delta_{ij}=\begin{cases}1, & \text{if } i=j,\\ 0, & \text{if } i\neq j.\end{cases}$$

The equation to be solved for $\hat{\rho}$ is the cubic equation

$$(1+\rho(N-1))nN(N-1)\rho(1-\rho)=(1+\rho(N-1))^2\sum_{i=1}^{N}U_i\Sigma^{-1}U_i'$$
$$-(1+\rho^2(N-1))\sum_{i=1}^{N}\sum_{j=1}^{N}U_i\Sigma^{-1}U_j'.$$

The equation for $\hat{\Sigma}$ is

$$(1-\hat{\rho})^2 N\hat{\Sigma} = \sum_{i=1}^{N} \hat{U}'_i\hat{U}_i - \frac{1+\hat{\rho}^2(N-1)}{(1+\hat{\rho}(N-1))^2}\sum_{i=1}^{N}\sum_{j=1}^{N} \hat{U}'_j\hat{U}_i,$$

and for $\hat{B}$ is

$$\hat{B} = \left[\sum_{i=1}^{N} Y'_iX_i - \frac{(1+\hat{\rho}^2(N-1))}{[1+\hat{\rho}(N-1)]^2}\sum_{i=1}^{N}\sum_{j=1}^{N} Y'_iX_j\right]$$
$$\times\left[\sum_{i=1}^{N} X'_iX_i - \frac{(1+\hat{\rho}^2(N-1))}{[1+\hat{\rho}(N-1)]^2}\sum_{i=1}^{N}\sum_{j=1}^{N} X'_iX_j\right]^{-1}.$$

2.2. *Least squares estimation*

Unlike the case where the $\boldsymbol{Y}_i$ were independent, when the $\boldsymbol{Y}_i$ are correlated random variables we cannot in general find optimal estimates of B (e.g., best linear unbiased estimates). One would hope that there would exist rules for choosing weight matrices W_i such that the consequent weighted least squares estimator would be optimal. This is not the case. In fact, as we shall soon see, the criterion of weighted least squares, as given above, is inadequate to yield optimal estimators.

We consider for simplicity the case where $n = 1$ and the y_i are correlated, with $\mathscr{C}(y_i, y_j) = \omega_{ij}$. Now let $\boldsymbol{Y} = (y_1, \ldots, y_N)$, with $\mathscr{E}\boldsymbol{Y} = BX'$, where B is a p-vector and X is an $N \times p$ matrix. Consider the class of linear (in $\boldsymbol{Y}$) unbiased estimators of B. They are of the form $\boldsymbol{B} = \boldsymbol{Y}A$, where $A = MX'(XMX')^{-1}$ and M is a positive definite $N \times N$ matrix. Since

$$\mathscr{C}(\boldsymbol{\beta}_j, \boldsymbol{\beta}_{j'}) = \sum_{k=1}^{N}\sum_{k'=1}^{N} a_{kj}a_{k'j'}\mathscr{C}(y_k, y_{k'})$$
$$= \sum_{k=1}^{N}\sum_{k'=1}^{N} a_{kj}a_{k'j'}\omega_{kk'},$$

we see that the covariance matrix of $\boldsymbol{B} = \boldsymbol{Y}A$ is

$$A'\Omega A = (XMX')^{-1}XM\Omega MX'(XMX')^{-1}.$$

When $M = \Omega^{-1}$, $A'\Omega A = (X\Omega^{-1}X')^{-1}$. Since, by the corollary to Theorem 12, the matrix

$$(XMX')^{-1}XM\Omega MX'(XMX')^{-1} - (X\Omega^{-1}X')^{-1}$$

is positive semidefinite (taking $\Omega^{-1} = TT'$, $A = XT$, and $B = XMT'^{-1}$), we see that $\boldsymbol{B} = Y\Omega^{-1}X'(X\Omega^{-1}X')^{-1}$ is the best linear unbiased estimator of B in this case.

This result is sometimes referred to as Aitken's generalization of least squares, and completely settles the problem of finding an optimal estimator of B when $n = 1$ in the face of heteroscedasticity and correlated dependent variables, *provided* that Ω is known. We will return to the problem of what to do if Ω is unknown shortly.

But first let us tie up a loose end. As stated before, the notion of weighted least squares defined earlier cannot lead to optimal estimates of B. This can be seen as follows. When $n = 1$, the W_i are now scalars, w_i, and the weighted least squares estimator of B reduces to

$$\hat{\boldsymbol{B}} = YWX'(XWX')^{-1},$$

where W is the $N \times N$ diagonal matrix with w_i as ith diagonal element. But from the above result, only if Ω is itself a diagonal matrix can a weighted least squares estimator be optimal, and then only if the weights are the reciprocals of the variances of the Y_i's.

Of course, the criterion of weighted least squares defined above provided a set of weight matrices for each of the N *independent* observations, whereas in the present context the N observations are correlated. Thus one might wish to define another notion of weighted least squares, applicable for dependent observations. The *method of weighted least squares for dependent samples* is one wherein $\hat{B}$ is to minimize

$$V^* = (Y^* - X^*(I \otimes B'))W(Y^* - X^*(I \otimes B'))',$$

where $Y^* = (Y_1, \ldots, Y_N)$, $X^* = (X_1, \ldots, X_N)$, and W is an $nN \times nN$ matrix. Then of course one could consider specially structured W's, such as $W = I$ (yielding ordinary least squares), W a block diagonal matrix with W_i as its ith block (yielding weighted least squares), and $W = W_1 \otimes W_2$, where W_1 is an $n \times n$ and W_2 an $n \times n$ matrix of weights (e.g., the specially structured covariance matrix $\Omega = \Phi \times \Sigma$ studied in section 2.2 above).

2.3. *Autoregressive errors*

We have not differentiated the three models, regression, structural relation, and functional relation, in dealing with the linear expected value model with correlated dependent vectors $\mathbf{Y}_i$ treated so far in section 2. Really, the only two cases to differentiate are the structural and functional relation, since, as footnoted earlier, the distinction between the regression and structural relation models, when there is error in the dependent vector in the latter model, is more pedantic than real. Also, the distinction between the structural and functional relations disappears when there is error in the dependent variable when we treat the structural relation as conditional on the value of the independent vectors, the X's.

What we shall do in this section is take a closer look at a particular circumstance in which a linear expected value model with correlated $\mathbf{Y}_i$'s arises and see, in the process, where the distinction in models comes into play.

First of all, let us introduce some nomenclature. Suppose we had an infinite sequence of independent, identically distributed random variables which, for later ease of notation, we write as the doubly infinite sequence, $\ldots, \mathbf{u}_{-2}, \mathbf{u}_{-1}, \mathbf{u}_0, \mathbf{u}_1, \mathbf{u}_2, \ldots$. Let $\mathscr{E}\mathbf{u}_i = 0$ and $\mathscr{V}\mathbf{u}_i = \sigma^2 < \infty$. Now consider the sequence, $\ldots, \mathbf{y}_{-2}, \mathbf{y}_{-1}, \mathbf{y}_0, \mathbf{y}_1, \mathbf{y}_2, \ldots$, where $\mathbf{y}_i = \rho\mathbf{y}_{i-1} + \mathbf{u}_i$. Such a sequence is called a *first-order autoregressive sequence.* (An nth-*order autoregressive sequence* is one which satisfies the equation $\mathbf{y}_i = \rho_i\mathbf{y}_{i-1} + \rho_2\mathbf{y}_{i-2} + \cdots + \rho_n\mathbf{y}_{i-n} + \mathbf{u}_i$.) By repeated substitution we see that the $\mathbf{y}_i$'s satisfy the relation

$$\sum_{t=0}^{\infty} \rho^t \mathbf{u}_{i-t} = \mathbf{y}_i,$$

so that $\mathscr{E}\mathbf{y}_i = 0$, $\mathscr{V}\mathbf{y}_i = \sigma^2 \sum_{t=0}^{\infty} \rho^{2t}$ which is finite and equal to $\sigma/(1-\rho^2)$ if and only if $|\rho| < 1$. Let us assume that this is so.

The interesting property of a first-order autoregressive sequence is that the $\mathbf{y}_i$ are not independent. They form a correlated sample, with

$$\begin{aligned}\mathscr{C}(\mathbf{y}_i, \mathbf{y}_j) &= \sum_{t=0}^{\infty}\sum_{t'=0}^{\infty} \rho^{t+t'}\,\mathscr{C}(\mathbf{u}_{i-t}, \mathbf{u}_{j-t'}) \\ &= \sum_{t=0}^{\infty} \rho^{t+(j-i+t)\sigma^2}, \qquad j > i,\end{aligned}$$

since $\mathscr{C}(\mathbf{u}_{i-t}, \mathbf{u}_{j-t'}) \neq 0$ only when $i - t = j - t'$.

Thus,

$$\mathscr{C}(\mathbf{y}_i, \mathbf{y}_j) = \rho^{|j-i|}\sigma^2/(1-\rho^2) = \rho^{|j-i|}\mathscr{V}\mathbf{y}_i,$$

for all i, j.

Notice what we have developed. The covariance matrix of the y_i's is one of the particular cases studied in detail in section 2.1. We see that in a functional relation, or in a structural relation conditional on the independent variables where the dependent variable is subject to error and the errors are from a first-order autoregressive sequence, we will then have a linear expected value model with correlated samples studied in section 2.1. To be more specific, suppose $y_i = \beta x_i$ and $y_i^* = y_i + v_i$, with $\mathscr{E}v_i = 0$, so that $\mathscr{E}y_i^* = \beta x_i$. Now if the v_i are a first-order autoregressive sequence, e.g., $v_i = \rho v_{i-1} + u_i$, where the u_i satisfy the aforementioned assumptions, then we have a model which gives rise to the case studied in section 2.1, where $\phi_{ij}(\rho) = \rho^{|i-j|}$.

There is a small problem with this description, namely, that any sample is one with a finite number n of elements. Thus, given observations on $y_1^*, \ldots, y_n^*$, we must define what we mean by v_0 so that v_1 can be defined by the equation $v_1 = \rho v_0 + u_1$. It is conventional to define $v_1 = u_1$, so that

$$v_i = \rho^{i-1}u_1 + \rho^{i-2}u_2 + \cdots + \rho u_{i-1} + u_i, \qquad i > 1,$$

and if $j > i$,

$$\begin{aligned}\mathscr{C}(y_i^*, y_j^*) &= \sum_{t=0}^{i-1}\sum_{t'=0}^{j-1} \rho^{t+t'}\mathscr{C}(u_{i-t}, u_{j-t'}) \\ &= \sum_{t=0}^{i-1} \rho^{t+(j-i+t)}\sigma^2 \\ &= \sigma^2\rho^{j-i}\sum_{t=0}^{i-1}\rho^{2t} \\ &= \frac{\sigma^2\rho^{j-i}(1-\rho^{2i})}{1-\rho^2},\end{aligned}$$

so that

$$\mathscr{C}(y_i^*, y_j^*) = \frac{\sigma^2\rho^{|i-j|}(1-\rho^{2\min(i,j)})}{1-\rho^2}.$$

Here again Ω, the covariance matrix of all the y's, is of the form $\Phi \otimes \Sigma$ where $\Sigma = \sigma^2 I$, but because of the difficulty in expressing Φ^{-1} succinctly and obtaining likelihood equations to solve for $\hat{\rho}$, one usually closes one's eyes to the definition of v_0 and pretends that the v_i form an untruncated autoregressive sequence, thus taking $\phi_{ij}(\rho) = \rho^{|i-j|}$.

The maximum likelihood estimator of ρ and B described in section 2.1 is appropriate only when the normality assumption holds. We have not, however, given a corresponding least squares estimator of B when ρ is unknown.

The ordinary least squares estimator is clearly not optimal, since, if ρ were known, we could do better with a weighted least squares estimator. Thus it stands to reason that the ordinary least squares estimator is not optimal when ρ is unknown.

Let us see what is involved in computing the least squares estimator of ρ and B (in fact, the parameters of a qth order autoregressive sequence of errors).

Since

$$y_i = \beta_1 x_{1i} + \cdots + \beta_p x_{pi} + v_i, \qquad i = 1, \ldots, N,$$

and

$$v_i + \rho_1 v_{i-1} + \cdots + \rho_q v_{i-q} = u_i, \qquad i = q+1, \ldots, N,$$

we see that

$$\begin{aligned} y_i + \rho_1 y_{i-1} + \cdots + \rho_q y_{i-q} = {} & \beta_1 x_{1i} + \cdots + \beta_p x_{pi} \\ & + \rho_1 \beta_1 x_{1,i-1} + \cdots + \rho_q \beta_p x_{p,i-q} \\ & + u_i, \qquad i = q+1, \ldots, N. \end{aligned}$$

The ordinary least squares estimator of $B = (\beta_1, \ldots, \beta_p)$ and $R = (\rho_1, \ldots, \rho_q)$ is the result of solving the equations derived from setting to zero the derivatives with respect to B and R of the function

$$\sum_{i=q+1}^{N} \left[y_i + \sum_{j=1}^{q} \rho_j y_{i-j} - \sum_{k=1}^{p} \beta_k x_{ki} - \sum_{j=1}^{q} \sum_{k=1}^{p} \rho_j \beta_k x_{k,i-j} \right]^2.$$

The equations to be solved are nonlinear and, hence, difficult to solve. There is, however, a procedure for estimating R and B which is computationally easier and whose resulting estimators have the same asymptotic covariance matrix as those resulting from ordinary least squares. It consists of the following steps:

(1) Find the values $\hat{R}$ and $\hat{G}$ of $R = (\rho_1, \ldots, \rho_q)$ and $G = (\gamma_1, \ldots, \gamma_r)$ which minimize

$$\sum_{i=q+1}^{N} [y_i + \rho_i y_{i-1} + \cdots + \rho_q y_{i-q} - \gamma_1 x_{1i} - \cdots - \gamma_r x_{ri}]^2,$$

where r is the number of linearly independent vectors of the set of $p(q+1)$ N-vectors,

$$X_{kj} = (x_{k,q+1-j}, \ldots, x_{k,N-j}), \qquad j = 0, 1, \ldots, q, \quad k = 1, \ldots, p.$$

(2) Let

$$\hat{v}_i = y_i + \hat{\rho}_1 y_{i-1} + \cdots + \hat{\rho}_q y_{i-q}, \qquad i = q+1, \ldots, N,$$

and

$$\hat{w}_{ki} = x_{ki} + \hat{\rho}_1 x_{k,i-1} + \cdots + \hat{\rho}_p x_{k,i-p}, \qquad k = 1, \ldots, p,$$
$$i = q+1, \ldots, N.$$

(3) Find the value $\hat{B}$ of $B = (\beta_1, \ldots, \beta_p)$ which minimize

$$\sum_{i=q+1}^{N} (\hat{v}_i - \beta_1 \hat{w}_{1i} - \cdots - \beta_p \hat{w}_{pi})^2.$$

Each of these steps is accomplished by using the ordinary least squares estimator, making the appropriate correspondence between the matrices X and Y defined in section 1.2 and the data of these two minimization problems.

3. Linear stochastic difference equations

The linear expected value model to be discussed in this section is sometimes called the *autoregressive model*, but, in order to avoid terminological confusion with the model treated in section 2.3, the linear expected value model with autoregressive errors, we will refer to this model by its pseudonym, the *linear stochastic difference equation*. In the case where $n = 1$, this model says that

$$\mathscr{E} y_i \,|\, y_{i-1}, \ldots, y_{i-p} = \beta_1 y_{i-1} + \cdots + \beta_p y_{i-p},$$

for $i = p+1, \ldots, N$. Thus the independent variables in this linear expected value model are lagged values of the dependent variables, rather than some other set of variables X.

One can estimate $B = (\beta_1, \ldots, \beta_p)$ by least squares methods, treating this model like any other linear expected value model. And the general remarks at the end of section 2.2 on the case where the independent variables are random apply here as well. We can, however, say more about properties of the least squares estimator of B in this case, since this model defines the explicit nature of the randomness of the independent variables. To do so, we first examine two aspects of the nature of this model, relating to the nature of the so-called "error term" in this model, i.e., that random term which, when superimposed on the non-random system of difference equations, would yield the model described, and the other relating to mathematical properties of the system of difference equations which would define the model if y were not random.

Our mode of expressing the linear stochastic difference equation as an expected value model covers over two major ways in which this model arises. The first, sometimes called the "errors-in-variables" model, assumes that there is a true structural relation

$$y_i^* = \beta_1 y_{i-1}^* + \cdots + \beta_p y_{i-p}^*,$$

but that we only observe $y_i = y_i^* + v_i$, so that

$$y_i = \beta_1 y_{i-1} + \cdots + \beta_p y_{i-p} + (v_i - \beta_1 v_{i-1} - \cdots - \beta_p v_{i-p}).$$

If $\mathscr{C}(v_i, y_i^*) = 0$ and $\mathscr{E}v_i = 0$ for all i, then

$$\mathscr{E}y_i \mid y_{i-1}, \ldots, y_{i-p} = \beta_1 y_{i-1} + \cdots + \beta_p y_{i-p}.$$

As we shall see in section 4, use of the ordinary least squares estimator in this context leads to an inconsistent estimator of $B = (\beta_1, \ldots, \beta_p)$. Indeed, it will be seen that under standard normality assumptions on the y^*'s and v's, B is unidentifiable.

The other context in which this model arises is sometimes called the "errors-in-equations" model. Briefly, it assumes that the true structural relation is $y_i = \beta_i y_{i-1} + \cdots + \beta_p y_{i-p} + v_i$, but that the v_i are unobservable. If v_i is independent of the y's and $\mathscr{E}v_i = 0$, then

$$\mathscr{E}y_i \mid y_{i-1}, \ldots, y_{i-p} = \beta_1 y_{i-1} + \cdots + \beta_p y_{i-p}.$$

The "errors-in-variables" model conceptually postulates a true relation between variables and explains the discrepancy between the model and our observations as due to observational error. The "errors-in-equations" model can be interpreted as saying that there are other random factors besides $y_{i-1}, \ldots, y_{i-p}$ which produce y_i, and they are unmeasurable, indeed perhaps unknown, but on the average contribute nothing to the expected value of y_i. Use of the least squares estimators provided in section 2.2 in the "errors-in-equations" context are quite appropriate here, as the model is a special case of that one.

(This discussion is relevant to both the material of sections 2.3 and 4. We have placed it here rather than in section 2.3 because the distinction between the models is clearer when the random independent variables are lagged dependent variables.)

The fundamental relationship before the introduction of errors to produce either the errors-in-variables or errors-in-equations model can be put in the form

$$z_k + \beta_1 z_{k-1} + \cdots + \beta_p z_{k-p} = 0.$$

There are implications from the structure of the model on the nature of the underlying variables, the z_k in this notation, the y_k or y_k^* in the two models. To see these implications, we digress to study the solution of non-stochastic linear difference equations with constant coefficients.

Suppose that $z_k = \theta^k$ is a solution of this equation. Then θ must be a root of the polynomial

$$\theta^k + \beta_1\theta^{k-1} + \cdots + \beta_p\theta^{k-p} = 0,$$

or, equivalently,

$$\theta^p + \beta_1\theta^{p-1} + \cdots + \beta_{p-1}\theta + \beta_p = 0.$$

This polynomial, called the characteristic polynomial, has p roots, $\theta_1, \ldots, \theta_p$; and indeed there are only p solutions of the difference equations, determined as follows:

(1) For each real unrepeated root θ there corresponds a solution of the form $C\theta^k$.

(2) For each real root θ which is repeated r times, there corresponds a solution of the form $(C_1 + C_2k + C_3k^2 + \cdots + C_rk^{r-1})\theta^k$.

(3) For each pair of unrepeated complex conjugate roots of the form $\theta = a \pm b_i$, there corresponds a solution of the form

$$A\rho^k \cos(k\omega + B),$$

where

$$\rho = \sqrt{(a^2 + b^2)} \quad \text{and} \quad \omega = \tan^{-1}(b/a).$$

(4) For each pair of complex conjugate roots of the form $\theta_j = a \pm b_j$ which are repeated r times, there corresponds a solution of the form

$$\rho^k[A_1\cos(k\omega + B_1) + A_2k\cos(k\omega + B_2) + \cdots + A_rk^{r-1}\cos(k\omega + B_r)].$$

Now if economic variables z_k satisfy this linear difference equation, they must be real. It is often reasonable to assume that the sequence of variables $\{z_k\}$ is stable, i.e., that $\lim_{k\to\infty} z_k$ exists and is a solution of the equation for any and all possible initial values. In economic terms this assumes that, given no further interference, the fluctuations in the variable z_k over time tend to die away and are only initially influenced by the initial values which set the time series in motion. This is at variance with the view that the economic system is basically unstable, so that the behavior of z_k depends so greatly on initial influences that it has no limiting value, and that only new exogenous interferences to the economic system keep z_k on track. We restrict ourselves to stable models only because to model an essentially unstable system one must in addition model the exogenous variables which steer the system, thus creating both difficult modeling and statistical problems. On the other hand, it is very easy to characterize stable models. A necessary and sufficient condition for stability is that the modulus, i.e., the sum of squares of the real and imaginary parts, of each of the roots of the polynomial associated with the equation be less than 1.

Another technical reason for assuming that our model is stable is that in certain circumstances the above model is unidentifiable, in a sense to be made precise in a moment, and one convenient way to make the model identifiable in that case is to impose the restriction of stability of the model. To determine the particular circumstance in which this arises, let us assume that the distribution of the solution of the linear stochastic difference equation, y_t, has the nice property in that it is *stationary*, i.e., that

$$F_{y_{t+\tau}}(y) = F_{y_t}(y),$$

for all τ. This assumption means that the distribution of the random sequence $\{y_t\}$ is unaffected by a shift in the "time axis".

Clearly, y_t cannot involve solutions of the non-stochastic linear difference equation based on roots of the characteristic polynomial with modulus either greater than or less than 1. For if that were the case, since $\{y_t\}$ would either diverge or tend to zero as $t \to \infty$, its distribution would not be stationary. Thus, the assumption of stationarity requires that y_t be a linear combination of solutions based on roots with modulus equal to 1, i.e.,

$$y_t = \sum_{i=1}^{r} a_i \cos(t\omega_i + b_i).$$

Note that the requirement of stationarity and stability of y_t demand conflicting properties of the roots of the characteristic equation. Stationarity requires that the roots have modulus equal to 1; stability requires that the roots have modulus less than 1. We must give up one of these properties, and so we give up stationarity. But we don't give it up entirely. Instead, let us require at least that the random variable $y = \lim_{t\to\infty} y_t$ is stationary even though y_t is not. To see what this condition, asymptotic stationarity, requires, we examine more closely the properties of characteristic equations all of whose roots have modulus equal to 1.

Let us first record some properties of complex numbers.

(1) If $z = x + iy$, then $\bar{z}$, the *complex conjugate* of z, is defined by $\bar{z} = x - iy$. Note that the squared modulus of z, $|z|^2$ is just $z\bar{z} = x^2 + y^2$.

(2) If $z = x + iy$, then e^z is defined by

$$e^z = e^x(\cos y + i \sin y).$$

Thus z can be rewritten as

$$z = r(\cos\theta + i\sin\theta) = r\,e^{i\theta},$$

where

$$r = \sqrt{(x^2 + y^2)} \quad \text{and} \quad \theta = \tan^{-1}(y/x).$$

(3) If $z = r\,e^{i\theta}$, then $\bar{z} = r\,e^{-i\theta}$.

Now consider the squared modulus of the characteristic polynomial, i.e.,

$$\psi(z) = |z^p + \beta_1 z^{p-1} + \cdots + \beta_{p-1}z + \beta_p|^2 = 0,$$

and suppose z_1 is a root of the polynomial. What we will soon see is that so is $\bar{z}_1^{-1}$, the reciprocal of the complex conjugate of z_1. For, letting $\beta_0 = 1$,

$$\begin{aligned}
\psi(z) &= \sum_{j=0}^{p} \beta_j z^{p-j} \sum_{j'=0}^{p} \beta_{j'} \bar{z}^{p-j'} \\
&= \sum_{j=0}^{p} \sum_{j'=0}^{p} \beta_j \beta_{j'}\, e^{i(p-j)}\, e^{-i(p-j')} \\
&= \sum_{j=0}^{p} \sum_{j'=0}^{p} \beta_j \beta_{j'}\, e^{i(j'-j)} \\
&= \sum_{k=-p}^{p} \gamma_k z^{p+k},
\end{aligned}$$

where $\gamma_{-k} = \gamma_k$. Then,

$$\begin{aligned}\psi(\bar{z}_1^{-1}) &= \sum_{k=-p}^{p} \gamma_k \bar{z}_1^{-(p+k)} \\ &= \bar{z}_1^{-2p} \sum_{k=-p}^{p} \gamma_k \bar{z}_1^{p-k} \\ &= \bar{z}_1^{-2p} \sum_{k=-p}^{p} \gamma_k \bar{z}_1^{p+k} \\ &= \bar{z}_1^{-2p}\, \overline{\psi(z_1)}.\end{aligned}$$

Thus if $\psi(z_1) = 0$, we see that $\psi(\bar{z}_1^{-1}) = 0$. One of the pair z_1, $\bar{z}_1^{-1}$ must be a root of the characteristic polynomial, but there is no way of determining which from this development.

We may group the roots into pairs $(z_1, \bar{z}_1^{-1}), \ldots, (z_p, \bar{z}_p^{-1})$ and rewrite $\psi(z)$ as the square of the modulus of a polynomial of degree p, viz,

$$\psi(z) = \left|\prod_{i=1}^{p} (z - \xi_i)\right|^2,$$

where ξ_i is either z_i, the ith root, or $\bar{z}_i^{-1}$. There are two different representations of $\psi(z)$ in this manner, depending on choices of the ξ_i.

For example, if

$$\psi(z) = 8z^4 - 54z^3 + 101z^2 - 54z + 8,$$

with roots $z_1 = 4$, $z_2 = 2$, $\bar{z}_1^{-1} = \frac{1}{4}$, $\bar{z}_2^{-1} = \frac{1}{2}$, we can express $\psi(z)$ as

$$\psi(z) = 8|(z-4)(z-2)|^2,$$

or

$$\psi(z) = 2|(z-4)(2z-1)|^2,$$

or

$$\psi(z) = \tfrac{1}{4}|(4z-1)(z-2)|^2,$$

or

$$\psi(z) = \tfrac{1}{8}|(4z-1)(2z-1)|^2.$$

Thus, we see that the squared modulus of the characteristic polynomial of every pth order difference equation can be represented as the square of the modulus of a polynomial $\psi^*(z)$ whose roots, are all smaller than 1.

What does this imply for linear stochastic difference equations?

Consider first the example

$$z_t - 6z_{t-1} = 0,$$

the non-zero root of whose characteristic polynomial exceeds 1.

This equation has as counterpart the equation

$$z_t - \tfrac{1}{6}z_{t-1} = 0,$$

the non-zero root of whose characteristic polynomial is less than 1. Thus, given data on the y's, one cannot uniquely determine β_1 in the relation

$$y_t - \beta_1 y_{t-1} = v_t,$$

since both

$$y_t = \sum_{j=0}^{\infty} \beta_1^j v_{t-j}$$

and

$$y_t = -\sum_{j=1}^{\infty} \frac{1}{\beta_1^j} v_{t+j}$$

satisfy the relation and when $\beta_1 = 6$ the first expression for y_t is not asymptotically stationary and when $\beta_1 = \frac{1}{6}$ the second expression for y_t is not asymptotically stationary.

It is reasonable to make the convention that the form of the first of the above relations is the "solution" (though both forms are), since it relates y_t to errors v_{t-j} earlier in time. This convention, though, has the effect in this example of constraining β_1, the root of the characteristic polynomial, to be less than 1.

The generalization of this convention to the solutions of more general stochastic difference equations, that the form of y_t only involve v_{t-j} for $j > 0$, has as its generalized counterpart that the roots of the characteristic polynomial of the linear stochastic difference equation all have modulus less than 1.

The proof of this generalization is beyond the scope of this book, as it involves notions of spectral analysis. The basic ingredients of this proof, however, are all given, at least by example, in the above development.

As an aid in linking this material with that of spectral analysis, let me point out that the spectral density of a linear stochastic difference equation is proportional to the reciprocal of the squared modulus of the characteristic polynomial, and so the spectral representation of the solution is couched in terms of a "square root" of this squared modulus. The convention adopted of expressing y_t in terms only of v_{t-j} for $j \geqslant 0$ translates directly into choosing as "square root" the polynomial all of whose roots have modulus less than 1.

4. Errors-in-variables models

4.1. *Models*

In the models studied in sections 1 and 2, we were given N independent observations on the n-vector $\boldsymbol{Y}^*$ whose expected value is $\mathscr{E}\boldsymbol{Y}^* = XB'$, where X is a known p-vector and B is an $n \times p$ matrix of parameters. However, suppose we are in a situation where, whatever the nature of X, be it a non-random vector or the value of a random vector $\boldsymbol{X}$, we observe not X but the random vector $\boldsymbol{X}^* = X + \boldsymbol{U}$. (Note that since we have introduced an error in the observation of X, we reintroduce the * on $\boldsymbol{Y}^*$ to highlight the fact that $\boldsymbol{Y}^* = Y + \boldsymbol{V}$ when the underlying model is a functional relation and that $\boldsymbol{Y}^* = \boldsymbol{Y} + \boldsymbol{V}$ when the underlying model is either a structural relation or a linear regression.)

Let us specialize our model to the case where $n = 1$, $p = s + 1$, and where the first coordinate of X (or $\boldsymbol{X}$) is always 1. Thus $\mathscr{E}\boldsymbol{y}^* = \beta_1 + \beta_2 x_2 + \cdots + \beta_{s+1}x_{s+1}$, or, as the x's and β's are usually labeled,

$$\mathscr{E}\boldsymbol{y}^* = \beta_0 + \beta_1 x_1 + \cdots + \beta_s x_s.$$

The usual assumptions about $\boldsymbol{v}$ and $\boldsymbol{U}$ are that $(\boldsymbol{U}, \boldsymbol{v})$ is distributed as $N(0, \Omega)$ and that, in the structural relation situation, $(\boldsymbol{U}, \boldsymbol{v})$ is independent of $\boldsymbol{X} = (\boldsymbol{x}_1, \ldots, \boldsymbol{x}_s)$, and hence of $\boldsymbol{y} = \beta_0 + \sum_{i=1}^{s} \beta_i \boldsymbol{x}_i$. Thus, in the case of a structural relation, when $\boldsymbol{X}$ is distributed as $N(\mu, \psi)$, so that $\boldsymbol{y}$ is distributed as $N\left(\beta_0 + \sum_{i=1}^{j} \beta_i \mu_i, B\psi B'\right)$, where $B = (\beta_1, \ldots, \beta_s)$, the vector $(\boldsymbol{X}^*, \boldsymbol{y}^*)$ of observations is distributed as $\left(\left(\mu, \beta_0 + \sum_{i=1}^{s} \beta_i \mu_i\right), \Sigma\right)$, where

$$\Sigma = \begin{bmatrix} \psi & \psi B' \\ B\psi & B\psi B' \end{bmatrix} + \Omega.$$

Let us count the number of sufficient parameters of the distribution of $(\boldsymbol{X}^*, \boldsymbol{y}^*)$. Since Σ is an $(s+1)\times(s+1)$ matrix, it embodies $(s+1)\times$

$(s+2)/2$ distinct parameters. Adding $s+1$ parameters to $\mathscr{E}(\boldsymbol{X}^*, \boldsymbol{y}^*)$ brings the total to $(s+1)(s+4)/2$.

Now let us count the number of parameters of our underlying model, that which generates the observed $(\boldsymbol{X}^*, \boldsymbol{y}^*)$. There are $s+1$ β's, s μ's, $s(s+1)/2$ distinct elements of ψ, and at least $s+1$ elements in Ω (assuming that it is merely a diagonal matrix, i.e., that the errors are uncorrelated with each other). This makes a total of at least $[(s+1)\times(s+4)/2]+s$ parameters. Thus there are at least s more model parameters than the number of sufficient parameters. This should indicate that the model parameters are not identifiable.

Exercise: For $s=1$, construct two sets of model parameters which are consistent with the same set of sufficient parameters of the distribution of $(\boldsymbol{x}^*, \boldsymbol{y}^*)$.

A rather startling fact is that, for the structural relation with normally distributed errors in variables, the model is unidentifiable if and only if the distribution of $\boldsymbol{X}$ (and hence of $\boldsymbol{y}$) is normal.

The proof of this fact is relatively easy when $s=1$. As there is a one-to-one correspondence between a density function $f_X(X)$ and its Fourier transform,

$$\varphi_X(T) = \int_{-\infty}^{\infty} \exp\{iTX'\} f_X(X)\, dX,$$

sometimes called its characteristic function, it suffices to prove that the characteristic function of the $(\boldsymbol{x}_i^*, \boldsymbol{y}_i^*)$, $i=1,\ldots,N$, is non-unique if and only if the $(\boldsymbol{x}_i, \boldsymbol{y}_i)$ are normally distributed.

Exercise: Let $\boldsymbol{X}$ be distributed as $N(\mu, \Sigma)$. Show that $\varphi_X(T) = \exp\{iT\mu' - \frac{1}{2}T\Sigma T'\}$.

Let $T=(t_1, t_2)$, and let Λ be the covariance matrix of $(\boldsymbol{u}, \boldsymbol{v})$. Then the characteristic function of $(\boldsymbol{u}, \boldsymbol{v})$ is

$$\begin{aligned}\varphi_{u,v}(T) &= \int_{-\infty}^{\infty}\int_{-\infty}^{\infty} \exp\{i(t_1u + t_2v)\}\, f_{u,v}(u, v)\, du\, dv \\ &= \exp\{-\tfrac{1}{2}T\Lambda T'\},\end{aligned}$$

when $(\boldsymbol{u}, \boldsymbol{v})$ is distributed as $N(0, \Lambda)$.

The characteristic function of $(\boldsymbol{x}, \boldsymbol{y})$ is

$$\varphi_{x,y}(T) = \int_{-\infty}^{\infty} \int_{-\infty}^{\infty} \exp\{\mathrm{i}(t_1 x + t_2 y)\} f_{x,y}(x, y)\, \mathrm{d}x\, \mathrm{d}y$$

$$\times \exp\{\mathrm{i}t_2\alpha\} \int_{-\infty}^{\infty} \exp\{\mathrm{i}(t_1 + \beta t_2)x\} f_x(x)\, \mathrm{d}x$$

$$= \exp\{\mathrm{i}t_2\alpha\}\, \varphi_x(t_1 + \beta t_2),$$

for arbitrary density for $\boldsymbol{x}$. Then

$$\varphi_{x^*,y^*}(T) = \varphi_{x,y}(T)\varphi_{u,v}(T)$$
$$= \exp\{\mathrm{i}t_2\alpha - \tfrac{1}{2}T\Lambda T'\}\, \varphi_x(t_1 + \beta t_2).$$

Now suppose the model is unidentifiable, i.e., that there exist two sets of parameters, (α, β, Λ) and $(\alpha^*, \beta^*, \Lambda^*)$, and two characteristic functions φ_x and φ_x^* such that

$$\varphi_{x^*,y^*}(T) = \exp\{\mathrm{i}t_2\alpha - \tfrac{1}{2}T\Lambda T'\}\, \varphi_x(t_1 + \beta t_2)$$
$$= \exp\{\mathrm{i}t_2\alpha^* - \tfrac{1}{2}T\Lambda T'\}\, \varphi_x^*(t_1 + \beta^* t_2).$$

Suppose $\beta = \beta^*$. Then let T be given by

$$T = (z \quad 0)\begin{pmatrix} 1 & 1 \\ \beta & \beta^* \end{pmatrix}^{-1} = \frac{z}{\beta - \beta^*}(-\beta^*, 1),$$

where z is arbitrary. Then, expressing $\varphi_{x^*,y^*}(T)$ as a function of z, we have

$$\varphi_{x^*,y^*}(T) = \exp\left\{\frac{\mathrm{i}z\alpha}{\beta - \beta^*} - \frac{z^2}{2(\beta - \beta^*)^2}(-\beta^*, 1)\Lambda(-\beta^*, 1)'\right\} \varphi_x(z)$$

$$= \exp\left\{\frac{\mathrm{i}z\alpha^*}{\beta - \beta^*} - \frac{z^2}{2(\beta - \beta^*)^2}(-\beta^*, 1)\Lambda^*(-\beta^*, 1)'\right\} \varphi_x(0).$$

Since $\varphi_x(0) = 1$, we see that the characteristic function of $\boldsymbol{x}$ is

$$\varphi_x(z) = \exp\left\{\mathrm{i}z\frac{(\alpha^* - \alpha)}{\beta - \beta^*} - \frac{z^2}{2(\beta - \beta^*)^2}(-\beta^*, 1)(\Lambda^* - \Lambda)(-\beta^*, 1)'\right\},$$

that is, the characteristic function of a random variable with distribution

$$N\left(\frac{\alpha^* - \alpha}{\beta - \beta^*}, \frac{(-\beta^*, 1)(\Lambda^* - \Lambda)(-\beta^*, 1)'}{(\beta - \beta^*)^2}\right).$$

Thus unidentifiability of the model implies normality of $\boldsymbol{x}$. That normality implies unidentifiability can be shown easily by first noting that there are only five parameters for the distribution of $(\boldsymbol{x}^*, \boldsymbol{y}^*)$, yet six (if Λ is diagonal) or more structural parameters, and then constructing two distinct sets of structural parameters, where $\beta \neq \beta^*$, which lead to the same set of parameters for the distribution of $(\boldsymbol{x}^*, \boldsymbol{y}^*)$.

Exercise: Find such a pair of structural parameter sets.

The identifiability situation for the linear functional relation is not as clear-cut as was that for the linear structural relation. In fact, there is even a problem of definition of what is meant by identifiability of the linear functional relation. This is because the observed sample members (y_i^*, x_i^*), $i = 1, \ldots, N$, are not identically distributed, and the number of parameters of the distribution increases with N. The parameters are $\alpha, \beta, \sigma_u^2, \sigma_v^2$ and $x_i, \ldots, x_n$. Thus our earlier definition of identifiability cannot be used here.

We can, however, distinquish between two sets of parameters, *structural* parameters and *incidental* parameters. In general, given a set of random vectors $\boldsymbol{Z}_1, \ldots, \boldsymbol{Z}_n$, with joint density function $f_{\boldsymbol{Z}}(Z; \Psi)$, where $\boldsymbol{Z} = (\boldsymbol{Z}_1, \ldots, \boldsymbol{Z}_n)$ and Ψ is a vector of parameters, we say that Ψ_i is an incidental parameter if the marginal distribution of some $\boldsymbol{Z}_k$ does not depend on Ψ_i; otherwise Ψ_i is a structural parameter. In our example, $\boldsymbol{Z}_i = (\boldsymbol{x}_i^*, \boldsymbol{y}_i^*)$, the $\boldsymbol{Z}_i$ are independent, and $\Psi = (\alpha, \beta, \sigma_u^2, \sigma_v^2, x_1, \ldots, x_n)$. Clearly $(\alpha, \beta, \sigma_u^2, \sigma_v^2)$ are structural parameters and $x_1, \ldots, x_n$ are incidental.

Now let Θ be a vector of structural parameters and Ξ be a vector of incidental parameters of $\boldsymbol{X}$. We say that Θ is *identifiable* only if $\Theta_1 \neq \Theta_2$ implies that, for some X and Ξ, $F_{\boldsymbol{X}}(X; \Theta_1, \Xi) \neq F_{\boldsymbol{X}}(X; \Theta_2, \Xi)$. It is not known whether the parameters $(\alpha, \beta, \sigma_u^2, \sigma_v^2)$ of the linear functional relation are identifiable if the errors are normally distributed. The only result that indicates that the linear functional relation may not be identifiable in this case is that there exists no uniformly consistent estimator of $\Theta = (\alpha, \beta, \sigma_u^2, \sigma_v^2)$.

4.2. *Estimation in non-normal structural relations*

A consequence of the identifiability result is that only if our true data are non-normally distributed will we have an identifiable model. For such a model, one can estimate the parameters by the method of maximum likelihood and, under standard regularity conditions, the estimators will be consistent. We will not discuss non-normal models in this book, as the essence of econometric models is the normality assumption about data and errors. However, let me record herewith a simple non-maximum likelihood estimator of the β's which is consistent for non-normal data. Suppose for simplicity that $\mathscr{E}\boldsymbol{y}^* = \mathscr{E}\boldsymbol{x}_1^* = \cdots = \mathscr{E}\boldsymbol{x}_s^* = 0$. (If not, one can redefine our problem in terms of the correspondence $y_i^* \leftrightarrow y_i^* - \bar{y}^*$, $x_{ji}^* \leftrightarrow x_{ji}^* - \bar{x}_j^*$, $j = 1, \ldots, s$, $i = 1, \ldots, N$, where $N\bar{y}^* = \sum_{i=1}^N y_i^*$, $N\bar{x}_j^* = \sum_{i=1}^N x_{ji}^*$, and then proceed.)

To explain this method of estimation most expeditiously, I must digress and introduce to you the cumulants of a multivariate distribution. Consider the characteristic function $\phi_X(T)$ of the multivariate distribution whose density is $f_X(X)$. Now suppose we can expand $\log \phi_X(T)$ in powers of the t_i's, that is,

$$\log \phi_X(T) = \sum_{j=1}^{\infty} \sum_{j_1 + \cdots + j_s = j} \kappa_X(j_1, \ldots, j_s) \frac{(it_1)^{j_1} \cdots (it_s)^{j_s}}{j_1! \cdots j_s!}.$$

The coefficient $\kappa_X(j_1, \ldots, j_s)$ of $t_1^{j_1} \cdots t_s^{j_s}$ is called the $(j_1, \ldots, j_s)$th *cumulant* of $f_X(X)$. Cumulants have some very nice properties, the most useful to us being those given in the following exercises.

Exercise: (1) If $f_X(X) = \prod_{i=1}^s f_{X_i}(x_i)$, then $\kappa_X(j_1, \ldots, j_s) = 0$ if $j_k, j_l > 0$ for some k, l with $k \neq l$.

(2) Let $\boldsymbol{X}$ and $\boldsymbol{Y}$ be independent s-vectors, with $\kappa_X(j_1, \ldots, j_s)$ and $\kappa_Y(j_1, \ldots, j_s)$ the $(j_1, \ldots, j_s)$th cumulant of $\boldsymbol{X}$ and $\boldsymbol{Y}$, respectively. Let $\boldsymbol{Z} = \boldsymbol{X} + \boldsymbol{Y}$. Then,

$$\kappa_Z(j_1, \ldots, j_s) = \kappa_X(j_1, \ldots, j_s) + \kappa_Y(j_1, \ldots, j_s).$$

(The property given in this exercise is especially handy, as there is no comparable property for moments of sums of independent vectors.)

Now consider the $(j_0, \ldots, j_s)$th cumulant of $\boldsymbol{Z} = (\boldsymbol{y}, \boldsymbol{x}_1, \ldots, \boldsymbol{x}_s)$, $\kappa_Z(j_0, \ldots, j_s)$. Since

$$\begin{aligned}
\boldsymbol{Z} &= (\beta_1 \boldsymbol{x}_1^* + \cdots + \beta_s \boldsymbol{x}_s^* + \boldsymbol{v}, \boldsymbol{x}_1^* + \boldsymbol{u}_1, \ldots, \boldsymbol{x}_s^* + \boldsymbol{u}_s) \\
&= (\beta_1 \boldsymbol{x}_1^* + \cdots + \beta_s \boldsymbol{x}_s^*, \boldsymbol{x}_1^*, \ldots, \boldsymbol{x}_s^*) + (\boldsymbol{v}, \boldsymbol{u}_1, \ldots, \boldsymbol{u}_s) \\
&= \boldsymbol{Z}^* + \boldsymbol{W},
\end{aligned}$$

where $\boldsymbol{W}$ and $\boldsymbol{Z}^*$ are independent, we see that

$$\kappa_Z(j_0, \ldots, j_s) = \kappa_{Z^*}(j_0, \ldots, j_s) + \kappa_W(j_0, \ldots, j_s).$$

Since $\boldsymbol{v}, \boldsymbol{u}_1, \ldots, \boldsymbol{u}_s$ are all independent, if $j_k, j_l > 0$ for some $k, l, k \neq l$, we note that $\kappa_W(j_0, \ldots, j_s) = 0$ in that case, so that

$$\kappa_Z(j_0, \ldots, j_s) = \kappa_{Z^*}(j_0, \ldots, j_s).$$

Let $\kappa_{X^*}(j_1, \ldots, j_s)$ be the $(j_1, \ldots, j_s)$th cumulant of $\boldsymbol{X}^*$. Let us express $\kappa_{Z^*}(j_0, \ldots, j_s)$ in terms of cumulants of $\boldsymbol{X}^*$. If $T = (t_0, t_1, \ldots, t_s)$, then

$$TZ^{*\prime} = (t_0\beta_1 + t_1)x_1^* + \cdots + (t_s\beta_s + t_s)x_n^*.$$

Now

$$\log \phi_{X^*}(R) = \sum_{j=1}^{\infty} \sum_{j_1+\cdots+j_s=j} \frac{\kappa_{X^*}(j_1, \ldots, j_s)}{j_1! \cdots j_s!} r_1^{j_1} \cdots r_s^{j_s},$$

so that

$$\begin{aligned}
\log \phi_{Z^*}(T) &= \sum_{j=1}^{\infty} \sum_{j_1+\cdots+j_s=j} \frac{\kappa_{X^*}(j_1, \ldots, j_s)}{j_1! \cdots j_s!} \\
&\quad \times (t_0\beta_1 + t_1)^{j_1} \cdots (t_0\beta_s + t_s)^{j_s} \\
&= \sum_{j=1}^{\infty} \sum_{j_1+\cdots+j_s=j} \frac{\kappa_{X^*}(j_1, \ldots, j_s)}{j_1! \cdots j_s!} \\
&\quad \times \sum_{i_1=0}^{j_1} \cdots \sum_{i_n=0}^{j_s} \binom{j_1}{i_1} \cdots \binom{j_s}{i_s} \\
&\quad \times \beta_1^{j_1-i_1} \cdots \beta_s^{j_s-i_s} t_0^{j-i_1-\cdots-i_s} t_1^{i_1} \cdots t_s^{i_s}.
\end{aligned}$$

Thus,

$$\begin{aligned}
\frac{\kappa_{Z^*}(i_0, i_1, \ldots, i_s)}{i_0! \cdots i_s!} &= \sum_{\substack{j_1+\cdots+j_s \\ = i_0+\cdots+i_s \\ j_k \geq i_k}} \frac{\kappa_{X^*}(j_1, \ldots, j_s)}{j_1! \cdots j_s!} \\
&\quad \times \beta_1^{j_1-i_1} \cdots \beta_n^{j_s-i_s} \binom{j_1}{i_1} \cdots \binom{j_s}{i_s},
\end{aligned}$$

or

$$\begin{aligned}
\kappa_{Z^*}(i_0, i_1, \ldots, i_s) = i_0! &\sum_{\substack{j_1+\cdots+j_s \\ = i_0+\cdots+i_s \\ j_k \geq i_k}} \frac{\kappa_{X^*}(j_1, \ldots, j_s)}{(j_1 - i_1)! \cdots (j_s - i_s)!} \\
&\times \beta_1^{j_1-i_1} \cdots \beta_s^{j_s-i_s}.
\end{aligned}$$

Consequently,

$$\begin{aligned}
\kappa_{Z^*}(i_0 + 1, i_1, \ldots, i_s) &= \beta_1\kappa_{Z^*}(i_0, i_1 + 1, i_2, \ldots, i_s) \\
&\quad + \beta_2\kappa_{Z^*}(i_0, i_1, i_2 + 1, i_3, \ldots, i_s) \\
&\quad + \cdots + \beta_s\kappa_{Z^*}(i_0, i_1, \ldots, i_{s-1}, i_s + 1).
\end{aligned}$$

Exercise: Check this.

The β's are then determined by the solution of s linearly independent linear equations of the above sort based on s different choices of $(i_0, i_1, \ldots, i_s)$, if s such choices can be found. For example, when $s = 2$, one might take (i_0, i_1, i_2) to be $(1, 1, 3)$ and $(0, 1, 2)$, and solve

$$\kappa_{Z^*}(2, 1, 3) = \beta_1 \kappa_{Z^*}(1, 2, 3) + \beta_2 \kappa_{Z^*}(1, 1, 4),$$
$$\kappa_{Z^*}(1, 1, 2) = \beta_1 \kappa_{Z^*}(0, 2, 2) + \beta_2 \kappa_{Z^*}(0, 1, 3),$$

for β_1, β_2.

The cumulants of a multivariate distribution can be estimated unbiasedly and consistently by the so-called sample k-statistics. As the cumulants are functions of the moments of the distribution, which are consistently (though not unbiasedly) estimated by the sample moments, one can also estimate the cumulants consistently by rewriting the cumulants in terms of the moments and replacing these moments by their estimates, the sample moments. In either event, the solution of the resulting s linear equations based on the estimates of the cumulants as coefficients of the β's is a consistent estimator of the vector of β's.

That if $\boldsymbol{X}^*$ is normally distributed there will be no set of s choices of $(i_0, i_1, \ldots, i_s)$ such that the equations based on these choices are linearly independent is a consequence of the following observation. Note that

$$\phi_{X^*}(T) = \exp\{\mathrm{i}T\mu' - \tfrac{1}{2}T\Sigma T'\},$$

if and only if

$$\log \phi_{X^*}(T) = \mathrm{i}T\mu' - \tfrac{1}{2}T\Sigma T',$$

i.e., if and only if

$$\kappa_{X^*}(i_1, i_2, \ldots, i_s) = 0 \qquad \text{for } \sum_{j=1}^{s} i_j > 2.$$

Therefore because of the one-to-one correspondence between distribution function and characteristic function, $\boldsymbol{X}^*$ is normally distributed if and only if $\kappa_{X^*}(i_1, \ldots, i_s) = 0$ for $\sum_{j=1}^{s} i_j > 2$.

4.3. *Instrumental variables*

Since the structural relation model is unidentifiable when the true data are normally distributed, we might consider altering the model in some manner by embedding it into either a simpler or more complex, but identifiable, model. Such an altered model can take on two forms. Either it leaves the number of sufficient parameters unchanged but reduces the number of unknown model parameters (e.g., in the case where $s = 1$, suppose we know σ_u^2 or σ_v^2 or even σ_u^2/σ_v^2) or it increases the number of sufficient parameters (and possibly the number of model parameters) in such a way that the number of sufficient parameters is at least as great as the number of model parameters. The main example of a model in which the latter is the case is the instrumental variable model.

In this model we suppose that we have in addition N observations on l other normally distributed variables z_i, $i = 1, \ldots, l$, but with normally distributed error $\boldsymbol{w}_i$. What we really observe is $\boldsymbol{z}_i^* = z_i + \boldsymbol{w}_i$, $i = 1, \ldots, l$, where $\mathscr{E}\boldsymbol{w}_i = 0$ and the $\boldsymbol{w}_i$ are uncorrelated with the $\boldsymbol{u}$'s, $\boldsymbol{v}$'s, z's, and $\boldsymbol{x}$'s. We further assume that the $\boldsymbol{x}_j$'s are linearly related to the z's, so that we can express $\boldsymbol{x}_j$ via the linear structural relation

$$\boldsymbol{x}_j = \gamma_{j0} + \gamma_{j1}z_1 + \cdots + \gamma_{jl}z_l,$$

for $j = 1, \ldots, s$.

Suppose for simplicity that $\gamma_{j0} = 0$ for $j = 1, \ldots, n$, and that $\beta_0 = 0$. (To put it another way, suppose each of our N observations on $\boldsymbol{y}^*$, the $\boldsymbol{x}_i^*$, and the $\boldsymbol{z}_i^*$ are measured from their sample means $\bar{\boldsymbol{y}}^*$, $\bar{\boldsymbol{x}}^*$, and $\bar{z}^*$, respectively.) This is really not much of a restriction, since, once we have consistent estimators $\hat{\boldsymbol{\beta}}_1, \ldots, \hat{\boldsymbol{\beta}}_s$ of $\beta_1, \ldots, \beta_s$ and $\hat{\boldsymbol{\gamma}}_{j1}, \ldots, \hat{\boldsymbol{\gamma}}_{jl}$ of $\gamma_{j1}, \ldots, \gamma_{jl}$, then $\hat{\boldsymbol{\beta}}_0 = \bar{\boldsymbol{y}}^* - \hat{\boldsymbol{\beta}}_1\bar{\boldsymbol{x}}_1^* - \cdots - \hat{\boldsymbol{\beta}}\bar{\boldsymbol{x}}^*$ is a consistent estimator of β_0 and $\hat{\boldsymbol{\gamma}}_{j0} = \bar{\boldsymbol{x}}_j^* - \hat{\boldsymbol{\gamma}}_{j1}\bar{z}_1 - \cdots - \hat{\boldsymbol{\gamma}}_{jl}\bar{z}_l$ is a consistent estimator of γ_{j0}.

Let $\boldsymbol{Z} = (z_1, \ldots, z_l)$ be distributed as $N(\nu, \Xi)$, and let Γ be the $s \times l$ matrix whose jth row is $(\gamma_{j1}, \ldots, \gamma_{jl})$. Then $\boldsymbol{X} = \boldsymbol{Z}\Gamma'$ so that, if $\boldsymbol{X}$ is distributed as $N(\mu, \psi)$, then $\mu = \nu\Gamma'$ and $\psi = \Gamma\Xi\Gamma'$. In order for ψ to be of full rank, s, we need $l \geqslant s$ and Γ must be of full rank.

Let $\boldsymbol{W} = (\boldsymbol{w}_1, \ldots, \boldsymbol{w}_l)$, and suppose that $(\boldsymbol{W}, \boldsymbol{U}, \boldsymbol{v})$ is distributed as $N(0, \Delta)$, where Δ is a diagonal matrix. (This is consonant with the minimal assumption made earlier about the number of non-zero elements of Ω.) Then the observable vector $(\boldsymbol{Z}^*, \boldsymbol{X}^*, \boldsymbol{y}^*)$ is distributed as $N((\nu, \nu\Gamma', \nu\Gamma'B'), \Sigma)$, where $B = (\beta_1, \ldots, \beta_s)$, and

$$\Sigma = \begin{bmatrix} \Sigma_{Z^*Z^*} & \Sigma_{Z^*X^*} & \Sigma_{Z^*y^*} \\ \Sigma_{X^*Z^*} & \Sigma_{X^*X^*} & \Sigma_{X^*y^*} \\ \Sigma_{y^*Z^*} & \Sigma_{y^*X^*} & \Sigma_{y^*y^*} \end{bmatrix} = \begin{bmatrix} \Xi & \Xi\Gamma' & \Xi\Gamma'B' \\ \Gamma\Xi & \Gamma\Xi\Gamma' & \Gamma\Xi\Gamma'B' \\ B\Gamma\Xi & B\Gamma\Xi\Gamma' & B\Gamma\Xi\Gamma'B' \end{bmatrix} + \Delta.$$

Counting first the number of sufficient parameters of the distribution of $(\boldsymbol{Z}^*, \boldsymbol{X}^*, \boldsymbol{y}^*)$, we find that this number is $(s+l+1)(s+l+4)/2$. Now let's count the number of model parameters. There are s β's, l ν's, sl elements of Γ, $l(l+1)/2$ distinct elements of Ξ, and $s+l+1$ elements of Δ. Including β_0 and the γ_{j0} as model parameters, we have a total of $(l^2+2sl+6s+sl+4)/2$ model parameters. As the difference between the number of sufficient parameters and model parameters is $s(s-1)$, independent of l, we see that for all $l \geqslant s$ the augmented model has increased the number of sufficient parameters to at least as many as the number of model parameters.

Consider the cross-covariance matrix between $\boldsymbol{y}^* - \boldsymbol{X}^*B'$ and $\boldsymbol{Z}^*$, i.e., the $1 \times l$ matrix whose ith element is $\mathscr{C}(\boldsymbol{y}^* - \boldsymbol{X}^*B', \boldsymbol{z}_i^*) = \mathscr{E}(\boldsymbol{y}^* - \boldsymbol{X}^*B')\boldsymbol{z}_i^* = \mathscr{E}\boldsymbol{y}^*\boldsymbol{z}_i^* - B\mathscr{E}\boldsymbol{X}^{*\prime}\boldsymbol{z}_i^*$. One might adopt as a heuristic description of the instrumental variable estimator of B that vector $\hat{B}$ which makes $\boldsymbol{y}^* - \boldsymbol{X}^*\hat{B}'$ "most uncorrelated" with the vector $\boldsymbol{Z}^*$, i.e., for which $\mathscr{E}\boldsymbol{y}^*\boldsymbol{z}_i^* - \hat{B}\mathscr{E}\boldsymbol{X}^{*\prime}\boldsymbol{z}_i^*$ is in some sense as close to 0 as possible for all $i = 1, \ldots, l$.

However, for $l > s$ it is impossible in general to find a B such that $\Sigma_{y^*Z^*} - B\Sigma_{X^*Z^*} \equiv 0$. We must then define precisely what we mean by "most uncorrelated". We can, for example, say that $\boldsymbol{y}^* - \boldsymbol{X}^*B'$ is most uncorrelated with $\boldsymbol{Z}^*$ if $\|\Sigma_{y^*Z^*} - B\Sigma_{X^*Z^*}\|$ is minimum. This leads us, by Theorem 15, to $B = \Sigma_{y^*Z^*}\Sigma^{+}_{X^*Z^*} = \Sigma_{y^*Z^*}\Sigma'_{X^*Z^*}(\Sigma_{X^*Z^*}\Sigma'_{X^*Z^*})^{-1}$, and thus to $\hat{\boldsymbol{B}} = \boldsymbol{y}^*\boldsymbol{Z}^{*\prime}\boldsymbol{Z}^*\boldsymbol{X}^{*\prime}(\boldsymbol{X}^*\boldsymbol{Z}^{*\prime}\boldsymbol{Z}^*\boldsymbol{X}^{*\prime})^{-1}$. More generally, one can use the arbitrary generalized solution $B = \Sigma_{y^*Z^*}M\Sigma'_{X^*Z^*}(\Sigma_{X^*Z^*}M\Sigma'_{X^*Z^*})^{-1}$, where M is a positive definite $l \times l$ matrix. This solution minimizes $\|(\Sigma_{y^*Z^*} - B\Sigma_{X^*Z^*})T\|$, where $M = TT'$ and T is triangular, that is, it minimizes a weighted norm.

Another way of interpreting the condition that $\boldsymbol{y}^* - \boldsymbol{X}^*B'$ is "most uncorrelated" with $\boldsymbol{Z}^*$ is the following. Consider the random variable $A\boldsymbol{Z}^{*\prime}$, where $A = (\alpha_1, \ldots, \alpha_l)$ is chosen such that $\mathscr{V}(A\boldsymbol{Z}^{*\prime}) = A\Sigma_{Z^*Z^*}A' = 1$. Let $\Phi = (\phi_0, \phi_1, \ldots, \phi_s)$, and consider the random variable $\phi_0\boldsymbol{y}^* + (\phi_1, \ldots, \phi_s)\boldsymbol{X}^{*\prime}$, where Φ is so chosen that $\mathscr{V}(\phi_0\boldsymbol{y}^* + (\phi_1, \ldots, \phi_s)\boldsymbol{X}^{*\prime}) = 1$. Let us find vectors A and Φ which minimize the covariance between these two random variables.

This requires that we look at the Lagrangian

$$\xi = A[\Sigma_{Z^*y^*} \;\; \Sigma_{Z^*X^*}]\Phi' - \frac{\lambda_1}{2}(A\Sigma_{Z^*Z^*}A' - 1)$$

$$-\frac{\lambda_2}{2}\left(\Phi\begin{bmatrix}\Sigma_{y^*y^*} & \Sigma_{y^*X^*}\\ \Sigma_{X^*y^*} & \Sigma_{X^*X^*}\end{bmatrix}\Phi' - 1\right).$$

Since

$$\frac{\partial \xi}{\partial A} = [\Sigma_{Z^*y^*} \ \ \Sigma_{Z^*X^*}]\Phi' - \lambda_1 \Sigma_{Z^*Z^*} A' = 0,$$

$$\frac{\partial \xi}{\partial \Phi} = [\Sigma_{Z^*y^*} \ \ \Sigma_{Z^*X^*}]' A' - \lambda_2 \Sigma^* \Phi' = 0,$$

where

$$\Sigma^* = \begin{bmatrix} \Sigma_{y^*y^*} & \Sigma_{y^*X^*} \\ \Sigma_{X^*y^*} & \Sigma_{X^*X^*} \end{bmatrix},$$

we see that

$$\lambda_1 = A[\Sigma_{Z^*y^*} \ \ \Sigma_{Z^*X^*}]\Phi',$$

$$\lambda_2 = \Phi[\Sigma_{Z^*y^*} \ \ \Sigma_{Z^*X^*}]' A',$$

or

$$\lambda_1 = \lambda_2 = \Phi[\Sigma_{Z^*y^*} \ \ \Sigma_{Z^*X^*}]' A'.$$

Then A and Φ satisfy

$$\Phi[\Sigma_{Z^*y^*} \ \ \Sigma_{Z^*X^*}]' \Sigma_{Z^*Z^*}^{-1} = \{\Phi[\Sigma_{Z^*y^*} \ \ \Sigma_{Z^*X^*}]' A'\} A,$$

as can be seen from solving the first equation. Also, substituting this expression for A into the second equation, we see that

$$[\Sigma_{Z^*y^*} \ \ \Sigma_{Z^*X^*}]' \Sigma_{Z^*Z^*}^{-1} [\Sigma_{Z^*y^*} \ \ \Sigma_{Z^*X^*}]\Phi = \{\Phi[\Sigma_{Z^*y^*} \ \ \Sigma_{Z^*X^*}]' A'\}^2 \Sigma^* \Phi'.$$

Thus Φ is a characteristic vector, corresponding to characteristic root $\{\Phi[\Sigma_{Z^*y^*} \ \ \Sigma_{Z^*X^*}]' A'\}^2$, of the matrix

$$\Sigma^{*-1}[\Sigma_{Z^*y^*} \ \ \Sigma_{Z^*X^*}]' \Sigma_{Z^*Z^*}^{-1} [\Sigma_{Z^*y^*} \ \ \Sigma_{Z^*X^*}].$$

Renormalizing Φ so that $\phi_0 = 1$, we find that $\beta_i = -\phi_i/\phi_0$, $i = 1, \ldots, s$.

The sample correlative of this B has an intrinsic geometric interpretation. Define the cosine of the angle between two n-vectors C and D as

$$\cos \angle C, D = \frac{CD'}{\sqrt{(CC'DD')}}.$$

This is just the cosine of the angle formed by the two lines from 0 to C and from 0 to D in n-space. Let C be a vector in the subspace $\mathscr{C}$ of n-space, and D be a vector in the subspace $\mathscr{D}$ of n-space. Define the cosine of the angle between $\mathscr{C}$ and $\mathscr{D}$ as

$$\cos \angle \mathscr{C}, \mathscr{D} = \min_{C \in \mathscr{C}, D \in \mathscr{D}} \cos \angle C, D.$$

Let $C_1, \ldots, C_p$ be a basis for $\mathscr{C}$, $D_1, \ldots, D_q$ be a basis for $\mathscr{D}$. Then

$$\cos \angle \mathscr{C}, \mathscr{D} = \min_{\{\epsilon_i, \delta_j\}} \cos \angle \sum_{i=1}^{p} \epsilon_i C_i, \sum_{j=1}^{q} \delta_j D_j.$$

There is no loss of generality in assuming that the basis vectors are normalized so that their lengths are 1. Then

$$\cos \angle \mathscr{C}, \mathscr{D} = \min_{\{\epsilon_i, \delta_j\}} \sum_{i=1}^{p} \sum_{j=1}^{q} \epsilon_i \delta_j C_i D'_j.$$

Now make the correspondence $n = N$, $p = s+1$, $q = l$, $C_1 = (y_1^*, \ldots, y_N^*)$, $C_2 = (x_{11}^*, \ldots, x_{1N}^*), \ldots,$ $C_p = (x_{s1}^*, \ldots, x_{sN}^*)$, $D_1 = (z_{11}^*, \ldots, z_{1N}^*), \ldots,$ $D_q = (z_{l1}^*, \ldots, z_{lN}^*)$, $(\epsilon_1, \ldots, \epsilon_p) = (\phi_0, \ldots, \phi_s) = \Phi$, $(\delta_1, \ldots, \delta_q) = (\alpha_1, \ldots, \alpha_l) = A$. Then,

$$\cos \angle \mathscr{C}, \mathscr{D} = \min_{A,\, \Phi} A[\hat{\Sigma}_{Z^*y^*}, \hat{\Sigma}_{Z^*X^*}]\Phi',$$

subject to the normalizations $A\hat{\Sigma}_{Z^*Z^*}A' = 1$, $\Phi\hat{\Sigma}^{*\prime}\Phi' = 1$. This minimization problem is the same as the previous one, except that population parameters are replaced by sample estimates. Thus the instrumental variable estimator obtained in this way has the interpretation of minimizing the cosine of the angle between $\mathscr{C}$ and $\mathscr{D}$. In the limit in probability as $N \to \infty$ this estimator minimizes the covariance between $y^* - X^*B'$ and $AX^{*\prime}$.

When $l = s$, this estimator takes on the simple form

$$\hat{B} = \hat{\Sigma}_{y^*Z^*}\,\hat{\Sigma}_{X^*Z^*}^{-1} = \left(\sum_{i=1}^{N} y_i^* Z_i^*\right)\left(\sum_{i=1}^{N} X_i^{*\prime} Z_i^*\right)^{-1}.$$

We motivated the rationale for the method of instrumental variables by considering the structural relation and counting the number of sufficient parameters and model parameters in this case. Yet our heuristic and eventual rigorous description of the instrumental variable estimator of B was in terms of the observables y^*, X^* and Z^*, quite independent of whether the underlying model was a structural or functional relation. Thus, the method of instrumental variables produces a consistent estimator of B in either case.

There is a special method of estimating $\beta = \beta_1$ when $s = 1$, known as the method of grouping which can be interpreted as an application of the use of an instrumental variable in the following way. Let $l = 1$ and define

$$z_i = \begin{cases} 1, & \text{if} \quad x_i^* \leqslant x_{(p_1)}^*, \\ 0, & \text{if} \quad x_{(p_1)}^* < x_i^* < x_{(p_2)}^*, \\ -1, & \text{if} \quad x_i^* \geqslant x_{(p_2)}^*, \end{cases}$$

where $x_{(p_1)}^*$ and $x_{(p_2)}^*$ are the p_1th and p_2th ordered values of the x_i^*, $p_1 < p_2$. Suppose further that $w_i = 0$ for all $i = 1, \ldots, N$. Then

$$\hat{\beta} = \frac{\sum_{i=1}^{N} y_i^* z_i}{\sum_{i=1}^{N} x_i z_i} = \frac{\sum_{i \in G_1} y_i^* - \sum_{i \in G_2} y_i^*}{\sum_{i \in G_1} x_i^* - \sum_{i \in G_2} x_i^*}$$

where G_1 is the set of all i for which $x_i^* \leqslant x_{(p_1)}^*$ and G_2 is the set of all i for which $x_i^* \geqslant x_{(p_2)}^*$.

Though this estimator is formally obtained using z as an instrumental variable, the estimator should not be construed as one based on the method of instrumental variables for the following reasons: (1) z_i is correlated with $\boldsymbol{u}_i$, as $\boldsymbol{z}_i$ is defined in terms of the observable $\boldsymbol{x}_i^*$'s, not the $\boldsymbol{x}_i$'s, and (2) it is inconceivable that $\boldsymbol{x}_i$ is linearly structurally related to $\boldsymbol{z}_i$ as defined. Objection (1) is the critical one. In fact, it can be shown that, unless the distribution of $\boldsymbol{x}$ has "gaps" (i.e., intervals of zero probability) of sufficient length at "appropriate places", $\hat{\boldsymbol{\beta}}$ is not a consistent estimator of β. Similar remarks can be made about the generalization of this estimator for $s > 1$.

4.4. *Maximum likelihood estimation in restricted models*

As mentioned earlier, another way of altering the model to produce an identifiable model is to reduce the number of unknown model parameters. The main case in which a maximum likelihood estimate of B is determined for such a model is in the functional relation wherein Ω, the covariance matrix of the errors, is of the form $\Omega = \omega A$, when A is a known $(s+1) \times (s+1)$ matrix and ω is a single parameter. In this case the likelihood function of $(\boldsymbol{X}^*, \boldsymbol{y}^*)$ is

$$\prod_{i=1}^{N} f_{\boldsymbol{X}_i^*, \boldsymbol{y}_i^*}(X_i^*, y_i^*) = (2\pi) - \frac{(s+1)N}{2} \omega^{-N(s+1)/2} |A|^{-N/2}$$
$$\times \exp\left\{-\left(\frac{1}{2\omega}\right) \sum_{i=1}^{N} \left(X_i^* - X_i, y_i^* - \sum_{j=1}^{s} \beta_j x_{ij}\right)\right.$$
$$\left. \times A^{-1} \left(X_i^* - X, y_i^* - \sum_{j=1}^{s} \beta_j x_{ij}\right)'\right\},$$

(where, as above, $\boldsymbol{X}_i^*$, $\boldsymbol{y}_i^*$ are measured from their sample mean, so that we can take $\beta_0 = 0$). It is better to define $W_i^* = (X_i^*, y_i^*)$ and $W_i = (X_i, y_i)$ with the constraints that

$$w_{i,s+1} = \sum_{j=1}^{s} \beta_j w_{ij}, \qquad i = 1, \dots, N.$$

Then our problem is to maximize

$$\frac{-N(s+1)}{2} \log \omega - \frac{1}{2\omega} \sum_{i=1}^{N} (W_i^* - W_i)A^{-1}(W_i^* - W_i)',$$

subject to these constraints.

Obviously, given the $\hat{W}_i$, the maximum likelihood estimate of the W_i, the maximum likelihood estimate of ω is

$$\hat{\omega} = \sum_{i=1}^{N} \frac{(W_i^* - \hat{W}_i)A^{-1}(W_i^* - \hat{W}_i)'}{N(s+1)}.$$

Our problem then reduces to that of maximizing $(-N(s+1)/2) \log \hat{\omega}$, or, better yet, minimizing $\hat{\omega}$ with respect to the $\hat{W}_i$ and the $\hat{\beta}_j$ subject to the constraint that

$$\hat{w}_{i,s+1} = \sum_{j=1}^{s} \hat{\beta}_j \hat{w}_{ij}, \qquad i = 1, \dots, N.$$

Let W^* be the $N \times (s+1)$ matrix whosc ith row is W_i^* and W be the $N \times (s+1)$ matrix whose ith row is W_i. Our problem is to minimize $\operatorname{tr}(W^* - W)A^{-1}(W^* - W)'$ with respect to W and $B = (\beta_1, \dots, \beta_s)$, subject to the constraint

$$(-1, B)W' = 0.$$

Let $A^{-1} = TT'$, and $Z^* = W^*T$, $Z = WT$. Then the constraint is

$$(-1, B)T^{-1\prime}Z' = 0,$$

and we must minimize $Q = \operatorname{tr}(Z^* - Z)(Z^* - Z)'$. To simplify the problem still further, let $D = Z^* - Z$. Then $Q = \operatorname{tr} DD' = \sum_{j=1}^{N} D_j D_j'$, where D_j is the jth row of D. The constraint is

$$(-1, B)T^{-1\prime}(D - Z^*)' = 0,$$

or

$$(-1, B)T^{-1\prime}Z_j^{*\prime} - (-1, B)T^{-1\prime}D_j' = 0, \qquad j = 1, \dots, N,$$

where Z^*_j is the jth row of Z^*. Thus our problem separates into N constrained minimizations in the N vectors D_j.

Let

$$\mathcal{L}_j = D_jD'_j + 2\lambda_j((-1, B)T^{-1\prime}Z^{*\prime}_j - (-1, B)T^{-1\prime}D'_j)$$

be the Lagrangian for the jth minimization problem, with $2\lambda_j$ the Lagrange multiplier. Then,

$$\frac{\partial \mathcal{L}_j}{\partial D_j} = 2D_j - 2\lambda_j(-1, B)T^{-1\prime} = 0$$

implies that

$$D_j = \lambda_j(-1, B)T^{-1\prime}.$$

Substituting this into the constraint, we have

$$0 = (-1, B)T^{-1\prime}Z^{*\prime}_j - \lambda_j(-1, B)T^{-1\prime}T^{-1}\begin{pmatrix}-1\\ B'\end{pmatrix},$$

or

$$\lambda_j = \frac{(-1, B)T^{-1\prime}Z^{*\prime}_j}{(-1, B)A^{-1}\begin{pmatrix}-1\\ B'\end{pmatrix}}.$$

Thus

$$\begin{aligned} Q &= \sum_{j=1}^{N} D_jD'_j \\ &= \sum_{j=1}^{N} \lambda_j^2(-1, B)A^{-1}\begin{pmatrix}-1\\ B'\end{pmatrix} \\ &= \sum_{j=i}^{N} \frac{[(-1, B)T^{-1\prime}Z'_j]^2}{(-1, B)A^{-1}\begin{pmatrix}-1\\ B'\end{pmatrix}}, \end{aligned}$$

which is to be minimized with respect to B. To achieve this end, let $G'_j = T^{-1\prime}Z^{*\prime}_j$, $G = \sum_{j=1}^{N} G'_jG_j$, and $C = (-1, B)$. Then

$$Q = \sum_{j=1}^{N} \frac{(CG'_j)^2}{CA^{-1}C'} = \sum_{j=1}^{N} \frac{CG'_jG_jC'}{CA^{-1}C'} = \frac{CGC'}{CA^{-1}C'}$$

But minimizing Q is equivalent to minimizing

$$q = \log Q = \log CGC' - \log CA^{-1}C'.$$

As

$$\frac{\partial q}{\partial G} = \frac{2CG}{CGC'} - \frac{2CA^{-1}}{CA^{-1}C'} = 0,$$

if, and only if, $CG = \xi CA$, or $CT^{-1\prime} \sum_{j=1}^{N} Z_j^{*\prime} Z_j^{*} T^{-1} = \xi CT^{-1\prime} T^{-1}$, or

$$C \sum_{j=1}^{N} Z_j^{*\prime} Z_j^{*} = \xi C,$$

where $\xi = CA^{-1}C'/CGC'$, we see that C must be a characteristic vector associated with characteristic root ξ of the matrix $\sum_{j=1}^{N} Z_j^{*\prime} Z_j^{*}$.

The appropriate root must be the smallest root, as

$$Q = \xi \frac{GAGAG'}{GAG'}$$

is monotone, increasing in ξ.

In summary, to estimate B, we first find the characteristic vector C associated with the smallest characteristic root of $\sum_{j=1}^{N} Z_j^{*\prime} Z_j^{*}$, then normalize C so that its first coordinate is -1, and finally take B as the last s coordinates of this normalized C. Since

$$\sum_{i=j}^{N} Z_j^{*\prime} Z_j^{*} = T' \sum_{j=1}^{N} W_j^{*} W_j^{*} T,$$

the appropriate characteristic root also satisfies the determinantal equation

$$\left| \sum_{j=1}^{N} W_j^{*\prime} W_j^{*} - \xi A \right| = 0,$$

and is presented in most texts in this form.

5. References

Though there are many books written on the subject matter of this chapter, "regression analysis", none organizes the material in quite the form done here. The best general text containing an exposition of the material in this chapter is:

Malinvaud, E., 1966, Statistical methods of econometrics (Rand McNally, Chicago).

Chapters 5 and 6 parallel sections 1.1, 1.2, 2.1 and 2.2, chapter 13 parallels section 2.3, chapter 14 parallels section 3, and chapter 10 parallels section 4.

Some of the material in section 2 relates to the problem of pooling cross-section and time series data. A good reference to this problem is:

Balestra, P. and M. Nerlove, 1966, Pooling cross section and time series data in the estimation of a dynamic model: The demand for natural gas, Econometrica 34, pp. 585–612.

The distinction between the three cases, functional relation, regression, and structural relation was first made in:

Kendall, M. G., 1951, Regression, structure, and functional relationships, Part I, Biometrika 38, pp. 11–25.

The regression relation and the structural relation with error in the dependent variable have been dubbed first "unbiased predictor" and later "eo ipso predictor" in:

Wold, H. O. A., 1961, Unbiased predictors, Fourth Berkeley Symposium on Mathematical Statistics and Probability, vol. 1 (University of California Press, Berkeley) pp. 719–761.

Wold, H. O. A., 1963, On the consistency of least squares regression, Sankhya 25, pp. 211–215.

In their chapter 13, Wold and Jurgen distinguish between the Gauss–Fischer specification and the Galton–Yule specification of regression analysis. In our terminology, given error only in the dependent variable, the Gauss–Fisher specification corresponds to the functional relation and the Galton–Yule specification corresponds to the (indistinguishable ex post) regression relation and structural relation. See:

Wold, H. O. A. and L. Jureen, 1952, Demand analysis (Wiley, New York).

There is now a great literature on the relation between the generalized inverse and the problems of this chapter. A fine reference for section 7 of chapter I and the least squares material in this chapter is:

Rao, C. R. and S. K. Mitra, 1971, Generalized inverse of matrices and its applications (Wiley, New York).

The reasoning behind the interest in linear unbiased estimators given in section 1.2 is taken from unpublished notes by W. H. Kruskal. However, the following paper contains some parallels to this argument:

Barnard, G. A., 1963, The logic of least squares, Journal of the Royal Statistical Society B, 25, pp. 124–127.

Some of the material in section 1.2 on the effect of X being random is based on chapter 6, "Linear regression with stochastic regressors", of:

Goldberger, A. S., 1964, Econometric theory (Wiley, New York).

The only sampling properties of $\hat{\boldsymbol{B}}$ given in this chapter were the three results in section 1.2 that

(1) $\hat{\boldsymbol{B}}^* = (\hat{\boldsymbol{\beta}}_{11}, \ldots, \hat{\boldsymbol{\beta}}_{1p}, \hat{\boldsymbol{\beta}}_{21}, \ldots, \hat{\boldsymbol{\beta}}_{2p}, \ldots, \hat{\boldsymbol{\beta}}_{n1}, \ldots, \hat{\boldsymbol{\beta}}_{np})$ is distributed as $N(B^*, \Sigma \otimes (XX')^{-1})$, where

$$B^* = (\beta_{11}, \ldots, \beta_{1p}, \beta_{21}, \ldots, \beta_{2p}, \ldots, \beta_{n1}, \ldots, \beta_{np}).$$

(2) If the columns of $\boldsymbol{X}$ are independent and identically distributed (or more generally if the $\boldsymbol{Y}_i$ conditional on the values of the $\boldsymbol{X}_i$, are independent and homoscedastic), then $\mathscr{E}\hat{\boldsymbol{B}}^* = B^*$ and

$$\mathscr{V}\hat{\boldsymbol{B}}^* = \Sigma \otimes \mathscr{E}_{\boldsymbol{X}}(\boldsymbol{X}\boldsymbol{X}')^{-1}.$$

(3) If $\text{plim}_{N\to\infty} (1/N)\boldsymbol{X}\boldsymbol{X}' = \Xi$ is non-singular, then

$$\underset{N\to\infty}{\text{plim}} \frac{1}{N} \mathscr{V}_{\boldsymbol{Y}|\boldsymbol{X}}\hat{\boldsymbol{B}}^* = \Sigma \otimes \Xi^{-1}.$$

We did not discuss sampling properties of $\hat{\boldsymbol{B}}^*$ when the $\boldsymbol{Y}_i$ were correlated or in the case of linear stochastic difference equations, primarily due to the paucity and complexity of results. In the case of the maximum likelihood estimators of section 2.1, we fall back upon the general asymptotic properties of these estimators and expect that the regularity conditions for them to hold are met. In the case considered in section 2.2, where $n = 1$, $\hat{\boldsymbol{B}}$ is a linear transformation of $\boldsymbol{Y}$, and so $\hat{\boldsymbol{B}}$ is normally distributed if $\boldsymbol{Y}$ is. The expected value and variance of $\hat{\boldsymbol{B}}$ are given in section 2.2. If $\boldsymbol{X}$ is random, then a result similar to (3) above holds in this case.

In the case of autoregressive errors treated in section 2.3, the only asymptotic properties studied are those of the ordinary least squares estimator and the Aitken generalization (when Ω is known) in this case. The arguments lean heavily on spectral analysis and the results are so couched, and so are not cited here. However, for the interested reader the relevant literature is:

Rosenblatt, M., 1956, On the estimation of regression coefficients of a vector-valued time series with a stationary residual, Annals of Mathematical Statistics 27, pp. 99–121.

Hannan, E. J., 1961, A central limit theorem for systems of regressions, Proceedings of the Cambridge Philosophical Society 57, pp. 583–588.

Eicher, F., 1963, Asymptotic normality and consistency of the least squares estimators for families of linear regressions, Annals of Mathematical Statistics 34, pp. 447–456.

Eicher, F., 1965, Limit theorems for regressions with unequal and dependent errors, in: J. Neyman, ed., Proceedings of the Fifth Berkeley Symposium on Mathematical Statistics and Probability, vol. 1 (University of California Press, Berkeley) pp. 59–82.

In the case of linear stochastic difference equations, Mann and Wald show that the ordinary least squares estimator is consistent and asymptotically normal in case all the roots of the characteristic polynomial are of modulus less than 1:

Mann, H. B. and A. Wald, 1943, On the statistical treatment of linear stochastic difference equations, Econometrica 11, pp. 173–220.

Key papers covering asymptotic theory of least squares estimators in the "explosive" case, where at least one root has modulus exceeding 1, are:

Anderson, T. W., 1959, On asymptotic distributions of estimates of parameters of stochastic difference equations, Annals of Mathematical Statistics 30, pp. 676–687.

Rao, M. M., 1961, Consistency and limit distributions of estimators of parameters in explosive stochastic difference equations, Annals of Mathematical Statistics 32, pp. 195–218.

The estimation procedure of section 2.3 is taken from the next reference, where also is shown that the asymptotic distribution of this estimator is the same as that of the ordinary least squares estimator:

Durbin, J., 1960, Estimation of parameters in time-series regression models, Journal of the Royal Statistical Society B, 22, pp. 139–153.

A good basic reference for linear difference equation theory is:

Goldberg, S., 1958, Introduction to difference equations (Wiley, New York).

The argument given in section 3 about the non-uniqueness of the solution of the linear stochastic difference equation is based on chapter I (section 3) of:

Hannan, E. J., 1960, Time series analysis (Methuen, London).

The identifiability theorem for the structural relation is proven in:

Reiersol, O., 1950, Identifiability of a linear relation between variables which are subject to error, Econometrica 18, pp. 375–389.

The proof that in the functional relation case there is no uniformly consistent estimator of the structural parameters is given and the distinction between structural and incidental parameters is first exposited in:

Neyman, J. and E. L. Scott, 1948, Consistent estimators based on partially consistent observations, Econometrica 16, pp. 1–32.

The material of section 4.2 is taken from:

Geary, R. C., 1942, Inherent relations between random variables, Proceedings of the Royal Irish Academy 47, pp. 63–67.

A good exposition of cumulants and k-statistics is:

Kendall, M. G. and A. Stuart, 1963, The advanced theory of statistics, vol. 1 (Griffin, London).

The method of instrumental variables described here is given in:

Geary, R. C., 1949, Determination of linear relations between systematic parts of variables with errors of observation the variances of which are unknown, Econometrica 17, pp. 30–59.

The interpretations of this estimator are taken from:

Durbin, J., 1954, Errors in variables, Revue de l'Institut International de Statistique 22, pp. 23–32.

Sargan, J. D., 1958, The estimation of economic relationships using instrumental variables, Econometrica 26, pp. 393–415.

The "method of grouping" has a long history, primarily as a "quick-and-dirty" method of estimating slopes of straight lines when the independent variable is not measured with error. It was first formally studied in the errors-in-variables context in:

Wald, A., 1940, Fitting of straight lines if both variables are subject to errors, Annals of Mathematical Statistics 11, pp. 284–300.

The objection to this method referred to in the text is given in:

Neyman, J. and E. L. Scott, 1954, On certain methods of estimating the linear structural relation, Annals of Mathematical Statistics 22, pp. 352–361; and 1952, Correction, vol. 23, p. 115.

Other work on this method either assumes that the random independent variable x is observed without error and theoretically determines an optimal grouping procedure based on the distribution of x or performs model sampling experiments to determine optimal grouping procedures empirically.

The material in section 4.4 is referred to in some texts as the method of *weighted regression* and is due to:

Van Uven, M. J., 1930, Adjustment of N points (in n-dimensional space) to the best linear $(n-1)$-dimensional space, Koninklijke Akademie Van Wetenschappen te Amsterdam, Proceedings of the Section of Sciences 33, pp. 143–157, 307–326.

For the relation between Van Uven's work and the method of maximum likelihood, see:

Koopmans, T. C., 1937, Linear regression analysis of economic time series (De Erven F. Bohn, Haarlem, Netherlands).

It is parenthetically interesting to note that if one observes replicated values of x_i, i.e., if one observes $\boldsymbol{x}^*_{i1} = x_i + \boldsymbol{u}_{i1}, \ldots, \boldsymbol{x}^*_{ij_i} = x_i + \boldsymbol{u}_{ij_i}$ and concomitant $\boldsymbol{y}^*_{i1}, \ldots, \boldsymbol{y}^*_{ij_i}$, for $i = 1, \ldots, N$, then the model is identifiable. A simple procedure for obtaining the maximum likelihood estimator of B is given in:

Villegas, C., 1961, Maximum likelihood estimation of a linear functional relationship, Annals of Mathematical Statistics 32, pp. 1048–1062.

It is based on obtaining the maximum likelihood estimate of Ω based on the replicated data and then using the procedure of section 4.4 with $\hat{\Omega}$ replacing Ω.

IV

Simultaneous equation estimation

In this chapter we will add an underlying structure to the coefficient matrix in the linear expected value model, a structure which has proved quite useful to econometric modelers, and review methods of estimating the structural parameters. Suppose that $\mathbf{Z}_i$ is distributed as $N(-X_i\Gamma', \Sigma)$, for $i = 1, \ldots, N$, where $\mathbf{Z}_i$ is an n-vector and X_i is a p-vector, and that we make the transformation $\mathbf{Y}_i = \mathbf{Z}_i B'^{-1}$ so that $\mathbf{Y}_i$ is distributed as $N(-X_i\Gamma' B'^{-1}, B^{-1}\Sigma B'^{-1}) = N(X_i\Pi', \Omega)$. Given observations on the $\mathbf{Y}_i$'s and concomitant X_i's we can estimate Π and Ω using appropriate methods from chapter III, for this is a linear expected value model. If the $\mathbf{Y}_i$ are independent, then Π is optimally estimated by least squares.

Suppose, however, that we are interested in estimating B, Γ, and Σ in this model, with no data on the $\mathbf{Z}_i$'s but data merely on $\mathbf{Y}_i$ and X_i. This is the fundamental problem to be treated in this chapter. As with most models relating manifest parameters (Π and Ω in this case) with latent parameters (B, Γ and Σ in this case), the identifiability problem must be dealt with. We do this in section 1. It may be the case that, though B, Γ, and Σ are not identifiable, a particular row of B and Γ and the corresponding diagonal element of Σ are identifiable, and that the modeler is only interested in that identifiable subset of parameters embedded in a non-identifiable model. Thus the major part of section 1 will be directed to this situation.

Letting $\mathbf{V}_i = \mathbf{Y}_i - X_i\Pi'$ and $\mathbf{U}_i = \mathbf{V}_i B'$, we see that $\mathbf{U}_i = \mathbf{Y}_i B' + X_i\Gamma'$ is distributed as $N(0, \Sigma)$. The parlance "simultaneous equation estimation" stems from the similarity of the expression $\mathbf{Y}_i B' + X_i\Gamma' = \mathbf{U}_i$ to a system of simultaneous linear equations with unknown coefficients, the elements of B and Γ. The linear expected value model $\mathscr{E}\mathbf{Y}_i = X_i\Pi'$, $\mathscr{V}\mathbf{Y}_i = \Omega$ is called the *reduced form* of the simultaneous equations model.

In section 2 we derive the maximum likelihood estimator of the elements of a given row of B and Γ, i.e., of the coefficients of a single equation in the set of simultaneous equations. In section 3 we derive the maximum likelihood estimator of B and Γ and its asymptotic distribution when the system of equations is identifiable. Section 5 contains a general treatment of the case of the method of instrumental variables in estimating B and Γ, viewing the relation $\boldsymbol{Y}_i B' + X_i \Gamma' = \boldsymbol{U}_i$ as an "errors-in-variables" linear expected value model. This is followed by a description of two-stage and three-stage least squares estimates, k-class estimates, principal components estimates. Simultaneous and iterative least squares estimates are considered in sections 4 and 6, respectively.

The variables appearing as elements of $\boldsymbol{Y}_i$ are called *endogenous* variables and those appearing as elements of X_i are called *exogenous* variables. Because we take as our origin for this model the general linear hypothesis, in which the X_i are not random, we will not admit random exogenous variables in the main developments in this chapter. The problem of how to deal with such exogenous variables will be considered in section 7. The most common situation in which this condition hamstrings us is when i indexes time and $x_{ij} = y_{i-l,k}$ for some j, k, l, i.e., when x_{ij} is y_k as observed $i-l$ time periods ago. Then the exogenous variable x_{ij} is a *lagged endogenous* variable and should be treated as a random variable. Though we will not treat any X_i as random in dealing with estimation of a single row of B and Γ, where we deal with all the equations simultaneously, we will take into account the possibility that an exogenous variable is a lagged endogenous variable.

A large degree of difficulty in reading the econometric literature on simultaneous equation estimation stems from both (a) the existence of two standard sets of notation, one invented by the Cowles Commission for Research in Economics and one invented by the Econometric Institute of the Netherlands School of Economics, and (b) the different ways of expressing the underlying model, each convenient for a particular derivation or application of a standard estimation procedure. We have taken it as a task to invent a standard notation which will have the virtue of being mnemonic (the others are not) and as consistent as possible across estimation approaches and alternative expressions of the underlying model.

To begin with, we point out that, since the generic random n-vector is written as $\boldsymbol{Y} = (\boldsymbol{y}_1, \ldots, \boldsymbol{y}_n)$, it would be most natural to express the ith observation of the vector $\boldsymbol{Y}$ as $\boldsymbol{Y}_i = (\boldsymbol{y}_{1i}, \ldots, \boldsymbol{y}_{ni})$, $i = 1, \ldots, N$. This is contrary to the standard rules of naming elements of vectors, where the jth element of a vector named Y_i would be y_{ij}, and not, as here, y_{ji}. But we adopt this natural usage anyway.

We will need to refer to the $N \times n$ matrix Y whose ith row is Y_i, and equally often to the jth column of Y. We might refer to the jth column as Y'_j, i.e., the jth row of Y', but this notation is ambiguous, as it doesn't distinguish between the jth row of Y' and the transpose of the jth row of Y. To eliminate this ambiguity, we will always refer to the matrix Y and call its ith row $Y_{.i}$ and the jth column of Y, expressed as a row-vector, $Y_{j.}$. (The position of the . is to remind you of whether we are considering rows or columns of Y.) Thus $Y'_{j.}$ is the jth column of Y, not the jth column of Y' expressed as a row vector and

$$Y = \begin{bmatrix} Y_{.1} \\ \cdot \\ \cdot \\ \cdot \\ Y_{.N} \end{bmatrix} = [Y'_{1.} \cdots Y'_{n.}].$$

We adopt similar notational conventions for rows and columns of the $N \times p$ matrix X and the $N \times n$ matrix U.

Much of our discussion will focus around the problem of estimating the parameters of a single equation of the system of simultaneous equations, and we can for this purpose adopt the convenience that the equation of interest is the first of the n equations. However, we will need from time to time to refer to the jth equation,

$$\sum_{k=1}^{n} \beta_{jk} y_{ki} + \sum_{k=1}^{p} \gamma_{jk} x_{ki} = u_{ji},$$

for $i = 1, \ldots, N$. When we study the jth equation by itself, we will assume for convenience that all the non-zero β_{jk} precede all the β_{jk} known a priori (from economic theory) to be identically zero, and similarly that all the non-zero γ_{jk} precede the γ_{jk} known to be zero. We let n_j be the number of non-zero β_{jk} and p_j be the number of non-zero γ_{jk}. Thus the jth equation is

$$\sum_{k=1}^{n_j} \beta_{jk} y_{ki} + \sum_{k=1}^{p_j} \gamma_{jk} x_{ki} = u_{ji}, \qquad i = 1, \ldots, N.$$

If B is the $n \times n$ matrix of β_{jk}'s, with jth row B_j, and Γ is the $n \times p$ matrix of γ_{jk}'s with jth row Γ_j, then the jth equation is expressible as

$$Y_{.i} B'_j + X_{.i} \Gamma'_j = u_{ji}, \qquad i = 1, \ldots, N.$$

Defining B_{*j} as the vector consisting of the first n_j elements of B_j, Γ_{*j} as the vector consisting of the first p_j elements of Γ_j, $\boldsymbol{Y}_{j.i}$ as the vector consisting of the first n_j elements of $\boldsymbol{Y}_{.i}$, and $X_{j.i}$ as the vector consisting of the first p_j elements of $X_{.i}$, we can rewrite the jth equation as

$$\boldsymbol{Y}_{j.i}B'_{*j} + X_{j.i}\Gamma'_{*j} = \boldsymbol{u}_{ji}, \qquad i = 1, \ldots, N.$$

We will call this the *simultaneous form* of the jth equation.

There is a usual normalization (to be explained in detail in section 1) of the matrix B wherein $\beta_{jj} = -1$ for all $j = 1, \ldots, n$. Let us further modify the simultaneous form to take explicit account of this normalization. Let $\boldsymbol{Y}_{(j).i}$ be the $(n_j - 1)$-vector consisting of the elements of $\boldsymbol{Y}_{j.i}$ with y_{ji} removed and $B_{*(j)}$ be the $(n_j - 1)$-vector consisting of the elements of B_{*j} with β_{jj} removed. Then we can rewrite the jth equation as

$$y_{ji} = \boldsymbol{Y}_{(j).i}B'_{*(j)} + X_{j.i}\Gamma'_{*j} - \boldsymbol{u}_{ji}, \qquad i = 1, \ldots, N.$$

We will call this the *regression form* of the jth equation.

Mnemonically, one can tell from the subscripts of B whether we are dealing with the jth row (B_j), the first n_j (i.e., the non-zero) elements of the jth row (B_{*j}), or the first n_j elements excluding β_{jj} ($B_{*(j)}$).

When dealing with the regression form of the jth equation, it is often convenient to treat the N observations on the jth equation in vector form. We will let $\boldsymbol{Y}_{*(j)}$ and X_{*j} be respectively the $N \times (n_j - 1)$ and $N \times p_j$ matrices whose ith rows are $\boldsymbol{Y}_{(j).i}$ and $X_{j.i}$. Then the N equations in the regression form can be rewritten as

$$\boldsymbol{Y}'_{j.} = \boldsymbol{Y}_{*(j)}B'_{*(j)} + X_{*j}\Gamma'_{*j} - \boldsymbol{U}'_{j.}.$$

It will be necessary for us in what follows to consider for the jth equation not only the exogenous variables appearing in that equation, i.e., the vector $X_{j.i}$, but also the remaining exogenous variables. We will define $X_{\bar{j}.i}$ as the $(p - p_j)$-vector of the ith observation on the $p - p_j$ exogenous variables whose coefficients are zero in the jth equation. Thus for a given j we assume that $X_{.i}$ is ordered as

$$X_{.i} = (X_{j.i}, X_{\bar{j}.i}),$$

so that X_{*j} has as its ith row the vector $X_{j.i}$, and we define $X_{*\bar{j}}$ as the $N \times (p - p_j)$ matrix whose ith row is the vector $X_{\bar{j}.i}$.

Since the order of the columns in Y (and those in X) depend on the equation under consideration, it might be considered worthwhile to append some notation to Y and X to indicate the equation which dictates the order of the columns. This we shall not do. It will be apparent from context, as well as from expressions such as

$$Y = [Y_{*j} \quad Y_{*\bar{j}}],$$
$$X = [X_{*j} \quad X_{*\bar{j}}],$$

(where Y_{*j} and $Y_{*\bar{j}}$ are defined similarly to X_{*j} and $X_{*\bar{j}}$).

With this notation established, we can rewrite the N equations in the simultaneous form matricially as

$$\boldsymbol{Y}_{*j}B'_{*j} + \boldsymbol{X}_{*j}\Gamma'_{*j} = \boldsymbol{U}'_{j}.$$

(A word of apology is in order for the subscript $*$ being used. It is used as a reminder that the $\boldsymbol{Y}_{.i}$ and $X_{.i}$, $i = 1, \ldots, N$, as well as B_j and Γ_j, are being trimmed appropriately of extraneous elements. Since in $\boldsymbol{Y}_{j.i}$ and $X_{j.i}$ the subscript j preceding the $.i$ does double-duty, in telling you that we are trimming based on the jth equation, we do not append the redundant $*$.)

We can express the simultaneous form of all n equations compactly as

$$\boldsymbol{Y}\boldsymbol{B}' + \boldsymbol{X}\boldsymbol{\Gamma}' = \boldsymbol{U}.$$

However, this form masks the information we have about the zero elements of B and Γ as well as the normalization. To express the regression form of all n equations, and thereby take explicit account of this information, we define the $\sum_{j=1}^{n} (n_j - 1)$-vectors

$$\vec{\boldsymbol{Y}} = (\boldsymbol{Y}_{1.}, \boldsymbol{Y}_{2.}, \ldots, \boldsymbol{Y}_{n.}),$$

and

$$\vec{\boldsymbol{U}} = (\boldsymbol{U}_{1.}, \boldsymbol{U}_{2.}, \ldots, \boldsymbol{U}_{n.}),$$

the $N \times (n_j + p_j - 1)$ matrix $\boldsymbol{Z}_j$ as $\boldsymbol{Z}_j = [\boldsymbol{Y}_{*(j)}, X_{*j}]$, the block diagonal $nN \times \sum_{j=1}^{n} (n_j + p_j - 1)$ matrix $\boldsymbol{Z}$ whose jth diagonal block is $\boldsymbol{Z}_j$, $r_j = (n_j + p_j - 1)$, $r = \sum_{j=1}^{n} r_j$ and the r-vector of parameters

$$\begin{aligned}\Delta &= (B_{*(1)}, \Gamma_{*1}, B_{*(2)}, \Gamma_{*2}, \ldots, B_{*(n)}, \Gamma_{*n}) \\ &= (\Delta_1, \Delta_2, \ldots, \Delta_n),\end{aligned}$$

where $\Delta_j = (B_{*(j)}, \Gamma_{*j})$. Then the regression form of the jth equation is

$$\boldsymbol{Y}'_{j.} = \boldsymbol{Z}_j\Delta'_j - \boldsymbol{U}'_{j}.$$

and the regression form of all n equations is

$$\vec{\mathbf{Y}}' = \mathbf{Z}\boldsymbol{\Delta}' - \vec{\mathbf{U}}'.$$

A consequence of considering the jth equation and partitioning the endogenous and exogenous variables into sets which have and sets which do not have coefficients in the jth equation is that Ω must be similarly partitioned. We will write

$$\Omega = \begin{bmatrix} \Omega_{jj} & \Omega_{j\bar{j}} \\ \Omega_{\bar{j}j} & \Omega_{\bar{j}\bar{j}} \end{bmatrix},$$

where Ω_{jj} is an $n_j \times n_j$ submatrix of the $n \times n$ matrix Ω.

We will also find it useful to partition the $n \times p$ matrix Π of reduced form coefficients to reflect (a) consideration of only the jth equation, (b) ordering the columns of Π in such a way that the exogenous variables appearing in the jth equation precede those which do not appear in that equation, and (c) ordering the rows of Π such that the first row corresponds to y_j, the next rows correspond to the other endogenous variables which appear in the jth equation, and the remaining rows correspond to the remaining endogenous variables.

We let Π_j denote the jth row of Π, and $\Pi_j = (\Pi_{jj}, \Pi_{j\bar{j}})$, where Π_{jj} is the subvector composed of the columns of Π corresponding to the elements of X_{*j}. Thus,

$$\mathbf{Y}'_{j.} = X_{*j}\Pi'_{jj} + X_{*\bar{j}}\Pi'_{j\bar{j}} + \mathbf{V}'_{j.},$$

where $\mathbf{V}_{j.}$ is defined similarly to $\boldsymbol{U}_{j.}$ and is the reduced form error term.

Similarly, let Π_{*j} be the $(n_j - 1) \times p_j$ matrix of reduced form coefficients of the rows of X_{*j} and $\Pi_{*\bar{j}}$ be the $(n_j - 1) \times (p - p_j)$ matrix of reduced form coefficients of the rows of $X_{*\bar{j}}$. Then,

$$\mathbf{Y}_{*(j)} = X_{*j}\Pi'_{*j} + X_{*\bar{j}}\Pi'_{*\bar{j}} + \mathbf{V}_{*(j)}.$$

We can thus define the $n_j \times p$ matrix $\Pi_{(j)}$ as

$$\Pi_{(j)} = \begin{bmatrix} \Pi_{jj} & \Pi_{j\bar{j}} \\ \Pi_{*j} & \Pi_{*\bar{j}} \end{bmatrix} = [\Pi_{(jj)} \quad \Pi_{(j\bar{j})}].$$

The matrix Π can then be expressed as

$$\Pi = \begin{bmatrix} \Pi_{(j)} \\ \Pi_{(\bar{j})} \end{bmatrix} = \begin{bmatrix} \Pi_{(jj)} & \Pi_{(j\bar{j})} \\ \Pi_{(\bar{j}j)} & \Pi_{(\bar{j}\bar{j})} \end{bmatrix},$$

where $\Pi_{(\bar{j}j)}$ and $\Pi_{(\bar{j}\bar{j})}$ are appropriate $(n-n_j)\times p_j$ and $(n-n_j)\times(p-p_j)$ matrices of reduced form coefficients.

The following will be useful as a handy means of reference to our notation, as well as a comparative notational dictionary between our notation and that of the Cowles Commission and the Econometric Institute.

Endogenous variables

Arbitrary order of columns

$$Y = \begin{bmatrix} y_{11} & \cdots & y_{n1} \\ \cdot & & \cdot \\ \cdot & & \cdot \\ \cdot & & \cdot \\ y_{1N} & & y_{nN} \end{bmatrix} = \begin{bmatrix} Y_{.1} \\ \cdot \\ \cdot \\ \cdot \\ Y_{.N} \end{bmatrix} = [Y'_{1.} \cdots Y'_{n.}].$$

Columns ordered on non-zero coefficients of jth *equation*

$$Y_{.i} = [Y_{j.i} \quad Y_{\bar{j}.i}]$$
$$= [(y_{1i}, \ldots, y_{n_j i}), (y_{n_j+1 i}, \ldots, y_{ni})],$$

$$Y_{*j} = \begin{bmatrix} Y_{j.1} \\ \cdot \\ \cdot \\ \cdot \\ Y_{j.N} \end{bmatrix}, \qquad Y_{*\bar{j}} = \begin{bmatrix} Y_{\bar{j}.1} \\ \cdot \\ \cdot \\ \cdot \\ Y_{\bar{j}.N} \end{bmatrix},$$

$$Y = [Y_{*j} \quad Y_{*\bar{j}}].$$

Upon removal of y_{ji}, $i = 1, \ldots, N$

$$Y_{(j).i} = (y_{1i}, \ldots, y_{j-1,i}, y_{j+1,i}, \ldots, y_{n_j i}),$$

$$Y_{*(j)} = \begin{bmatrix} Y_{(j).1} \\ \cdot \\ \cdot \\ \cdot \\ Y_{(j).N} \end{bmatrix}.$$

Exogenous variables

Arbitrary order of columns

$$X = \begin{bmatrix} x_{11} & \cdots & x_{p1} \\ \cdot & & \cdot \\ \cdot & & \cdot \\ \cdot & & \cdot \\ x_{1N} & \cdots & x_{pN} \end{bmatrix} = \begin{bmatrix} X_{.1} \\ \cdot \\ \cdot \\ \cdot \\ X_{.N} \end{bmatrix} = [X'_{1.} \cdots X'_{p.}].$$

Columns ordered on non-zero coefficients of the jth *equation*

$$\begin{aligned} X_{.i} &= [X_{j.i} \quad X_{\bar{j}.i}] \\ &= [(x_{1i}, \ldots, x_{p_j i}), (x_{p_{j+1},i}, \ldots, x_{pi})], \end{aligned}$$

$$X_{*j} = \begin{bmatrix} X_{j.1} \\ \cdot \\ \cdot \\ \cdot \\ X_{j.N} \end{bmatrix}, \qquad X_{*\bar{j}} = \begin{bmatrix} X_{\bar{j}.1} \\ \cdot \\ \cdot \\ \cdot \\ X_{\bar{j}.N} \end{bmatrix},$$

$$X = [X_{*j} \quad X_{*\bar{j}}].$$

Parameters

Arbitrary order of columns

$$B = \begin{bmatrix} \beta_{11} & \cdots & \beta_{1n} \\ \cdot & & \cdot \\ \cdot & & \cdot \\ \cdot & & \cdot \\ \beta_{n1} & \cdots & \beta_{nn} \end{bmatrix} = \begin{bmatrix} B_{.1} \\ \cdot \\ \cdot \\ \cdot \\ B_{.n} \end{bmatrix} = [B'_{1.} \cdots B'_{n.}],$$

$$\Gamma = \begin{bmatrix} \gamma_{11} & \cdots & \gamma_{1p} \\ \cdot & & \cdot \\ \cdot & & \cdot \\ \cdot & & \cdot \\ \gamma_{n1} & \cdots & \gamma_{np} \end{bmatrix} = \begin{bmatrix} \Gamma_{.1} \\ \cdot \\ \cdot \\ \cdot \\ \Gamma_{.n} \end{bmatrix} = [\Gamma'_{1.} \cdots \Gamma'_{p.}].$$

Columns ordered on non-zero coefficients of the jth *equation*

$$B_{*j} = (\beta_{j1}, \dots, \beta_{jn_j}),$$
$$B_j = (B_{*j} \quad 0),$$
$$\Gamma_{*j} = (\gamma_{j1}, \dots, \gamma_{jp_j}),$$
$$\Gamma_j = (\Gamma_{*j} \quad 0).$$

Upon removal of β_{jj}

$$B_{*(j)} = (\beta_{j1}, \dots, \beta_{j,j-1}, \beta_{j,j+1}, \dots, \beta_{jn_j}).$$

Equations

Simultaneous form

jth equation – per observation: $\boldsymbol{Y}_{j.i}B'_{*j} + X_{j.i}\Gamma'_{*j} = \boldsymbol{u}_{ji}, \quad i = 1, \dots, N,$

– all observations: $\boldsymbol{Y}_{*j}B'_{*j} + X_{*j}\Gamma'_{*j} = \boldsymbol{U}'_{j.}.$

All equations – per observation: $\boldsymbol{Y}_{.i}B' + X_{.i}\Gamma' = \boldsymbol{U}_{.i}, \quad i = 1, \dots, N,$

– all observations: $\boldsymbol{Y}B' + X\Gamma' = \boldsymbol{U}.$

Regression form

jth equation – per observation: $\boldsymbol{y}_{ji} = \boldsymbol{Y}_{(j).i}B'_{*(j)} + X_{j.i}\Gamma'_{*j} - \boldsymbol{u}_{ji}, \quad i = 1, \dots, N,$

– all observations: $\begin{cases} \boldsymbol{Y}'_{j.} = \boldsymbol{Y}_{*(j)}B'_{*(j)} + X_{*j}\Gamma'_{*j} - \boldsymbol{U}'_{j.}, \\ \boldsymbol{Y}'_{j.} = \boldsymbol{Z}_j\Delta'_j - \boldsymbol{U}'_{j.}. \end{cases}$

All equations – all observations: $\vec{\boldsymbol{Y}}' = \boldsymbol{Z}\Delta' - \vec{\boldsymbol{U}}'.$

Definitions:

$$\boldsymbol{Z}_j = (\boldsymbol{Y}_{*(j)}, X_{*j}),$$
$$\boldsymbol{Z} = \begin{bmatrix} \boldsymbol{Z}_1 & & 0 \\ & \ddots & \\ 0 & & \boldsymbol{Z}_n \end{bmatrix},$$

$$\Delta_j = (B_{*(j)} \quad \Gamma_{*j}),$$
$$\Delta = (\Delta_1, \ldots, \Delta_n),$$
$$\vec{\boldsymbol{Y}} = (\boldsymbol{Y}_{1.}, \ldots, \boldsymbol{Y}_{n.}) = (\boldsymbol{y}_{11}, \ldots, \boldsymbol{y}_{1N}, \boldsymbol{y}_{21}, \ldots, \boldsymbol{y}_{2N}, \ldots, \boldsymbol{y}_{n1}, \ldots, \boldsymbol{y}_{nN}).$$

Reduced form

$$\boldsymbol{Y} = X\Pi' + \boldsymbol{V}.$$

jth equation–all observations: $\boldsymbol{Y}'_{j.} = X\Pi'_j + \boldsymbol{V}'_{j.}$
$= X_{*j}\Pi'_{jj} + X_{*\bar{j}}\Pi'_{j\bar{j}} + \boldsymbol{V}'_{j.}$.

All equations–all observations: $\boldsymbol{Y}_{*(j)} = X_{*j}\Pi'_{*j} + X_{*\bar{j}}\Pi'_{*\bar{j}} + \boldsymbol{V}_{*(j)}$.

Definitions:

$$\Pi_{(j)} = \begin{bmatrix} \Pi_{jj} & \Pi_{j\bar{j}} \\ \Pi_{*j} & \Pi_{*\bar{j}} \end{bmatrix} = [\Pi_{(jj)} \quad \Pi_{(j\bar{j})}],$$

$$\Pi = \left[\begin{array}{c|c} \Pi_{jj} & \Pi_{j\bar{j}} \\ \Pi_{*j} & \Pi_{*\bar{j}} \\ \hline \Pi_{(\bar{j}j)} & \Pi_{(\bar{j}\bar{j})} \end{array}\right] = \begin{bmatrix} \Pi_{(j)} \\ \Pi_{(\bar{j})} \end{bmatrix},$$
$$= \begin{bmatrix} \Pi_{(jj)} & \Pi_{(j\bar{j})} \\ \Pi_{(\bar{j}j)} & \Pi_{(\bar{j}\bar{j})} \end{bmatrix}.$$

Notational dictionary

Our	*Cowles Commission**	*Econometric Institute*
N	T	T
n	G	M
n_j	G^{Δ}	$m_j + 1$
p	K	Λ
p_j	K^*	l_j
r		n
r_j		n_j
B_{*j}	β_{Δ}	$(-1, \gamma_j)$
Γ_{*j}	γ_*	β_j
Y_{*j}	y_{Δ}	$[y \quad Y_j]$
$Y_{*\bar{j}}$	$y_{\Delta\Delta}$	–
X_{*j}	z_*	X_j
$X_{*\bar{j}}$	B_{**}	–
Z_j		Z_j
Δ_j		δ'_j

Notational dictionary *(continued)*

Our	*Cowles Commission**	*Econometric Institute*
Δ		δ'
$\vec{Y}$		y'
$Y_{j.}$		y_j'
$Y_{*(j)}$		Y_j
$B_{*(j)}$		γ_j
$\Pi = \begin{bmatrix} \Pi_{(jj)} & \Pi_{(j\bar{j})} \\ \Pi_{(\bar{j}j)} & \Pi_{(\bar{j}\bar{j})} \end{bmatrix}$	$\Pi = \begin{bmatrix} \Pi_{\Delta *} & \Pi_{\Delta.**} \\ \Pi_{\Delta\Delta.*} & \Pi_{\Delta\Delta.**} \end{bmatrix}$	–
$\Omega = \begin{bmatrix} \Omega_{jj} & \Omega_{j\bar{j}} \\ \Omega_{\bar{j}j} & \Omega_{\bar{j}\bar{j}} \end{bmatrix}$		

* Note that the Cowles Commission notation is based on a consideration of the first equation as the one to be estimated.

1. Identification of a single equation

It is clear from simply counting equations and unknowns that B, Γ, and Σ cannot in general be determined uniquely from knowledge of Π and Ω. More subtly, let $\tilde{\Gamma} = P\Gamma$, $\tilde{B} = PB$, and $\tilde{\Sigma} = P\Sigma P'$, where P is non-singular. Then,

$$\Pi' = -\Gamma' B'^{-1} = -\tilde{\Gamma}' P^{-1\prime} P' \tilde{B}^{-1} = -\tilde{\Gamma}' \tilde{B}^{-1},$$

and

$$\Omega = B^{-1} \Sigma B'^{-1} = \tilde{B}^{-1} P \Sigma P' \tilde{B}'^{-1} = \tilde{B}^{-1} \tilde{\Sigma} \tilde{B}'^{-1},$$

so that $\tilde{B}$, $\tilde{\Gamma}$, and $\tilde{\Sigma}$ are equally consistent with Π and Ω.

Suppose we were only interested in whether the first rows of B and Γ are identifiable. Without loss of generality, we can define the matrices B and Γ so that all the non-zero elements of the first row of these matrices precede the elements that one knows a priori (from economic theory) are zero. Let n_1 be the number of non-zero elements of the first row B_1 of B, and p_1 be the number of non-zero elements of the first row Γ_1 of Γ. Let $\Gamma_1 = [\Gamma_{*1} \;\; 0]$, $B_1 = [B_{*1} \;\; 0]$, where Γ_{*1} is $1 \times p_1$ and B_{*1} is $1 \times n_1$.

Let

$$\Pi = \begin{bmatrix} \Pi_{(11)} & \Pi_{(1\bar{1})} \\ \Pi_{(\bar{1}1)} & \Pi_{(\bar{1}\bar{1})} \end{bmatrix},$$

where $\Pi_{(11)}$ is $n_1 \times p_1$. Then the first equation in the relation

$$-B\Pi = \Gamma$$

can be written as the two relations

$$-B_{*1}\Pi_{(11)} = \Gamma_{*1},$$
$$-B_{*1}\Pi_{(1\bar{1})} = 0.$$

Of course these equations cannot be satisfied uniquely by B_{*1}, Γ_{*1} even now, for any scalar multiple of these two vectors will satisfy the equation. For this reason, we must introduce some normalization of B_{*1}. A standard normalization is $\beta_{11} = -1$. Then B_{*1} is identifiable if and only if $B_{*1}\Pi_{(1\bar{1})} = 0$ determines B_{*1} uniquely; and then Γ_{*1} is identifiable also, as $\Gamma_{*1} = -B_{*1}\Pi_{(11)}$.

Now $\Pi_{(1\bar{1})}$ is a $n_1 \times (p - p_1)$ matrix, and we have assumed that $\Pi = B^{-1}\Gamma$ for at least one pair of matrices B, Γ. Therefore there is at least one vector B_{*1} satisfying $B_{*1}\Pi_{(1\bar{1})} = 0$, so that the n_1 rows of $\Pi_{(1\bar{1})}$ are linearly dependent, and so the rank of $\Pi_{(1\bar{1})}$ is at most $n_1 - 1$.

If the rank of $\Pi_{(1\bar{1})}$ is smaller than $n_1 - 1$, then every subset of $n_1 - 1$ rows of $\Pi_{(1\bar{1})}$ are linearly dependent. Suppose then that $\sum_{i=2}^{n_1-1} a_i\Pi_{(1\bar{1})i} = \Pi_{(1\bar{1})n_1}$, where $\Pi_{(1\bar{1})i}$ is the ith row of $\Pi_{(1\bar{1})}$. If $B_{*1}\Pi_{(1\bar{1})} = 0$, then

$$B^*_{*1} = B_{*1} + [0, a_2, \ldots, a_{n_1-1}, -1]$$

also satisfies $B^*_{*1}\Pi_{(1\bar{1})} = 0$.

Therefore, a necessary and sufficient condition for B_{*1} to be identifiable is for the rank of $\Pi_{(1\bar{1})}$ to be $n_1 - 1$. This condition is called the *rank condition* for identifiability. Of course, if $p - p_1 < n_1 - 1$, then this condition cannot be fulfilled, as then the rank of $\Pi_{(1\bar{1})}$ would be at most $p - p_1$. Thus it is necessary for $p - p_1$ to be at least $n_1 - 1$. This latter condition, called the *order condition* for identifiability, is easy to check in practice; on the other hand, the rank condition is hard to check, because typically we do not *know* Π but only have a maximum likelihood estimate of Π, and it may be merely due to random variation in the estimate that the rank condition is met when the true Π doesn't meet it, or contrarily (and a much less likely event), that the rank condition is not met when the true Π does satisfy the condition. We shall return to this problem in section 6 of chapter VI.

Recalling that

$$\Pi'_{(1\bar{1})} = [\Pi'_{1\bar{1}} \quad \Pi'_{*\bar{1}}],$$

we can deduce another necessary and sufficient condition for identifiability, namely that the rank of $\Pi_{*\bar{1}}$ must equal $n_1 - 1$. The sufficiency follows from the fact that $B_{*1}\Pi_{(1\bar{1})} = 0$ implies that the rank of $\Pi_{(1\bar{1})}$ is at most $n_1 - 1$, and since the rank of $\Pi_{*\bar{1}}$ equals $n_1 - 1$ implies that the rank of $\Pi_{(1\bar{1})}$ is at least $n_1 - 1$, we see that the rank of $\Pi_{(1\bar{1})}$ is equal to $n_1 - 1$.

The necessity follows from noting that if the rank of $\Pi_{*\bar{1}}$ were less than $n_1 - 1$ then there is some non-zero vector A such that $A\Pi_{*\bar{1}} = 0$. Then,

$$\begin{aligned} \boldsymbol{Y}_{*(1)}A' &= X_{*1}\Pi'_{*1}A' + X_{*\bar{1}}\Pi'_{*\bar{1}}A' + \boldsymbol{V}_{*(1)}A' \\ &= X_{*1}(\Pi'_{*1}A') + \boldsymbol{V}_{*(1)}A', \end{aligned}$$

and so

$$\boldsymbol{Y}'_{1.} = \boldsymbol{Y}_{*(1)}[B'_{*(1)} - A'] + X_{*1}[\Gamma'_{*1} + \Pi'_{*1}A'] + [\boldsymbol{V}_{*(1)}A' - \boldsymbol{U}'_{1.}].$$

This equation, with $A \neq 0$, is indistinguishable from the original equation

$$\boldsymbol{Y}'_{1.} = \boldsymbol{Y}_{*(1)}B'_{*(1)} + X_{*1}\Gamma'_{*1} - \boldsymbol{U}'_{1.},$$

and so the model is unidentifiable.

One other condition for identifiability is usually alluded to in various texts by example but never treated systematically, namely the restriction that Σ be diagonal or, more generally, block-diagonal. Note in our general example of unidentifiability where both B, Γ, Σ and PB, $P\Gamma$, $P\Sigma P'$ are consistent with Π and Ω that when Σ is block-diagonal $P\Sigma P'$ need not be. Thus we are immediately restricted by the block-diagonality of Σ to those non-singular P's such that $P\Sigma P'$ is block-diagonal as candidates for transformations of the parameter space which produce unidentifiability.

Let us consider the block-diagonality condition in conjunction with specification of zeros in B and Γ to determine necessary and sufficient conditions for identifiability of the first rows of B and Γ. We can write these zero restrictions as

$$[B_{.i} \;\; \Gamma_{.i}]\psi_i = 0, \qquad i = 1, \ldots, n,$$

where ψ_i is an $(n+p)\times(n+p)$ matrix with a 1 in the (j, j)th position if the jth element of the vector $[B_{.i} \;\; \Gamma_{.i}]$ is zero and zeros elsewhere. Now let

$$P = \begin{bmatrix} P_{11} & P_{12} \\ P_{21} & P_{22} \end{bmatrix},$$

and

$$\Sigma = \begin{bmatrix} \Sigma_{11} & \Sigma_{12} \\ \Sigma_{21} & \Sigma_{22} \end{bmatrix},$$

where the partitioning is defined such that none of the elements of the first row of the $n_1^* \times n_1^*$ matrix Σ_{11} are zero and such that all of the elements of the first row of Σ_{12} are zero. Let P_1 be the first row of P. Then the last $n - n_1^*$ elements of the first row of $P\Sigma P'$, i.e.,

$$P_1\Sigma \begin{bmatrix} P'_{21} \\ P'_{22} \end{bmatrix},$$

must equal zero. Also $P_1[B \;\; \Gamma]$ must satisfy the same zero restriction as did $[B_{.i} \;\; \Gamma_{.i}]$, i.e.,

$$P_1[B \;\; \Gamma]\psi_1 = 0.$$

Thus if the first equation is identified then

$$P_1 \left[\Sigma \begin{bmatrix} P'_{21} \\ P'_{22} \end{bmatrix}, [B \;\; \Gamma]\psi_1 \right] = [0, 0],$$

so that the rank of the matrix

$$M = \left[\Sigma \begin{bmatrix} P'_{21} \\ P'_{22} \end{bmatrix}, [B \;\; \Gamma]\psi_1 \right]$$

is at most $n - 1$ for every non-singular P such that $\tilde{B}$, $\tilde{\Gamma}$, $\tilde{\Sigma}$ satisfy the 0 restrictions. If it has even smaller rank, then there is a vector P_1^* different from P_1 also satisfying the equation $P_1^*M = 0$, contradicting the assumption of identifiability. Therefore a necessary condition for identifiability is that the rank of M is exactly $n - 1$.

Taking $P = I$, we obtain the corollary result that a necessary (but not sufficient) condition for identifiability of the first equation given the zero restrictions on B and Γ described by $[B \;\; \Gamma]\psi_1 = 0$ and that the first row of Σ_{12} is zero is that the matrix

$$\left[\begin{bmatrix} \Sigma_{12} \\ \Sigma_{22} \end{bmatrix}, [B \;\; \Gamma]\psi_1 \right]$$

has rank $n - 1$.

Let us see why the more general necessary condition is in this case not sufficient for identifiability. If the whole model were identifiable, then P would have to equal I; for the first equation to be identifiable, then P_1 would have to equal E_1. Now suppose $n = 2$ and there are no zero restrictions on B and Γ, with the restriction on Σ being that it is diagonal. Then the rank of

$$\Sigma\begin{bmatrix}P'_{21}\\P'_{22}\end{bmatrix}=\begin{bmatrix}\sigma_{11} & 0\\0 & \sigma_{22}\end{bmatrix}\begin{bmatrix}p_{21}\\p_{22}\end{bmatrix}=\begin{bmatrix}\sigma_{11} & p_{21}\\\sigma_{22} & p_{22}\end{bmatrix}$$

is 1 unless $p_{21}=p_{22}=0$. Does this imply that $P_1=E_1$? Well, consider the condition

$$0=p_1\Sigma\begin{bmatrix}P'_{21}\\P'_{22}\end{bmatrix}=p_{11}\sigma_{11}p_{21}+p_{12}\sigma_{22}p_{22}.$$

This can be satisfied for many values of (p_{11},p_{12}) other than $(1,0)$, provided that $p_{11}p_{22}\neq p_{12}p_{21}$, i.e., that P is non-singular. Thus the rank condition is not sufficient for identifiability.

If, however, it is known that $p_{21}=0$ and $p_{22}\neq 0$, then $p_{12}=0$ and, because of normalization conventions, $p_{11}=1$. In the jargon of identifiability, knowing that $p_{21}=0$ is knowing that "the second equation is identifiable with respect to the first equation".

Note that if none of the elements of the first row of Σ are zero, i.e., if there are no restrictions on the covariance matrix relating to the first equation, then the condition reduces to the condition that the rank of $[B\ \Gamma]\psi_1$ is $n-1$. That this is equivalent to the condition given earlier, that the rank of $\Pi_{(1\bar{1})}$ is n_1-1, can be seen by noting that, since

$$\psi_1=\begin{bmatrix}0 & & 0\\ & I_0 & \\0 & & I\end{bmatrix},$$

and since rank $([B\ \Gamma]\psi_1)=$ rank $(B^{-1}[B\ \Gamma]\psi_1)=$ rank $([I-\Pi]\psi_1)$, then $n-1=n-n_1+\text{rank}\,(\Pi_{(1\bar{1})})$. Note however that in this case the condition is also sufficient for identifiability.

An example at this point may be helpful to fix ideas. Let $Y_i=(y_{i1},y_{i2})$, $X_i=(x_{i1},x_{i2})$,

$$B=\begin{bmatrix}1 & \beta_{12}\\\beta_{21} & 1\end{bmatrix},\qquad \Gamma=\begin{bmatrix}0 & 0\\\gamma_{21} & \gamma_{22}\end{bmatrix},$$

so that we know a priori that $\gamma_{11}=\gamma_{12}=0$. The matrix ψ_1 is of the form

$$\psi_1=\begin{bmatrix}0&0&0&0\\0&0&0&0\\0&0&1&0\\0&0&0&1\end{bmatrix}.$$

Then $n_1 = 2$, $p_1 = 0$, and

$$\Pi_{(1\bar{1})} = \Pi = \frac{1}{1-\beta_{12}\beta_{21}}\begin{bmatrix} 1 & -\beta_{12} \\ -\beta_{21} & 1 \end{bmatrix}\begin{bmatrix} 0 & 0 \\ \gamma_{21} & \gamma_{22} \end{bmatrix}.$$

The rank of $\Pi_{(1\bar{1})}$ is $n_1 - 1 = 1$ unless $\gamma_{21} = \gamma_{22} = 0$ or $\beta_{12}\beta_{21} = 1$. Thus if B is non-singular and $\Gamma \neq 0$, the first equation is identifiable.

Viewed another way, taking B and Γ as general matrices, the matrix

$$[B \;\; \Gamma]\psi_1 = \begin{bmatrix} 0 & 0 & \gamma_{11} & \gamma_{12} \\ 0 & 0 & \gamma_{21} & \gamma_{22} \end{bmatrix}$$

has rank 1 when $\gamma_{11} = \gamma_{12} = 0$. Thus, under the restrictions of this situation the first equation is identifiable. Moreover, this more general view of this situation tells us that the first equation is identifiable for all matrices Γ of rank 1, i.e., so long as $\gamma_{11}\gamma_{22} = \gamma_{12}\gamma_{21}$ and $\Gamma \neq 0$.

Since $\psi_2 = 0$, the rank of $[B \;\; \Gamma]\psi_2$ is 0. But $n_2 = 2$. Thus the second equation is unidentified.

Now suppose we have as a restriction on Σ that it is a diagonal matrix. Then,

$$\begin{bmatrix} \Sigma_{11} & \\ \Sigma_{21} & [B \;\; \Gamma]\psi_2 \end{bmatrix} = \begin{bmatrix} 0 & 0 & 0 & 0 & 0 \\ \sigma_{22} & 0 & 0 & 0 & 0 \end{bmatrix},$$

which has rank $n_2 - 1 = 1$. Thus the necessary condition for identifiability of the second equation does hold. This, of course, does not imply that the equation is identified, but if it didn't hold we could conclude that the equation is not identified.

Exercise: Consider the case where $n = 3$, $p = 2$, $\sigma_{12} = \sigma_{13} = 0$ and $\gamma_{11} = \gamma_{22} = 0$. What are necessary conditions for each of the equations to be identified?

2. Maximum likelihood estimation of a single equation

Let us assume that we *know* that B_{*1} and Γ_{*1} are identifiable, and wish to obtain maximum likelihood estimates of these vectors when there is no restriction on Σ. Thus we wish to maximize the likelihood function of $Y_{1.1}, \ldots, Y_{1.N}$ with respect to B_{*1}, Γ_{*1} and σ_{11} subject to the constraint $B_{*1}\Pi_{(1\bar{1})} = 0$ and to the generalized normalization condition $B_{*1}\Phi B'_{*1} = 1$, where Φ is a known symmetric matrix, $Y_{1.i}$ is the subvector consisting of the first n_1 elements of $Y_{.i}$, and $\Pi_{(1)} = [\Pi_{(11)}\ \ \Pi_{(1\bar{1})}]$. (The special normalization given above takes Φ to be a matrix with $\varphi_{11} = 1$, $\varphi_{ij} = 0$ otherwise.)

However, before we do this, let us make a change in the independent variables $X_{.i}$, by taking $R_i = X_{1.i}$ and $S_i = X_{\bar{1}.i} - X_{1.i}(X'_{*1}X_{*1})^{-1}(X'_{*1}X_{*\bar{1}})$, where $X_{1.i}$ is the subvector of $X_{.i}$ consisting of the first p_1 components, X_{*1} is the $N \times p_1$ matrix whose ith row is $X_{1.i}$, and $X_{*\bar{1}}$ is the $N \times (p - p_1)$ matrix whose ith row is $X_{\bar{1}.i}$. Then

$$\begin{aligned}\mathscr{E}\mathbf{Y}_{1.i} &= X_{\bar{1}.i}\Pi'_{(1\bar{1})} + X_{1.i}\Pi'_{(11)} \\ &= S_i\Pi'_{(1\bar{1})} + R_i[(X'_{*1}X_{*1})^{-1}(X^{*\prime}_{*\bar{1}}X_{*\bar{1}})\Pi'_{(1\bar{1})} + \Pi'_{(11)}]\end{aligned}$$

so that $\mathbf{Y}_{1.i}$ is distributed as $N(R_i\Pi^{*\prime}_{(11)} + S_i\Pi'_{(1\bar{1})}, \Omega_{11})$, where Ω_{11} is the leading $n_1 \times n_1$ submatrix of Ω and

$$\Pi^*_{(11)} = \Pi_{(11)} + \Pi_{(1\bar{1})}(X'_{*\bar{1}}X_{*1})(X'_{*1}X_{*1})^{-1}.$$

The purpose of this transformation is that, without altering the constraints, it simplifies some equations later. For let S be the $N \times (p - p_1)$ matrix whose ith row is S_i and R be the $N \times p_1$ matrix whose ith row is R_i. Then $R = X_{*1}$ and $S = X_{*\bar{1}} - X_{*1}(X'_{*1}X_{*1})^{-1}(X'_{*1}X_{*\bar{1}})$ so that $R'S = 0$. It is readily seen that

$$X(X'X)^{-1}X' = R(R'R)^{-1}R' + S(S'S)^{-1}S'.$$

Exercise: Check this.

Our likelihood function is

$$L = (2\pi)^{-n_1N/2}|\Omega_{11}|^{-N/2}$$
$$\times \exp\left\{-\frac{1}{2}\sum_{i=1}^{N}(\mathbf{Y}_{1.i} - R_i\Pi^{*\prime}_{(11)} - S_i\Pi'_{(1\bar{1})})\Omega_{11}^{-1}(\mathbf{Y}_{1.i} - R_i\Pi^{*\prime}_{(11)} - S_i\Pi'_{(1\bar{1})})'\right\},$$

and to maximize it subject to the constraints, we must find the extremum of the Lagrangian expression

$$\mathscr{L} = \log L + B_{*1}\Pi_{(1\bar{1})}\Lambda' + \upsilon(B_{*1}\Phi B'_{*1} - 1),$$

where Λ is a $p - p_1$ vector of Lagrange multipliers and υ is another Lagrange multiplier.

Since

$$\frac{\partial\mathscr{L}}{\partial B_{*1}} = \Pi_{(1\bar{1})}\Lambda' + 2\upsilon\Phi B'_{*1} = 0$$

implies that

$$B_{*1}\Pi_{(1\bar{1})}\Lambda' + 2\upsilon B_{*1}\Phi B'_{*1} = 0,$$

and since $B_{*1}\Pi_{(1\bar{1})} = 0$ and $B_{*1}\Phi B'_{*1} = 1$, we see that $\upsilon = 0$. Thus the choice of Φ will not affect the extremum of $\mathscr{L}$, and so we shall, in the course of finding this extremum, find it convenient to redefine Φ in order to simplify some of the mathematics involved in obtaining the maximum likelihood estimator.

As a function of Ω_{11} the likelihood function is of the form to which we can apply the results of Theorem 19 so that

$$\hat{\Omega}_{11} = \frac{1}{N}\sum_{i=1}^{N}(Y_{1.i} - R_i\Pi^{*\prime}_{(11)} - S_i\Pi'_{(1\bar{1})})' \times (Y_{1.i} - R_i\Pi^{*\prime}_{(11)} - S_i\Pi'_{(1\bar{1})}).$$

We now need only determine $\hat{\Pi}_{(1\bar{1})}$ and $\hat{\Pi}^{*}_{(11)}$. Substituting this value into L, we see that, even without knowledge of $\hat{\Pi}_{(1\bar{1})}$ and $\hat{\Pi}^{*}_{(11)}$, the exponent of e is constant so that our Lagrangian is

$$\mathscr{L}^{*} = -\frac{N}{2}\log\left|\frac{1}{N}\sum_{i=1}^{N}(Y_{1.i} - R_i\Pi^{*\prime}_{(11)} - S_i\Pi'_{(1\bar{1})})' \times (Y_{1.i} - R_i\Pi^{*\prime}_{(11)} - S_i\Pi'_{(1\bar{1})})\right| + B_{*1}\Pi_{(1\bar{1})}\Lambda'.$$

Now

$$\frac{\partial\mathscr{L}^{*}}{\partial\Pi_{(1\bar{1})}} = \hat{\Omega}_{11}^{-1}\left[\sum_{i=1}^{N} Y'_{1.i}S_i - \hat{\Pi}_{(1\bar{1})}\sum_{i=1}^{N} S'_iS_i\right] + \hat{B}'_{*1}\hat{\Lambda}$$
$$= \hat{\Omega}_{11}^{-1}[Y'_{*1}S - \hat{\Pi}_{(1\bar{1})}S'S] + \hat{B}'_{*1}\hat{\Lambda} = 0,$$

$$\frac{\partial\mathscr{L}^{*}}{\partial\Pi^{*}_{(11)}} = \hat{\Omega}_{11}^{-1}\left[\sum_{i=1}^{N} Y'_{1.i}R_i - \hat{\Pi}^{*}_{(11)}\sum_{i=1}^{N} R'_iR_i\right]$$
$$= \hat{\Omega}_{11}^{-1}[Y'_{*1}R - \hat{\Pi}^{*}_{(11)}R'R] = 0,$$

and in addition

$$\frac{\partial\mathscr{L}^{*}}{\partial B_{*1}} = \hat{\Pi}_{(1\bar{1})}\hat{\Lambda}' = 0$$

must be solved to obtain the maximum likelihood estimates, where, as defined earlier, R is the $N \times p_1$ matrix whose ith row is R_i, S is the $N \times (p - p_1)$ matrix whose ith row is S_i, and Y_{*1} is the matrix whose ith row is $Y_{1.i}$.

We obtain at once that

$$\hat{\Pi}^*_{(11)} = Y'_{*1}R(R'R)^{-1},$$
$$\hat{\Pi}_{(1\bar{1})} = [\hat{\Omega}_{11}\hat{B}'_{*1}\hat{\Lambda} + Y'_{*1}S][S'S]^{-1},$$

so that

$$0 = \hat{B}_{*1}\hat{\Pi}_{(1\bar{1})} = \hat{B}_{*1}\hat{\Omega}_{11}\hat{B}'_{*1}\hat{\Lambda}(S'S)^{-1} + \hat{B}_{*1}Y'_{*1}S(S'S)^{-1},$$

or, using the normalization $B_{*1}\Phi B'_{*1} = B_{*1}\hat{\Omega}_{11}B'_{*1} = 1$, i.e., taking $\Phi = \hat{\Omega}_{11}$,

$$\hat{\Lambda} = -\hat{B}_{*1}Y'_{*1}S,$$

and

$$\hat{\Pi}_{(1\bar{1})} = [I - \hat{\Omega}_{11}\hat{B}'_{*1}\hat{B}_{*1}]Y'_{*1}S(S'S)^{-1}.$$

Let us now write

$$N\hat{\Omega}_{11} = Y'_{*1}Y'_{*1} - \hat{\Pi}^*_{(11)}R'Y_{*1} - \hat{\Pi}_{(1\bar{1})}S'Y_{*1} - Y'_{*1}R\hat{\Pi}^{*\prime}_{(11)}$$
$$- Y'_{*1}S\hat{\Pi}'_{(1\bar{1})} + \hat{\Pi}^*_{(11)}R'R\hat{\Pi}^{*\prime}_{(11)} + \hat{\Pi}_{(1\bar{1})}S'S\hat{\Pi}'_{(1\bar{1})},$$

remembering that $RS' = 0$. Substituting the above values of $\hat{\Pi}^*_{(11)}$ and $\hat{\Pi}_{(1\bar{1})}$, we obtain

$$\begin{aligned}N\hat{\Omega}_{11} &= Y'_{*1}Y'_{*1} - 2Y'_{*1}R(R'R)^{-1}R'Y_{*1} + \hat{\Omega}_{11}\hat{B}'_{*1}\hat{B}_{*1}Y'_{*1}S(S'S)^{-1}S'Y_{*1}\\ &\quad - 2Y_{*1}S(S'S)^{-1}S' + Y'_{*1}S(S'S)^{-1}S'Y_{*1}\hat{B}'_{*1}\hat{B}_{*1}\\ &\quad + Y'_{*1}R(R'R)^{-1}R'Y_{*1} + Y'_{*1}S(S'S)^{-1}S'Y_{*1}\\ &\quad + \hat{\Omega}_{11}\hat{B}'_{*1}\hat{B}_{*1}Y'_{*1}S(S'S)^{-1}S'Y_{*1}\hat{B}'_{*1}\hat{B}_{*1}\hat{\Omega}_{11}\\ &\quad - \hat{\Omega}_{11}\hat{B}'_{*1}\hat{B}_{*1}Y'_{*1}S(S'S)^{-1}S'Y_{*1} - Y'_{*1}S(S'S)^{-1}S'Y_{*1}\hat{B}'_{*1}\hat{B}_{*1}\hat{\Omega}_{11}\\ &= Y'_{*1}Y_{*1} - Y'_{*1}R(R'R)^{-1}R'Y_{*1} - Y'_{*1}S(S'S)^{-1}S'Y_{*1}\\ &\quad + \hat{\Omega}_{11}\hat{B}'_{*1}\hat{B}_{*1}Y'_{*1}S(S'S)^{-1}S'Y_{*1}\hat{B}'_{*1}\hat{B}_{*1}\hat{\Omega}_{11},\end{aligned}$$

so that

$$\hat{\Omega}_{11} = W + \hat{\Omega}_{11}\hat{B}'_{*1}\mu\hat{B}_{*1}\hat{\Omega}_{11},$$

where

$$W = \frac{1}{N}(Y'_{*1}Y_{*1} - Y'_{*1}R(R'R)^{-1}R'Y_{*1} - Y'_{*1}S(S'S)^{-1}S'Y_{*1}),$$

and

$$\mu = \frac{1}{N}\hat{B}_{*1}Y'_{*1}S(S'S)^{-1}S'Y_{*1}\hat{B}'_{*1}.$$

Since $NW = Y'_{*1}Y_{*1} - Y'_{*1}X(X'X)^{-1}X'Y_{*1}$, by Theorem 12 W is positive semidefinite. As W is the maximum likelihood estimate of Ω_{11} in the linear expected value model in which $\boldsymbol{Y}'_{*1}$ is distributed as $N(X\Pi'_{(1)}, \Omega_{11})$, where $\Pi_{(1)} = (\Pi_{(11)}\Pi_{(1\bar{1})})$, and since Ω_{11} is non-singular, with probability one W is positive definite. We shall assume this is so henceforth. Then, using the normalization $\hat{B}_{*1}\hat{\Omega}_{11}\hat{B}'_{*1} = 1$, we see that

$$\hat{B}_{*1}\hat{\Omega}_{11}\hat{B}'_{*1} = \hat{B}_{*1}W\hat{B}'_{*1} + \mu\hat{B}_{*1}\hat{\Omega}_{11}\hat{B}'_{*1}\hat{B}_{*1}\hat{\Omega}_{11}\hat{B}'_{*1},$$

or

$$\mu = 1 - \hat{B}_{*1}W\hat{B}'_{*1}.$$

To simplify notation, let us define W^* by the equation

$$N(W^* - W) = Y'_{*1}S(S'S)^{-1}S'Y_{*1},$$

so that

$$\mu = \hat{B}_{*1}(W^* - W)\hat{B}'_{*1}.$$

We also obtain from this normalization that

$$\hat{\Omega}_{11}\hat{B}'_{*1} = W\hat{B}'_{*1} + \mu\hat{\Omega}_{11}\hat{B}'_{*1},$$

or

$$\hat{\Omega}_{11}\hat{B}'_{*1} = (1 - \mu)^{-1}W\hat{B}'_{*1}.$$

Referring back to an earlier equation and substituting, we have

$$\begin{aligned} 0 &= \hat{\Pi}_{(1\bar{1})}\hat{\Lambda}' = -\hat{\Pi}_{(1\bar{1})}S'Y_{*1}\hat{B}'_{*1} \\ &= -(I - \hat{\Omega}_{11}\hat{B}'_{*1}\hat{B}_{*1})N(W^* - W)\hat{B}'_{*1}, \end{aligned}$$

or

$$(W^* - W)\hat{B}'_{*1} - \mu\hat{\Omega}_{11}\hat{B}'_{*1} = 0.$$

Then $\hat{B}'_{*1}$ satisfies

$$((W^* - W) - \theta W)\hat{B}'_{*1} = 0,$$

where $\theta = \mu/(1 - \mu)$, or $\mu = \theta/(1 + \theta)$, i.e., θ is a characteristic root and $\hat{B}_{*1}$ is a characteristic vector of the matrix $Q = W^{-1}(W^* - W)$.

But which root? The one which yields the maximum of L. Since L is proportional to $|\hat{\Omega}_{11}|^{-N/2}$, we need only calculate $|\hat{\Omega}_{11}|$. But

$$\begin{aligned} \hat{\Omega}_{11} &= W + \frac{\mu}{(1 - \mu)^2} W\hat{B}'_{*1}\hat{B}_{*1}W \\ &= W + \theta(1 + \theta)W\hat{B}'_{*1}\hat{B}_{*1}W, \end{aligned}$$

so that $|\hat{\Omega}_{11}| = |W||I + \theta(1+\theta)W\hat{B}'_{*1}\hat{B}_{*1}|$. Let B^* be the orthogonal matrix of characteristic vectors of Q, with $\hat{B}'_{*1}$ the vector corresponding to the smallest θ as its first column.

Then,

$$|B^{*\prime}||\hat{\Omega}_{11}||B^*| = |\hat{\Omega}_{11}| = |W||I + \theta(1+\theta)B^{*\prime}W\hat{B}'_{*1}\hat{B}_{*1}B^*|.$$

Since $\hat{B}_{*1}B^* = [1 \; 0 \cdots 0]$, and $\hat{B}'_{*1}\hat{B}_{*1}B^* = [\hat{B}'_{*1} \; 0 \cdots 0]$, we see that $I + \theta(1+\theta)B^*W\hat{B}'_{*1}\hat{B}_{*1}B^*$ is a triangular matrix whose determinant is just the (1, 1)th element of the matrix. Since the (1, 1)th element is $1 + \theta(1+\theta)\hat{B}_{*1}W\hat{B}'_{*1}$, we see that

$$\begin{aligned}|\hat{\Omega}_{11}| &= |W|(1 + \theta(1+\theta)\hat{B}_{*1}W\hat{B}'_{*1})\\ &= |W|(1 + \theta(1+\theta)(1-\mu))\\ &= |W|(1+\theta)\end{aligned}$$

is monotonically increasing in θ. Since $|\hat{\Omega}_{11}|$ enters into the likelihood function as $|\hat{\Omega}_{11}|^{-N/2}$, we see that the vector associated with the smallest root θ is the maximum likelihood estimate of B_{*1}, and is called the limited information maximum likelihood (LIML) estimator of B_{*1}.

Finally, $\hat{\Gamma}_{*1} = -\hat{B}_{*1}\hat{\Pi}_{(11)}$ and the (1, 1)th element of Σ is easily seen to be estimated by $\hat{\sigma}_{11} = \hat{B}_{*1}\hat{\Omega}_{11}\hat{B}'_{*1}$.

One interpretation of the characteristic vector associated with the smallest characteristic root θ_1 of Q is that it is the vector which minimizes the ratio

$$\frac{B_{*1}(Y'_{*1}Y_{*1} - Y'_{*1}R(R'R)^{-1}R'Y_{*1})B'_{*1}}{B_{*1}WB'_{*1}} = \frac{B_{*1}W^*B'_{*1}}{B_{*1}WB'_{*1}}.$$

This ratio, whose minimum value is $1 + \theta_1$, has the interpretation of being the ratio of residual variance when Y_{*1} is regressed on R to residual variance when Y_{*1} is regressed on X, and a "principle" of estimation has grown around this interpretation, called the "least-variance-ratio" principle. As this principle of estimation has no far-reaching applications, aside from the sole application in the problem wherein the "principle" was discovered, we play down completely this principle and the interpretation of the LIML estimator in this light, and instead stress the application of the maximum likelihood principle to this problem to find the LIML estimators.

Suppose $p - p_1 = n_1 - 1$. Then the equations

$$B_{*1}\Pi_{(1\bar{1})} = 0$$

can be rewritten as

$$(-1, B^*_{*1})\begin{bmatrix}\Pi_{1\bar{1}}\\ \Pi_{*\bar{1}}\end{bmatrix}=0$$

where $\Pi_{1\bar{1}}$ is the first row of $\Pi_{(1\bar{1})}$ and $\Pi_{*\bar{1}}$ is $(n_1-1)\times(p-p_1)$, i.e., a square matrix. We take $\Pi_{*\bar{1}}$ to be non-singular. (All we know is that the rank of $\Pi_{(1\bar{1})}$ is n_1-1, so that there exists *some* non-singular submatrix of $\Pi_{(1\bar{1})}$. We thus assume that we have selected our normalization and ordering of the endogenous variables so that $\Pi_{*\bar{1}}$ is this non-singular submatrix.) Then

$$\hat{B}^*_{*1}=\hat{\Pi}_{1\bar{1}}\hat{\Pi}^{-1}_{*\bar{1}}$$

is called the *indirect least squares* estimate of B^*_{*1}, where $\hat{\Pi}_{(1\bar{1})}$ is the maximum likelihood estimate of $\Pi_{(1\bar{1})}$, based on the results in chapter III on the general linear hypothesis.

Now

$$[\hat{\Pi}^*_{(11)}\hat{\Pi}_{(1\bar{1})}]=Y'_{*1}(R\ S)\begin{bmatrix}R'R & 0\\ 0 & S'S\end{bmatrix}^{-1}$$
$$=\begin{bmatrix}Y'_{*1}R(R'R)^{-1}\\ Y'_{*1}S(S'S)^{-1}\end{bmatrix},$$

so that $(-1,\hat{B}^*_{*1})Y'_{*1}S(S'S)^{-1}=0$ defines $\hat{B}^*_{*1}$.

In general, the pair of equations,

$$\hat{B}_{*1}Y'_{*1}S(S'S)^{-1}=0,$$

and

$$\hat{B}_{*1}\Phi\hat{B}_{*1}=1,$$

determines $\hat{B}_{*1}$ uniquely, where Φ is the normalization matrix.

To see that this result is readily obtainable from limited information maximum likelihood, note that

$$|Q-\theta I|=0,$$

if and only if

$$|Y'_{*1}S(S'S)^{-1}S'Y_{*1}-\theta W|=0,$$

or

$$|Y'_{*1}S(S'S)^{-1}S'Y_{*1}-(\xi-1)W|=0,$$

or

$$|Y'_{*1}Y_{*1} - Y'_{*1}R(R'R)^{-1}R'Y_{*1} - \xi(Y'_{*1}Y_{*1} - Y'_{*1}R(R'R)^{-1}R'Y_{*1}$$
$$- Y'_{*1}S(S'S)^{-1}S'Y_{*1}| = 0.$$

This equation is of the form

$$|E - \xi(E - F)| = 0,$$

where E and F are positive semidefinite and $E - F$ is positive definite. If V satisfies $VE = \xi V(E - F)$, then, since

$$VEV' = \xi V(E - F)V',$$

we see that $\xi \geqslant 0$ and

$$(1 - \xi)VEV' = -\xi VFV',$$

so that $\xi \geqslant 1$. Since $\theta = \xi - 1$, θ must be at least zero.

Now check that the vector $\hat{B}_{*1}$ based on indirect least squares satisfies

$$\hat{B}_{*1}Y'_{*1}S(S'S)^{-1} = 0,$$

and so *a fortiori* $\hat{B}_{*1}$ satisfies the equation

$$\hat{B}_{*1}Y_{*1}S(S'S)^{-1}S'Y_{*1} = 0 = 0 \cdot \hat{B}_{*1}W,$$

and so it is the vector associated with the smallest possible root, $\theta = 0$.

Suppose one column of X, say the pth column $X'_{p.}$ is a vector of 1's. This arises when some equations of interest include a constant term. Then the number of exogenous variables may be reduced by 1 in the following way. Let

$$Y^* = Y - N^{-1}X'_{p.}X_{p.}Y,$$
$$X^* = \tilde{X}_p - N^{-1}X'_{p.}X_{p.}\tilde{X}_p,$$

where $\tilde{X}_p$ is the $N \times (p-1)$ submatrix of X with pth column deleted. The estimation problem reduces to one with Y^* as the matrix of endogenous variables and X^* as the matrix of exogenous variables. The coefficients of $X_{p.}$ are estimated by

$$\hat{\Gamma}'_{p.} = \frac{-\hat{B}Y'X'_{p.}}{N} - \frac{\hat{\hat{\Gamma}}\tilde{X}'_pX'_{p.}}{N},$$

where $\hat{B}$ and $\hat{\hat{\Gamma}}$ (the estimate of Γ upon excluding $\Gamma'_{p.}$) are estimated using Y^* and X^*.

This can be seen by noting that in the *reduced form*, i.e., in the general linear hypothesis model relating Y and X, the coefficients of $X_{p.}$, namely the last column of Π, are estimated as follows. Write the exponent of the likelihood function as

$$\operatorname{tr}(Y' - \Pi X')(Y' - \Pi X')'\Omega^{-1} = \operatorname{tr}(Y' - \tilde{\Pi}_p \tilde{X}_p' - \Pi_{p.}' X_{p.})$$
$$\times (Y' - \tilde{\Pi}_p \tilde{X}_p' - \Pi_{p.}' X_{p.})'\Omega^{-1},$$

where $\Pi_{p.}'$ is the last column of Π and $\tilde{\Pi}_p$ is the $n \times (p-1)$ submatrix of Π with last column deleted. Differentiating with respect to $\Pi_{p.}'$, setting the derivative equal to zero, and solving for $\hat{\Pi}_{p.}'$, we find that

$$\hat{\Pi}_{p.}' = \frac{(Y' - \hat{\tilde{\Pi}}_p \tilde{X}_p')X_{p.}'}{N}$$

(check this). Since $\hat{\Gamma} = -\hat{B}\hat{\Pi}$, $\hat{\Gamma}_{p.}' = -\hat{B}\hat{\Pi}_{p.}'$, or

$$\hat{\Gamma}_{p.}' = \frac{-\hat{B}Y'X_{p.}'}{N} - \frac{\hat{\tilde{\Gamma}}\tilde{X}_p' X_{p.}}{N},$$

as noted earlier.

Then

$$\hat{\Omega}^* = \frac{1}{N}\left(Y' - \frac{Y'X_{p.}'}{N} - \hat{\tilde{\Pi}}_p\left(\tilde{X}_p' - \frac{\tilde{X}_p' X_{p.}'}{N}\right)\right)$$
$$\times \left(Y' - \frac{Y'X_{p.}'}{N} - \hat{\tilde{\Pi}}_p\left(\tilde{X}_p' - \frac{\tilde{X}_p' X_{p.}'}{N}\right)\right)'$$
$$= \frac{1}{N}(Y^* - \hat{\tilde{\Pi}}_p X^*)(Y^* - \hat{\tilde{\Pi}}_p X^*)',$$

and this is to be used in place of $\hat{\Omega}$ in maximum likelihood estimation of B and Γ. Since the identifiability constraints did not involve $\Gamma_{p.}'$, they are unaltered in the maximization.

An interesting application of the limited information maximum likelihood estimator is to the problem of parameter estimation in the errors-in-variables linear structural relation. Suppose that the observed independent variables are functionally related to instrumental variables, so that

$$\boldsymbol{x}_j^* = \gamma_{j1} z_1 + \cdots + \gamma_{jl} z_l + \boldsymbol{r}_j, \qquad j = 1, \ldots, s.$$

Let us now write the system of simultaneous equations in the observed variables:

$$\boldsymbol{y}_i^* - \beta_1 \boldsymbol{x}_{1i}^* - \cdots - \beta_s \boldsymbol{x}_{si}^* = \boldsymbol{v}_i - \beta_1 \boldsymbol{u}_{1i} - \cdots - \beta_s \boldsymbol{u}_{si} = \boldsymbol{r}_0,$$

$$\boldsymbol{x}_{1i}^{*} - \gamma_{11} z_{1i} - \cdots - \gamma_{1l} z_{li} = \boldsymbol{r}_1,$$

$$\boldsymbol{x}_{si}^{*} - \gamma_{s1} z_{1i} - \cdots - \gamma_{sl} z_{li} = \boldsymbol{r}_s.$$

We treat the variables y^*, $x_1^*, \ldots, x_n^*$ as endogenous and $z_1, \ldots, z_l$ as exogenous. (If the relation between x^* and the z's is structural, then we treat the relation conditionally on the z's and reduce it to this case.)

Our problem is to estimate the coefficients of the first equation in this system, and so first ask under what conditions this equation is identified. Letting

$$B = \begin{bmatrix} -\beta_1 & \cdots & -\beta_s \\ 1 & & \\ \cdot & & \\ \cdot & 0 & \\ \cdot & & \\ 0 & & 1 \end{bmatrix},$$

and

$$\Gamma = -\begin{bmatrix} 0 & \cdots & 0 \\ \gamma_{11} & \cdots & \gamma_{1l} \\ \cdot & & \\ \cdot & & \\ \cdot & & \\ \gamma_{s1} & \cdots & \gamma_{sl} \end{bmatrix},$$

we see that, in our current notation, $n = s$, $p = l$, $n_1 = s$ and $p_1 = 0$. Since $\Pi_{(1\bar{1})} = -B^{-1}\Gamma$ must have rank $n_1 - 1 = s - 1$ and B has full rank s, the first row of B is identifiable if and only if the rank of Γ is $s - 1$. Thus, we see that a necessary condition for the method of instrumental variables to lead to identifiability is that $l \geqslant s$.

In the case where $l = s$, one can use the identity of indirect least squares with limited information maximum likelihood estimation to write an explicit equation for the estimate of the vector $B = (\beta_1, \ldots, \beta_s)$ as follows. Defining Z, X^*, and Y^* as matrices whose N columns are the observations on y^*, $x_1^*, \ldots, x_s^*$, $z_1, \ldots, z_s$, we see that the LIML estimate of B is

$$\hat{B} = Y^* Z'(X^* Z')^{-1},$$

which is precisely the estimator obtained earlier.

Further, if $l > s$, we are required to find the characteristic vector corresponding to the smallest characteristic root of the matrix

$$Q = \frac{W^{-1}Y_{*1}S(S'S)^{-1}S'Y_{*1}}{N},$$

where in this case

$$Y_{*1} = [Y^{*\prime}X^{*\prime}],$$

$$R = 0,$$

$$S = Z'.$$

Now Q is of the form $(A - C)^{-1}C = (C^{-1}A - I)^{-1}$, where

$$C = \begin{bmatrix} Y^* \\ X^* \end{bmatrix} Z'(ZZ')^{-1}Z[Y^{*\prime}X^{*\prime}]/N$$

$$= \begin{bmatrix} \hat{\Sigma}_{y^*Z} \\ \hat{\Sigma}_{X^*Z} \end{bmatrix} \hat{\Sigma}_{ZZ}^{-1}[\hat{\Sigma}_{Zy^*}\hat{\Sigma}_{ZX^*}],$$

and

$$A = [Y^{*\prime}X^{*\prime}][Y^*X^*]$$

$$= \begin{bmatrix} \hat{\Sigma}_{y^*y^*} & \hat{\Sigma}_{y^*X^*} \\ \hat{\Sigma}_{X^*y^*} & \hat{\Sigma}_{X^*X^*} \end{bmatrix}$$

$$= \hat{\Sigma}^*.$$

Finding the smallest characteristic root of Q is equivalent to finding the smallest characteristic root of

$$A^{-1}C = \hat{\Sigma}^{*-1}[\hat{\Sigma}_{Zy^*}\ \hat{\Sigma}_{ZX^*}]'\hat{\Sigma}_{ZZ}^{-1}[\hat{\Sigma}_{Zy^*}\ \hat{\Sigma}_{ZX^*}],$$

i.e., to the instrumental variable estimate given in section 4.3 of chapter III.

3. Maximum likelihood estimation of a system of simultaneous equations

If all the equations are identified, then one can apply the procedure of the previous section for each equation separately. However, it does not make use of all the information available from the other equations in obtaining estimates of the coefficients of a given equation. In contrast, let us look at the full model again.

The vector $\vec{U}$ can easily be seen to be distributed as $N(0, \Sigma \otimes I)$.

Since $\vec{Y} = \vec{U} + \Delta Z'$, let us determine the distribution of $\vec{Y}$. Since

$$f_{\vec{U}}(\vec{U}) = (2\pi)^{-Nn/2}|\Sigma \otimes I|^{-\frac{1}{2}} \exp\{-\vec{U}(\Sigma^{-1} \otimes I)\vec{U}'/2\},$$

we see that

$$f_{\vec{Y}}(\vec{Y}) = (2\pi)^{-Nn/2}|\Sigma \otimes I|^{-\frac{1}{2}} \times \exp\{-(\vec{Y} - \Delta Z')(\Sigma^{-1} \otimes I)(\vec{Y} - \Delta Z')'/2\} J(\vec{U} \to \vec{Y}).$$

However, we cannot compute the Jacobian directly from the relation $\vec{Y} = \vec{U} + \Delta Z'$, as some of the elements of Z may be lagged endogenous variables, i.e., y's.

But

$$u_{ji} = \sum_{k=1}^{n} y_{ki}\beta_{jk} + \sum_{k=1}^{p} x_{ki}\gamma_{jk},$$

so that

$$\frac{\partial u_{ji}}{\partial y_{j'i'}} = \begin{cases} \beta_{jj'}, & \text{if } i = i', \\ \gamma_{jj'}, & \text{if } i > i' \text{ and } x_{j'i} = y_{j'i'} \\ & \text{(i.e., if } x_{j'i'} \text{ is a lagged endogenous variable)}, \\ 0, & \text{otherwise.} \end{cases}$$

Ordering the rows and columns of the Jacobian matrix by superscript and within superscript by subscript (e.g., the first few rows correspond to $u_{11}, u_{21}, \ldots$), we see that

$$J = \begin{vmatrix} B & 0 & & & 0 \\ * & B & 0 & & \\ * & * & B & & \\ & & & \ddots & \\ & & & & 0 \\ & & & & \\ * & * & & & B \end{vmatrix},$$

where the * represents a matrix which may have some $\gamma_{jj'}$'s in it. Then $J = (|B|^n)^+$ and the logarithm of the likelihood function of $\vec{Y}$ is

$$L = -\frac{Nn}{2} \log 2\pi - \frac{N}{2} \log |\Sigma| + N \log |B|^+ - \frac{1}{2}(\vec{Y} - \Delta Z')(\Sigma^{-1} \otimes I)(\vec{Y} - \Delta Z')'.$$

Since

$$(\vec{Y}-\Delta Z')(\Sigma^{-1}\otimes I)(\vec{Y}-\Delta Z')' = \sum_{i=1}^{n}\sum_{j=1}^{n}(Y_{i.}-\Delta_i Z_i')(Y_{j.}-\Delta_j Z_j')'\sigma^{ij},$$

where σ^{ij} is the (i, j)th element of Σ^{-1}, and $\Delta_i = (B_{*(i)}\Gamma_{*i})$, we see that

$$\begin{aligned}\frac{\partial L}{\partial \sigma^{ij}} &= -\frac{1}{2}(Y_{i.}-\Delta_i Z_i')(Y_{j.}-\Delta_j Z_j')' + \frac{N}{2}\frac{\Sigma_{ij}^{-1}}{|\Sigma^{-1}|}\\ &= -\frac{1}{2}(Y_{i.}-\Delta_i Z_i')(Y_{j.}-\Delta_j Z_j')' + \frac{N}{2}\sigma_{ij} = 0.\end{aligned}$$

Thus,

$$\hat{\sigma}_{ij} = ((Y_{i.}-\Delta_i Z_i')(Y_{j.}-\Delta_j Z_j')')/N.$$

Substituting this into L leaves us with

$$L = -\frac{Nn}{2}\log 2\pi - \frac{N}{2} - \frac{N}{2}\log|\hat{\Sigma}| + N\log|B|^{+}.$$

Let

$$p(\Delta) = \frac{\partial \log|B|^{+}}{\partial \Delta}, \qquad q(\Delta) = -\frac{1}{2}\frac{\partial \log|\hat{\Sigma}|}{\partial \Delta}.$$

Then we must solve the equation

$$p(\Delta)+q(\Delta)=0$$

for the maximum likelihood estimate of Δ. In general, these equations are nonlinear, and must be solved by iterative methods. The solution is called the full-information maximum likelihood (FIML) estimate of Δ.

Exercise: Consider a system of n simultaneous linear equations, each of which are just identifiable, i.e., for each j $n_j - 1 = p - p_j$ and rank $\Pi_{(j\bar{j})} = n_j - 1$. Derive the FIML estimator of the coefficients of the system of equations in this case.

In the special case where B is triangular, since our normalization makes the diagonal elements of B equal to -1, $|B|^{+} = 1$ for all Δ, so that $p(\Delta) = 0$. If, further, Σ were diagonal, then $\log|\hat{\Sigma}| = \sum_{i=1}^{n}\log\hat{\sigma}_{ii}$ and

$$q(\Delta) = (1/2N)\sum_{i=1}^{n}\frac{Z_i'(Y_{i.}-\Delta_i Z_i')}{\hat{\sigma}_{ii}} = 0,$$

when each term is zero, i.e., when

$$Z_i'(Y_{i.} - \hat{\Delta}_i Z_i')' = 0,$$

or

$$\hat{\Delta}_i = Y_{i.} Z_i (Z_i' Z_i)^{-1}.$$

Consider now the FIML estimator of B, Γ, Σ, or alternatively of $\Theta = (\Delta, \vec{\Sigma})$ where $\vec{\Sigma}$ is the $n(n+1)/2$ vector of elements of Σ. Its asymptotic covariance matrix is the inverse of the matrix

$$A = -\mathscr{E}\begin{bmatrix} \dfrac{\partial^2 \log f_{\vec{Y}}(\vec{Y};\Theta)}{\partial\Delta'\,\partial\Delta} & \dfrac{\partial^2 \log f_{\vec{Y}}(\vec{Y};\Theta)}{\partial\Delta'\,\partial\vec{\Sigma}} \\ \dfrac{\partial^2 \log f_{\vec{Y}}(\vec{Y};\Theta)}{\partial\vec{\Sigma}'\,\partial\Delta} & \dfrac{\partial^2 \log f_{\vec{Y}}(\vec{Y};\Theta)}{\partial\vec{\Sigma}'\,\partial\vec{\Sigma}} \end{bmatrix}$$

$$= \begin{bmatrix} A_1 & A_2 \\ A_2' & A_3 \end{bmatrix}.$$

The asymptotic covariance matrix of $\hat{\Delta}$ alone is given by the upper left-hand block of $J_0 = A^{-1}$, which can easily be seen to be $(A_1 - A_2 A_3^{-1} A_2')^{-1}$. But this block is also obtained directly by inverting

$$-E\left[\frac{\partial^2 \log f_{\vec{Y}}(\vec{Y};\Theta^*)}{\partial\Delta'\,\partial\Delta}\right],$$

where $f_{\vec{Y}}(\vec{Y},\Theta^*) = f_{\vec{Y}}(\vec{Y};\Delta,\hat{\vec{\Sigma}}(\Delta))$. This can be seen by the following argument.

Since

$$\left.\frac{\partial \log f_{\vec{Y}}(\vec{Y};\Theta)}{\partial\vec{\Sigma}}\right|_{\vec{\Sigma}=\hat{\vec{\Sigma}}(\Delta)} = 0 \quad \text{for all} \quad \Delta,$$

differentiating with respect to Δ yields the equation

$$\left.\frac{\partial^2 \log f_{\vec{Y}}(\vec{Y};\Theta)}{\partial\vec{\Sigma}'\,\partial\Delta} + \frac{\partial^2 \log f_{\vec{Y}}(\vec{Y};\Theta)}{\partial\vec{\Sigma}'\,\partial\vec{\Sigma}}\frac{\partial\hat{\vec{\Sigma}}(\Delta)}{\partial\Delta}\right|_{\vec{\Sigma}=\hat{\vec{\Sigma}}(\Delta)} = 0,$$

or

$$\frac{\partial\hat{\Sigma}(\Delta)}{\partial\Delta} = -\left[\frac{\partial^2 \log f_{\vec{Y}}(\vec{Y};\Theta)}{\partial\vec{\Sigma}'\,\partial\vec{\Sigma}}\right]^{-1}\frac{\partial^2 \log f_{\vec{Y}}(\vec{Y};\Theta)}{\partial\vec{\Sigma}'\,\partial\Delta}.$$

But $\log f_{\vec{Y}}(\vec{Y},\Theta^*) = \log f_{\vec{Y}}(\vec{Y};\Delta,\vec{\Sigma}(\Delta))$, so that

$$\frac{\partial \log f_{\vec{Y}}(\vec{Y};\Theta^*)}{\partial\Delta} = \left.\frac{\partial \log f_{\vec{Y}}(\vec{Y};\Theta)}{\partial\Delta}\right|_{\Sigma=\hat{\Sigma}(\Delta)},$$

and

$$\frac{\partial^2 \log f_{\vec{Y}}(\vec{Y};\Theta^*)}{\partial \Delta'\,\partial \Delta} = \frac{\partial^2 \log f_{\vec{Y}}(\vec{Y};\Theta)}{\partial \Delta'\,\partial \Delta} + \frac{\partial^2 \log f_{\vec{Y}}(\vec{Y};\Theta)}{\partial \Delta'\,\partial \vec{\Sigma}}\,\frac{\partial \hat{\Sigma}(\Delta)}{\partial \Delta}\bigg|_{\Sigma=\hat{\Sigma}(\Delta)}$$

$$= \frac{\partial^2 \log f_{\vec{Y}}(\vec{Y};\Theta)}{\partial \Delta'\,\partial \Delta} - \frac{\partial^2 \log f_{\vec{Y}}(\vec{Y};\Theta)}{\partial \Delta'\,\partial \vec{\Sigma}} \times \left[\frac{\partial^2 \log f_{\vec{Y}}(\vec{Y};\Theta)}{\partial \vec{\Sigma}'\,\partial \vec{\Sigma}}\right]^{-1} \times \frac{\partial^2 \log f_{\vec{Y}}(\vec{Y};\Theta)}{\partial \vec{\Sigma}'\,\partial \Delta}\bigg|_{\Sigma=\hat{\Sigma}(\Delta)},$$

for all Δ. Taking expected values of both sides, we see that

$$\mathscr{E}\left[\frac{\partial^2 \log f_{\vec{Y}}(\vec{Y},\Theta^*)}{\partial \Delta'\,\partial \Delta}\right]^{-1} = A_1 - A_2 A_3^{-1} A_2'.$$

To determine the asymptotic covariance matrix of $\hat{\Delta}$, we will find it easier to determine the matrix whose typical element is

$$\frac{\partial \log f_{\vec{Y}}(\vec{Y};\Theta)}{\partial \delta_{i\alpha}}\,\frac{\partial \log f_{\vec{Y}}(\vec{Y};\Theta)}{\partial \delta_{j\beta}}.$$

In our above notation, $\partial \log f_{\vec{Y}}(\vec{Y};\Theta)/\partial \delta_{i\alpha} = p(\delta_{i\alpha}) + q(\delta_{i\alpha})$, where

$$p(\delta_{i\alpha}) = \begin{cases} \beta^{lk}, & \text{if } \delta_{i\alpha} = \beta_{kl}, \\ 0, & \text{otherwise,} \end{cases}$$

$$q(\delta_{i\alpha}) = \frac{1}{N}\sum_{k=1}^{n} \hat{\sigma}^{ki}[(Y_{k.} - \Delta_k Z_k')Z_i]_\alpha,$$

β^{lk} is the (l, k)th element of B^{-1}, $\hat{\sigma}^{ki}$ is the (k, i)th element of $\hat{\Sigma}^{-1}$, and $[(Y_{k.} - \Delta_k Z_k')Z_i]_\alpha$ is the αth element of the vector $[(Y_{k.} - \Delta_k Z_k')Z_i]$.

Thus the asymptotic covariance matrix is the probability limit of

$$q'(\Delta)q(\Delta) + q'(\Delta)p(\Delta) + p'(\Delta)q(\Delta) + p'(\Delta)p(\Delta).$$

To obtain $q(\Delta)$ we must digress and reconsider the reduced form to define some necessary quantities.

Recalling that $\mathbf{Y}_{.i} = X_{.i}\Pi' + \mathbf{U}_{.i}B'^{-1}$, define $\mathbf{V}_{.i} = \mathbf{U}_{.i}B'^{-1}$. Now rewrite the matrix $\mathbf{Y}_{*j}$ as $\bar{Y}_{*j} + \mathbf{V}_{*j}$, where $\bar{Y}_{*j}$ is a matrix of constants involving the exogenous variables and the matrix Π, and $\mathbf{V}_{*j}$ is the $N \times (n_j - 1)$ matrix

$$V_{*j} = \begin{bmatrix} v_{j_1 1} & \cdots & v_{j_{n_j-1} 1} \\ v_{j_1 2} & \cdots & v_{j_{n_j-1} 2} \\ \cdot & & \\ \cdot & & \\ \cdot & & \\ v_{j_1 N} & \cdots & v_{j_{n_j-1} N} \end{bmatrix},$$

and $j_1, \ldots, j_{n_j-1}$ are the indices of the endogenous variables (excluding the jth) which have non-zero coefficients in the jth equation.

Similarly, rewrite the matrix Z as $Z = \bar{Z} + V$, where

$$\bar{Z} = \begin{bmatrix} \bar{Y}_{*1} X_{*1} & & & & 0 \\ & \bar{Y}_{*2} X_{*2} & & & \\ & & \cdot & & \\ & & & \cdot & \\ & & & & \cdot \\ 0 & & & & \bar{Y}_{*n} X_{*n} \end{bmatrix},$$

and

$$V = \begin{bmatrix} V_{*1}\begin{matrix}0\\0\end{matrix} & & & & & \\ & V_{*2}\begin{matrix}0\\0\end{matrix} & & & & \\ & & V_{*3} & & & \\ & & & \cdot & & \\ & & & & \cdot & \\ & & & & & \cdot \\ & & & & & V_{*n} 0 \end{bmatrix}.$$

Now $q(\Delta) = U(\hat{\Sigma}^{-1} \otimes I)(\bar{Z} + V)/N$, so

$$\begin{aligned} N^2 q'(\Delta) q(\Delta) = {} & \bar{Z}'(\hat{\Sigma}^{-1} \otimes I)\vec{U}'\vec{U}(\hat{\Sigma}^{-1} \otimes I)\bar{Z} \\ & + \bar{Z}'(\Sigma^{-1} \otimes I)\vec{U}'\vec{U}(\Sigma^{-1} \otimes I)V \\ & + V'(\Sigma^{-1} \otimes I)\vec{U}'\vec{U}(\Sigma^{-1} \otimes I)\bar{Z} \\ & + V'(\Sigma^{-1} \otimes I)\vec{U}'\vec{U}(\Sigma^{-1} \otimes I)V. \end{aligned}$$

Since $\text{plim}_{N\to\infty} (\vec{U}'\vec{U}/N) = \Sigma \otimes I$, $\text{plim}_{N\to\infty} \hat{\Sigma} = \Sigma$, and $\text{plim}_{N\to\infty} (V'M/N) = 0$, for any matrix of constants M, we see that

$$\begin{aligned} \underset{N\to\infty}{\text{plim}}\, q'(\Delta)q(\Delta) = {} & \underset{N\to\infty}{\text{plim}} \frac{\bar{Z}'(\Sigma^{-1} \otimes I)\bar{Z}}{N} \\ & + \underset{N\to\infty}{\text{plim}} \frac{V'(\Sigma^{-1} \otimes I)\vec{U}'\vec{U}(\Sigma^{-1} \otimes I)V}{N^2}. \end{aligned}$$

Also,

$$Nq'(\Delta)p(\Delta) = \bar{Z}'(\Sigma^{-1} \otimes I)\vec{U}'p(\Delta) + V'(\Sigma^{-1} \otimes I)\vec{U}'p(\Delta),$$

and, since $\text{plim}_{N\to\infty}(\vec{U}'M/N) = 0$ for any matrix of constants M, we see that

$$\underset{N\to\infty}{\text{plim}}\, q'(\Delta)p(\Delta) = \underset{N\to\infty}{\text{plim}} \frac{V'(\Sigma^{-1} \otimes I)\vec{U}'p(\Delta)}{N}.$$

Finally, $p(\Delta)$ is a vector of constants and is described by

$$p(\Delta) = (\beta^{1_1 1}, \ldots, \beta^{1_{n_1-1}1}, 0, \ldots, 0, \beta^{2_1 2}, \ldots, \beta^{2_{n_2-1}2}, 0, \ldots, 0, \ldots, \beta^{n_1 n}, \ldots, \beta^{n_{n_n-1}n}, 0, \ldots, 0).$$

The only piece of this jigsaw puzzle that we still have to evaluate further is

$$\underset{N\to\infty}{\text{plim}} \frac{V'(\Sigma^{-1} \otimes I)\vec{U}'}{N}.$$

Recalling that $U_{j.} = -(u_{j1}, \ldots, u_{jn})$, we see that

$$V'(\Sigma^{-1} \otimes I)\vec{U}' = -\begin{bmatrix} \sigma^{11}V'_{*1} & \sigma^{12}V'_{*1} & \cdots & \sigma^{1n}V'_{*1} \\ 0 & & & 0 \\ \sigma^{21}V'_{*2} & \sigma^{22}V'_{*2} & \cdots & \sigma^{2n}V'_{*2} \\ 0 & & & 0 \\ \cdot & & & \\ \cdot & & & \\ \cdot & & & \\ \sigma^{n1}V'_{*n} & \sigma^{n2}V'_{*n} & \cdots & \sigma^{nn}V'_{*n} \\ 0 & & & 0 \end{bmatrix} \begin{bmatrix} U'_{1.} \\ \cdot \\ \cdot \\ \cdot \\ U'_{n.} \end{bmatrix}$$

$$= -\begin{bmatrix} \sum_{j=1}^{n} \sigma^{1j}V'_{*1}U_{j.} \\ 0 \\ \sum_{j=1}^{n} \sigma^{2j}V'_{*2}U_{j.} \\ 0 \\ \cdot \\ \cdot \\ \cdot \\ \sum_{j=1}^{n} \sigma^{nj}V'_{*n}U_{j.} \\ 0 \end{bmatrix}.$$

Now express B and B^{-1} as

$$B = \begin{bmatrix} B_1 \\ \cdot \\ \cdot \\ \cdot \\ B_n \end{bmatrix},$$

and

$$B^{-1} = \begin{bmatrix} B^1 \\ \cdot \\ \cdot \\ \cdot \\ B^n \end{bmatrix},$$

where B_i and B^i are n-vectors. Then,

$$V_{.i} = U_{.i}B'^{-1} = U_{.i}[B^{1\prime} \cdots B^{n\prime}],$$

and

$$V_{*j} = \begin{bmatrix} U_{.1}B^{j_1\prime} \cdots U_{.1}B^{j_{n_j-1}\prime} \\ \cdot \\ \cdot \\ \cdot \\ U_{.N}B^{j_1\prime} \cdots U_{.N}B^{j_{n_j-1}\prime} \end{bmatrix}$$

$$= \begin{bmatrix} U_{.1} \\ \cdot \\ \cdot \\ \cdot \\ U_{.N} \end{bmatrix} [B^{j_1\prime} \cdots B^{j_{n_j-1}\prime}].$$

Then,

$$V'_{*i}U'_{j.} = \begin{bmatrix} B^{i_1} \\ \cdot \\ \cdot \\ \cdot \\ B^{i_{n_1-1}} \end{bmatrix} [U'_{.1} \cdots U'_{.N}]U'_{j.}.$$

Since $[U'_{.1} \cdots U'_{.N}]U'_{j.}$ is an $n \times 1$ matrix with lth element $\sum_{i=1}^{N} u_{l.i}u_{j.i}$, we see that

$$\underset{N\to\infty}{\text{plim}}\frac{1}{N}[\boldsymbol{U}'_{.1}\cdots\boldsymbol{U}'_{.N}]\boldsymbol{U}'_{j.}$$

is an $n\times 1$ matrix consisting of the lth column of Σ. Then $\text{plim}_{N\to\infty}(1/N)\boldsymbol{V}'(\Sigma\otimes I)\vec{\boldsymbol{U}}'$ has as its ith non-zero block the column vector

$$-\begin{bmatrix} B^{i_1} \\ \cdot \\ \cdot \\ \cdot \\ B^{i_{n_i-1}} \end{bmatrix}\sum_{j=1}^{n}\sigma^{ij}\begin{bmatrix} \sigma_{1j} \\ \cdot \\ \cdot \\ \cdot \\ \sigma_{nj} \end{bmatrix}=-\begin{bmatrix} B^{i_1} \\ \cdot \\ \cdot \\ \cdot \\ B^{i_{n_i-1}} \end{bmatrix}E'_i,$$

where E_i is the n-vector with 1 as ith coordinate and zeros elsewhere.

Looking carefully at this ith block, we see that it consists of the elements

$$\beta^{i_1 i},\beta^{i_2 i},\ldots,\beta^{i_{n_i-1}i},$$

that is, the ith block of $p(\Delta)$. Thus,

$$\underset{N\to\infty}{\text{plim}}\frac{\boldsymbol{V}'(\Sigma^{-1}\otimes I)\vec{\boldsymbol{U}}'}{N}=p'(\Delta).$$

To put the pieces together now,

$$\underset{N\to\infty}{\text{plim}}\,q'(\Delta)q(\Delta)=\underset{N\to\infty}{\text{plim}}\frac{\bar{Z}'(\Sigma^{-1}\otimes I)\bar{Z}}{N}+p'(\Delta)p(\Delta),$$

$$\underset{N\to\infty}{\text{plim}}\,q'(\Delta)p(\Delta)=-p'(\Delta)p(\Delta),$$

and so the asymptotic covariance matrix of the FIML estimate of Δ is

$$\underset{N\to\infty}{\text{plim}}\frac{\bar{Z}'(\Sigma^{-1}\otimes I)\bar{Z}}{N}.$$

4. Simultaneous least squares estimation

Note that in maximum likelihood estimation we are reduced to the problem of maximizing the function

$$L=-\frac{Nn}{2}\log 2\pi-\frac{N}{2}-\frac{N}{2}\log|\hat{\Sigma}|+N\log|B|^{+},$$

or equivalently minimizing $|B^{-1}\hat{\Sigma}B^{-1\prime}| = |\hat{\Omega}|$, the determinant of the covariance matrix of the reduced form model. This principle of estimation led to a system of nonlinear equations in $\hat{\Delta}$ to be solved.

As a computationally easier alternative estimation principle, it has been suggested that one minimize instead $\operatorname{tr}\hat{\Omega}$ with respect to Δ. Once again the equation

$$\frac{\partial \operatorname{tr}\hat{\Omega}}{\partial \Delta} = 0$$

is nonlinear and must be solved by iterative methods.

The reason this method is dubbed "simultaneous least squares" (SLS) is that $\operatorname{tr}\hat{\Omega}$ is the sum of the diagonal elements of $\hat{\Omega}$, where the jth diagonal element is the squared residual $(Y_{j.} - \Pi_j X')(Y_{j.} - \Pi_j X')'$, for $j = 1, \ldots, n$. This function, to be minimized with respect to Δ (since Π is a function of Δ) is in the form of the function minimized in the ordinary linear expected value model. The difference, which makes this procedure ad hoc rather than emerging as a consequence of the model considered in chapter III, is that the n residual vectors $Y_{j.} - \Pi_j X'$ are not independent, hence one cannot merely add the n squared residuals to attain the "best" function to be minimized. Instead one must incorporate in the quadratic form the covariance matrix between the residual vectors. If that matrix were incorporated into the quadratic form to be minimized, then we would once again have the same minimization problem as that of maximum likelihood estimation.

This point can be seen clearly by referring once again to the likelihood function of the reduced form,

$$L = -\frac{nN}{2}\log 2\pi - \frac{N}{2}\log|\Omega| - \frac{1}{2}\sum_{i=1}^{N}(Y_{.i} - X_{.i}\Pi')\Omega^{-1}(Y_{.i} - X_{.i}\Pi')'.$$

There are two routes to be taken in maximizing L. In one we note that L is maximized with respect to Ω if

$$\hat{\Omega} = \frac{1}{N}\sum_{i=1}^{N}(Y_{.i} - X_{.i}\Pi')'(Y_{.i} - X_{.i}\Pi'),$$

and, since in this case $\sum_{i=1}^{N}(Y_{.i} - X_{.i}\Pi')\hat{\Omega}^{-1}(Y_{.i} - X_{.i}\Pi')' = nN$, all that remains to be maximized is $-\log|\hat{\Omega}|$, as seen earlier. In the other route, we first try to maximize L with respect to Δ. Since only Π is a function of Δ, this reduces to minimizing

$$\sum_{i=1}^{N}(Y_{.i} - X_{.i}\Pi')\Omega^{-1}(Y_{.i} - X_{.i}\Pi')' = \operatorname{tr}(Y - X\Pi')'(Y - X\Pi')\Omega^{-1},$$

rather than the function minimized in simultaneous least squares, namely,

$$\sum_{j=1}^{n} (Y_{j.} - \Pi_j X')(Y_{j.} - \Pi_j X')' = \operatorname{tr}(Y - X\Pi')'(Y - X\Pi').$$

5. Simultaneous equation estimation via instrumental variables

Consider for the moment the jth equation

$$\boldsymbol{Y}'_{j.} = \boldsymbol{Y}_{*(j)}\boldsymbol{B}'_{*(j)} + \boldsymbol{X}_{*j}\boldsymbol{\Gamma}'_{*j} + \boldsymbol{U}'_{j.},$$

of a system of simultaneous equations, and assume that this equation is identifiable. This equation is a linear equation in which the vector $\Delta_j = (B_{*(j)}, \Gamma_{*j})$ of parameters is to be estimated. One can view this equation as telling us that, except for an error term, $\boldsymbol{U}'_{j.}$, the y's are related in a structural relation,

$$\boldsymbol{Y}'_{j.} = \boldsymbol{Y}_{*(j)}\boldsymbol{B}'_{*(j)} + \boldsymbol{X}_{*j}\boldsymbol{\Gamma}'_{*j}.$$

Since the system of equations is interdependent, i.e., elements of $\boldsymbol{Y}_{j.}$ are also elements of $\boldsymbol{Y}_{*(k)}$ for some $k \neq j$, one can view $\boldsymbol{Y}_{*(j)}$ as equal to some "true value" $\bar{Y}_{*(j)}$ plus an error, so that the jth equation is a structural relation with errors-in-variables.

We can treat the system of equations similarly. In the equation

$$\vec{\boldsymbol{Y}}' = \boldsymbol{Z}\Delta' + \vec{\boldsymbol{U}}',$$

as constructed earlier, we can view $\boldsymbol{Z}$ as of the form $\boldsymbol{Z} = \bar{Z} + \boldsymbol{W}$ and so the system of equations can be treated as a structural relation with errors-in-variables.

An omnibus approach to the problem of estimating Δ_j and/or Δ is via the use of an instrumental variable. In the various subsections of this section, we will treat all non-maximum likelihood methods for estimating the structural parameters, regardless of how the methods were originally derived or discovered, as applications of the selection and use of a particular instrumental variable.

For the jth equation, we seek an r_j-vector which is "most uncorrelated" with $y_{jk} - \boldsymbol{Y}_{(j).k}\boldsymbol{B}'_{*(j)} - X_{j.k}\Gamma'_{*j}$, the typical element of $\boldsymbol{Y}'_{j.} - \boldsymbol{Z}_j\Delta'_j$. If we restrict ourselves to $r_j = n_j + p_j - 1$ and let W_j be the $N \times r_j$ matrix of observations on the vector of instrumental variables to be used to estimate Δ_j, then

$$\hat{\Delta}_j = Y_{j.} W_j' (Z_j W_j')^{-1}$$

is the estimator of Δ_j.

Similarly, if we let W be the $nN \times r$ matrix

$$W = \begin{bmatrix} W_1 & & & & 0 \\ & W_2 & & & \\ & & \cdot & & \\ & & & \cdot & \\ 0 & & & \cdot & W_n \end{bmatrix}$$

then

$$\hat{\Delta} = \vec{Y}' W' (Z W')^{-1}.$$

Of course, this assumes that $Z_j W_j'$ and/or ZW' are invertible. If they are not invertible, the general theory given in section 4.3 of chapter III applies. We will in what follows assume the invertibility of these matrices, primarily for ease of exposition of results. In case lack of invertibility materially affects the applicability of the method of instrumental variables in its general form (e.g., if lack of invertibility is equivalent to unidentifiability), the fact will be duly noted.

Obviously if the instrumental variables are separately observed variables, i.e., not functions of the exogenous or endogenous variables in the system of equations, then we are using additional information to help us get out of an unidentifiable situation. But typically the instrumental variables used are functions of X, the matrix of exogenous variables. In this case, are we getting something for nothing by taking functions of the variables of the model and making, using these functions as instrumental variables, an identifiable situation out of an unidentifiable one?

One popular choice of form of W_j, exhibiting explicit functional dependence on X, is the form

$$W_j = (Y_{*(j)} - \tilde{W}_j \quad X_{*j}).$$

This form is used in the two-stage least squares, k-class, and characteristic vectors approaches to estimation of Δ_j, to be described later. With this choice of W_j, if the jth equation is not identifiable, then

$$Z_j'W_j = \begin{bmatrix} Y'_{*(j)} \\ X'_{*j} \end{bmatrix} [Y_{*(j)} - \tilde{W}_j \quad X_{*j}]$$

$$= \begin{bmatrix} Y'_{*(j)}Y_{*(j)} - Y'_{*(j)}\tilde{W}_j & Y'_{*(j)}X_{*j} \\ X'_{*j}Y_{*(j)} - X'_{*j}\tilde{W}_j & X'_{*j}X_{*j} \end{bmatrix}$$

should not be invertible. That indeed it is not is the consequence of the following theorem.

Theorem: *The columns of $\Pi_{*j}X'_{*j} + \Pi_{*\bar{j}}X'_{*\bar{j}}$ and those of X'_{*j} are linearly dependent if and only if the* jth *equation is not identifiable.*

Proof: Suppose the jth equation is not identifiable. Then, by the rank condition, the rank of $\Pi_{*\bar{j}}$ is less than $n_j - 1$, and therefore there is an n_j-vector $A \neq 0$ such that $\Pi'_{*\bar{j}}A' = 0$, so that

$$\boldsymbol{Y}_{*(j)}A' = X_{*j}\Pi'_{*j}A' + \boldsymbol{U}_{*(j)}\Pi'A'.$$

But

$$\boldsymbol{Y}_{*(j)}A' - \boldsymbol{U}_{*(j)}\Pi'A' = (X_{*j}\Pi'_{*j} + X_{*\bar{j}}\Pi'_{*\bar{j}})A'.$$

Therefore,

$$A(\Pi_{*j}X'_{*j} + \Pi_{*\bar{j}}X'_{*\bar{j}}) = (A\Pi_{*j})X'_{*j},$$

i.e., the columns of the two matrices are linearly dependent.

Conversely, suppose that there exist vectors C and D, not both the zero vector, such that

$$0 = C(\Pi_{*j}X' + \Pi_{*\bar{j}}X'_{*\bar{j}}) + DX'_{*j}$$
$$= C\boldsymbol{Y}'_{*(j)} + DX'_{*j} - CU'_{*(j)}.$$

Then, adding this equation to

$$\boldsymbol{Y}_{j.} = B_{*(j)}\boldsymbol{Y}'_{*(j)} + \Gamma_{*j}X'_{*j} - U'_{j.}$$

yields

$$\boldsymbol{Y}_{j.} = [C + B_{*(j)}]\boldsymbol{Y}'_{*(j)} + [D + \Gamma_{*j}]X'_{*j} - [C\boldsymbol{U}'_{*(j)} + \boldsymbol{U}'_{j.}],$$

which is indistinguishable from the jth equation.

Thus, if W_j is of the form $W_j = (Y_{*(j)} - W_j \ X_{*j})$, and the model is not identifiable, then the columns of X'_{*j} are linearly dependent on the columns of $\Pi_{*j}X'_{*j}+\Pi_{*\bar{j}}X'_{*\bar{j}}$. Thus,

$$\boldsymbol{Z}_j\boldsymbol{W}'_j=(\boldsymbol{Y}_{*(j)}\ X_{*j})\begin{pmatrix}\boldsymbol{Y}_{*(j)}-\boldsymbol{W}_j\\ X'_{*j}\end{pmatrix}$$

$$=(X_{*j}\Pi'_{*j}+X_{*\bar{j}}\Pi'_{*\bar{j}}+\boldsymbol{U}_{*(j)}\Pi'\ X_{*j})\begin{pmatrix}\boldsymbol{Y}_{*(j)}-\boldsymbol{W}_j\\ X'_{*j}\end{pmatrix}$$

$$=(X_{*j}A'+\boldsymbol{U}_{*(j)}\Pi'\ X_{*j})\begin{pmatrix}\boldsymbol{Y}_{*(j)}-\boldsymbol{W}_j\\ X'_{*j}\end{pmatrix}.$$

But since $\mathscr{E}\boldsymbol{U}_{*(j)}=0$, $\operatorname{plim}_{N\to\infty}(1/N)\boldsymbol{U}_{*(j)}\Pi'=0$, and so

$$\operatorname*{plim}_{N\to\infty}\left[\frac{1}{N}\boldsymbol{Z}_j\boldsymbol{W}'_j\right]=(X_{*j}A'\ X_{*j})\operatorname*{plim}_{N\to\infty}\begin{pmatrix}\boldsymbol{Y}_{*(j)}-\boldsymbol{W}_j\\ X'_{*j}\end{pmatrix}.$$

Since $(X_{*j}A'\ X_{*j})$ has rank at most p_j, not n_j+p_j-1, $\operatorname{plim}_{N\to\infty}[(1/N)\boldsymbol{Z}_j\boldsymbol{W}'_j]$ will not be an invertible matrix. Hence the method of instrumental variables will of necessity break down if the jth equation is not identifiable.

5.1. *Two-stage least squares estimate*

Briefly, the particular matrix of instrumental variables which forms the basis for the two-stage least squares estimate of Δ_j is the matrix

$$W_j=X(X'X)^{-1}X'Z_j,$$

where X is the $N\times p$ matrix whose ith row is $X_{.i}$, and where $Z_j=(Y_{*(j)}\ X_{*j})$. Then,

$$\hat{\Delta}_j=Y'_{j.}X(X'X)^{-1}X'Z_j[Z'_jX(X'X)^{-1}X'Z_j]^{-1}.$$

For the entire system of equations we can take

$$W=Q(Q'Q)^{-1}Q'Z,$$

and

$$\hat{\Delta}=\vec{Y}Q(Q'Q)^{-1}Q'Z[Z'Q(Q'Q)^{-1}Q'Z]^{-1},$$

where $Q=I_n\otimes X$ and I_n is the $n\times n$ identity matrix.

The two-stage least squares estimate is sometimes presented as, in our notation,

$$\hat{\Delta}_j=Y_{j.}[Y_{*(j)}-T_j,X_{*j}]\begin{bmatrix}Y'_{*(j)}Y_{*(j)}-T'_jT_j & Y'_{*(j)}X_{*j}\\ X'_{*j}Y_{*(j)} & X'_{*j}X_{*j}\end{bmatrix}^{-1},$$

where $T_j = [I - X(X'X)^{-1}X']Y_{*(j)}$. We shall now show that this is identical with the estimator we give.

As usual we assume that the $N \times p$ matrix X has as its first p_j columns the matrix X_{*j}. Thus,

$$X\begin{bmatrix} I \\ 0 \end{bmatrix} = X_{*j},$$

where I is a $p_j \times p_j$ matrix and 0 is a $(p - p_j) \times p_j$ matrix of zeros. Also $X(X'X)^{-1}X'Y_{*(j)} = Y_{*(j)} - T_j$, so that

$$[Y_{*(j)} - T_j, X_{*j}] = X\begin{bmatrix} (X'X)^{-1}X'Y_{*(j)} & I \\ & 0 \end{bmatrix}.$$

Now, since $X'T_j = X'Y_{*(j)} - X'X(X'X)^{-1}X'Y_{*(j)} = 0$, $X'_{*j}T_j = 0$ as well. Also $I - X(X'X)^{-1}X'$ is a projection matrix. Thus,

$$\begin{aligned}
\begin{bmatrix} Y'_{*(j)} - T'_j \\ X'_{*j} \end{bmatrix} [Y_{*(j)} - T_j, X_{*j}]
&= \begin{bmatrix} Y'_{*(j)}Y_{*(j)} - T'_jT_j & Y'_{*(j)}X_{*j} \\ X'_{*j}Y_{*(j)} & X'_{*j}X_{*j} \end{bmatrix} \\
&= \begin{bmatrix} Y'_{*(j)}X & (X'X)^{-1} \\ I & 0 \end{bmatrix} X'X \begin{bmatrix} (X'X)^{-1}X'Y_{*(j)} & I \\ & 0 \end{bmatrix} \\
&= \begin{bmatrix} Y'_{*(j)}X \\ X'_{*j}X \end{bmatrix} \begin{bmatrix} (X'X)^{-1}X'Y_{*(j)} & I \\ & 0 \end{bmatrix} \\
&= \begin{bmatrix} Y'_{*(j)}X(X'X)^{-1}X'Y_{*(j)} & Y'_{*(j)}X_{*j} \\ X'_{*j}X(X'X)^{-1}X'Y_{*(j)} & X'_{*j}X_{*j} \end{bmatrix}.
\end{aligned}$$

Since this matrix is symmetric, $Y'_{*(j)}X_{*j} = Y'_{*(j)}X(X'X)^{-1}X'X_{*j}$. Also,

$$\begin{aligned}
X'_{*j}X(X'X)^{-1}X'X_{*j} &= [I \quad 0]X'X(X'X)^{-1}X'X\begin{bmatrix} I \\ 0 \end{bmatrix} \\
&= [I \quad 0]X'X\begin{bmatrix} I \\ 0 \end{bmatrix} \\
&= X'_{*j}X_{*j}.
\end{aligned}$$

Thus,

$$\begin{bmatrix} Y'_{*(j)}Y_{*(j)} - T'_jT_j & Y'_{*(j)}X_{*j} \\ X'_{*j}Y_{*(j)} & X'_{*j}X_{*j} \end{bmatrix} = Z'_jX(X'X)^{-1}X'Z_j,$$

the matrix to be inverted in our estimator.

Finally, since

$$X(X'X)^{-1}X'X_{*j} = X(X'X)^{-1}X'X\begin{bmatrix} I \\ 0 \end{bmatrix}$$

$$= X\begin{bmatrix} I \\ 0 \end{bmatrix} = X_{*j},$$

we see that

$$[Y_{*(j)} - T_j, X_{*j}] = X(X'X)^{-1}X'Z_j.$$

Thus,

$$\hat{\Delta}_j = Y_{j.}[X(X'X)^{-1}X'Z_j][Z_j'X(X'X)^{-1}X'Z_j]^{-1}$$

$$= Y_{j.}[Y_{*(j)} - T_j, X_{*j}]\begin{bmatrix} Y'_{*(j)}Y_{*(j)} - T_j'T_j & Y'_{*(j)}X_{*j} \\ X'_{*j}Y_{*(j)} & X'_{*j}X_{*j} \end{bmatrix}^{-1}.$$

Neither the instrumental variable presentation nor the formal identity just derived give any clue into the origin of the name "two-stage least squares" for this estimator. The origin is as follows.

Let us pursue the point of view that we are estimating the parameters of a structural relation with errors-in-variables. Then a reasonable heuristic approach to this problem would be to replace $Y_{*(j)}$ by a good estimate of its true value. We could then treat the resulting relation as a structural relation with error only in the dependent variable, i.e., disregard the remaining error in the estimate of $Y_{*(j)}$ and use ordinary least squares to estimate Δ_j. Thus in the "first stage", we would use least squares on the reduced form equation

$$Y_{*(j)} = X[\Pi_{*j} \quad \Pi_{*\bar{j}}]' + V_{*(j)},$$

to obtain

$$[\hat{\Pi}_{*j} \quad \hat{\Pi}_{*\bar{j}}]' = (X'X)^{-1}X'Y_{*(j)},$$

and

$$\hat{Y}_{*(j)} = X(X'X)^{-1}X'Y_{*(j)},$$

and, using in the "second stage" the method of ordinary least squares on the equation

$$Y_{j.}' = \hat{Y}_{*(j)}B'_{*(j)} + X_{*j}\Gamma'_{*j} + U_{j.}',$$

we find that

$$\hat{\Delta}_j = Y_{j.}'[Y_{*(j)} \; X_{*j}]\begin{bmatrix} Y'_{*(j)}Y_{*(j)} & Y'_{*(j)}X_{*j} \\ X'_{*j}Y_{*(j)} & X'_{*j}X_{*j} \end{bmatrix}^{-1}.$$

Exercise: (1) Check that this formula for $\hat{\Delta}_j$ is equivalent to that given earlier.

(2) Suppose I renumbered my n y_j's, i.e., instead of dealing with Y I worked with $\tilde{Y} = YP$, where P is a permutation matrix, and $\tilde{B}' = P^{-1}B'$. What effect would this have on the set of n LIML estimators?, on the set of n 2SLS estimators?

5.2. *k-class estimate*

This estimator uses as instrumental variable

$$W_j = [Y_{*(j)} - kT_j, X_{*j}],$$

where $T_j = [I - X(X'X)^{-1}X']Y_{*(j)}$ and k is an arbitrary scalar. Then

$$\hat{\Delta}_j = Y_{j.}[Y_{*(j)} - kT_j, X_{*j}]\{Z_j'[Y_{*(j)} - kT_j, X_{*j}]\}^{-1}.$$

We can rewrite this estimator in its usual form by noting that

$$\begin{bmatrix} Y'_{*(j)} \\ X'_{*j} \end{bmatrix} [Y_{*(j)} - kT_j, X_{*j}] = \begin{bmatrix} Y'_{*(j)}Y_{*j} - kT_j'T_j & Y'_{*(j)}X_{*j} \\ X'_{*j}Y_{*(j)} & X'_{*j}X_{*j} \end{bmatrix},$$

so that

$$\hat{\Delta}_j = Y_{j.}[Y_{*(j)} - kT_j, X_{*j}] \begin{bmatrix} Y'_{*(j)}Y_{*(j)} - kT_j'T_j & Y'_{*(j)}X_{*j} \\ X'_{*j}Y_{*(j)} & X'_{*j}X_{*j} \end{bmatrix}^{-1}.$$

Note that when $k = 0$ this reduces to the ordinary least squares estimator of Δ_j and when $k = 1$ this reduces to the two-stage least squares estimator of Δ_j.

We record that the first two columns of $\{Z_j'[Y_{*(j)} - kT_j, X_{*j}]\}^{-1}$ are

$$\begin{bmatrix} I \\ -(X'_{*j}X_{*j})^{-1}X'_{*j}Y_{*(j)} \end{bmatrix}$$
$$\times [Y'_{*(j)}Y_{*(j)} - kT_j'T_j - Y'_{*(j)}X_{*j}(X'_{*j}X_{*j})^{-1}X'_{*j}Y_{*(j)}]^{-1}.$$

Thus,

$$\hat{B}_j = Y_{j.}[Y_{*(j)} - kT_j - X_{*j}(X'_{*j}X_{*j})^{-1}X'_{*j}Y_{*(j)}]$$
$$\times [Y'_{*(j)}Y_{*(j)} - kT_j'T_j - Y'_{*(j)}X_{*j}(X'_{*j}X_{*j})^{-1}X'_{*j}Y_{*(j)}]^{-1}.$$

When $k = \theta + 1$, where θ is the smallest characteristic root of $W^{-1}Y'_{*j}S(S'S)^{-1}S'Y_{*j}$, this estimate reduces to the LIML estimate. To see this, first note that k so defined is the smallest characteristic root of the equation

$$|Y'_{*j}(I-X_{*j}(X'_{*j}X_{*j})^{-1}X'_{*j})Y_{*j}-kY'_{*j}(I-X_{*j}(X'_{*j}X_{*j})^{-1}X'_{*j})Y_{*j}|=0.$$

To effect a correspondence with the notation of section 1, take $j=1$, in which case $Y_{*1}=[Y'_{1.}\ \ Y_{*(1)}]$. (For arbitrary j the relation between Y_{*j}, $Y'_{j.}$, and $Y_{*(j)}$ is not quite as simple, but can nonetheless be defined using auxiliary matrices of 0's and 1's.) We thus see that

$$Y'_{*1}(I-X_{*1}(X'_{*1}X_{*1})^{-1}X'_{*1})Y_{*1}=\begin{bmatrix} Y_{1.}P_1Y'_{1.} & Y_{1.}T_1 \\ T'_1Y'_{1.} & T'_1T_1 \end{bmatrix},$$

where $P_1=I-X_{*1}(X'_{*1}X_{*1})^{-1}X'_{*1}$. Then $\hat{B}_{*(1)}$ satisfies

$$\begin{bmatrix} Y_{1.} \\ Y'_{*(1)} \end{bmatrix}[I-X_{*1}(X'_{*1}X_{*1})^{-1}X'_{*1}][Y'_{1.}\ Y_{*(1)}]\begin{bmatrix} -1 \\ \hat{B}'_{*(1)} \end{bmatrix}=$$
$$k\begin{bmatrix} Y_{1.}P_1Y'_{1.} & Y_{1.}T_1 \\ T'_1Y'_{1.} & T'_1T_1 \end{bmatrix}\begin{bmatrix} -1 \\ \hat{B}'_{*(1)} \end{bmatrix},$$

so that

$$\begin{aligned}\hat{B}_{*(1)}=\ & Y_{1.}\{Y_{*1}-X_{*1}(X'_{*1}X_{*1})^{-1}X'_{*1}Y_{*1}-kT_1\} \\ & \times\{Y'_{*1}Y_{*1}-Y'_{*1}X_{*1}(X'_{*1}X_{*1})^{-1}X'_{*1}Y_{*1}-kT'_1T_1\}^{-1},\end{aligned}$$

i.e., is the k-class estimate given above. It is an easy matter to check that the LIML estimate of Γ_{*1},

$$\hat{\Gamma}_{*1}=-\hat{B}_{*(1)}Y'_{*1}X_{*1}(X'_{*1}X_{*1})^{-1},$$

is equal to the k-class estimate given above.

5.3. *Estimates based on characteristic vectors of functions of exogenous variables*

Rather than using $T_j=[I-X(X'X)^{-1}X']Y_{*(j)}$ in the two-stage least squares estimator of Δ_j, it has been suggested that T_j be replaced by

$$\tilde{T}_j=[I-\tilde{X}(\tilde{X}'\tilde{X})^{-1}\tilde{X}']Y_{*(j)},$$

where $\tilde{X}=[X_{*j}\ \ F']$, F being an $l\times N$ matrix such that $\tilde{X}$ is of full rank $l+p_j$. (Aside from the restrictions which this condition implies, l is arbitrary. The advantage of this variant is that in case X is not of full rank, so that one cannot use two-stage least squares, one may still be able to use this variant.) Use of such a T_j is equivalent to using as instrumental variable

$$W_j = [Y_{*(j)} - \tilde{T}_j, X_{*j}].$$

Many suggestions have been made for choices of F', to wit:

(1) $X_{*\bar{j}}$ times the matrix of characteristic vectors corresponding to the l largest characteristic roots of $X'_{*\bar{j}}X_{*\bar{j}}$;
(2) $X_{*\bar{j}}$ times the matrix of characteristic vectors corresponding to the l largest characteristic roots of $X_{*\bar{j}} - X_{*j}(X'_{*j}X_{*j})^{-1}X'_{*j}X_{*\bar{j}}$;
(3) X times the matrix of characteristic vectors corresponding to the l largest characteristic roots of $X'X$.

Other suggested choices involve an alternative ranking of the characteristic vectors of these matrices to eliminate those which are highly correlated with vectors in X_{*j}.

5.4. Comparison

We note the similarity of the form of the estimators presented in the last three sections. To compare them, consider now the matrix which one would formally use as the covariance matrix of $\hat{\Delta}_j$ if only the "independent" variables did not contain endogenous variables, i.e., the matrix

$$C = (W_jZ'_j)^{-1}W_j\mathscr{E}(Y'_{j.}Y_{j.})W'_j(Z_jW'_j)^{-1}.$$

Note that $\mathscr{E}(Y'_{j.}Y_{j.}) = \sigma_{jj}I$.

If we pretend that C is the covariance matrix of $\hat{\Delta}_j$, we can ask for characteristics of W_j which make this matrix relatively good. We consider three cases,

$$W_j^1 = [Y_{*(j)} - T_j\, X_{*j}],$$
$$W_j^2 = [Y_{*(j)} - \tilde{T}_j\, X_{*j}],$$
$$W_j^3 = [Y_{*(j)} - kT_j\, X_{*j}],$$

where

$$T_j = [I - X(X'X)^{-1}X']Y_{*(j)},$$
$$\tilde{T}_j = [I - \tilde{X}(\tilde{X}'\tilde{X})^{-1}\tilde{X}']Y_{*(j)},$$
$$\tilde{X}' = [X_{*j}F'].$$

Finally, we find it more convenient to study the inverse of C (disregarding the scalar σ_{jj}), namely

$$\sigma_{jj}C_m^{-1} = Z_j'W_j^m(W_j^{m\prime}W_j^m)^{-1}W_j^{m\prime}Z_j, \qquad m = 1, 2, 3.$$

For notational uniformity, let $W_j^m = [Y_{*j} - W_{mj} \; X_{*j}]$. Then,

$$W_j^{m\prime}W_j^m =$$

$$\begin{bmatrix} Y_{*(j)}'Y_{*(j)} - \tilde{W}_{mj}'Y_{*(j)} - Y_{*(j)}'\tilde{W}_{mj} + \tilde{W}_{mj}'\tilde{W}_{mj} & Y_{*(j)}'X_{*j} - \tilde{W}_{mj}'X_{*j} \\ X_{*j}'Y_{*(j)} - X_{*j}'\tilde{W}_{mj} & X_{*j}'X_{*j} \end{bmatrix}.$$

But $X_{*j}'\tilde{W}_{1j} = 0$, so that $X_{*j}'\tilde{W}_{3j} = 0$. Similarly, since $X_{*j} = \tilde{X}\left[\begin{smallmatrix} I \\ 0 \end{smallmatrix}\right]$, $X_{*j}'\tilde{W}_{2j} = 0$.

Also

$$\tilde{W}_{mj}'\tilde{W}_{mj} = \begin{cases} \tilde{W}_{mj}'Y_{*(j)}, & m = 1, 2, \\ k\tilde{W}_{mj}'Y_{*(j)}, & m = 3, \end{cases}$$

(since the multiplying $Y_{*(j)}$ in T_j or $\tilde{T}_j$ is a projection matrix) so that, letting

$$\phi_m = \begin{cases} 1 & m = 1, 2, \\ 2 - k & m = 3, \end{cases}$$

$$W_j^{m\prime}W_j^m = \begin{bmatrix} Y_{*(j)}'Y_{*(j)} - \phi_m\tilde{W}_{mj}'Y_{*(j)} & Y_{*(j)}'X_{*j} \\ X_{*j}'Y_{*(j)} & X_{*j}'X_{*j} \end{bmatrix}.$$

Similarly

$$Z_j'W_j^m = \begin{bmatrix} Y_{*(j)}' \\ X_{*j}' \end{bmatrix}[Y_{*(j)} - \tilde{W}_{mj} \quad X_{*j}]$$

$$= \begin{bmatrix} Y_{*(j)}'Y_{*(j)} - Y_{*(j)}'\tilde{W}_{mj} & Y_{*(j)}'X_{*j} \\ X_{*j}'Y_{*(j)} & X_{*j}'X_{*j} \end{bmatrix},$$

so that for $m = 1, 2$, $\sigma_{jj}C_m^{-1} = Z_j'W_j^m$.

For $m = 3$, $\sigma_{jj}C_3^{-1}$ is of the form

$$\sigma_{jj}C_3^{-1} = (Z_j'W_j^3)(Z_j'W_j^3 + G)^{-1}(Z_j'W_j^3),$$

where

$$G = \begin{bmatrix} (k-1)\tilde{W}_{3j}'Y_{*(j)} & 0 \\ 0 & 0 \end{bmatrix}.$$

But,

$$(Z_j'W_j^3 + G)^{-1} =$$

$$(Z_j'W_j^3)^{-1} - (Z_j'W_j^3)^{-1}G(G^* + G^*(Z_j'W_j^3)^{-1}G)^{-1}G^*(Z_j'W_j^3)^{-1},$$

where G^* is the matrix G augmented in its lower diagonal partition by the identity matrix. (This can be seen by using a result of chapter I with the correspondence

$$A \leftrightarrow Z_j'W_j^3,$$

$$U' \leftrightarrow \begin{bmatrix} I & 0 \\ 0 & 0 \end{bmatrix},$$

$$S \leftrightarrow \begin{bmatrix} (k-1)\tilde{W}_{3j}'Y_{*(j)} & 0 \\ 0 & I \end{bmatrix} = G^*,$$

$$U'S \leftrightarrow G,$$

$$V \leftrightarrow I.)$$

Thus for $m = 3$,

$$\begin{aligned} \sigma_{jj}C_3^{-1} &= Z_j'W_j^3 - G(G^* + G^*(Z_j'W_j^3G)^{-1}G^* \\ &= Z_j'W_j^3 - G(I + (Z_j'W_j^3)^{-1}G)^{-1} \end{aligned}$$

We are now in a position to compare the three cases. But first let $Q = I - X(X'X)^{-1}X'$ and $\tilde{Q} = [I - \tilde{X}(\tilde{X}'\tilde{X})^{-1}\tilde{X}']$, so that $T_j = QY_{*(j)}$ and $\tilde{T}_j = \tilde{Q}Y_{*(j)}$. Then Q and $\tilde{Q}$ are projection matrices, so that

$$Y_{*(j)}'\tilde{W}_{mj} = \begin{cases} Y_{*(j)}'QY_{*(j)}, & m = 1, \\ Y_{*(j)}'\tilde{Q}Y_{*(j)}, & m = 2, \\ kY_{*(j)}'QY_{*(j)}, & m = 3. \end{cases}$$

In comparing the first two cases, note that the difference in the inverses of the covariance matrices is the matrix

$$\begin{bmatrix} Y_{*(j)}'(Q - \tilde{Q})Y_{*(j)} & 0 \\ 0 & 0 \end{bmatrix},$$

and so the superiority of two-stage least squares over that of use of characteristic vectors of a function of the X matrix rests solely on the rank of Q and $\tilde{Q}$. (Being idempotent, both these matrices have only 0 and 1 as characteristic roots, the number of 1's being the rank of the matrix.) Equivalently, one must compare $\tilde{X}(\tilde{X}'\tilde{X})^{-1}\tilde{X}'$ and $X(X'X)^{-1}X'$. But each of these matrices are matrices of projection transformations, on the spaces whose bases are the rows of $\tilde{X}$ and X, respectively. Since both these matrices are of full rank, we see that $Q - \tilde{Q}$ is positive definite (and hence $C_1^{-1} - C_2^{-1}$ is positive definite, or $C_2 - C_1$ is positive definite, i.e., two-stage least squares is superior) if and only if rank $X <$ rank $\tilde{X}$, i.e., $p < l + p_j$. But typically this is not so, as l is usually less than $p - p_j$. Thus two-stage least squares is superior inferior to the modification using an arbitrary matrix F in place of $X_{*\bar{j}}$.

5.5. Iterative instrumental variable estimate

As seen from the exposition of the method of instrumental variables in section 4.3 of chapter III, the best instrumental variable is one which is "most uncorrelated" with $\mathbf{y}^* - \mathbf{X}^*\hat{B}'$. In the context of simultaneous equation estimators, this corresponds to finding $\mathbf{W}_j$ which are most uncorrelated with $\mathbf{Y}_{j.} - \mathbf{Z}_j\hat{\Delta}'_j$.

Obviously, if $\mathbf{Y}_{j.} = \mathbf{Z}_j\Delta'_j$, then $\mathbf{Y}_{j.} - \mathbf{Z}_j\Delta'_j$, being equal to 0, is uncorrelated with anything. So one might suggest taking $W_j = \mathbf{Y}_{j.} - \mathbf{Z}_j\Delta'_j$. But of course Δ'_j is unknown, so a "second best" suggestion is to take $W_j = \mathbf{Y}_{j.} - \mathbf{Z}_j\hat{\Delta}'_j$ for some $\hat{\Delta}'_j$ estimating Δ'_j. We begin to see here the germ of a self-iterative procedure which proceeds initially with some estimate $\hat{\Delta}_j^{(0)}$ of Δ_j, then uses $W_j^{(0)} = Y_{j.} - Z_j\hat{\Delta}_j'^{(0)}$ as instrumental variable to obtain

$$\hat{\Delta}_j^{(1)} = Y_{j.}W_j'^{(0)}(Z_jW_j'^{(0)})^{-1},$$

and thence, reestimating W_j as $W_j^{(1)} = Y_{j.} - Z_j\hat{\Delta}_j'^{(1)}$, reiterating the procedure until it converges.

5.6. Three-stage least squares estimate

As stated earlier, $\vec{\mathbf{Y}}' - \mathbf{Z}\Delta'$ is distributed as $N(0, \Sigma \otimes I)$. Thus one can estimate Σ by first obtaining an estimate $\hat{\Delta}$ of Δ, e.g., by two-stage least squares, and then estimating Σ from the residuals $\vec{Y} - Z\hat{\Delta}' = \hat{\vec{U}}$. Unfortunately, we do not know the distribution of the $\hat{\vec{U}}$'s, but we do know from maximum likelihood theory that if the $\hat{\vec{U}}$'s were distributed as $N(0, \Sigma \otimes I)$ then the maximum likelihood estimate of σ_{ij} would be $\hat{U}_{i.}\hat{U}'_{j.}/N$. (*Exercise*: Check this.) Thus, even if we have an estimate of Δ which is not a maximum likelihood estimate, we will still use this estimator of Σ unless otherwise specified.

Given an estimate $\hat{\Sigma}$ of Σ, we can then approximate the best estimator of Δ in a linear expected value model by recalculating $\hat{\Delta}$ as

$$\hat{\Delta} = \vec{Y}(\hat{\Sigma} \otimes I)^{-1}Z(Z'(\hat{\Sigma} \otimes I)^{-1}Z)^{-1}.$$

This is equivalent to the use of $W = (\hat{\Sigma} \otimes I)^{-1}Z$ as the matrix of instrumental variables for the entire system of equations. Since it was contemplated that Δ be estimated by two-stage least squares, then Σ be estimated by $\hat{\Sigma}$, and finally $\hat{\Delta}$ above be calculated in the "third stage" of the procedure, this method is dubbed "three-stage least squares". Note that it neither depends on two-stage least squares nor does it require three stages of computation.

Exercise: Consider a system of n simultaneous linear equations, all of which are identifiable, but wherein the first n^* are each just identifiable. What does the 3SLS estimator reduce to in this case?

Note that, since $\vec{\boldsymbol{Y}} = \Delta \boldsymbol{Z}' - \vec{\boldsymbol{U}}$,

$$\hat{\boldsymbol{\Delta}} = \Delta - \vec{\boldsymbol{U}}(\hat{\boldsymbol{\Sigma}} \otimes I)^{-1}\boldsymbol{Z}(\boldsymbol{Z}'(\hat{\boldsymbol{\Sigma}} \otimes I)^{-1}\boldsymbol{Z})^{-1}.$$

Assuming that $\vec{\boldsymbol{U}}$ is independent of $\boldsymbol{Z}$, then conditional on $\boldsymbol{Z}$ the covariance matrix of $\vec{\boldsymbol{U}}$ is that of $\vec{\boldsymbol{Y}}$, namely $\Sigma \otimes I$. Thus $\text{plim}_{N\to\infty} \vec{\boldsymbol{U}}'\vec{\boldsymbol{U}}/N = \Sigma \otimes I$.

If $\hat{\boldsymbol{\Sigma}}$ is a consistent estimator of Σ, then

$$\begin{aligned}
&\operatorname*{plim}_{N\to\infty} N(\hat{\boldsymbol{\Delta}}' - \Delta')(\hat{\boldsymbol{\Delta}} - \Delta) = \\
&\operatorname*{plim}_{N\to\infty} N(\boldsymbol{Z}'(\hat{\boldsymbol{\Sigma}} \otimes I)^{-1}\boldsymbol{Z})^{-1}\boldsymbol{Z}(\hat{\boldsymbol{\Sigma}} \otimes I)^{-1}\vec{\boldsymbol{U}}'\vec{\boldsymbol{U}}(\hat{\boldsymbol{\Sigma}} \otimes I)^{-1}\boldsymbol{Z}'(\boldsymbol{Z}'(\hat{\boldsymbol{\Sigma}} \otimes I)^{-1}\boldsymbol{Z})^{-1} = \\
&\operatorname*{plim}_{N\to\infty} N^2(\boldsymbol{Z}'(\Sigma \otimes I)^{-1}\boldsymbol{Z})^{-1}\boldsymbol{Z}'(\Sigma \otimes I)^{-1}(\Sigma \otimes I) \\
&\times (\Sigma \otimes I)^{-1}\boldsymbol{Z}(\boldsymbol{Z}'(\Sigma \otimes I)^{-1}\boldsymbol{Z})^{-1}.
\end{aligned}$$

Recalling that $\boldsymbol{Z} = \bar{Z} + \boldsymbol{V}$, where $\boldsymbol{Z}$ is a block-diagonal matrix of the $\boldsymbol{Z}_j$'s, $\boldsymbol{Z}_j = (\boldsymbol{Y}_{*(j)}, X_{*j})$, and $\bar{Z}_j = (\bar{Y}_{*(j)}, X_{*j}) = (X_{*j}\Pi'_{*j} + X_{*\bar{j}}\Pi'_{*\bar{j}}, X_{*j})$, we see that

$$\operatorname*{plim}_{N\to\infty} N(\boldsymbol{Z}'(\Sigma \otimes I)\boldsymbol{Z})^{-1} = (\bar{Z}(\Sigma \otimes I)^{-1}\bar{Z}')^{-1},$$

and so

$$\operatorname*{plim}_{N\to\infty} N(\hat{\boldsymbol{\Delta}}' - \Delta')(\hat{\boldsymbol{\Delta}} - \Delta) = (\bar{Z}(\Sigma \otimes I)^{-1}\bar{Z}')^{-1}.$$

6. Iterative least squares estimate

Continuing along the line of thought which led to two-stage least squares, wherein we would like to use ordinary least squares if only we had a good estimate of the true value of $Y_{*(j)}$, we can start with an arbitrary "first stage" estimate $Y^{(1)}_{*(j)}$, estimate $\Delta^{(1)}_j$ from the relation

$$Y'_{j.} = Y^{(1)}_{*(j)}B'_{*(j)} + X_{*j}\Gamma'_{*j} + U'_{j.}$$

using least squares, then re-estimate the $Y_{j.}$ by

$$Y^{(2)}_{j.} = Y^{(1)}_{*(j)}\hat{B}'^{(1)}_{*(j)} + X_{*j}\Gamma'^{(1)}_{*j}.$$

Reassembling the $Y^{(2)}_{j.}$'s into $Y^{(2)}_{*j}$, we can once again estimate $\hat{\Delta}^{(2)}_j$ from the relation

$$Y'_{j.} = Y^{(2)}_{*(j)}B'_{*(j)} + X_{*j}\Gamma'_{*j} + U'_{j},$$

and so on. This procedure yields, at the tth stage,

$$\hat{\Delta}^{(t)}_j = Y'_{j.}[Y^{(t)}_{*(j)}X_{*j}]\begin{bmatrix} Y^{(t)}_{*(j)}Y^{(t)\prime}_{*(j)} & Y^{(t)}_{*(j)}X'_{*j} \\ X_{*j}Y^{(t)\prime}_{*(j)} & X_{*j}X'_{*j}\end{bmatrix}^{-1}$$

$$= Y'_{j.}W^{(t)}_j[Z'^{(t)}_j W^{(t)}_j]^{-1},$$

where $Z'^{(t)}_j = (Y^{(t)}_{*(j)}X_{*j})$ and $W^{(t)}_j = X(X'X)^{-1}X'Z^{(t)}_j$. Thus it is not quite an instrumental variable estimator, as the independent variable is changing with t.

Since the iterative procedure is searching for a fix-point (in the y's) of the linear equations

$$Y'_{j.} = Y_{*(j)}B'_{*(j)} + X_{*j}\Gamma'_{*j},$$

standard arguments from the theory of functional analysis will lead to a proof of convergence of the iterations to the fix-point solution of the equations.

Exercise: A nice property of an estimator, called scale invariance, is that if we changed the units of our variables then, prior to renormalization, our estimators should change in a compensating way. More precisely, suppose instead of observing X and Y we observed $\tilde{X} = XD_1$ and $\tilde{Y} = YD_2$, where D_1 and D_2 are diagonal matrices of "scaling" constants. Let $\hat{B}$, $\hat{\Gamma}$ be our estimators of B and Γ in the model $YB' + X\Gamma' = U$. Let $\tilde{Y}\tilde{B}' + \tilde{X}\tilde{\Gamma}' = U$, where $\tilde{B} = BD_2^{-1}$ and $\tilde{\Gamma} = \Gamma D_1^{-1}$. Then we would like $\hat{\tilde{B}} = \hat{B}D_2^{-1}$ and $\hat{\tilde{\Gamma}} = \hat{\Gamma}D_1^{-1}$ prior to normalizing the "tilda-d" model.

Does the instrumental variables estimator have this property?, does the FIML estimator?, does the simultaneous least squares estimator?, does the iterative least squares estimator?

7. Random exogenous variables

In the development of estimators of the parameters of a single equation in a system of simultaneous equations, we have used as our starting point the linear expected value model known in this context as the reduced form. All our treatment in sections 1 and 2 have taken the exogenous variables as constants, not random variables. And our treatment in section 5 "eliminated" the randomness in the system of equations by viewing $\boldsymbol{Z}$, including the exogenous variables, as of the form $\boldsymbol{Z} = \bar{Z} + \boldsymbol{W}$, and so passing off the possible randomness of the exogenous variables as due to errors-in-variables. (We could have explicitly treated the single equation in section 5 in the same way. Instead we let X_{*j} be non-random in order to proceed with the development of section 5.4.) In this section we explore explicitly the implications of randomness of exogenous variables.

Obviously, in estimating a single equation we can fall back on treating all our work as a conditional analysis, conditional on the values of the exogenous variables. However, such treatment sweeps a knotty identifiability problem under the rug. If the exogenous variables are lagged endogenous variables, then the covariance matrix of $\vec{Y}$ is not $\Sigma \otimes I$, for in the ith equation some exogenous variable will equal some $y_{ki'}$ for $i' < i$. In this case, even with the order condition holding, a single equation in the system may not be identifiable.

This may be seen by considering the following example. Consider a system of two equations of the form

$$\beta_{11}\boldsymbol{y}_{1i} + \gamma_{11}\boldsymbol{x}_{1i} + \gamma_{12}\boldsymbol{x}_{2i} = \boldsymbol{u}_{1i},$$
$$\beta_{21}\boldsymbol{y}_{1i} + \beta_{22}\boldsymbol{y}_{2i} = \boldsymbol{u}_{2i},$$

where $\boldsymbol{x}_{1i} = \boldsymbol{y}_{1,i-1}$, $\boldsymbol{x}_{2i} = \boldsymbol{y}_{2,i-1}$.

(Thus the first equation is defined for $i = 2, \ldots, N$, and the second for $i = 1, \ldots, N$, unless one makes some assumption about the values of $\boldsymbol{y}_{10}$ and $\boldsymbol{y}_{20}$.)

Exercise: Check that if x_{1i} and x_{2i} are exogenous variables unrelated to the y's then these equations are identifiable.

Now consider a variant of the first equation, namely

$$\beta_{11}\boldsymbol{y}_{1i} + (\gamma_{11} + \alpha\beta_{21})\boldsymbol{x}_{1i} + (\gamma_{12} + \alpha\beta_{22})\boldsymbol{x}_{22} = \boldsymbol{u}^*_{1i},$$

where $u_{1i}^* = u_{1i} + \alpha u_{2,i-1}$. This equation is obtained by adding α times the second equation (when $i = i - 1$) to the first. If we make the assumption that the covariance matrix of $\vec{U}$ is of the form $\Sigma \otimes I$, then the first equation is still identifiable, for, though $\mathscr{C}(u_{1i}, u_{2,i-1}) = 0$, $\mathscr{C}(u_{1i}^*, u_{2,i-1})$ will not equal 0 (it will equal $\alpha^2 \mathscr{V}(u_{2,i-1})$).

However, if we assume more generally that the covariance matrix of $\vec{U}$ is of arbitrary structure, then we cannot distinguish this variant from the original first equation, and thus the first equation will not be identifiable. We see, therefore, the criticality of the assumption that the covariance matrix of $\vec{U}$ be block-diagonal. This assumption can be relaxed somewhat, but we shall not get into those conditions here.

One might argue that the critical ingredient of this example is that the second equation contains no exogenous variables. If it did, then the transformation used to produce a variant of the first equation would have produced one which was clearly distinguishable from the original first equation, as it would have contained those exogenous variables. In general, what one needs to construct such unidentifiable situations is to make sure that exogenous variables in other equations of the system but not in the equation of interest are "cancelled out" by the transformation and to construct, using those other equations, a variant of the equation of interest. Such unidentifiable situations cannot be constructed if those exogenous variables are not linearly related to the lagged endogenous variables in the equation of interest; if there is such a linear relation, it can conversely be used to construct a transformation "cancelling out" those exogenous variables and thence producing a variety of the equation of interest which cannot be distinguished from it.

8. References

The seminal general references to the problems of identification and the simultaneous form of simultaneous equations are the two Cowles Commission monographs:

Koopmans, T. C., ed., 1950, Statistical inference in dynamic economic models, Cowles Commission for Research in Economics Monograph no. 10 (Wiley, New York).

Hood, W. C. and T. C. Koopmans, eds., 1953, Studies in econometric method, Cowles Commission for Research in Economics Monograph no. 14 (Wiley, New York).

The fundamental general reference to the regression form of simultaneous equations, including the two-stage least squares and *k*-class estimators, is:

Theil, H., 1961, Economic forecasts and policy (North-Holland, Amsterdam).

The problem of identification in econometric models (including details on the material in section 7) is thoroughly described in:

Fisher, F. M., 1966, The identification problem in econometrics (McGraw-Hill, New York).

Our presentation in section 2 is based primarily on:

Anderson, T. W. and H. Rubin, 1949, Estimation of parameters of a single equation in a complete system of stochastic equations, Annals of Mathematical Statistics 20, pp. 46–63.

The presentation in section 3 is a variant of that given in:

Rothenberg, T. J. and C. T. Leenders, 1964, Efficient estimation of simultaneous equation systems, Econometrica 32, pp. 57–76.

The material of section 4 is based on:

Brown, T. M., 1960, Simultaneous least squares: A distribution free method of equation system structure estimation, International Economic Review 1, pp. 173–191.

The three-stage least squares estimate is given in:

Zellner, A. and H. Theil, 1962, Three-stage least squares: Simultaneous estimation of simultaneous equations, Econometrica 30, pp. 54–78.

The material of section 5.c is taken from:

Kloek, T. and L. B. M. Mennes, 1960, Simultaneous equation estimation based on principal components of predetermined variables, Econometrica 28, pp. 45–61.

The relationship between instrumental variable estimates and those given in section 5 is summarized well in:

Brundy, J. M. and D. W. Jorgenson, 1971, Efficient estimation of simultaneous equations by instrumental variables, Harvard Institute of Economic Research Discussion Paper no. 191.

Another approach to comparing the estimators considered in section 5.4 is given in:

Amemiya, T., 1966, On the use of principal components of independent variables in two-stage least squares estimation, International Economic Review 7, pp. 283–303.

The iterative least squares estimate was first presented in:

Wold, H., 1965, A fix-point theorem with econometric background, Arkiv for Matematik 6, pp. 209–240.

V

Multivariate statistical analysis

Hypothesis testing theory

This chapter continues the general discussion of statistical theory begun in chapter II, in this chapter concentrating on the theory of hypothesis testing. Section 1 describes hypothesis testing theory, section 2 presents certain sampling distributions useful in hypothesis testing, and section 3 gives a general framework for construction of tests of particular types of hypotheses, namely "linear hypotheses", in a particular version of the linear expected value model. We restrict our discussion to what is known as parametric hypothesis testing, i.e., to situations in which the form of the distribution of $\boldsymbol{X}$ is known and we have a hypothesis about the unknown parameter Θ that we wish to test.

The reason for this is the following: Econometric models are almost universally models involving a specified set of parameters and the only possible "non-parametric" aspect one might hope for in econometric practice is that the tests of hypotheses about the parameters do not depend on the probability distribution of $\boldsymbol{X}$. There is no formal theory of non-parametric test construction (and certainly nothing parallel to the "non-parametric" least squares procedures developed in point estimation theory), let alone construction of tests about parameters where the test doesn't depend on the distribution of the data. Such non-parametric test procedures as exist for econometric problems have been developed in an ad hoc fashion, and so, as appropriate, we will present those particular tests in chapter VI. The general theory presented in this chapter will suffice as background for understanding these procedures as well.

1. Hypothesis testing theory

Once again $\boldsymbol{X}$ is an n-vector valued random variable, the form of whose distribution is known, but where Θ is a k-vector of unknown parameters lying in a subset Ω of k-space. The problem of testing a hypothesis about Θ is the problem of deciding whether or not Θ belongs to a smaller subset Ω_0 of Ω or not. We usually call Ω_0 the *null hypothesis parameter space* and use $\Omega_1 = \Omega - \Omega_0$ as the symbol for the *alternative hypothesis parameter space.*

To test whether Θ is in Ω_0, we shall use a function of $\boldsymbol{X}$, $\phi(\boldsymbol{X})$, where $0 \leq \phi(\boldsymbol{X}) \leq 1$, in the following way:

(1) Observe $\boldsymbol{X} = X$.
(2) Construct a biased coin with probability $\phi(X)$ of heads and $1 - \phi(X)$ of tails (using for example a random number generator).
(3) Toss the coin (figuratively, if you're doing this with random numbers).
(4) If the result is a head, say that Θ is in Ω_1; if the result is a tail say that Θ is in Ω_0.

Such a function will be called a *test function.* The action "say that Θ is in Ω_0" is called *accepting the null hypothesis*; the action "say that Θ is in Ω_1" is called *rejecting the null hypothesis.*

Each test function has associated with it probabilities of making two types of errors, the *type I error* of rejecting the null hypothesis when it is true and the *type II error* of accepting the null hypothesis when it is false. We define the symbols of the probabilities of these types of errors as $\alpha(\Theta)$ and $\beta(\Theta)$, respectively. From the definition of $\phi(\boldsymbol{X})$, we see that

$$\alpha_\phi(\Theta) = \int \phi(X) f_{\boldsymbol{X}}(X; \Theta)\, \mathrm{d}X, \qquad \text{for} \quad \Theta \in \Omega_0,$$

and

$$\beta_\phi(\Theta) = \int (1 - \phi(X)) f_{\boldsymbol{X}}(X; \Theta)\, \mathrm{d}X, \qquad \text{for} \quad \Theta \in \Omega_1,$$

where the subscript ϕ denotes the test function being used. The problem of finding a good test function is then one of finding ϕ such that $\alpha_\phi(\Theta)$ and $\beta_\phi(\Theta)$ are, in some sense, as low as possible.

The classic theory of hypothesis testing balances off the risks of making each of these two types of errors in the following way. We consider that the worst of the two errors is the type I error. (This is because usually the null hypothesis is the hypothesis that nothing astounding can be learned from the observation on **X**, and rejecting this hypothesis may lead to, for example, unfounded acceptance of a new scientific proposition.) We therefore wish to control the risk of a type I error. We do this by establishing an upper bound α on $\alpha_\phi(\Theta)$ for all Θ in Ω_0. Then, among those test functions ϕ such that

$$\alpha_\phi(\Theta) = \mathscr{E}_\Theta \phi(\mathbf{X}) \leqslant \alpha,$$

we seek to find the function ϕ which "minimizes" $\beta_\phi(\Theta)$ for $\Theta \in \Omega_1$.

Though this general philosophy gives an intuitive picture of the error balancing used in hypothesis testing theory, it is not quite complete or rigorous. The reason for this lies primarily in the characteristic of $\beta_\phi(\Theta)$ and what it means to "minimize" it for $\Theta \in \Omega_1$. Clearly, if for *each* $\Theta \in \Omega_1$ $\beta_\phi(\Theta) \leqslant \beta_{\phi^*}(\Theta)$ for all other test functions ϕ^*, then we will have found a true minimizer ϕ. (When ϕ has such a property we call it a *uniformly most powerful test.*) But such a property is a lot to ask of a test function.

Let us study the issues involved in finding "minimizing" test functions more carefully. We call a hypothesis *simple* if the appropriate subset of Ω consists of only one point; we call a hypothesis *composite* otherwise. We first study the case where $\Omega_0 = \Theta_0$ and $\Omega_1 = \Theta_1$, i.e., both null and alternative hypotheses are simple. For this case, the minimization problem becomes a simple problem in the calculus of variations, whose techniques can be used to find the minimizing ϕ. The following theorem, called the *Neyman–Pearson Lemma* gives the result. Its proof is not constructive, but is instead very elementary.

Theorem: *Let S be a subset of the sample space of* **X** *given by*

$$S = \left\{ X \middle| \frac{f_X(X;\Theta_0)}{f_X(X;\Theta_1)} \leqslant k \right\}.$$

Then the best function for testing $\Theta = \Theta_0$ *against* $\Theta = \Theta_1$ *is*

$$\phi_S(X) = \begin{cases} 1, & \text{if } X \in S, \\ 0, & \text{if } X \notin S, \end{cases}$$

where k is determined by the equation $\mathscr{E}\Theta_0\phi_S(\mathbf{X}) = \alpha$.

Proof: Suppose T is another subset of the sample space of $\boldsymbol{X}$ with

$$\phi_T(X) = \begin{cases} 1, & \text{if} \quad X \in T, \\ 0, & \text{if} \quad X \notin T, \end{cases}$$

and $\mathscr{E}\Theta_0\phi_T(\boldsymbol{X}) = \alpha$.

Then,

$$\alpha = \int \phi_T(X) f_{\boldsymbol{X}}(X; \Theta_0)\, \mathrm{d}X = \int \phi_S(X) f_{\boldsymbol{X}}(X; \Theta_0)\, \mathrm{d}X.$$

Let $T \cap S$ be the points common to T and S, $T \cap \bar{S}$ be the points in T but not S, and $\bar{T} \cap S$ be the points in S but not T. Then,

$$S = (T \cap S) \cup (\bar{T} \cap S),$$
$$T = (T \cap S) \cup (T \cap \bar{S}),$$

and

$$\begin{aligned} \alpha &= \int_T f_{\boldsymbol{X}}(X; \Theta_0)\, \mathrm{d}X = \int_S f_{\boldsymbol{X}}(X; \Theta_0)\, \mathrm{d}X \\ &= \int_{X \in T \cap S} f_{\boldsymbol{X}}(X; \Theta_0)\, \mathrm{d}X + \int_{X \in \bar{T} \cap S} f_{\boldsymbol{X}}(X; \Theta_0)\, \mathrm{d}X \\ &= \int_{X \in T \cap S} f_{\boldsymbol{X}}(X; \Theta_0)\, \mathrm{d}X + \int_{X \in T \cap \bar{S}} f_{\boldsymbol{X}}(X; \Theta_0)\, \mathrm{d}X. \end{aligned}$$

Therefore,

$$\int_{X \in \bar{T} \cap S} f_{\boldsymbol{X}}(X; \Theta_0)\, \mathrm{d}X = \int_{X \in T \cap \bar{S}} f_{\boldsymbol{X}}(X; \Theta_0)\, \mathrm{d}X.$$

Now if Θ_1 is true, ϕ_S is a better test function than ϕ_T if $\mathscr{E}_{\Theta_1}(1 - \phi_S(\boldsymbol{X})) \leqslant \mathscr{E}_{\Theta_1}(1 - \phi_T(\boldsymbol{X}))$, i.e., when $\mathscr{E}_{\Theta_1}\phi_S(\boldsymbol{X}) \geqslant \mathscr{E}_{\Theta_1}\phi_T(\boldsymbol{X})$. This is equivalent to

$$\int_{S \cap \bar{T}} f_{\boldsymbol{X}}(X; \Theta_1)\, \mathrm{d}X - \int_{T \cap \bar{S}} f_{\boldsymbol{X}}(X; \Theta_1)\, \mathrm{d}X \geqslant 0.$$

But in $S \cap \bar{T}$,

$$f_{\boldsymbol{X}}(X; \Theta_1) \geqslant (1/k) f_{\boldsymbol{X}}(X; \Theta_0),$$

and in $T \cap \bar{S}$,

$$f_{\boldsymbol{X}}(X; \Theta_1) \leqslant (1/k) f_{\boldsymbol{X}}(X; \Theta_0).$$

Therefore,

$$\int_{X\in S\cap\bar{T}} f_X(X;\Theta_1)\,dX \geq \frac{1}{k}\int_{X\in S\cap\bar{T}} f_X(X;\Theta_0)\,dX,$$

and

$$\frac{1}{k}\int_{X\in T\cap\bar{S}} f_X(X;\Theta_0)\,dX \geq \int_{X\in T\cap\bar{S}} f_X(X;\Theta_1)\,dX,$$

so that

$$\int_{X\in S\cap\bar{T}} f_X(X;\Theta_1)\,dX - \int_{X\in T\cap\bar{S}} f_X(X;\Theta_1)\,dX \geq \frac{1}{k}\int_{X\in S\cap\bar{T}} f_X(X;\Theta_0)\,dX$$
$$-\frac{1}{k}\int_{X\in T\cap\bar{S}} f_X(X;\Theta_0)\,dX,$$

which, as we have seen above, equals 0.

As a simple example of the use of this lemma, let $\boldsymbol{X} = (\boldsymbol{x}_1, \ldots, \boldsymbol{x}_n)$ be distributed as $N(\mu, I)$, where $\mu = \theta(1, \ldots, 1)$. Let $\theta_0 = 0$ and $\theta_1 = 1$. Then,

$$S = \left\{ X \left| \frac{(2\pi)^{-n/2}\exp\left\{-\sum_{i=1}^{n} x_i^2/2\right\}}{(2\pi)^{-n/2}\exp\left\{-\sum_{i=1}^{n}(x_i-1)^2/2\right\}} \leq k \right.\right\}$$
$$= \left\{ X \left| \sum_{i=1}^{n} x_i \geq c \right.\right\},$$

where $c = (n/2) - \log k$ is so chosen that $\mathscr{E}_0\phi_S(\boldsymbol{X}) = \alpha$.

Since $\sum_{i=1}^{n} \boldsymbol{x}_i$ is distributed as $N(n\theta, n)$, we can easily determine c to be $n\theta + \sqrt{n}\,Z_\alpha$, where Z_α is the upper 100α % point of the $N(0, 1)$ distribution.

If the null hypothesis is composite but the alternative hypothesis is simple, there is no unfailing procedure for generating a "minimizing" ϕ. One procedure which works in many cases is to ask, "what value of Θ in Ω_0 would be hardest to discriminate from Θ_1?" (This question can be given precise mathematical formulation.) One would then take that value $\Theta^* \in \Omega_0$ and use the Neyman–Pearson Lemma to test Θ^* against Θ_1. A fortiori, if $\mathscr{E}_{\Theta^*}\phi(\boldsymbol{X}) = \alpha$, then $\mathscr{E}_\Theta\phi(\boldsymbol{X}) \leq \alpha$ for $\Theta \in \Omega_0$.

A simple example of this approach is to consider the situation treated above, where X is distributed as $N(\mu, I)$ where $\mu = \theta(1, \ldots, 1)$, and $\Omega_0 = \{\theta | \theta \leq 0\}$ and $\theta_1 = 1$. Here it is clear that $\theta^* = 0$ is the hardest value of $\theta \in \Omega_0$ to discriminate from θ_1, so that the test derived above is best for this pair of hypotheses also.

If the alternative is composite, then, whatever the nature of the null hypothesis, there is no procedure for finding a uniformly most powerful test. If the null hypothesis is simple, one procedure to use is to pick a $\Theta_1 \in \Omega_1$, use the Neyman–Pearson Lemma, and hope that the test does not depend on the choice of Θ_1. In that case the test is uniformly most powerful.

Once again we consider the previous example, but with $\theta_0 = 0$ and $\Omega_1 = \{\theta | \theta > 0\}$. Selecting $\theta_1 \in \Omega_1$ and using the Neyman–Pearson Lemma, we find that

$$S = \left\{ X \middle| \sum_{i=1}^{n} x_i \geq c \right\},$$

where $c = \theta_1 n/2 - (\log k)/\theta_1$. Since to satisfy the α requirement c must be $\sqrt{n}\, Z_\alpha$, independent of the choice of θ_1, we see that $\phi_S(X)$ is uniformly most powerful for this pair of hypotheses.

Exercise: Let $\Omega_1 = \{\theta | \theta \neq 0\}$. Show that no uniformly most powerful test exists. (*Hint*: Take two separate candidates for θ_1, one negative and the other positive, and find that the resulting test depends on the sign of the choice of θ_1.)

Often when the null and alternative hypotheses are composite and we know that no uniformly most powerful test exists we restrict our search for good test functions to a smaller class of tests with intuitively nice properties. One such class of tests is the class of *unbiased tests*, tests satisfying the inequality

$$1 - \beta_\phi(\Theta) \geq \alpha, \qquad \Theta \in \Theta_1,$$

i.e., one wherein it is more likely to reject the null hypothesis when it is false than when it is true. Another class of tests is the class of *invariant tests*, tests whose decisions do not change if we change the parameter space and the sample space by a natural transformation which leaves the problem unchanged (e.g., if Θ is the mean vector of the distribution of $\boldsymbol{X}$ and we change our measurement of $\boldsymbol{X}$ and Θ from feet to meters, this should not affect the result of the test function for the new problem). Except in very special circumstances, econometric practice has not investigated these restricted classes of tests.

What is primarily done when null and alternative hypotheses are composite is resort to a portmanteau procedure, the *likelihood ratio test*, which has two compelling features. First of all, it yields a test function. And secondly, if a uniformly most powerful test exists, it is the likelihood ratio test.

The likelihood ratio test is defined as follows:

$$\phi(\mathbf{X}) = \begin{cases} 1, & \text{if } \quad l^* = \dfrac{\max_{\Theta \in \Omega_0} f_{\mathbf{X}}(X;\Theta)}{\max_{\Theta \in \Omega_1} f_{\mathbf{X}}(X;\Theta)} \leq k^*, \\ 0, & \text{otherwise,} \end{cases}$$

where k^* is so chosen that $\int \phi(\mathbf{X}) f_{\mathbf{X}}(X;\Theta)\,\mathrm{d}X \leq \alpha$ for $\Theta \in \Omega_0$. This test function mimics in form the form of the best test function when both null and alternative hypotheses are simple.

This test function is most times given as

$$\phi(\mathbf{X}) = \begin{cases} 1, & \text{if } \quad l = \dfrac{\max_{\Theta \in \Omega_0} f_{\mathbf{X}}(X;\Theta)}{\max_{\Theta \in \Omega} f_{\mathbf{X}}(X;\Theta)} \leq k, \\ 0, & \text{otherwise.} \end{cases}$$

That these are equivalent is clear from noting that the denominator of l is that of l^* when $f_{\mathbf{X}}(X;\Theta)$ is maximized by a Θ in Ω_1 and that $l = 1$ if it is maximized by a Θ in Ω_0. [Both k^* and k must be less than 1. Otherwise the alternative hypothesis is less "likely" than the null and so we wouldn't want $\phi(\mathbf{X}) = 1$ in that case.] The latter form of $\phi(\mathbf{X})$ will be used by us, the main purpose of the first form being to demonstrate the relation to the Neyman–Pearson Lemma. One should note that $\max_{\Theta \in \Omega} f_{\mathbf{X}}(X;\Theta)$ is given by $f_{\mathbf{X}}(X;\hat{\Theta}(X))$, where $\hat{\Theta}(X)$ is the maximum likelihood estimate of Θ.

A major practical problem in hypothesis testing is the determination of the cutoff value k for use in likelihood ratio (or Neyman–Pearson Lemma) tests. To do this one needs the sampling distribution of l in order to determine the value of k such that

$$\alpha \leq \int_k^\infty f_l(l;\Theta)\,\mathrm{d}l, \qquad \Theta \in \Omega_0.$$

Equivalently, we can seek the sampling distribution of a monotonic function of l. Before embarking on the development of many of the standard tests of hypotheses in econometric work, we shall therefore digress and introduce some of the standard tabulated sampling distributions in use.

2. Sampling distributions

In principle the distribution of any function $y = h(\boldsymbol{X})$ of $\boldsymbol{X}$ can be determined via the methods given in chapter II. One need only begin with the density function of $\boldsymbol{X}$, make a change of variables to include as a new variable the function h of interest, determine the Jacobian of the transformation, and integrate out all extraneous variables, leaving only the density function of the variable of interest, y. One then integrates this density function and tabulates values of the integral for various values of y.

In practice this is very difficult. The integration of extraneous variables may not be accomplishable in closed form. And even if it is, the integration of the final density function of y may be difficult. Today with the help of computers the latter problem is easily surmounted using appropriate techniques from numerical analysis. The former problem, though, is quite onerous for the numerical analyst, but fortunately another computer-related technique is available. One can generate repeated observations on $\boldsymbol{X}$ via computer-generated random numbers drawn from the distribution of $\boldsymbol{X}$, then, for each observation, tabulate $h(\boldsymbol{X})$. Given a large enough sample of $\boldsymbol{X}$'s, one can get a good estimate of the distribution of $y = h(\boldsymbol{X})$ empirically. This technique is sometimes referred to as the *Monte Carlo method.* It has been put to good use in econometrics to investigate sampling distributions of some estimators and test functions which arise in econometric practice.

In this section, therefore, we will merely describe sampling distributions of functions of $\boldsymbol{X} = (x_1, \ldots, x_n)$, where $\boldsymbol{X}$ is distributed as $N(0, \sigma^2 I)$, whose densities have been derived in closed form and whose distribution functions have been well-tabulated.

2.1. Chi-square distribution

Let x be distributed as $N(0, 1)$. Then $y = h(x) = x^2$ is distributed as "chi-square with 1 degree of freedom" ($\chi^2(1)$). The parameter of the chi-squared distribution is called the "degrees of freedom". The density function of y is

$$f_y(y) = (2\sqrt{\pi}\sqrt{y})^{-1}\,e^{-y/2}, \qquad y > 0.$$

This can easily be seen by noting that the Jacobian of the transformation is $1/\sqrt{(2y)}$.

We shall say that y is distributed as "chi-square with n degrees of freedom" ($\chi^2(n)$) if its density function is

$$f_y(y) = (\Gamma(n/2)2^{n/2})^{-1} y^{(n/2)-1}\,e^{-y/2}, \qquad y > 0,$$

where

$$\Gamma(k) = \int_0^\infty y^{k-1}\,e^{-y}\,dy,$$

$$\Gamma(k) = (k-1)\Gamma(k-1), \qquad \text{for} \quad k > 1,$$

and

$$\Gamma(\tfrac{1}{2}) = \sqrt{(2\pi)}.$$

It can be demonstrated in a variety of manners that the $\chi^2(m)$ distribution can be characterized as the distribution of the sum of squares of m independent $N(0, 1)$ random variables.

This fact is useful in proving the following:

If $\boldsymbol{Y}$ is an n-vector distributed as $N(0, \Sigma)$, then $\boldsymbol{Y}\Sigma^{-1}\boldsymbol{Y}'$ is distributed as $\chi^2(n)$.

Proof: Let $\Sigma = T'^{-1}T^{-1}$. Consider the transformation $\boldsymbol{Z} = \boldsymbol{Y}T$. Then $\boldsymbol{Z}$ is distributed as $N(0, T'\Sigma T) = N(0, I)$. In that case $\boldsymbol{Z}\boldsymbol{Z}' = \boldsymbol{Y}\Sigma^{-1}\boldsymbol{Y}' = \sum_{i=1}^{n} z_i^2$. But each z_i is distributed as $N(0, 1)$ and the z_i are independent. Therefore $\boldsymbol{Y}\Sigma^{-1}\boldsymbol{Y}'$ is distributed as $\chi^2(n)$.

2.2. *F-distribution*

Let $\boldsymbol{u}$ be distributed as $\chi^2(m)$, let $\boldsymbol{v}$ be distributed as $\chi^2(n)$, and let $\boldsymbol{u}$ and $\boldsymbol{v}$ be independent. Let $\boldsymbol{w} = (\boldsymbol{u}/m) \div (\boldsymbol{v}/n)$. Then $\boldsymbol{w}$ has an "F-distribution with m and n degrees of freedom", $F(m, n)$. The density function of $\boldsymbol{w}$ is

$$f_w(w) = \Gamma\left(\frac{m+n}{2}\right) \Big/ \left\{\Gamma\left(\frac{m}{2}\right)\Gamma\left(\frac{n}{2}\right)\right\} \; w^{(m/2)-1} \Big/ \left(1 + \frac{mw}{n}\right)^{(m+n)/2}, \qquad w > 0.$$

This can be seen by starting with the joint density of $\boldsymbol{u}$ and $\boldsymbol{v}$, making the transformation

$$w = nu/mv, \qquad x = v,$$

with Jacobian mx/n, to obtain the joint density of $\boldsymbol{w}$ and $\boldsymbol{x}$, and integrating to obtain the marginal density of $\boldsymbol{w}$.

2.3. *t-distribution*

Let $\boldsymbol{u}$ be a $N(0, 1)$ random variable and $\boldsymbol{v}$ be independent of $\boldsymbol{u}$ and distributed as $\chi^2(n)$. Then $\boldsymbol{w} = \boldsymbol{u}/\sqrt{(\boldsymbol{v}/n)}$ is distributed as "t with n degrees of freedom" ($t(n)$). The density function of $\boldsymbol{w}$ is

$$f_{\mathbf{w}}(w) = \Gamma\left(\frac{n+1}{2}\right)\Big/\left\{\sqrt{(\pi n)}\Gamma\left(\frac{n}{2}\right)\right\}\ \left(1+\frac{w^2}{n}\right)^{-(n+1)/2}.$$

The same procedure for deriving the F-distribution above can be used starting from the joint density of $\boldsymbol{u}$ and $\boldsymbol{v}$. It is clear that if $\boldsymbol{w}$ is distributed as $t(n)$, then $\boldsymbol{w}^2$ is distributed as $F(1, n)$.

2.4. *Asymptotic distribution of likelihood ratio*

Consider the special case of testing a composite null against a composite alternative hypothesis wherein Ω_0 is a subset of m-space specified by $\theta_1 = \theta_1^0, \ldots, \theta_m = \theta_m^0$. [More generally, one can assume for what follows that there exist k functions $h_1(\Theta), \ldots, h_k(\Theta)$, representing a re-parameterization to new parameters $\xi_1 = h_1(\Theta), \ldots, \xi_k = h_k(\Theta)$, where the transformation from Θ to Ξ is an isomorphism, and where Ω_0 is specified by $\xi_1 = \xi_1^0, \ldots, \xi_m = \xi_m^0$. Since such generality clutters up the exposition with extraneous "bookkeeping", we make the simplifying assumption herein that the parameter Θ is so defined that the null hypothesis is simply specified as above.] We also consider the special case treated in section 4 of chapter II, where X is an nN-vector and where $f_{\mathbf{X}}(X; \Theta) = \prod_{i=1}^N f_{\mathbf{X}_i}(X_i; \Theta)$.

Then, for arbitrary Θ^*,

$$\log f_{\mathbf{X}}(X; \Theta^*) = \log f_{\mathbf{X}}(X; \hat{\Theta}(X)) + \sum_{\alpha=1}^{N}\sum_{i=1}^{k} \frac{\partial \log f_{\mathbf{X}_\alpha}(X_\alpha; \Theta)}{\partial \theta_i}\bigg|_{\Theta=\hat{\Theta}(X)} (\theta_i^* - \hat{\theta}_i(X))$$

$$+\sum_{\alpha=1}^{N}\sum_{i=1}^{k}\sum_{j=1}^{k}\frac{\partial^2\log f_{\mathbf{X}_\alpha}(X_\alpha;\Theta)}{\partial\theta_i\,\partial\theta_j}\bigg|_{\Theta=\hat{\Theta}(X)}$$
$$\times\{(\theta_i^*-\hat{\theta}_i(X))(\theta_j^*-\hat{\theta}_j(X))/2\}$$
$$+\sum_{\alpha=1}^{N}\sum_{h,i,j=1}^{k}\frac{\partial^3\log f_{\mathbf{X}_\alpha}(X_\alpha;\Theta)}{\partial\theta_h\,\partial\theta_i\,\partial\theta_j}\bigg|_{\Theta=\Theta^+}$$
$$\times\{(\theta_h^*-\hat{\theta}_h(X))(\theta_i^*-\hat{\theta}_i(X))(\theta_j^*-\hat{\theta}_j(X))/6\},$$

where Θ^+ lies between Θ^* and $\hat{\Theta}(X)$, where $\hat{\Theta}(X)$ is the maximum likelihood estimator of $\Theta\in\Omega$.

First, taking $\Theta^*\in\Omega$, we see from similar arguments to those in section 4 of chapter II, that

$$\operatorname*{plim}_{N\to\infty}\frac{1}{N}\log f_{\mathbf{X}}(\mathbf{X};\Theta^*)=\operatorname*{plim}_{N\to\infty}\frac{1}{N}\log f_{\mathbf{X}}(\mathbf{X};\hat{\Theta}(X))$$
$$+\sum_{i=1}^{k}\sum_{j=1}^{k}g_{0ij}(\theta_i^*-\hat{\theta}_i(\mathbf{X}))(\theta_j^*-\hat{\theta}_j(\mathbf{X}))/2,$$

where

$$g_{0ij}=-\mathscr{E}\left[\frac{\partial^2\log f_{\mathbf{X}}(\mathbf{X};\Theta)}{\partial\theta_i\,\partial\theta_j}\bigg|_{\Theta=\Theta^0}\right],$$

and Θ^0 is the true value of Θ.

Thus, maximizing $\log f_{\mathbf{X}}(X;\Theta^*)$ with respect to $\Theta^*\in\Omega$ yields $\Theta^*=\hat{\Theta}(X)$ as maximizer, so that

$$\operatorname*{plim}_{N\to\infty}\frac{1}{N}\max_{\Theta^*\in\Omega}\log f_{\mathbf{X}}(\mathbf{X};\Theta^*)=\operatorname*{plim}_{N\to\infty}\frac{1}{N}\log f_{\mathbf{X}}(\mathbf{X};\hat{\Theta}(\mathbf{X})).$$

Second, taking $\Theta^*\in\Omega_0$ (so that the first m elements of Θ^* are $\theta_1^0,\ldots,\theta_m^0$), we see that

$$\operatorname*{plim}_{N\to\infty}\frac{1}{N}\log f_{\mathbf{X}}(\mathbf{X};\Theta^*)=\operatorname*{plim}_{N\to\infty}\frac{1}{N}\log f_{\mathbf{X}}(\mathbf{X};\hat{\Theta}(\mathbf{X}))$$
$$+\sum_{i=1}^{m}\sum_{j=1}^{m}g_{0ij}(\theta_i^0-\hat{\theta}_i(\mathbf{X}))(\theta_j^*-\hat{\theta}_j(\mathbf{X}))/2$$
$$+\sum_{i=1}^{m}\sum_{j=m+1}^{k}g_{0ij}(\theta_i^0-\hat{\theta}_i(\mathbf{X}))(\theta_j^*-\hat{\theta}_j(\mathbf{X}))/2$$
$$+\sum_{i=m+1}^{k}\sum_{j=1}^{m}g_{0ij}(\theta_i^*-\hat{\theta}_i(\mathbf{X}))(\theta_j^0-\hat{\theta}_j(\mathbf{X}))/2$$
$$+\sum_{i=m+1}^{k}\sum_{j=m+1}^{k}g_{0ij}(\theta_i^*-\hat{\theta}_i(\mathbf{X}))(\theta_j^*-\hat{\theta}_j(\mathbf{X}))/2.$$

Thus, maximizing $\log f_{\mathbf{X}}(X;\Theta^*)$ with respect to the last $k-m$ elements of Θ yields $\Theta = \hat{\Theta}_0(X)$ as maximizer, so that

$$\operatorname*{plim}_{N\to\infty} \frac{1}{N} \max_{\Theta\in\Omega_0} \log f_{\mathbf{X}}(\mathbf{X}; \Theta^*) = \operatorname*{plim}_{N\to\infty} \frac{1}{N} f_{\mathbf{X}}(\mathbf{X}; \hat{\Theta}(\mathbf{X})) + \max_{\theta_1^0,\ldots,\theta_m^0} \sum_{i=1}^{m}\sum_{j=1}^{m} g_{0ij}(\hat{\theta}_i(\mathbf{X}) - \theta_i^0)(\hat{\theta}_j(\mathbf{X}) - \theta_j^0)/2.$$

We see then that

$$\begin{aligned}\operatorname*{plim}_{N\to\infty} \frac{1}{N} \log l &= \operatorname*{plim}_{N\to\infty} \frac{1}{N} \max_{\Theta\in\Omega} \log f_{\mathbf{X}}(\mathbf{X}; \Theta) \\ &\quad - \operatorname*{plim}_{N\to\infty} \frac{1}{N} \max_{\Theta\in\Omega} \log f_{\mathbf{X}}(\mathbf{X}; \Theta) \\ &= -\sum_{i=1}^{m}\sum_{j=1}^{m} g_{0ij}(\theta_i^0 - \hat{\theta}_i(\mathbf{X}))(\theta_j^0 - \hat{\theta}_j(\mathbf{X}))/2.\end{aligned}$$

But $\sqrt{N}\,(\hat{\theta}_1(\mathbf{X}), \ldots, \hat{\theta}_m(\mathbf{X}))$ is distributed asymptotically under the null hypothesis as $N(\sqrt{N}\,(\theta_1^0, \ldots, \theta_m^0), G_{00}^{-1})$, where G_{00} is the upper left-hand $m \times m$ submatrix of G_0. Thus $-2 \log l$ is asymptotically distributed as

$$N \sum_{i=1}^{m}\sum_{j=1}^{m} (\hat{\theta}_i(\mathbf{X}) - \theta_i^0)(\hat{\theta}_j(\mathbf{X}) - \theta_j^0) g_{0ij}.$$

If one considers the vector $\sqrt{N}\,(\hat{\theta}_1(\mathbf{X}) - \theta_1^0, \ldots, \hat{\theta}_m(\mathbf{X}) - \theta_m^0)G_{00}^{1/2} = \mathbf{Y}$, we see that $y_1, \ldots, y_m$ are independent $N(0, 1)$ random variables, so that the asymptotic distribution of $-2 \log l$ is that of $\sum_{i=1}^{m} y_i^2$, i.e., it is $\chi^2(m)$.

2.5. *Pearson family approximation*

Many tabulated sampling distributions satisfy the differential equation

$$\frac{df_x(x)}{dx} = \frac{x + \alpha_3}{\alpha_0 + \alpha_1 x + \alpha_2 x^2} f_x(x),$$

for appropriate choices of α_0, α_1, α_2, and α_3.

The family of density functions satisfying this differential equation is called the *Pearson family*. It can be shown that knowledge of the first four moments of the distribution is sufficient to determine $f_x(x)$ completely. That is, the parameters α_0, α_1, α_2, and α_3 of the density function $f_x(x)$ satisfying the above differential equation are completely determined from knowledge of the first four moments of $\mathbf{x}$. The first four moments of $f_x(x)$ satisfy the following relationship:

$$\begin{bmatrix} 0 & 1 & 2\mu_1 & 1 \\ \mu_0 & 2\mu_1 & 3\mu_2 & \mu_1 \\ 2\mu_1 & 3\mu_2 & 4\mu_3 & \mu_2 \\ 3\mu_2 & 4\mu_3 & 5\mu_4 & \mu_3 \end{bmatrix} \begin{bmatrix} \alpha_0 \\ \alpha_1 \\ \alpha_2 \\ \alpha_3 \end{bmatrix} = \begin{bmatrix} -\mu_1 \\ -\mu_2 \\ -\mu_3 \\ -\mu_4 \end{bmatrix}.$$

With this fact in mind, one can obtain an approximation to the sampling distribution of any statistic, given knowledge of its first four moments, by adopting as the approximation the appropriate member of the Pearson family. For example, consider the member of the family given by

$$f_x(x) = \frac{\Gamma(p+q)}{\Gamma(p)\Gamma(q)} x^{p-1}(1-x)^{q-1}$$

for $0 < x < 1$. Here $\alpha_0 = 0$, $\alpha_1 = -1/(p+q-2)$, $\alpha_2 = 1/(p+q-2)$, and $\alpha_3 = -(p-1)/(p+q-2)$. This density, that of the *beta distribution*, has as its first two moments

$$\mathscr{E}\boldsymbol{x} = p/(p+q),$$
$$\mathscr{V}\boldsymbol{x} = pq/(p+q)^2(p+q+1).$$

Thus one can approximate the sampling distribution of a random variable $\boldsymbol{x}$ defined over the range (0, 1) by the beta distribution with parameters determined from the first two moments of $\boldsymbol{x}$. More generally, if $\boldsymbol{x}$ is distributed over a finite range (a, b), then $\boldsymbol{y} = (\boldsymbol{x} - a)/(b - a)$ is distributed over the range (0, 1) and so the above approximation can be used for the density of $\boldsymbol{y}$ and transformed to obtain an approximation to the density of $\boldsymbol{x}$.

3. Tests of linear hypotheses

In this section we consider a very special situation, namely one where $\boldsymbol{X} = (\boldsymbol{x}_1, \ldots, \boldsymbol{x}_n)$ is distributed as $N(\mu, \sigma^2 I)$, where $\Theta = (\mu, \sigma^2)$ is unknown, and where we make very restrictive assumptions about the nature of Ω and Ω_0. We assume that the n-vector $\mu = (\mu_1, \ldots, \mu_n)$ is known to lie in a given p-dimensional subspace of n-space, so that Ω is a p-dimensional subspace of n-space. Further, all hypotheses we consider will be hypotheses which restrict μ further to some q-dimensional subspace Ω_0 of n-space (and hence Ω_0 is a subspace of Ω as well). In this formulation $\Omega_1 = \Omega - \Omega_0$ is orthogonal to Ω_0.

A simple example of the restrictiveness of this assumption is that of the one-tailed t-test situation. In that situation, $\mu = \theta(1, \ldots, 1)$, so that $p = 1$, but the one-tailedness assumption is that $\theta \leqslant 0$, say. But this definition of Ω no longer defines a subspace of n-space, and so the results of this section cannot apply to this problem. Nontheless, this assumption about the nature of Ω and Ω_0 is sufficiently rich to include tests of most hypotheses of interest about parameters of linear expected value models, as will soon be seen.

In preparation for deriving the likelihood ratio test of the hypothesis that Θ is in Ω_0 against the alternative that it is in $\Omega - \Omega_0$, let us first establish some notational conventions regarding bases in n-space, the p-dimensional subspace Ω, and the q-dimensional subspace Ω_0. With these conventions established, we will assume herewith that the coordinates of both $\boldsymbol{X}$ and μ will be given relative to the basis in n-space.

Let $U_1, \ldots, U_n$ be a basis for n-space. It would be nice if the U_i had the following properties:

(1) $U_1, \ldots, U_q$ are a basis for Ω_0.
(2) $U_1, \ldots, U_p$ are a basis for Ω.
(3) $U_1, \ldots, U_q$ are orthogonal to $U_{q+1}, \ldots, U_p$.
(4) $U_1, \ldots, U_p$ are orthogonal to $U_{p+1}, \ldots, U_n$.

Of course, if $U_1, \ldots, U_n$ were an orthogonal basis, then (3) and (4) would be satisfied. So let us assume that this is so, and further that (1) and (2) are satisfied and that the U_i have length 1. After all, such a basis does exist and so can be constructed from the definitions of Ω and Ω_0.

To illustrate this, consider the following situation. Let $\mu = (\theta_1, \theta_1, \theta_2, \theta_2, \theta_2)$ so that Ω is a 2-dimensional subspace of 5-space. Let our null hypothesis be that $3\theta_1 - 2\theta_2 = 0$, so that Ω_0 is a 1-dimensional subspace. A basis for Ω_0 is the vector $V = (2, 2, 3, 3, 3)$; a basis for Ω are the vectors $W_1 = (1, 1, 0, 0, 0)$ and $W_2 = (0, 0, 1, 1, 1)$. We can, using the Gram–Schmidt procedure, construct the required basis $U_1, \ldots, U_5$ from appropriately selected vectors from the basis for Ω_0, Ω, and the elementary basis of 5-space.

We begin by taking

$$U_1 = \frac{1}{\sqrt{35}}\, V = \frac{1}{\sqrt{35}}\,(2, 2, 3, 3, 3).$$

Augmenting U_1 with W_2 and using the Gram–Schmidt procedure we obtain

$$U_2 = \frac{1}{\sqrt{210}}(-9, -9, 4, 4, 4).$$

Using in turn the additional vectors E_1, E_3 and E_4 in the Gram–Schmidt procedure, we obtain

$$U_3 = \frac{1}{\sqrt{2}}(1, -1, 0, 0, 0),$$

$$U_4 = \frac{1}{\sqrt{6}}(0, 0, 2, -1, -1).$$

$$U_5 = \frac{1}{\sqrt{2}}(0, 0, 0, 1, -1).$$

These vectors have the required properties (1)–(4).

If X is an n-vector whose coordinates are expressed in terms of the elementary basis, so that $X = x_1E_1 + \cdots + x_nE_n$, then, relative to the basis of U's the vector X is expressible as $X = v_1U_1 + \cdots + v_nU_n$. The coordinates $v_1, \ldots, v_n$ are easily determined as follows. Since

$$\begin{aligned} XU_i' &= v_1U_1U_i' + \cdots + v_nU_nU_i' \\ &= v_i, \end{aligned}$$

we see that $v_i = \sum_{j=1}^{n} x_ju_{ij}$. If U is the matrix whose ith row is U_i, then the coordinates of X relative to the basis of U_i's is given by XU'. Since U is an orthogonal matrix, if X is distributed as $N(\mu, \sigma^2I)$, XU' is distributed as $N(\mu U', \sigma^2 I)$, i.e., the only change is that the mean vector is now expressed as well in terms of the basis of U's.

Assume that the coordinates x_i of X are expressed not in terms of the elementary basis but rather in terms of the basis of U's, i.e., that

$$X = x_1U_1 + \cdots + x_nU_n.$$

What about the coordinates of μ? First of all, under Ω, since $\mu \in \Omega$, the coordinates of μ corresponding to the last $n-p$ basis elements $U_{p+1}, \ldots, U_n$ must be zero. Similarly, under Ω_0, since $\mu \in \Omega_0$, the last $n-q$ coordinates of μ must be zero. (In our example, $\mu U_2' = (-18\theta_1 + 12\theta_2)$ so that the second coordinate of μ is 0 if $3\theta_1 - 2\theta_2 = 0$. Also check that $\mu U_i' = 0$ for $i = 3, 4, 5$ in any event.) Then the likelihood ratio is

$$\lambda = \frac{\max\limits_{\Theta \in \Omega_0} f_{\mathbf{x}}(X; \Theta)}{\max\limits_{\Theta \in \Omega} f_{\mathbf{x}}(X'; \Theta)}$$

$$= \frac{\max\limits_{\theta \in \Omega_0} (2\pi)^{-n/2}\sigma^{-n/2} \exp\left\{-\left[\sum_{i=1}^{q} (x_i - \theta_i)^2 + \sum_{i=q+1}^{n} x_i^2\right] \Big/ 2\sigma^2\right\}}{\max\limits_{\theta \in \Omega} (2\pi)^{-n/2}\sigma^{-n/2} \exp\left\{-\left[\sum_{i=1}^{p} (x_i - \theta_i)^2 + \sum_{i=p+1}^{n} x_i^2\right] \Big/ 2\sigma^2\right\}}$$

$$= \frac{\max\limits_{\sigma^2} (2\pi)^{-n/2}\sigma^{-n/2} \exp\left\{-\sum_{i=q+1}^{n} x_i^2/2\sigma^2\right\}}{\max\limits_{\sigma^2} (2\pi)^{-n/2}\sigma^{-n/2} \exp\left\{-\sum_{i=p+1}^{n} x_i^2/2\sigma^2\right\}}$$

$$= \frac{(2\pi)^{-n/2}\left(\sum_{i=q+1}^{n} x_i^2/n\right)^{n/2} \exp\{-n/2\}}{(2\pi)^{-n/2}\left(\sum_{i=p+1}^{n} x_i^2/n\right)^{-n/2} \exp\{-n/2\}}.$$

This is a monotonic function of

$$\sum_{i=q+1}^{p} x_i^2 \Big/ \sum_{i=p+1}^{n} x_i^2,$$

and so this is an appropriate test statistic. But noting that the $\mathbf{x}_i$ are $N(0, \sigma^2)$ for $i = q+1, \ldots, p$, under Ω_0 and for $i = p+1, \ldots, n$, under Ω, and are independent, we see that by dividing numerator and denominator by σ^2 we will have as numerator and denominator independent $\chi^2(p-q)$ and $\chi^2(n-p)$ distributed random variables. Thus we know that

$$\mathbf{w} = \sum_{i=q+1}^{p} (\mathbf{x}_i^2/(p-q)) \Big/ \sum_{i=p+1}^{n} (\mathbf{x}_i^2/(n-p))$$

is distributed as $F(p-q, n-p)$. We would reject Ω_0 if the observed value of $\mathbf{w}$ is greater than the appropriate upper α percentile of the $F(p-q, n-p)$ distribution. [As a brief aside, if σ^2 is known, the likelihood ratio test is a monotonic function of $\sum_{i=q+1}^{p} \mathbf{x}_i^2/\sigma^2$, which is distributed as $\chi^2(p-q)$, and so this is the test statistic we would use then.]

For the example introduced earlier, that of testing whether $3\theta_1 - 2\theta_1 = 0$ when $\mu = (\theta_1, \theta_1, \theta_2, \theta_2, \theta_2)$, the test statistic is:

$$w=\frac{(\boldsymbol{X}U_2')^2}{[(\boldsymbol{X}U_3')^2+(\boldsymbol{X}U_4')^2+(\boldsymbol{X}U_5')^2]/3}$$

$$=\frac{[-9(\boldsymbol{x}_1+\boldsymbol{x}_2)+4(\boldsymbol{x}_3+\boldsymbol{x}_4+\boldsymbol{x}_5)]^2/210}{\left[\dfrac{(\boldsymbol{x}_1-\boldsymbol{x}_2)^2}{2}+\dfrac{(2\boldsymbol{x}_3-\boldsymbol{x}_4-\boldsymbol{x}_5)^2}{6}+\dfrac{(\boldsymbol{x}_4-\boldsymbol{x}_5)^2}{2}\right]\Big/3}$$

$$=\frac{[-9(\boldsymbol{x}_1+\boldsymbol{x}_2)+4(\boldsymbol{x}_3+\boldsymbol{x}_4+\boldsymbol{x}_5)]^2/210}{\left[\dfrac{(\boldsymbol{x}_1-\boldsymbol{x}_2)^2}{2}+\dfrac{2}{3}(\boldsymbol{x}_3^2+\boldsymbol{x}_4^2+\boldsymbol{x}_5^2-\boldsymbol{x}_3\boldsymbol{x}_4-\boldsymbol{x}_3\boldsymbol{x}_5-\boldsymbol{x}_4\boldsymbol{x}_5)\right]\Big/3}$$

which is distributed as $F(1,3)$.

The test statistic $\boldsymbol{w}$ has a geometric interpretation which is useful to learn as most of the derivations of specific applications of this general test procedure will be couched in terms of this geometric interpretation. Consider the picture given in figure 6. Although Ω and Ω_0 are pictured as 2- and 1-dimensional, respectively, this is only done to enable us to draw a picture of these p- and q-dimensional spaces. Pictured are X, $P_\Omega(X)$,

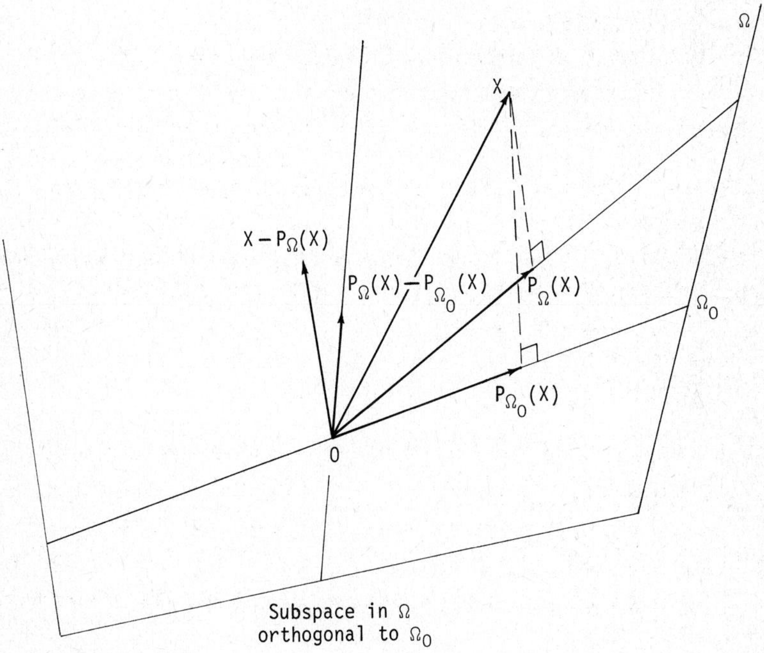

FIGURE 6

the orthogonal projection of X onto Ω, and $P_{\Omega_0}(X)$, the orthogonal projection of X onto Ω_0. The sum $\sum_{i=q+1}^{p} x_i^2$ is the squared length of the vector $P_{\Omega_0}(X)-P_\Omega(X)$. Roughly speaking, if this length is "large" the null hypothesis is rejected. The normalization yardstick of how large "large" is, in case σ^2 is known, is σ^2, and, in case σ^2 is not known, is an estimate of σ^2, namely the squared length $\sum_{i=p+1}^{n} x_i^2$ of the vector from X orthogonal to $P_\Omega(X)$.

This geometric interpretation has been made without reference to the practical problem of finding these projections when the vector $\boldsymbol{X}$ is expressed relative to the elementary basis, as is practically always the case, and we don't have at hand the vectors $U_1, \ldots, U_n$ to transform the problem. It turns out that we don't need the full set of vectors $U_1, \ldots, U_n$ in order to perform the calculations necessary for actually carrying out the test of significance (we merely needed them all in principle in order to derive the test). The reason is this. All we need to find are two vectors, $P_\Omega(X)$ and $P_{\Omega_0}(X)$. Then all we must calculate are the squared length of $P_\Omega(X)-P_{\Omega_0}(X)$ and the squared length of $X-P_\Omega(X)$, the two ingredients of the test statistic.

To obtain these projections all we need concern ourselves with is a basis, not necessarily orthogonal, for each of the spaces Ω and Ω_0. Let $V_1, \ldots, V_q$ be a basis for Ω_0, and let V be the $q \times n$ matrix whose ith row is V_i. Then $P_{\Omega_0}(X)$ is given by XV^+V. Similarly if $W_1, \ldots, W_p$ is a basis for Ω and W is the $p \times n$ matrix whose ith row is W_i, then $P_\Omega(X)$ is given by XW^+W.

To return once again to our example, we can use the natural basis vector $V=(2,2,3,3,3)$ to obtain

$$
\begin{aligned}
P_{\Omega_0}(X) &= XV'(VV')^{-1}V \\
&= \frac{1}{35} X \begin{bmatrix} 4 & 4 & 6 & 6 & 6 \\ 4 & 4 & 6 & 6 & 6 \\ 6 & 6 & 9 & 9 & 9 \\ 6 & 6 & 9 & 9 & 9 \\ 6 & 6 & 9 & 9 & 9 \end{bmatrix} \\
&= \frac{1}{35}(4s_1+6s_2, 4s_1+6s_2, 6s_1+9s_2, 6s_1+9s_2, 6s_1+9s_2),
\end{aligned}
$$

where $s_1 = x_1+x_2$ and $s_2 = x_3+x_4+x_5$.

We can also use the natural basis $W_1=(1,1,0,0,0)$ and $W_2=(0,0,1,1,1)$ for Ω to obtain

$$P_\Omega(X) = XW'(WW')^{-1}W$$

$$= X\begin{bmatrix}1 & 0\\ 1 & 0\\ 0 & 1\\ 0 & 1\\ 0 & 1\end{bmatrix}\begin{bmatrix}2 & 0\\ 0 & 3\end{bmatrix}^{-1}\begin{bmatrix}1 & 1 & 0 & 0 & 0\\ 0 & 0 & 1 & 1 & 1\end{bmatrix}$$

$$= \begin{bmatrix}\frac{s_1}{2} & \frac{s_1}{2} & \frac{s_2}{3} & \frac{s_2}{3} & \frac{s_2}{3}\end{bmatrix}.$$

Then the squared length of $P_{\Omega_0}(X) - P_\Omega(X)$ is

$$\sum_{i=1}^{2}\left[\frac{4s_1+6s_2}{35} - \frac{s_1}{2}\right]^2 + \sum_{i=3}^{5}\left[\frac{6s_1+9s_2}{35} - \frac{s_2}{3}\right]^2 =$$

$$\frac{1}{(210)^2}[2[36s_2 - 81s_1]^2 + 3[36s_1 - 16s_2]^2] =$$

$$\frac{(9s_1 - 4s_2)^2}{210}.$$

Note the ease with which this calculation is made, without involved changes of bases to find a common orthogonal set of basis vectors for Ω_0, Ω, and n-space.

The squared length of $X - P_\Omega(X)$ is just

$$\sum_{i=1}^{2}\left(x_i - \frac{s_1}{2}\right)^2 + \sum_{i=3}^{5}\left(x_i - \frac{s_2}{3}\right)^2 =$$

$$2\left(\frac{x_1 - x_2}{2}\right)^2 + \left(\frac{2x_3 - x_4 - x_5}{3}\right)^2 + \left(\frac{2x_4 - x_3 - x_5}{3}\right)^2 + \left(\frac{2x_5 - x_3 - x_4}{3}\right)^2 =$$

$$\frac{(x_1 - x_2)^2}{2} + \frac{2}{3}[x_3^2 + x_4^2 + x_5^2 - x_3x_4 - x_3x_5 - x_4x_5].$$

A comparison of this derivation with the direct derivation of the denominator of the test statistic given earlier shows that this is much easier to perform.

Sometimes it is easier to determine $P_\Omega(Y) - P_{\Omega_0}(Y)$ using the following argument. Consider the subspace of Ω which is orthogonal to Ω_0. Let $Q_{\Omega_0}(Y)$ denote the orthogonal projection of Y onto that subspace. Then $Q_{\Omega_0}(Y) = P_\Omega(Y) - P_{\Omega_0}(Y)$.

If Ω_0 is defined "by negation", i.e., by defining the subspace of Ω which, under the null hypothesis, gets mapped into the 0 vector and defining Ω_0 as the set of coordinates of μ which do not get mapped into 0, then it may be easier by virtue of this definition to determine $Q_{\Omega_0}(Y)$

than $P_{\Omega_0}(Y)$ directly. An example of this will be seen prominently in section 1 of chapter VI.

4. References

The landmark work on hypothesis testing theory is:

Lehmann, E. L., 1959, Testing statistical hypotheses (Wiley, New York).

A good reference to the sampling distributions given above and their derivations is:

Hogg, R. V. and A. T. Craig, 1959, Introduction to mathematical statistics (MacMillan, New York).

The asymptotic distribution of the likelihood ratio is briefly derived in:

Kendall, M. G. and A. Stuart, 1961, The advanced theory of statistics, vol. 2 (Griffin, London).

Wilks, S. S., 1938, The large-sample distribution of the likelihood ratio for testing composite hypotheses, Annals of Mathematical Statistics 9, pp. 60–62.

A thorough treatment of the Pearson family is given in:

Elderton, W. P., 1938, Frequency curves and correlation (Cambridge University Press, Cambridge).

A good reference for the theory of testing linear hypothesis is:

Scheffe, H., 1959, Analysis of variance (Wiley, New York).

The coordinate-free approach taken here is described in:

Kruskal, W., 1961, The coordinate-free approach to Gauss–Markov estimation, and its application to missing and extra observations, in: J. Neyman, ed., Proceedings of the Fourth Berkeley Symposium on Mathematical Statistics and Probability, vol. I (University of California Press, Berkeley) pp. 435–451.

VI

Tests of hypotheses in econometric models

In this chapter we apply the general principles of hypothesis test construction given in chapter VI to frequently encountered hypothesis testing situations in econometric practice. The first set of principles to be applied are those used in constructing tests of linear hypotheses. We begin by deriving the one-way analysis of variance, not so much because it is used in econometric practice as because pedagogically it is a simple application of the material of section 3 of chapter V. In this example the structure of μ, and hence of the bases for Ω and Ω_0, is quite transparent.

Our next sections deal with the multiple regression model, i.e., the linear expected value model wherein $n = 1$. Section 2 treats the general problem of testing a linear hypothesis about the regression coefficients, and section 3 treats the problem of testing the equality of T regressions.

In section 4 the notion of a simple index of "goodness" of the linear expected value model is introduced and a test of whether this index, the multiple correlation coefficient, is a specified value is constructed.

One of the most vital assumptions in deriving estimators and tests in econometric models is that vectors $\boldsymbol{Y}_1, \ldots, \boldsymbol{Y}_N$ (or variables $y_1, \ldots, y_N$) are independent. In section 5 we test this null hypothesis against a particular alternative hypothesis, namely that these variables are serially correlated.

In section 6 we study a test for identifiability of an equation in a system of simultaneous equations. Clearly such a test is necessary, as the condition for identifiability relates to the rank of a matrix of unknown parameters.

1. One-way analysis of variance

In this application of the theory of construction of tests of linear hypotheses, we consider the case in which we take a random sample of size J from each of I independent normally distributed random variables with common variance σ^2. Thus, letting

$$\boldsymbol{X} = (\boldsymbol{x}_{11}, \ldots, \boldsymbol{x}_{1J}, \boldsymbol{x}_{21}, \ldots, \boldsymbol{x}_{2J}, \ldots, \boldsymbol{x}_{I1}, \ldots, \boldsymbol{x}_{IJ}),$$

we see that

$$\mu = (\mu_1, \ldots, \mu_1, \mu_2, \ldots, \mu_2, \ldots, \mu_I, \ldots, \mu_I),$$

where each μ_i is repeated J times.

The null hypothesis in the one-way analysis of variance is that $\mu_1 = \mu_2 = \cdots = \mu_I$. Clearly, a basis for the one-dimensional subspace Ω_0 is the IJ-vector $U = (1, \ldots, 1)$. Also, letting U_i be of the form

$$U_i = (0, \ldots, 0, 1, \ldots, 1, 0, \ldots, 0),$$

where the 1's are elements $(i-1)J+1, \ldots, iJ$, for $i = 1, \ldots, I$, we see that $U_1, \ldots, U_I$ are an orthogonal basis for Ω.

To find the denominator of the test statistic for our null hypothesis, we must first find $P_\Omega(X)$. But

$$P_\Omega(X) = \sum_{i=1}^{I} P_{U_i}(X) = \sum_{i=1}^{I}\sum_{j=1}^{J} \frac{x_{ij}}{J} U_i$$

$$= (\bar{x}_{1.}, \ldots, \bar{x}_{1.}, \bar{x}_{2.}, \ldots, \bar{x}_{2.}, \ldots, \bar{x}_{I.}, \ldots, \bar{x}_{I.}),$$

where $\bar{x}_{i.} = \sum_{j=1}^{J} x_{ij}/J$. Thus,

$$X - P_\Omega(X) = (x_{11} - \bar{x}_{1.}, \ldots, x_{1J} - \bar{x}_{1.}, \ldots, x_{I1} - \bar{x}_{I.}, \ldots, x_{IJ} - \bar{x}_{I.}),$$

and the denominator of the test statistic is

$$\sum_{i=1}^{I}\sum_{j=1}^{J} (x_{ij} - \bar{x}_{i.})^2/(IJ - I).$$

To find the numerator of the test statistic, note that

$$P_{\Omega_0}(X) = \sum_{i=1}^{I}\sum_{j=1}^{J} (x_{ij}/IJ)U = \bar{x}_{..}U,$$

so that

$$P_\Omega(X) - P_{\Omega_0}(X) = \sum_{i=1}^{I} (\bar{x}_{i.} - \bar{x}_{..})U_i,$$

and the squared length of this vector is $J\sum_{i=1}^{I}(\bar{x}_{i.}-\bar{x}_{..})^2$.

Putting together all our calculations, we see that

$$w=\frac{J\sum_{i=1}^{I}(\bar{x}_{i.}-\bar{x}_{..})^2/(I-1)}{\sum_{i=1}^{I}\sum_{j=1}^{J}(x_{ij}-\bar{x}_{i.})^2/(IJ-I)}$$

is distributed as $F(I-1, IJ-I)$ and is the test statistic for testing the hypothesis of equality of means of the I populations.

Exercise (Two-way analysis of variance): Consider the above setting, modified as follows. Let $\mathscr{E}x_{ij}=\mu+\alpha_i+\beta_j$, with $\sum_{i=1}^{I}\alpha_i=\sum_{j=1}^{J}\beta_j=0$. Test the hypothesis that $\alpha_1=\cdots=\alpha_I$. Test the hypothesis that $\beta_1=\cdots=\beta_J$.

2. Tests of linear hypotheses in regression models

Consider the linear regression model where Y is an N-vector distributed as $N(BX', \sigma^2I)$, B is a p-vector of parameters, and X is an $N\times p$ matrix of observations on the so-called "independent" variables. Note that we have assumed a special structure for the covariance matrix of Y, namely $\Sigma=\sigma^2I$. In this case μ is the N-vector BX'. We assume that $p<N$ and that the rank of X (which is at most p) is equal to p. Then μ lies in a p-dimensional subspace Ω of N-space.

Writing $X=[X_1',\ldots,X_p']$, it becomes clear that the vectors $X_1,\ldots,X_p$ are a basis for Ω (since every μ is of the form $\mu=\sum_{i=1}^{p}\beta_iX_i$ and the X_i are linearly independent). Thus, whatever the linear null hypothesis about μ (and hence about B) may be, we can once and for all determine the denominator of the appropriate test statistic. Its basic ingredient is the squared length of the vector $Y-P_\Omega(Y)$, i.e., the squared length of $Y-YX'^{+}X'=Y(I-X(X'X)^{-1}X')$, so that the denominator is $Y(I-X(X'X)^{-1}X')Y'$ divided by $N-p$.

Exercise: Let $p=2$, $X_1=(1,\ldots,1)$ and $X_2=(x_1,\ldots,x_N)$. Determine $Y(I-X(X'X)^{-1}X')Y'$ in this case.

The general linear hypothesis is one which introduces m homogeneous linear constraints on the vector B of the form $BA' = 0$, where A is an $m \times p$ matrix of rank m. The null hypothesis space Ω_0 is then a $(p-m)$-dimensional subspace of N-space whose basis is constructed as follows. Augment the matrix A with a $(p-m)\times p$ matrix consisting of the $(p-m)\times(p-m)$ identity matrix and the $(p-m)\times m$ zero matrix, to wit

$$C = \begin{bmatrix} & A & \\ I & & 0 \end{bmatrix}.$$

Then $BC' = [0 \;\; \beta_1 \cdots \beta_{p-m}] = [0 \;\; \dot{B}]$, so that B can be expressed in terms of $\dot{B}$ as $B = [\alpha \;\; \dot{B}](C^{-1})'$. Let A^* denote the last $(p-m)$ rows of $(C^{-1})'$. Then $B = \dot{B}A^*$. Since $\mu = \mathscr{E}Y = BX' = \dot{B}A^*X'$, we see that the $p-m$ rows of A^*X' are a basis for Ω_0.

However, to calculate the appropriate test statistics one need not calculate A^* explicitly. Instead note that $AA^{*\prime} = 0$, so that the columns of $[A' \;\; A^{*\prime}]$ are linearly independent. Thus the matrix

$$D = \begin{bmatrix} A \\ A^* \end{bmatrix}$$

is of full rank and DX' is a basis for Ω. Let $U_1, \ldots, U_m$ denote the row vectors of AX' and $Z_1, \ldots, Z_{p-m}$ denote the row vectors of A^*X'. Then relative to this basis,

$$\mu = (\mu_1, \ldots, \mu_p) = \mu_1 U_1 + \cdots + \mu_m U_m + \mu_{m+1} Z_1 + \cdots + \mu_p Z_{p-m}.$$

When μ is in Ω_0, we have $\mu_1 = \cdots = \mu_m = 0$. Then μ is expressible as

$$\mu = (\mu_1, \ldots, \mu_m, 0, \ldots, 0) + (0, \ldots, 0, \mu_{m+1}, \ldots, \mu_p) = V + W,$$

where W is in Ω_0^I and V and W are orthogonal. Therefore V is in Ω_0^I, the subspace in Ω orthogonal to Ω_0. Since V is expressible as $V = \mu_1 U_1 + \cdots + \mu_m U_m$, we see that $U_1, \ldots, U_m$, i.e., the rows of AX', are a basis for Ω_0^I.

Let $Q_{\Omega_0}(Y)$ be the orthogonal projection on this subspace. Then $P_\Omega(Y) = Q_{\Omega_0}(Y) + P_{\Omega_0}(Y)$, so that the numerator of the test statistic is the squared length of $Q_{\Omega_0}(Y)$ divided by m, i.e.,

$$Y(XA'(AX'XA')^{-1}AX')^{-1}Y'/m.$$

As an example of the calculation of this numerator, consider the case $p = 2$, $X_1 = (x_{11}, \ldots, x_{1N})$, $X_2 = (x_{21}, \ldots, x_{2N})$, $m = 1$, and $A = (1, -a)$, i.e., our null hypothesis is that $\beta_1 - a\beta_2 = 0$. Only if this is true will we have the relation $X_1 - aX_2 = 0$ regardless of the value of the coordinates of the basis vectors X_1, X_2. Then

$$AX' = (x_{11} - ax_{21}, \ldots, x_{1N} - ax_{2N}),$$

$$AX'XA' = \sum_{i=1}^{N} (x_{1i} - ax_{2i})^2,$$

and

$$Y(XA'(AX'XA')^{-1}AX')Y' = \sum_{i=1}^{N} y_i^2(x_{1i} - ax_{2i})^2 \Big/ \sum_{i=1}^{N} (x_{1i} - ax_{2i})^2.$$

When $a = 0$, i.e., if our hypothesis is $\beta_1 = 0$, this reduces to

$$\sum_{i=1}^{N} y_i^2 x_{1i}^2 \Big/ \sum_{i=1}^{N} x_{1i}^2.$$

If instead we were interested in testing a different null hypothesis about B, say $B = B_0$, the methods given in chapter V do not automatically apply, since Ω_0 as defined is not a subspace of Ω. (Recall that any subspace must contain the 0 vector.) In general, to treat such a hypothesis one can reparameterize the problem, defining $\delta_i = \beta_i - \beta_{i0}$, $\Delta = (\delta_1, \ldots, \delta_p)$, $\mu = \Delta X'$, and $Z = Y - B_0 X'$. Then, replacing Y by Z in the above expressions, one obtains the appropriate test statistic. (Similar modifications will handle the hypothesis that a subvector of B has a specific null-hypothesized value.) In the above example, if the null hypothesis is that $\beta_1 = \beta_{10}$, then the numerator of the test statistic is

$$\sum_{i=1}^{N} (y_i - \beta_{10}x_{1i})^2 x_{1i}^2 \Big/ \sum_{i=1}^{N} x_{1i}^2,$$

and the denominator is

$$\left[\sum_{i=1}^{N} (y_i - \beta_{10}x_{1i})^2 - \left(\sum_{i=1}^{N} (y_i - \beta_{10}x_{1i})^2 x_{1i}^2 \Big/ \sum_{i=1}^{N} x_{1i}^2\right)\right] \Big/ (N-2).$$

3. Test of equality of regressions

We consider herein the situation where we have observed T independent samples of N-vectors $\mathbf{Y}_1, \ldots, \mathbf{Y}_T$, where $\mathbf{Y}_t = (y_{1t}, \ldots, y_{Nt})$ is distributed as $N(B_t X_t', \sigma^2 I)$, X_t' is the $p \times N$ matrix whose ith row is $(x_{i1t}, \ldots, x_{iNt})$, and $B_t = (\beta_{1t}, \ldots, \beta_{pt})$.

We are interested in testing the special linear hypothesis that $B_1 = \cdots = B_T$, i.e., that the T regressions have identical parameters.

Now, letting $\boldsymbol{Y} = (\boldsymbol{Y}_1, \ldots, \boldsymbol{Y}_T)$, $B = (B_1, \ldots, B_T)$, and

$$X' = \begin{bmatrix} X_1' & & 0 \\ & \cdot & \\ & & \cdot \\ 0 & & \cdot \\ & & X_T' \end{bmatrix} = \begin{bmatrix} X_{11}' \cdots X_{p1}' & & 0 \\ & \cdot & \\ & & \cdot \\ 0 & & \cdot \\ & & X_{1T}' \cdots X_{pT}' \end{bmatrix},$$

we see that $\boldsymbol{Y}$ is distributed as $N(BX', \sigma^2 I)$. We shall apply to this model the general test construction procedure in section 3 of chapter V.

Here

$$\mu = \sum_{t=1}^{T} \sum_{i=1}^{p} \beta_{it} X_{it}',$$

so that the pT vectors X_{it}, $i = 1, \ldots, p$, $t = 1, \ldots, T$, are a basis for the parameter space Ω. Thus, following the arguments of the preceding section, the denominator of the test statistic for any linear hypothesis about the β's is

$$Y(I - X(X'X)^{-1}X')Y'/(NT - pT).$$

To obtain the numerator of the test statistic for the hypothesis that $\beta_{i1} = \cdots = \beta_{iT}$, $i = 1, \ldots, p$, one first notes that under this hypothesis the p vectors $\sum_{t=1}^{T} X_{it}$, $i = 1, \ldots, p$, are a basis for Ω_0. Letting $X_{i.} = \sum_{t=1}^{T} X_{it}$ and $X_.' = [X_{1.}' \cdots X_{p.}']$, we see that the squared length of $P_{\Omega_0}(Y)$ is $Y(I - X_.(X_.'X_.)^{-1}X_.')Y'$. Thus the numerator of the test statistic is

$$Y(X(X'X)^{-1}X' - X_.(X_.'X_.)^{-1}X_.')Y'/(pT - p).$$

Exercise: (1) Derive the result of this section from those of the previous section. (After all, isn't this hypothesis simply a linear hypothesis in an expanded model?)

(2) The material in this section is developed for equal-sized samples. Instead, for $T = 2$, suppose $\boldsymbol{Y}_1$ were an N_1-vector and $\boldsymbol{Y}_2$ were an N_2-vector. Test the hypothesis that $B_1 = B_2$. (Remember to consider the case where N_1 or N_2 are less than p.) Compare with the Chow–Fisher test (see page 207 of Johnston, *Econometric methods*, McGraw-Hill Book Company, New York, 1972).

(3) Let $B_1^* = (\beta_{11}, \ldots, \beta_{r1})$, $B_2^* = (\beta_{12}, \ldots, \beta_{r2})$ where $r < p$. Test the hypothesis that $B_1^* = B_2^*$.

4. Testing that multiple regression coefficient is zero

Let $(\mathbf{y}, \mathbf{X})$ be distributed as $N(\mu, \Sigma)$, where $\mathbf{X}$ is a p-vector and Σ is positive definite. Let $B = \Sigma_{22}^{-1}\Sigma_{21}$ be the p-vector of regression coefficients of $\mathbf{y}$ on X. We recall from section 2 of chapter II that the squared multiple correlation coefficient is the proportion of the variance of $\mathbf{y}$ due to $\mathbf{X}$. Suppose we were interested in testing the hypothesis that the multiple correlation coefficient is 0, i.e., that knowledge of $\mathbf{X} = X$ yields no reduction in the variance of $\mathbf{y}$. This is equivalent to the hypothesis that $\Sigma_{12}\Sigma_{22}^{-1}\Sigma_{21} = 0$, which, because Σ_{22}^{-1} is positive definite, is equivalent to $\Sigma_{12} = 0$.

We know under Ω that, given N independent observations (y_i, X_i), $i = 1, \dots, N$, of $(\mathbf{y}, \mathbf{X})$, the likelihood function is maximized by

$$\hat{\mu} = (\bar{y}, \bar{X}) = \frac{1}{N}\sum_{i=1}^{N}(y_i, X_i),$$

$$\hat{\Sigma} = \frac{1}{N}\sum_{i=1}^{N}(y_i - \bar{y}, X_i - \bar{X})'(y_i - \bar{y}, X_i - \bar{X}),$$

and its maximum value is

$$(2\pi)^{-N(p+1)/2}N^{N(p+1)/2}\exp\{-N(p+1)/2\}|N\hat{\Sigma}|^{N/2}.$$

Under Ω_0 the likelihood function can be decomposed into two factors,

$$g_1 = (2\pi)^{-\frac{1}{2}}\sigma_{11}^{-N/2}\exp\left\{-\sum_{i=1}^{N}(y_i - \mu_1)^2/2\sigma_{11}\right\},$$

and

$$g_2 = (2\pi)^{-Np/2}|\Sigma_{22}|^{-N/2}\exp\left\{-\sum_{i=1}^{N}(X_i - \ddot{\mu})'\Sigma_{22}^{-1}(X_i - \ddot{\mu})/2\right\}.$$

Applying Theorem 19 to each factor separately and putting the results together, we see that under Ω_0 the likelihood function's maximum value is

$$(2\pi)^{-N(p+1)/2}N^{N(p+1)/2}\,e^{-N(p+1)/2}(N\hat{\sigma}_{11})^{-N/2}|N\hat{\Sigma}_{22}|^{-N/2},$$

where $\hat{\sigma}_{11}$ is the (1, 1)th element of $\hat{\Sigma}$, and $\hat{\Sigma}_{22}$ is the lower right-hand $p \times p$ block submatrix of $\hat{\Sigma}$ as defined above. Therefore the likelihood ratio is

$$\boldsymbol{l} = \frac{|N\hat{\boldsymbol{\Sigma}}|^{N/2}}{(N\hat{\boldsymbol{\sigma}}_{11})^{N/2}|N\hat{\boldsymbol{\Sigma}}_{22}|^{N/2}} = (1 - \hat{\boldsymbol{\rho}}^2)^{N/2},$$

where $\hat{\boldsymbol{\rho}}$ is the maximum likelihood estimate of the multiple correlation coefficient under Ω. The likelihood ratio test is thus equivalent to a test based directly on $\hat{\boldsymbol{\rho}}^2$.

It will be more convenient for us to find the sampling distribution of

$$\boldsymbol{w} = \frac{\hat{\boldsymbol{\rho}}^2}{1-\hat{\boldsymbol{\rho}}^2} = \frac{\hat{\boldsymbol{\Sigma}}_{12}\hat{\boldsymbol{\Sigma}}_{22}^{-1}\hat{\boldsymbol{\Sigma}}_{21}}{\hat{\boldsymbol{\sigma}}_{11}-\hat{\boldsymbol{\Sigma}}_{12}\hat{\boldsymbol{\Sigma}}_{22}^{-1}\hat{\boldsymbol{\Sigma}}_{21}}$$

and this will suffice, as $\boldsymbol{l}$ is a monotonic function of $\boldsymbol{w}$ and so a test based on $\boldsymbol{w}$ will be equivalent to one based on $\boldsymbol{l}$.

One first notes that $\hat{\boldsymbol{\sigma}}_{11.2} = \hat{\boldsymbol{\sigma}}_{11} - \hat{\boldsymbol{\Sigma}}_{12}\hat{\boldsymbol{\Sigma}}_{22}^{-1}\hat{\boldsymbol{\Sigma}}_{21}$ is the maximum likelihood estimate of $\mathscr{V}\boldsymbol{y}$ given $\boldsymbol{X} = X$. It can be shown that the distribution of $N\hat{\boldsymbol{\sigma}}_{11.2}$ is that of the sum of $N-p$ independent variables of the form z^2 where z is distributed as $N(0, \sigma_{11.2})$. Thus in this case N times the denominator of $\boldsymbol{w}$ is distributed as $\sigma_{11.2}$ times a $\chi^2(N-p)$ random variable.

To obtain the distribution of N times the numerator of $\boldsymbol{w}$, we record that $N\hat{\boldsymbol{\Sigma}}$ is distributed as $\sum_{i=1}^{N-1} \boldsymbol{Z}_i'\boldsymbol{Z}_i$, where $\boldsymbol{Z}_i$ is distributed as $N(0, \Sigma)$ and the $\boldsymbol{Z}_i$ are independent. Then z_{1i}, the first element of $\boldsymbol{Z}_i$, is distributed conditionally on $\ddot{\boldsymbol{Z}}_i = (z_{2i}, \ldots, z_{pi}) = (z_{2i}, \ldots, z_{pi}) = \ddot{Z}_i$ as $N(\ddot{Z}_i\Sigma_{22}^{-1}\Sigma_{21}, \sigma_{11.2})$. Now let $H = \sum_{i=1}^{N-1} \ddot{Z}_i'\ddot{Z}_i = N\hat{\Sigma}_{22}$ and $G = \sum_{i=1}^{N-1} z_{1i}\ddot{Z}_iH^{-1} = \hat{\Sigma}_{12}\hat{\Sigma}_{22}^{-1}$. What we shall show is that $\boldsymbol{GHG}'$ (i.e. N times the numerator of $\boldsymbol{w}$) is distributed as $\sigma_{11.2}$ times a $\chi^2(p-1)$ random variable under the null hypothesis.

First, let $H = TT'$, $\ddot{Z} = (\ddot{Z}_1', \ldots, \ddot{Z}_{N-1}')$, and $\ddot{D} = T^{-1}\ddot{Z}$. Then $\ddot{D}\ddot{D}' = T^{-1}\ddot{Z}\ddot{Z}'T^{-1\prime} = T^{-1}HT^{-1\prime} = I$. Augment the $p \times (N-1)$ matrix D with $N-p-1$ rows $\dot{D}$ such that the augmented $(N-1)\times(N-1)$ matrix

$$D = \begin{bmatrix} \dot{D} \\ \ddot{D} \end{bmatrix}$$

is orthogonal. Now let $\dot{\boldsymbol{Z}}_1 = (z_{11}, \ldots, z_{N-1,1})$, and define $\boldsymbol{U} = \dot{\boldsymbol{Z}}_1 D'$. Then

$$\begin{aligned} \mathscr{E}\boldsymbol{U} &= \mathscr{E}\dot{\boldsymbol{Z}}_1 D' \\ &= \Sigma_{12}\Sigma_{22}^{-1}\ddot{Z}D' \\ &= \Sigma_{12}\Sigma_{22}^{-1}T\ddot{D}D' \\ &= \Sigma_{12}\Sigma_{22}^{-1}T[0 \quad I] \\ &= [0 \quad \Sigma_{12}\Sigma_{22}^{-1}T], \end{aligned}$$

and

$$\mathscr{V}\boldsymbol{U} = D\mathscr{V}\dot{\boldsymbol{Z}}'D' = D(\sigma_{11.2}I)D' = \sigma_{11.2}DD' = \sigma_{11.2}I.$$

Now

$$\begin{aligned} GHG' &= (\dot{Z}_1\ddot{Z}'H^{-1})H(H^{-1}\ddot{Z}\dot{Z}_1') \\ &= UD\ddot{D}'(T'H^{-1}T)\ddot{D}D'U' \\ &= U\begin{bmatrix}0\\ I\end{bmatrix}[0 \quad I]U' \\ &= \sum_{i=N-p+1}^{N-1} u_i^2. \end{aligned}$$

Therefore $\boldsymbol{GHG}'$ is distributed as the sum of squares of $p-1$ independent normally distributed random variables $\boldsymbol{u}_i$ with variance $\sigma_{11.2}$. Under the null hypothesis, $\Sigma_{12} = 0$, and so $\mathscr{E}\boldsymbol{U} = 0$. Thus, when H_0 is true, $\boldsymbol{GHG}'$ is distributed as $\sigma_{11.2}$ times a $\chi^2(p-1)$ random variable.

Moreover,

$$\dot{\boldsymbol{Z}}_1'\dot{\boldsymbol{Z}}_1' = \boldsymbol{UU}' = \sum_{i=1}^{N-p} \boldsymbol{u}_i^2 + \boldsymbol{GHG}',$$

where $\boldsymbol{GHG}'$ is independent of $\sum_{i=1}^{N-p-1} u_i^2$. But $\dot{\boldsymbol{Z}}_1\dot{\boldsymbol{Z}}_1' = \hat{\sigma}_{11}$, so that $\sum_{i=1}^{N-p} \boldsymbol{u}_i^2 = \hat{\boldsymbol{\sigma}}_{11} - \boldsymbol{GHG}' = \hat{\boldsymbol{\Sigma}}_{12}\hat{\boldsymbol{\Sigma}}_{11}^{-1}\hat{\boldsymbol{\Sigma}}_{21}$. Thus the numerator and denominator of $\boldsymbol{w}$ are independent.

We conclude that under the null hypothesis the distribution of $[(N-p)/(p-1)]\boldsymbol{w}$ is $F(p-1, N-p)$.

Exercise: (1) Derive the result of this section from that of section 2 where the null hypothesis is $B = 0$.

(2) Specialize this result to one which tests that the ordinary correlation coefficient between two normally distributed random variables is zero.

5. Testing for independence

As can be seen from the structure of chapter III, quite a difference in the properties of the estimator, if not in the estimator itself, can result from altering the assumption about the nature of the $\boldsymbol{Y}_i$'s from being independent samples to being correlated samples. In this section we will study procedures for testing whether we have independent samples.

There are many alternatives to independence. The one we have studied most closely is that of autocorrelated errors (see section 2.3 of chapter III). We shall focus on that model as our alternative hypothesis in this section.

However, the problem of testing for independence in a linear expected value model is a composite of two separable issues, namely "How does one test for independence in a nonstructured model?" and "What further features are added to the testing problem when a structured model such as the linear expected value model obtains?"

We restrict ourselves to the case $n = 1$, so that $\mathscr{E}\mathbf{y} = XB'$, and have N observations on $\mathbf{y}$ and X. Let us first look at the case where $\mathscr{E}\mathbf{y}_i = 0$ for $i = 1, \ldots, N$, and see what form the test for independence of the $\mathbf{y}_i$ takes. Our null hypothesis is that $\mathbf{Y} = (\mathbf{y}_i, \ldots, \mathbf{y}_N)$ is distributed as $N(0, \Delta)$, where Δ is a known diagonal matrix. We take as the first alternative hypothesis for consideration that $\mathbf{Y}$ is distributed as $N(0, \Sigma)$, where Σ is a known matrix. Since in this case our hypotheses are simple, we can determine from the Neyman–Pearson Lemma that the best test rejects the null hypothesis when

$$\frac{(2\pi)^{-N/2}|\Delta|^{-\frac{1}{2}}\exp\{-Y\Delta^{-1}Y'/2\}}{(2\pi)^{-N/2}|\Sigma|^{-\frac{1}{2}}\exp\{-Y\Sigma^{-1}Y'/2\}} \leqslant k.$$

This is equivalent to rejecting H_0, when

$$\mathbf{Y}\Sigma^{-1}\mathbf{Y}'/\mathbf{Y}\Delta^{-1}\mathbf{Y}' \leqslant k'.$$

Since Δ is known, we might as well take $\Delta = I$. (Otherwise, just redefine our random vector as $\mathbf{Y} = (\mathbf{y}_1/\sqrt{\delta_{11}}, \ldots, \mathbf{y}_N/\sqrt{\delta_{NN}})$ and proceed.) Also, taking $\Sigma^{-1} = \Gamma\Theta\Gamma'$, where Γ is orthogonal and Θ is diagonal, we can redefine our test statistic as

$$\mathbf{r} = \mathbf{Z}\Theta\mathbf{Z}'/\mathbf{Z}\mathbf{Z}' = \sum_{i=1}^{N}\theta_i\mathbf{z}_i^2\Big/\sum_{i=1}^{N}\mathbf{z}_i^2,$$

where $\mathbf{Z} = \mathbf{Y}\Gamma$.

Exercise: Suppose Δ and Σ are known up to a common but unknown multiplicative constant θ. Show that the above test is uniformly most powerful for testing these hypotheses as well. (Because of this we will always take $\Delta = I$ as our standard null hypothesis in what follows, despite the fact that we can be slightly more general and introduce an unknown multiplicative constant θ as a parameter.)

The exact distribution of $\mathbf{r}$ is unknown except for some special cases.

One can, however, approximate its distribution by obtaining its first four moments and using a Pearson family approximation. To do this, note first that $r = u/v$, where $u = \sum_{i=1}^{N} \theta_i z_i^2$, $v = \sum_{i=1}^{N} z_i^2$, and where, again by appropriate scaling of variables, we can take the z_i to be independent $N(0, 1)$ random variables. Then v is distributed as $\chi^2(N)$.

To see that r and v are independent, consider the transformation

$$
\begin{aligned}
z_1 &= w \sin a_1 &&= wg_1(A),\\
z_2 &= w \cos a_1 \sin a_2 &&= wg_2(A),\\
&\;\;\vdots\\
z_{N-2} &= w \cos a_1 \cos a_2 \cdots \cos a_{N-3} \sin a_{N-2} &&= wg_{N-2}(A),\\
z_{N-1} &= w \cos a_1 \cos a_2 \cdots \cos a_{N-1} \sin a_{N-1} &&= wg_{N-1}(A),\\
z_N &= w \cos a_1 \cos a_2 \cdots \cos a_{N-2} \cos a_{N-1} &&= wg_N(A),
\end{aligned}
$$

Then $v = \sum_{i=1}^{N} z_i^2 = w^2$, and

$$u = \sum_{i=1}^{N} \theta_i z_i^2 = w^2 \sum_{i=1}^{N} \theta_i g_i^2(A),$$

so that

$$r = u/v = \sum_{i=1}^{N} \theta_i g_i^2(A)$$

is only a function of $A = (a_1, \ldots, a_{N-1})$ and v is only a function of w.

The Jacobian of this transformation can be verified to be $w^{N-1} \prod_{i=1}^{N-2} \cos^{N-1-i} a_i$. Since the density function of $Z = (z_1, \ldots, z_N)$ is

$$f_Z(Z) = (2\pi)^{-N/2} \exp\left\{-\sum_{i=1}^{N} z_i^2/2\right\},$$

we see that the density function of w and A is

$$f_{w,A}(w, A) = (2\pi)^{-N/2} w^{N-1} \exp\{-w^2/2\} \prod_{i=1}^{N-2} \cos^{N-1-i} a_i,$$

i.e., w and A are independent. From this we conclude that r and v are independent. As a consequence of this, we can calculate all the moments of r from the relation

$$\mathscr{E} r^s = \mathscr{E} u^s / \mathscr{E} v^s.$$

Let $\bar{\theta} = \sum_{i=1}^{N} \theta_i/N$. Then it is an easy exercise to determine that

$$\mathscr{E}\boldsymbol{r} = \bar{\theta},$$

$$\mathscr{V}\boldsymbol{r} = \frac{2\sum_{i=1}^{N}(\theta_i - \bar{\theta})^2}{N(N+2)},$$

$$\mu_3 = \frac{8\sum_{i=1}^{N}(\theta_i - \bar{\theta})^3}{N(N+2)(N+4)},$$

$$\mu_4 = \frac{48\sum_{i=1}^{N}(\theta_i - \bar{\theta})^4 + 12\left[\sum_{i=1}^{N}(\theta_i - \bar{\theta})^2\right]^2}{N(N+2)(N+4)(N+6)}.$$

The reason we considered the case where $\mathscr{E}\boldsymbol{Y} = 0$ is that, if B were known, we could use the above result to test for independence by replacing each y_i by $y_i - X_iB'$. One approach when B is unknown is to use the above result as a test statistic, replacing $y_i - X_iB'$ by $y_i - X_i\hat{\boldsymbol{B}}'$, where $\hat{\boldsymbol{B}}$ is the least squares estimator of B.

We note that if X is the $p \times N$ matrix with ith column X_i', then $\hat{\boldsymbol{B}} = \boldsymbol{Y}X'(XX)^{-1}$, so that

$$\boldsymbol{Y} - \hat{\boldsymbol{B}}X = \boldsymbol{Y}(I - X'(XX')^{-1}X),$$

where the matrix $P = I - X'(XX')^{-1}X$ is a projection matrix. If $\boldsymbol{Y}$ is distributed as $N(BX, \Sigma)$, then $\boldsymbol{Y} - \hat{\boldsymbol{B}}X$ is distributed as $N(0, P\Sigma P)$.

We now wish to identify this problem with the previous one. Since P is an $N \times N$ projection matrix of rank $N - p$, there is an orthogonal matrix Ξ such that

$$\Xi P \Xi' = \begin{pmatrix} I & 0 \\ 0 & 0 \end{pmatrix} = I_*,$$

where I is an $(N-p)\times(N-p)$ identity matrix. Then

$$\begin{aligned} \Xi P \Sigma^{-1} P \Xi' &= \Xi P \Xi' \Xi \Sigma^{-1} \Xi' \Xi P \Xi' \\ &= \begin{pmatrix} I & 0 \\ 0 & 0 \end{pmatrix} \Xi \Sigma^{-1} \Xi' \begin{pmatrix} I & 0 \\ 0 & 0 \end{pmatrix} \\ &= \begin{pmatrix} \Sigma_* & 0 \\ 0 & 0 \end{pmatrix}, \end{aligned}$$

where Σ_* is the upper left $(N-p)\times(N-p)$ submatrix of $\Xi\Sigma^{-1}\Xi'$.

We can simplify the test statistic somewhat by taking $\Sigma_* = \Gamma_* \Theta_* \Gamma_*'$, where Γ_* is orthogonal and Θ_* is diagonal, and letting

$$\Gamma = \begin{pmatrix} \Gamma_* & 0 \\ 0 & I \end{pmatrix}.$$

Then,

$$\begin{aligned} \Gamma' \Xi P \Sigma^{-1} P \Xi' \Gamma &= \Gamma \begin{pmatrix} \Sigma_* & 0 \\ 0 & 0 \end{pmatrix} \Gamma' \\ &= \begin{pmatrix} \Gamma_*' \Sigma_* \Gamma_* & 0 \\ 0 & 0 \end{pmatrix} \\ &= \begin{pmatrix} \Theta_* & 0 \\ 0 & 0 \end{pmatrix} \\ &= \Theta. \end{aligned}$$

Also,

$$\begin{aligned} \Gamma' \Xi P \Xi' \Gamma &= \Gamma' I_* \Gamma \\ &= \begin{pmatrix} \Gamma_*' & 0 \\ 0 & I \end{pmatrix} \begin{pmatrix} I & 0 \\ 0 & 0 \end{pmatrix} \begin{pmatrix} \Gamma_* & 0 \\ 0 & I \end{pmatrix} \\ &= \begin{pmatrix} \Gamma_*' \Gamma_* & 0 \\ 0 & 0 \end{pmatrix} \\ &= I_*. \end{aligned}$$

The test statistic under consideration is

$$\hat{\boldsymbol{r}} = \frac{(\boldsymbol{Y} - \hat{\boldsymbol{B}}' X) \Sigma^{-1} (\boldsymbol{Y} - \hat{\boldsymbol{B}}' X)'}{(\boldsymbol{Y} - \hat{\boldsymbol{B}}' X)(\boldsymbol{Y} - \hat{\boldsymbol{B}}' X)'},$$

where $\hat{\boldsymbol{B}}$ replaces B in the test statistic which would ordinarily be used if B were known. This can be rewritten as

$$\begin{aligned} \hat{\boldsymbol{r}} = \frac{\boldsymbol{Y} P \Sigma^{-1} P \boldsymbol{Y}'}{\boldsymbol{Y} P \boldsymbol{Y}'} &= \frac{\boldsymbol{Y} P^2 \Sigma^{-1} P^2 \boldsymbol{Y}'}{\boldsymbol{Y} P^3 \boldsymbol{Y}'} \\ &= \frac{\boldsymbol{Z} \Gamma' \Xi P \Sigma^{-1} P \Xi' \Gamma \boldsymbol{Z}'}{\boldsymbol{Z} \Gamma' \Xi P \Xi' \Gamma \boldsymbol{Z}'} \\ &= \frac{\boldsymbol{Z} \Theta \boldsymbol{Z}'}{\boldsymbol{Z} I_* \boldsymbol{Z}'}, \end{aligned}$$

where $\boldsymbol{Z} = \boldsymbol{Y} P \Xi' \Gamma$.

Since we are only considering the first $N - p$ elements of $\boldsymbol{Z}$, let us define $\boldsymbol{Z}_*$ to be the first $N-p$ element of $\boldsymbol{Z}$. Then

$$\hat{r} = \frac{\boldsymbol{Z}_* \Theta_* \boldsymbol{Z}_*'}{\boldsymbol{Z}_* \boldsymbol{Z}_*'} = \sum_{i=1}^{N-p} \theta_i z_i^2 \Big/ \sum_{i=1}^{N-p} z_i^2.$$

If we let Σ_{**} be the upper left $p \times p$ submatrix of $\Xi\Sigma\Xi'$, we can write the covariance matrix of $\boldsymbol{Z}$ as

$$\begin{aligned} \Gamma'\Xi P\Sigma P\Xi'\Gamma &= \Gamma'\Xi P\Xi'\Xi\Sigma\Xi'\Xi P\Xi'\Gamma \\ &= \Gamma'\begin{pmatrix} I & 0 \\ 0 & 0 \end{pmatrix}\Xi\Sigma\Xi'\begin{pmatrix} I & 0 \\ 0 & 0 \end{pmatrix}\Gamma \\ &= \Gamma'\begin{pmatrix} \Sigma_{**} & 0 \\ 0 & 0 \end{pmatrix}\Gamma \\ &= \begin{pmatrix} \Gamma_*'\Sigma_{**}\Gamma_* & 0 \\ 0 & 0 \end{pmatrix}. \end{aligned}$$

Under the "null hypothesis" that $\boldsymbol{Y} - \hat{\boldsymbol{B}}'X = \boldsymbol{Y}P$ has the identity matrix as its covariance matrix (this being analogous to the true null hypothesis that $\boldsymbol{Y} - B'X$ has the identity matrix as its covariance matrix), we note that $\boldsymbol{Z} = \boldsymbol{Y}P\Xi'\Gamma$ has covariance matrix $\Gamma'\Xi I\Xi'\Gamma = I$ as well. Thus under the "null hypothesis" the z_i are $N(0, 1)$ random variables as in the case of $\boldsymbol{r}$ above.

In the case of $\boldsymbol{r}$ we had defined $\Theta = \Gamma'\Sigma^{-1}\Gamma$, i.e., the diagonal matrix of characteristic roots of Σ^{-1}. In this case, $\hat{\boldsymbol{r}}$ is defined in terms of the characteristic roots of the upper left $p \times p$ submatrix Σ_* of $\Xi\Sigma^{-1}\Xi'$, where Ξ is the orthogonal matrix of characteristic vectors of P.

Making the correspondences

$$\begin{aligned} &\boldsymbol{r} \leftrightarrow \hat{\boldsymbol{r}}, \\ &N \leftrightarrow N-p, \\ &\Sigma^{-1} \leftrightarrow \Sigma_*, \end{aligned}$$

the results for $\boldsymbol{r}$ carry over for $\hat{\boldsymbol{r}}$. (Of course, one should be reminded that this is all based on nonstochastic regressors, i.e., X being a matrix of fixed variables.)

The problems with the above approach are apparent. First of all, one does not in practice know Σ, the covariance matrix of the alternative hypothesis. (Indeed, one does not usually even know Δ, the null diagonal covariance matrix.) Secondly, even when Σ is known, it is not clear that working by analogy and using $\hat{\boldsymbol{r}}$ as test statistic is the best test procedure. It is true that if $\Sigma = I$ then the covariance matrix of $\boldsymbol{Z}_*$ is also I. Thus rejecting H_0 using $\hat{r}$ is a conservative test of H_0. However, it is not conversely true that if the covariance matrix of Z_* is I then $\Sigma = I$.

As an example of this let $\Sigma = I + [\rho/(1-\rho)]J$, where J is a matrix all of whose elements are 1, let $p = 2$, and let

$$X = \begin{bmatrix} 1 & \cdots & 1 \\ x_1 & \cdots & x_N \end{bmatrix}.$$

Then $P = I - X'(XX')^{-1}X$, and, since $XPX' = 0$, we can take the last two rows of Ξ to be

$$\begin{bmatrix} 1/\sqrt{N} & \cdots & 1/\sqrt{N} \\ (x_1 - \bar{x})\Big/\left(\sqrt{\sum_{i=1}^{N}(x_i - \bar{x})^2}\right) & \cdots & (x_N - \bar{x})\Big/\left(\sqrt{\sum_{i=1}^{N}(x_i - \bar{x})^2}\right) \end{bmatrix}.$$

Since Σ_{**} is the upper left $(N-2)\times(N-2)$ submatrix of $\Xi\Sigma\Xi'$, only the first $N-2$ rows of Ξ enter into the calculation of Σ_{**}. But these rows are all orthogonal to the rows of X.

Now let us study Σ in more detail. It has two characteristic roots, $1 + N\rho/(1-\rho)$, with associated characteristic vector $[1/\sqrt{N}, \ldots, 1/\sqrt{N}]$, and 1, with multiplicity $N-1$. Therefore the first $N-2$ rows of Ξ, being orthogonal to $(1/\sqrt{N}, \ldots, 1/\sqrt{N})$, are also characteristic vectors of Σ. And so the upper left $(N-2)\times(N-2)$ submatrix of $\Xi\Sigma\Xi'$ is the diagonal matrix of characteristic roots corresponding to these characteristic vectors, to wit, $\Sigma_{**} = I$.

One step away from complete knowledge of Σ (yet not taking the deep plunge toward complete ignorance of Σ) is to assume that Σ is of a special known structure but with unknown parameters. The particular structure to be studied herein is one where Σ is of the form

$$\Sigma^{-1} = I + \xi Y,$$

where Y is a known symmetric matrix, and ξ is an unknown parameter constrained only by the requirement that Σ is positive definite. Our null hypothesis is that $\xi = 0$ and our alternative is $\xi \neq 0$.

This structure has as important special cases, to which we will return later, the cases studied in section 2.1 of chapter III. In one of these cases, $\mathscr{C}(y_i, y_j) = \rho/(1-\rho)$ for all i, j, so that

$$\Sigma = I + [\rho/(1-\rho)]J,$$

and

$$\Sigma^{-1} = I - [\rho/(1+(N-1)\rho)]J.$$

In the other, $\mathscr{C}(y_i, y_j) = \rho^{|i-j|}(1-\rho)^2/(1-\rho^2)$, so that

$$\Sigma = \frac{(1-\rho)^2}{1-\rho^2}\begin{bmatrix} 1 & \rho & \rho^2 & \cdots \rho^{N-1} \\ \rho & 1 & \rho & \cdots \rho^{N-2} \\ \cdot & \cdot & \cdot & \cdot \\ \cdot & \cdot & \cdot & \cdot \\ \cdot & \cdot & \cdot & \cdot \\ \rho^{N-1} & \rho^{N-2} & \rho^{N-3} & \cdots 1 \end{bmatrix}$$

and

$$\Sigma^{-1} = \frac{1}{(1-\rho)^2}\begin{bmatrix} 1 & -\rho & 0 & 0 \cdots 0 & 0 & 0 \\ -\rho & 1+\rho^2 & -\rho & 0 \cdots 0 & 0 & 0 \\ 0 & -\rho & 1+\rho^2 & -\rho \cdots 0 & 0 & 0 \\ \cdot & \cdot & \cdot & \cdot & \cdot & \cdot & \cdot \\ \cdot & \cdot & \cdot & \cdot & \cdot & \cdot & \cdot \\ \cdot & \cdot & \cdot & \cdot & \cdot & \cdot & \cdot \\ 0 & 0 & 0 & 0 \cdots -\rho & 1+\rho^2 & -\rho \\ 0 & 0 & 0 & 0 \cdots 0 & -\rho & 1 \end{bmatrix}.$$

If Σ^{-1} has $1+\rho^2-\rho$ instead of 1 in its upper left and lower right corners, then it would be of the form

$$I + [\rho/(1-\rho)^2]A,$$

where

$$A = \begin{bmatrix} 1 & -1 & 0 & \cdots & 0 & 0 & 0 \\ -1 & 2 & -1 & \cdots & 0 & 0 & 0 \\ 0 & -1 & 2 & \cdots & 0 & 0 & 0 \\ \cdot & \cdot & \cdot & & \cdot & \cdot & \cdot \\ \cdot & \cdot & \cdot & & \cdot & \cdot & \cdot \\ \cdot & \cdot & \cdot & & \cdot & \cdot & \cdot \\ 0 & 0 & 0 & \cdots & -1 & 2 & 1 \\ 0 & 0 & 0 & \cdots & 0 & 0 & 1 \end{bmatrix}.$$

Thus in the second case we can say that Σ^{-1} is approximately of the form $I + \lambda Y$.

Returning to the general case, let Π be an orthogonal matrix and Λ a diagonal matrix such that

$$\Pi Y \Pi' = \Lambda.$$

Then the density function of $\boldsymbol{Y}$ is

$$f_Y(Y;\xi,B)=(2\pi)^{-N/2}|I+\zeta Y|^{\frac{1}{2}}\exp\{-(Y-BX')(I+\zeta Y)(Y-BX')'/2\}$$
$$=(2\pi)^{-N/2}\prod_{i=1}^{N}(1+\xi\lambda_i)^{\frac{1}{2}}\exp\{-[(Y-BX')(I+\xi\Pi'\Lambda\Pi)(Y-BX')']/2\}.$$

We assume in what follows that the $N\times p$ matrix X' is expressible as a linear transformation of some p columns of Π', which for convenience we take to be the first p columns. (We will review the implications of this assumption later. At this juncture, we take the assumption as a mathematical convenience to enable us to make the testing problem tractable.) Then there is some non-singular $p\times p$ matrix C such that $X'=\Pi_1'C$, where Π_1' is the $N\times p$ matrix consisting of the first p columns of Π'. Defining

$$I_*=\begin{bmatrix}I\\0\end{bmatrix},$$

where I is $p\times p$ and I_* is $N\times p$, we see that we can express X' as $X'=\Pi'I_*C$.

Now making the transformation $\mathbf{Z}=\mathbf{Y}\Pi'$, we see that

$$f_Z(Z;\xi,B)=(2\pi)^{-N/2}\prod_{i=1}^{N}(1+\xi\lambda_i)^{\frac{1}{2}}$$
$$\times\exp\{-[(Z-BCI_*)\Pi(I+\xi\Pi'\Lambda\Pi)\Pi'(Z-BCI_*)']/2\}.$$

We can reparameterize the problem so that our regression parameters are $B^*=BC$ or, more conveniently, take $C=I$, so that we continue to use B as our vector of regression parameters. Then,

$$f_Z(Z;\xi,B)=(2\pi)^{-N/2}\prod_{i=1}^{N}(1+\xi\lambda_i)^{\frac{1}{2}}$$
$$\times\exp\left\{-\left[\sum_{i=1}^{p}(1+\xi\lambda_i)(z_i-\beta_i)^2+\sum_{i=p+1}^{N}(1+\xi\lambda_i)z_i^2\right]\Big/2\right\}.$$

Now suppose we are interested in testing the null hypothesis $\xi=0$ against the alternative $\xi\neq 0$. Since under either hypothesis the maximum likelihood estimate of β_i is z_i, the likelihood ratio is

$$l=\max_B f_Z(Z;0,B)\Big/\max_{\xi,B}f_Z(Z;\xi,B)$$
$$=\frac{\exp\left\{-\sum_{i=p+1}^{N}z_i^2/2\right\}}{\max_\xi\prod_{i=1}^{N}(1+\xi\lambda_i)^{\frac{1}{2}}\exp\left\{-\sum_{i=p+1}^{N}(1+\xi\lambda_i)z_i^2/2\right\}}$$
$$=\min_\xi\prod_{i=1}^{N}(1+\xi\lambda_i)^{-\frac{1}{2}}\exp\left\{\xi\sum_{i=p+1}^{N}\lambda_i z_i^2/2\right\}.$$

If $\hat{\xi}$ minimizes l, then $\hat{\xi}$ satisfies the equation

$$\sum_{i=1}^{N} \lambda_i (1+\hat{\xi}\lambda_i)^{-1} = \sum_{i=p+1}^{N} \lambda_i z_i^2.$$

Let $u = \sum_{i=p+1}^{N} \lambda_i z_i^2$. Then taking the derivative with respect to u of the equation defining $\hat{\xi}$ we find that

$$-\sum_{i=1}^{N} \lambda_i^2 (1+\hat{\xi}\lambda_i)^{-2} \frac{d\hat{\xi}}{du} = 1,$$

so that $\hat{\xi}$ is a monotonically decreasing function of u.

Let us now study the derivative of $-2 \log l$ with respect to u. We see that

$$-2 \log l = \sum_{i=1}^{N} \log (1+\hat{\xi}(u)\lambda_i) - u\hat{\xi}(u),$$

and

$$\frac{\partial(-2 \log l)}{\partial u} = \sum_{i=1}^{N} \lambda_i (1+\hat{\xi}(u)\lambda_i)^{-1} \frac{\partial \hat{\xi}(u)}{\partial u} - \hat{\xi}(u) - u \frac{\partial \hat{\xi}(u)}{\partial u}$$
$$= u \frac{\partial \hat{\xi}(u)}{\partial u} - \hat{\xi}(u) - u \frac{\partial \hat{\xi}(u)}{\partial u}.$$

Thus $-2 \log l$ is monotonically increasing in u if $\hat{\xi}$ is negative and decreasing in u if $\hat{\xi}$ is positive. Since $\hat{\xi}$ is monotonically decreasing in u, we see that rejecting H_0 if $l \leq k$ is equivalent to rejecting H_0 if $u_1 < \boldsymbol{u} < u_2$, where $\hat{\xi}(u_1) < 0 < \hat{\xi}(u_2)$.

In order to determine the critical values u_1 and u_2, we must study the distribution of $\boldsymbol{u}$. But $\boldsymbol{u} = \sum_{i=p+1}^{N} \lambda_i \boldsymbol{z}_i^2$, where the z_i are independent $N(0, (1+\xi\lambda_i)^{-1})$ distributed variables. Then $(1+\xi\lambda_i)\boldsymbol{z}_i^2$ is distributed as $\chi^2(1)$, and so when H_0 is true $\boldsymbol{z}_i^2$ is distributed as $\chi^2(1)$. The distribution of $\boldsymbol{u}$ is then under H_0 that of a linear combination of $\chi^2(1)$ variables.

Exercise: Suppose Σ were of the form $\Sigma^{-1} = \theta(I+\xi Y)$, where θ is an unknown parameter, Y is a known matrix, and that we are interested in testing the null hypothesis $\xi = 0$. Show that

$$-2 \log l = \sum_{i=1}^{N} \log (1+\hat{\xi}\lambda_i) - N \log (1+\hat{\xi}r)$$

where

$$r = u/v, \qquad u = \sum_{i=p+1}^{N} \lambda_i z_i^2, \qquad v = \sum_{i=p+1}^{N} z_i^2.$$

Show that $\hat{\xi}$ is a monotonically increasing function of r. Show also that the sign of the derivative of $\log l$ with respect to r is the sign of $\hat{\xi}$, so that l is monotonically decreasing in r for $\hat{\xi} < 0$ and increasing in r for $\hat{\xi} > 0$.

The result of this exercise is that for this model the appropriate test of H_0 is to reject H_0 if $r_1 < \boldsymbol{r} < r_2$. The reader should contrast the cases considered by the two exercises in this section. The first assumed a known covariance matrix, and there we saw that introduction of an unknown scalar multiple as a parameter did not change the test. The second assumed a covariance matrix of known structure but with an unknown parameter, and there we saw that introduction of an unknown scalar multiple as a parameter did change the test.

One should note about these tests that if our alternative hypothesis was not $\xi \neq 0$, but instead $\xi > 0$, then our critical region would only consist of $\boldsymbol{u} < u_2$ or $\boldsymbol{r} < r_2$. Similarly, if our alternative were $\xi < 0$, then the critical region would be $\boldsymbol{u} > u_1$ or $\boldsymbol{r} > r_1$.

A more satisfactory formulation of $\boldsymbol{u}$ and $\boldsymbol{r}$, involving only parameters of the original problem, can be obtained as follows. Let $\tilde{\boldsymbol{Z}} = (\boldsymbol{Y} - \hat{\boldsymbol{B}}X)\Pi'$, where $\hat{\boldsymbol{B}}$ is the maximum likelihood estimator of B. Since $BX\Pi' = BC'I_*\Pi\Pi' = B^*$, $\hat{\boldsymbol{B}}X\Pi' = \hat{\boldsymbol{B}}^*$. Then $\tilde{\boldsymbol{Z}} = \boldsymbol{Y}\Pi' - \hat{\boldsymbol{B}}^* = \boldsymbol{Z} - \hat{\boldsymbol{B}}^*$, i.e.,

$$\tilde{z}_i = \begin{cases} 0, & \text{if} \quad i = 1, \ldots, p, \\ z_i, & \text{if} \quad i = p+1, \ldots, N. \end{cases}$$

Then $\sum_{i=p+1}^{N} \lambda_i z_i^2 = \sum_{i=1}^{N} \lambda_i \tilde{z}_i^2 = (\boldsymbol{Y} - \hat{\boldsymbol{B}}X)\Pi'\Lambda\Pi(\boldsymbol{Y} - \hat{\boldsymbol{B}}X)' = (\boldsymbol{Y} - \hat{\boldsymbol{B}}X) \times Y(\boldsymbol{Y} - \hat{\boldsymbol{B}}X)'$ and $\sum_{i=p+1}^{N} z_i^2 = (\boldsymbol{Y} - \hat{\boldsymbol{B}}X)(\boldsymbol{Y} - \hat{\boldsymbol{B}}X)'$.

Let us recapitulate. *Case I*: If B is known and we have both known (or known up to a scalar multiplicative parameter) null diagonal covariance matrix Δ and known alternative covariance matrix Σ, then the best test statistic for independence is

$$\boldsymbol{r} = \frac{(\boldsymbol{Y} - BX)\Sigma^{-1}(\boldsymbol{Y} - BX)'}{(\boldsymbol{Y} - BX)\Delta^{-1}(\boldsymbol{Y} - BX)'} = \sum_{i=1}^{N} \theta_i z_i^2 \Big/ \sum_{i=1}^{N} z_i^2,$$

where the θ_i are characteristic roots of Σ^{-1}, Γ is the matrix of characteristic vectors of Σ^{-1}, and $\boldsymbol{Z} = (\boldsymbol{Y} - BX)\Gamma$.

Case II: If B is unknown and we wish to use the above statistic with $\hat{\boldsymbol{B}}$ replacing B, then this is equivalent to using

$$\boldsymbol{r} = \sum_{i=1}^{N-p} \theta_i z_i^2 \Big/ \sum_{i=1}^{N-p} z_i^2,$$

where, letting $P = I - X'(XX')^{-1}X$ and Ξ be the matrix of characteristic vectors of P, the θ_i are the characteristic roots of $\Xi P\Sigma^{-1}P\Xi'$, Γ is the matrix of characteristic vectors of $\Xi P\Sigma^{-1}P\Xi'$, and $\mathbf{Z} = (\mathbf{Y} - \hat{\mathbf{B}}X)\Xi'\Gamma$.

Case III: If, further, B is unknown and Σ^{-1} is of the form

$$\Sigma^{-1} = \theta(I + \xi \Upsilon),$$

where Υ is known and θ and ξ are unknown parameters, and if $X' = \Pi_1' C$, where Π_1' is an $N \times p$ matrix consisting of the p characteristic vectors of Υ and C is a nonsingular $p \times p$ matrix, then the best test statistic for independence is

$$\boldsymbol{r} = \frac{(\mathbf{Y} - \hat{\mathbf{B}}X)\Upsilon(\mathbf{Y} - \hat{\mathbf{B}}X)'}{(\mathbf{Y} - \hat{\mathbf{B}}X)(\mathbf{Y} - \hat{\mathbf{B}}X)'} = \sum_{i=p+1}^{N} \lambda_i \boldsymbol{z}_i^2 \Big/ \sum_{i=p+1}^{N} \boldsymbol{z}_i^2,$$

where the λ_i are the characteristic roots of Υ, Π is the matrix of characteristic vectors of Υ, and $\mathbf{Z} = \mathbf{Y}\Pi'$. (If θ is known, then the test statistic is $\boldsymbol{u} = \sum_{i=p+1}^{N} \lambda_i \boldsymbol{z}_i^2$.)

In all three cases we are interested in the distribution of a statistic of the same form, namely the ratio of a weighted sum of independent $\chi^2(1)$ variables to the sum of those $\chi^2(1)$ variables. The usual situation is to use a Pearson family member to approximate the distribution of r.

Returning to the simplifying mathematical assumption in Case III that X' is a linear transformation of p columns of Π, following is an example wherein it does not hold. Let $p = 1$, $N = 3$, $X = (1, 0, 0)$, and

$$\Upsilon = \begin{bmatrix} 1 & 1 & 1 \\ 1 & 1 & 0 \\ 1 & 0 & 1 \end{bmatrix}.$$

Then,

$$\Upsilon = \frac{1}{16}\begin{bmatrix} 0 & 2\sqrt{2} & -2\sqrt{2} \\ 2\sqrt{2} & 2 & 2 \\ -2\sqrt{2} & 2 & 2 \end{bmatrix}\begin{bmatrix} 1 & 0 & 0 \\ 0 & 1+\sqrt{2} & 0 \\ 0 & 0 & 1-\sqrt{2} \end{bmatrix}\begin{bmatrix} 0 & 2\sqrt{2} & -2\sqrt{2} \\ 2\sqrt{2} & 2 & 2 \\ -2\sqrt{2} & 2 & 2 \end{bmatrix}.$$

Since in this case C must be a 1×1 matrix, we ask whether X' can be a scalar multiple of any of the columns of Π. Clearly none of the columns of Π are colinear with X'. We see from this that the simplifying mathematical assumption is quite constraining. Without it we do not obtain the likelihood ratio test procedure developed above.

Situations in which this assumption holds also have another associated bonus feature. If Σ^{-1} were known (or known up to a scalar multiple), then the best linear unbiased estimator of B would be

$$\begin{aligned}\hat{B} &= Y\Sigma^{-1}X'(X\Sigma^{-1}X')^{-1}\\ &= Y(I+\xi\Pi'\Lambda\Pi)\Pi_1'(\Pi_1(I+\xi\Pi'\Lambda\Pi)\Pi_1')^{-1}\\ &= Y(\Pi_1'+\xi\Pi'\Lambda I_*)(I+\xi I_*'\Lambda I_*)^{-1}\\ &= Y(\Pi_1'+\xi\Pi_1'\Lambda_1)(I+\xi\Lambda_1)^{-1}\\ &= Y\Pi_1'(I+\xi\Lambda_1)(I+\xi\Lambda_1)^{-1}\\ &= YX'(XX')^{-1},\end{aligned}$$

where Λ_1 is the upper $p\times p$ submatrix of Λ and where for convenience we take $X'=\Pi_1'$, i.e., $C=I$ in the linear relationship between X and the selected p columns of Π. In short, when this assumption holds, then, even though ξ is unknown and $\Sigma\neq I$, we see that the best linear unbiased estimator of B reduces to the ordinary least squares estimator.

Let us get back to our two examples of specially structured covariance matrices which occur in practice, namely those where $\Sigma = I+[\rho/(1-\rho)]J$ and where $\Sigma^{-1}=I+[\rho/(1-\rho)^2]A$, and A is of special tridiagonal form given above. These two cases are usually referred to not by the structure of the covariance matrix of $\boldsymbol{Y}$ but rather by a description of a model regarding the "errors", i.e., the deviations $\boldsymbol{Y}-BX$. Let $\boldsymbol{U}=\boldsymbol{Y}-BX$. The first case corresponds to the model $\boldsymbol{u}_i = \sqrt{(\rho/(1-\rho))}\boldsymbol{w}+\boldsymbol{v}_i$, where the $\boldsymbol{v}_i$ are independent with zero mean and unit variance, $\boldsymbol{w}$ has zero mean and unit variance, and $\boldsymbol{w}$ and the $\boldsymbol{v}_i$ are independent. For then

$$\mathscr{C}(\boldsymbol{u}_i,\boldsymbol{u}_j)=\begin{cases}\rho/(1-\rho), & \text{if } i\neq j,\\ \rho/(1-\rho)+1, & \text{if } i=j.\end{cases}$$

The second case corresponds to the model

$$\begin{aligned}&\boldsymbol{u}_1=\boldsymbol{v}_1,\\ &\boldsymbol{u}_i=\rho\boldsymbol{u}_{i-1}+\boldsymbol{v}_i, \qquad i=2,\ldots,N,\end{aligned}$$

where the $\boldsymbol{v}_i$ are independent with zero mean and variance $(1-\rho)^2/(1-\rho^2)$ and where $\mathscr{C}(\boldsymbol{v}_i,\boldsymbol{u}_j)=0$ for $j<i$. For then

$$\mathscr{C}(\boldsymbol{u}_i,\boldsymbol{u}_{i-1})=\rho\mathscr{V}(\boldsymbol{u}_{i-1}),$$

and, for $j<i$,

$$\mathscr{C}(\boldsymbol{u}_i,\boldsymbol{u}_j)=\rho^{i-j}\mathscr{V}(\boldsymbol{u}_j)$$

Assuming that $\mathcal{V}(\boldsymbol{u}_j)$ is independent of j, we see that $\mathcal{V}(\boldsymbol{u}_j)=\mathcal{V}(\boldsymbol{u}_1)=\mathcal{V}(\boldsymbol{v}_1)=(1-\rho)^2/(1-\rho^2)$.

In the case where $\Sigma = I+[\rho/(1-\rho)]J$, since the rank of J is 1, all but one of its characteristic roots are 0. The non-zero characteristic root is N, with associated characteristic vector the vector $E=(1/\sqrt{N})(1,\ldots,1)$. The remaining characteristic vectors are a set of $N-1$ vectors orthogonal to each other and to E. Nonetheless, even with this arbitrary choice of remaining characteristic vectors, it is not necessarily the case that a given matrix X' is expressible as $\Pi_1'C$, where Π_1' is an $N\times p$ submatrix of Π'.

In this case, though, if X' is expressible as $\Pi_1'C$, then the test statistic is either identically 0 (when the vector E' is not a column of Π_1'), identically 1 (when $p=N-1$), or

$$\boldsymbol{u} = Nz_j^2, \qquad \text{when } \theta \text{ is known,}$$

$$\boldsymbol{r} = Nz_j^2 \Big/ \sum_{i=p+1}^{N} z_i^2, \qquad \text{when } \theta \text{ is unknown,}$$

where j is the index of the coordinate of $\boldsymbol{Z}=\boldsymbol{Y}\Pi'$ associated with the characteristic vector E, i.e., $z_j=(1/\sqrt{N})\sum_{i=1}^{N} y_i$, and the $N-p$ z_i^2 are associated with the columns of Π' not included in Π_1'.

One should note that here the distribution of a monotonic function of $\boldsymbol{r}$ is easy to obtain. Let $s=(N/\boldsymbol{r}-1)/(N-p)$. Then s is distributed as $F(N-p,1)$.

As an example to clarify the construction of the test statistic in this case, let $p=2$, $N=4$,

$$X' = \begin{bmatrix} 1 & 2 \\ -1 & 3 \\ 1 & 2 \\ -1 & 3 \end{bmatrix},$$

$$\Pi' = \frac{1}{2}\begin{bmatrix} 1 & \sqrt{2} & 0 & 1 \\ 1 & 0 & \sqrt{2} & -1 \\ 1 & -\sqrt{2} & 0 & 1 \\ 1 & 0 & -\sqrt{2} & -1 \end{bmatrix},$$

so, taking

$$\Pi_1' = \frac{1}{2}\begin{bmatrix} 1 & 0 \\ -1 & \sqrt{2} \\ 1 & 0 \\ -1 & -\sqrt{2} \end{bmatrix},$$

and

$$C = \begin{bmatrix} 2 & 4 \\ 0 & 5\sqrt{2} \end{bmatrix},$$

we see that $X' = \Pi_1' C$.

Now let $\boldsymbol{Z} = \boldsymbol{Y}\Pi'$, and rearrange the coordinates of $\boldsymbol{Z}$ so that the first two correspond to the columns of Π' included in Π_1', i.e.,

$$2z_3 = y_1 + y_2 + y_3 + y_4,$$
$$2z_4 = \sqrt{2}(y_1 - y_3),$$
$$2z_1 = \sqrt{2}(y_2 - y_4),$$
$$2z_2 = y_1 - y_2 + y_3 - y_4,$$

and $B^* = BC$, so that

$$\beta_1^* = 2\beta_1,$$
$$\beta_2^* = 4\beta_1 + 5\sqrt{2}\,\beta_2.$$

(In this case, $\hat{\boldsymbol{\beta}}_1^* = z_1$, $\hat{\boldsymbol{\beta}}_2^* = z_2$, so that

$$\hat{\boldsymbol{\beta}}_1 = (1/2)z_1 = (1/2\sqrt{2})(y_2 - y_4),$$
$$\hat{\boldsymbol{\beta}}_2 = (1/5\sqrt{2})(\hat{\boldsymbol{\beta}}_2^* - 4\hat{\boldsymbol{\beta}}_1)$$
$$= (1/10\sqrt{2})(y_1 - (1 + 2\sqrt{2})y_2 + y_3 - (1 - 2\sqrt{2})y_4).$$

Then

$$\boldsymbol{u} = 4z_3^2 = (y_1 + y_2 + y_3 + y_4)^2,$$

and

$$\boldsymbol{r} = \frac{4z_3^2}{z_3^2 + z_4^2} = \frac{4(y_1 + y_2 + y_3 + y_4)^2}{(y_1 + y_2 + y_3 + y_4)^2 + 2(y_1 - y_3)^2}.$$

Our other example is one in which $\Sigma^{-1} = I + [\rho/(1-\rho)^2]A$, where

$$A = \begin{bmatrix} 1 & -1 & 0 \cdots & 0 & 0 & 0 \\ -1 & 2 & -1 \cdots & 0 & 0 & 0 \\ \cdot & \cdot & \cdot & \cdot & \cdot & \cdot \\ \cdot & \cdot & \cdot & \cdot & \cdot & \cdot \\ \cdot & \cdot & \cdot & \cdot & \cdot & \cdot \\ 0 & 0 & 0 \cdots & -1 & 2 & -1 \\ 0 & 0 & 0 \cdots & 0 & -1 & 1 \end{bmatrix}.$$

Here the characteristic roots of A are

$$\lambda_j = 2\left[1 - \cos\frac{\pi(j-1)}{N}\right], \qquad j = 1, \ldots, N,$$

and the associated characteristic vectors Π'_j have coordinates proportional to

$$\pi_{jk} = 2\cos\left[\frac{2k-1}{2}\cdot\frac{\pi(j-1)}{N}\right].$$

For $N = 3$, for example

$$\Pi = \frac{1}{\sqrt{6}}\begin{bmatrix} \sqrt{2} & \sqrt{2} & \sqrt{2} \\ \sqrt{3} & 0 & -\sqrt{3} \\ 1 & -2 & 1 \end{bmatrix},$$

and

$$\Lambda = \begin{bmatrix} 0 & 0 & 0 \\ 0 & 1 & 0 \\ 0 & 0 & 3 \end{bmatrix}.$$

Again the choice of $N - p\lambda_j$'s in the test statistic depend critically on which p rows of Π can be linearly transformed into the $p \times N$ matrix X. But here, writing the test statistic in terms of its original variables, we see that

$$\begin{aligned} \boldsymbol{r} &= \frac{(\boldsymbol{Y} - \hat{\boldsymbol{B}}X)A(\boldsymbol{Y} - \hat{\boldsymbol{B}}X)'}{(\boldsymbol{Y} - \hat{\boldsymbol{B}}X)(\boldsymbol{Y} - \hat{\boldsymbol{B}}X)'} = \frac{\boldsymbol{Y}PAP\boldsymbol{Y}'}{\boldsymbol{Y}P\boldsymbol{Y}'} \\ &= \frac{\boldsymbol{U}A\boldsymbol{U}}{\boldsymbol{U}\boldsymbol{U}'}, \end{aligned}$$

say. The numerator can be expressed as

$$\begin{aligned} \boldsymbol{U}A\boldsymbol{U}' &= \boldsymbol{u}_1^2 + \boldsymbol{u}_N^2 + 2\sum_{i=2}^{N-1} \boldsymbol{u}_i^2 - 2\sum_{i=2}^{N} \boldsymbol{u}_i\boldsymbol{u}_{i-1} \\ &= \sum_{i=2}^{N} (\boldsymbol{u}_i - \boldsymbol{u}_{i-1})^2. \end{aligned}$$

Thus the statistic is expressible without reference to specific rows of Π.

The ratio $\boldsymbol{r}$ in this case is called the *von. Neumann ratio*, and its distribution has been tabulated in the case where $\hat{\boldsymbol{B}}$ is replaced by B. When $\hat{\boldsymbol{B}}$ is explicitly used in determining $\boldsymbol{r}$, one would like to approximate its distribution via a Pearson family member. However, the moments, as given above, depend on the λ_j's. In particular,

$$\begin{aligned} (N-p)\mathscr{E}\boldsymbol{r} = \sum_{i=p+1}^{N} \lambda_i &= \operatorname{tr} PAP = \operatorname{tr} AP \\ &= \operatorname{tr} A(I - X(X'X)^{-1}X') \end{aligned}$$

$$= \operatorname{tr} A - \operatorname{tr}(X'X)^{-1}X'AX$$
$$= 2N - 2 - \operatorname{tr}(X'X)^{-1}X'AX.$$

Also

$$\sum_{i=p+1}^{N} (\lambda_i - \bar{\lambda})^2 = \sum_{i=p+1}^{N} \lambda_i^2 - (N-p)(\mathscr{E}r)^2$$

and

$$\sum_{i=p+1}^{N} \lambda_i^2 = \operatorname{tr}(PAP)^2 = \operatorname{tr} A^2P$$
$$= \operatorname{tr} A^2 - \operatorname{tr} A^2X(X'X)^{-1}X'$$
$$= 6N - 8 - \operatorname{tr} A^2X(X'X)^{-1}X'.$$

Neglecting the tr terms in the above expression, one obtains as approximations that

$$\mathscr{E}r \simeq \frac{2(N-1)}{N-p},$$

$$\mathscr{V}r \simeq \frac{2(6N-8)-(N-p)\mathscr{E}r)^2}{(N-p)(N-p+2)}$$

$$= \frac{4(N^2-3pN+4p-2)}{(N-p)^2(N-p+2)}.$$

One can similarly obtain

$$\mu_3 \simeq \frac{-32(p-1)(N^2-5pN+8p-4)}{(N-p)^3(N-p+2)(N-p+4)},$$

$$\mu_4 \simeq (3-6/N)[\mathscr{V}r]^2.$$

These can be used to approximate the distribution of

$$w = \frac{N^2r-(4p^2-1)}{4N^2-4p^2+2}$$

by a Beta distribution with parameters α and β determined by

$$\alpha = (N+p)/2,$$

$$\beta = (N-p+2)/2.$$

To summarize the state-of-the-art with regard to testing for independence in the linear expected value model, we know the following:

(a) If $\Sigma^{-1} = \theta(I + \xi A)$ and X is a linear combination of p characteristic vectors of A, then a test based on $\boldsymbol{r}$ (or equivalently on $\boldsymbol{w}$) is the likelihood ratio procedure.

(b) If $\Sigma^{-1} = \theta(I + \xi A)$ and X is not a linear combination of some p characteristic vectors of A, then nothing is known about properties of a test based on $\boldsymbol{r}$. In either case (a) or (b), though, the approximate distribution of $\boldsymbol{w}$ is appropriate.

(c) If Σ^{-1} is not of the form $\theta(I + \xi A)$ but is of the form $\Sigma^{-1} = \theta(I + \xi Y)$, then the likelihood ratio test described above depends on the characteristic roots of Y and on the assumption that X is a known combination of p characteristic vectors of Y. The approximate distribution of $\boldsymbol{r}$ has not been obtained for any particular choices of Y other than $Y = J$.

(d) If Σ is known, then the likelihood ratio procedure is based on $\boldsymbol{r}$ as given in case I.

(e) If Σ^{-1} is unknown and not of the form $\theta(I + \xi Y)$, nothing is known about test procedures for testing independence in the linear expected value model. Common practice is to use $\boldsymbol{r}$ as in (d) and use the a fortiori test procedure.

Exercise: Let $\Sigma = I + \rho A'C$, where A and C are known N-vectors. What is the likelihood ratio test of the hypothesis $\rho = 0$, given a sample $\boldsymbol{Y} = (\boldsymbol{y}_1, \ldots, \boldsymbol{y}_N)$ distributed as $N(BX, \Sigma)$ where B is an unknown p vector and X is a known $p \times N$ matrix?

6. Testing for identifiability

We consider here the problem of testing for the identifiability of a single equation in a system of simultaneous equations. We know that a necessary and sufficient condition for the first equation to be identifiable is that the rank of $\Pi_{(1\bar{1})}$ is $n_1 - 1$. There are two ways of interpreting the assignment of providing a test for identifiability. One is to test the rank condition against the hypothesis that the rank of $\Pi_{(1\bar{1})}$ is n_1. This corresponds to testing the model against the hypothesis that no structural equation holds. Another is to test the rank condition against the hypothesis that the rank of $\Pi_{(1\bar{1})}$ is at most $n_1 - 2$. This corresponds to testing the model against the hypothesis that a structural equation holds but is not unique.

In both tests we shall be using the likelihood function under the hypothesis that the rank of $\Pi_{(1\bar{1})}$ is $n_1 - 1$, which we saw in section 2 of chapter IV, was $(2\pi)^{-n_1N/2} e^{-N/2}$ times the quantity

$$\min_{B_{*1}} |\hat{\Omega}_{11}|^{-N/2} = |W|^{-N/2}(1+\theta_1)^{-N/2},$$

where θ_1 is the smallest characteristic root and $\hat{B}_{*1}$ the associated characteristic vector of $W^{-1}(W^* - W)$ defined above. Since W^* is positive semidefinite and W is assumed to be positive definite, by an easy extension of Theorem 8 we see that

$$|W^{-1}(W^* - W) - \theta I| = 0$$

implies that $\theta_1 \geqslant 0$, or $1 + \theta_1 \geqslant 1$. But this can be rewritten as

$$|(W^* - W) - \theta W| = 0.$$

We note that

$$\begin{aligned} N(\boldsymbol{W}^* - W) &= \boldsymbol{Y}'_{*1} S(S'S)^{-1} S' \boldsymbol{Y}_{*1} \\ &= (I - \hat{\boldsymbol{\Omega}}_{11} \hat{\boldsymbol{B}}'_{*1} \hat{\boldsymbol{B}}_{*1})^{-1} \hat{\boldsymbol{\Pi}}_{(1\bar{1})}(S'S) \\ &\quad \times \boldsymbol{\Pi}'_{(1\bar{1})}(I - \hat{\boldsymbol{\Omega}}_{11} \hat{\boldsymbol{B}}'_{*1} \hat{\boldsymbol{B}}_{*1})^{-1}. \end{aligned}$$

Now if the rank of $\Pi_{(1\bar{1})}$ is $n_1 - 1$, as $N \to \infty$ the plim of $\boldsymbol{\theta}_1$ will be 0, since the plim of $\boldsymbol{W}^* - \boldsymbol{W}$ will be the product of matrices one of which ($\Pi_{(1\bar{1})}$) will not be of full rank. If, however, the rank of $\Pi_{(1\bar{1})}$ is n_1, then as $N \to \infty$ the plim of $\boldsymbol{\theta}_1$ will be some positive number.

We are now ready to study the likelihood function for the two hypotheses of interest. In the case where the rank of $\Pi_{(1\bar{1})}$ is n_1, let us take the Λ matrix in the development of the likelihood function in section 2 of chapter IV to be the zero matrix. Then the likelihood function reduces to

$$(2\pi)^{-n_1N/2} e^{-N/2} |W|^{-N/2},$$

so that the likelihood ratio is

$$l = (1+\theta_1)^{-N/2}.$$

To test the null hypothesis that the rank of $\Pi_{(1\bar{1})}$ is $n_1 - 1$ against the alternative that it is n_1, we use $-2 \log \boldsymbol{l} = N \log(1 + \boldsymbol{\theta}_1)$ which is asymptotically distributed as a $\chi^2(p - p_1 - n_1 + 1)$ random variable. The degrees of freedom are obtained by noting that restricting the rank of the $n_1 \times (p - p_1)$ matrix $\Pi_{(1\bar{1})}$ to $n_1 - 1$ places $p - p_1 - (n_1 - 1)$ restrictions on $\Pi_{(1\bar{1})}$.

In the case where the rank of $\Pi_{(1\bar{1})}$ is $n_1 - 2$, let us reinterpret B_{*1} as a $2 \times n_1$ matrix and Λ as a $2 \times (p - p_1)$ matrix in the development of the likelihood function in section 2 of chapter IV. Then the likelihood function will be of the same form as in the case when the rank of $\Pi_{(1\bar{1})}$ is $n_1 - 1$, namely,

$$(2\pi)^{-n_1 N/2} \mathrm{e}^{-N/2} \min_{B_{*1}} |\hat{\Omega}_{11}|^{-N/2},$$

where $\hat{\Omega}_{11} = W + \theta(1+\theta) W \hat{B}'_{*1} \hat{B}_{*1} W$. Since here we require $\hat{B}_{*1}$ to be a $2 \times n_1$ matrix whose rows are not scalar multipliers of each other, we see that these rows must be the characteristic vectors associated with the two smallest characteristic roots of $W^{-1}(W^* - W)$.

The likelihood ratio is then

$$l = \frac{(1+\theta_1)^{-N/2}}{(1+\theta_1)^{-N/2}(1+\theta_2)^{-N/2}} = (1+\theta_2)^{N/2},$$

where we have set up the pair of hypotheses so that the null hypothesis is that the rank of $\Pi_{(1\bar{1})}$ is $n_1 - 2$ and the alternative hypothesis is that the rank is $n_1 - 1$, i.e., so that the null hypothesis is more restrictive of the parameter space than is the alternative. Nonetheless, we cannot in this case use $-2 \log \boldsymbol{l}$ as a χ^2 variable under the null hypothesis. This is due to the fact that under H_0 plim $\boldsymbol{\theta}_2$ = plim $\boldsymbol{\theta}_1 = 0$, and this "asymptotic confusion" between $\boldsymbol{\theta}_2$ and $\boldsymbol{\theta}_1$ violates some of the assumptions inherent in developing the asymptotic χ^2 distribution of $-2 \log \boldsymbol{l}$. One procedure, though, which leads to an approximate χ^2 test is to use $N \log(1+\boldsymbol{\theta}_1) + N \log(1+\boldsymbol{\theta}_2)$ as a test statistic, and this statistic is asymptotically distributed as a $\chi^2(p - p_1 - n_1 + 2)$ random variable.

7. References

The material in sections 1–3 are direct applications of the results of section 3 in chapter V above. The development in section 4 is based on:

Anderson, T. W., 1958, An introduction to multivariate statistical analysis (Wiley, New York).

The basic references for our treatment of testing for independence are:

Anderson, T. W., 1948, On the theory of testing serial correlation, Skandinavisk Aktuarietidskrift 31, pp. 88–116.

Durbin, J. and G. S. Watson, 1950, Testing for serial correlation in least squares regression, I, Biometrika 37, pp. 409–428.

The approximate distribution of r is based on:

Theil, H. and A. L. Nagar, 1965, Testing the independence of regression disturbances, Journal of the American Statistical Association 60, pp. 1067–1079.

The a fortiori test procedure is described in:

Kadiyala, K. R., 1970, Testing for the independence of regression disturbances, Econometrica 38, pp. 97–117.

The material on testing for identifiability is based on chapter VI (pp. 112–199) of the Hood–Koopmans book cited in section 8 of chapter IV, entitled "The estimation of simultaneous linear economic relationships", especially its section 8 and appendix G.

VII

A prolegomenon to econometric model building

The title of this chapter is pompous for a purpose, namely to attract you to this chapter and yet warn you not to read it with the same intensity with which you might read other chapters of this book. The intent of this chapter is to introduce to you issues in modelling which have been heretofore not mentioned, primarily because they do not fit into the assumption–theorem–proof style adopted throughout the book.

A prolegomenon is more than a prologue and less than a guidebook. It is a philosophical disquisition on a given subject. Since our subject is statistical methods as applied to econometric models, one might wonder why a prolegomenon on this subject appears at the end rather than the beginning of the book. The reason, if you have plowed through this far, is clear – the relation between econometric modeling and statistical methods for parameter estimation and hypothesis testing is that the former lags behind the latter. Since statistical methods are so complex for such simple-to-state models as the linear expected value model and its relative, the system of simultaneous linear equations, there is great incentive for econometric models to be a form for which statistical methods of estimation are well developed.

Note that all models studied earlier were formulated as linear in both the variables and the parameters. The critical linearity, though, is the linearity in the parameters, for it is this linearity which reflects itself in the ease with which parameter estimation methods can and have been developed. The purpose of this chapter is to describe prototypical sets of assumptions made in econometric modeling leading to model types which are linear in their parameters. We focus first on single-equation modeling in order to introduce some of these assumptions in a mathematically uncluttered context.

The rich variety of single-equation models linear in their parameters studied earlier include the structural and functional relation, the conditional expected value in a multivariate normal distribution, and the linear stochastic difference equation. The underlying motivation behind the use of such model types is their simplicity. This, buttressed by the central limit theorem which "justifies" the normality assumptions typically made in these models and by Taylor's theorem, which "justifies" the linearity as an approximation to whatever the true function is, leads modelers to develop linear single equation models as a matter of course.

The two major issues in single equation modeling are the proper interpretation of the so-called "error term" and the appropriate imputation of "causality" to the independent variables. We shall treat each of these issues in turn.

1. The error term in economic modeling

The task of economics is to describe, analyze, and explain, or, in one word, understand, economic phenomena. To understand a given economic phenomenon, one must first *identify all the factors* which together produce the phenomenon of interest. One must then be able to explain precisely how these factors interact and produce this phenomenon. This explanation may very well be a *narrative account* of what underlies the phenomenon. Usually, however, the relevant factors are all quantifiable factors, or, borrowing a term from mathematics, variables. One might then press on and *translate this narrative explanation into mathematical terms* as far as possible. This has the advantage of exhibiting concisely which economic variables are functionally related. It also has the advantage of exposing any incompleteness in the narrative.

Consider, for example, the following narrative: the current price of butter depends on the current available quantity of butter and the current price and quantity of margarine, and that as quantity of butter and/or margarine increase the price of butter will decrease and as price of margarine decreases the price of butter will decrease. If we let p_{B} and p_{M} be the price of butter and margarine and q_{B} and q_{M} be the quantity of butter and margarine, then we would rewrite this narrative as:

$$p_{\mathrm{B}} = f(q_{\mathrm{B}}, p_{\mathrm{M}}, q_{\mathrm{M}}),$$

$$\frac{\partial f(q_{\mathrm{B}}, p_{\mathrm{M}}, q_{\mathrm{M}})}{\partial q_{\mathrm{B}}} < 0,$$

$$\frac{\partial f(q_B, p_M, q_M)}{\partial p_M} > 0,$$

$$\frac{\partial f(q_B, p_M, q_M)}{\partial q_M} < 0.$$

One is then struck with the obvious incompleteness in the narrative: the function f is unspecified.

This narrative or these mathematical expressions suffice for some purposes, for example, to help a butter manufacturer decide whether or not to increase production of butter at a time when he is well satisfied with the current high price of butter. You will agree, however, that the task of economics to understand how and why the price of butter rises and falls is not completed with the pronouncement of these expressions. The function f must be specified.

We might rewrite our definition of the task of economics, then, as follows: the task of economics is to determine the specific relationships between the variables relevant to economic phenomena. Usually, though, the economist can only give the form of the relationships but not numeric formulae for the relationships. For example, one might be able to say that

$$p_B = f(q_B, p_M, q_M) = \alpha + \beta q_B + \gamma p_M + \delta q_M,$$

but he may not know the values of the coefficients α, β, γ, δ in the expression for f.

You might reply to this that all the economist must do is obtain observations on p_B, q_B, p_M, and q_M at four different times, $(p_B^{(1)}, q_B^{(1)}, p_M^{(1)}, q_M^{(1)})$, $(p_B^{(2)}, p_B^{(2)}, p_M^{(2)}, q_M^{(2)})$, $(p_B^{(3)}, q_B^{(3)}, p_M^{(3)}, q_M^{(3)})$, and $(p_B^{(4)}, q_B^{(4)}, p_M^{(4)}, q_M^{(4)})$, say, and solve the four linear equations

$$p_B^{(1)} = \alpha + \beta q_B^{(1)} + \gamma p_M^{(1)} + \delta q_M^{(1)},$$
$$p_B^{(2)} = \alpha + \beta q_B^{(2)} + \gamma p_M^{(2)} + \delta q_M^{(2)},$$
$$p_B^{(3)} = \alpha + \beta q_B^{(3)} + \gamma p_M^{(3)} + \delta q_M^{(3)},$$
$$p_B^{(4)} = \alpha + \beta q_B^{(4)} + \gamma p_M^{(4)} + \delta q_M^{(4)},$$

for α, β, γ, and δ.

This is of course correct, but suppose he does this and then observes a set $(p_B^{(5)}, q_B^{(5)}, p_M^{(5)}, q_M^{(5)})$ which does not satisfy the equation

$$p_B^{(5)} = \alpha + \beta q_B^{(5)} + \gamma p_M^{(5)} + \delta\delta q_M^{(5)},$$

where α, β, γ, and δ have been determined from the aforementioned four sets of observations. Should the economist then admit that his relationship is incorrect and renew his effort to understand how and why the price of butter fluctuates?

The answer to this question depends entirely on whether or not the economist has identified *all* the factors which together produce the phenomenon of interest. If he has, then he may still argue that the relationship is correct but that his observations are measurements of the relevant quantities which are obscured by error. He must then try to understand the nature of the errors in order to complete his understanding of the butter price fluctuations. Alternatively, he might argue that the relationship

$$p_B = \alpha + \beta q_B + \gamma p_M + \delta q_M$$

is merely a first-order approximation to the true relationship

$$p_B = f(q_B, p_M, q_M),$$

and that the discrepancy is due merely to this approximation.

If the economist has *not* identified all the factors, he might still argue that the effect of the additional unidentified factors is separable from that of those isolated, and so he might, in our example, say that

$$p_B = f(q_B, p_M, q_M) + g(\text{all other factors}),$$

where g is some unspecified function. The discrepancy between $p_B^{(5)}$ and $\alpha + \beta q_B^{(5)} + \gamma p_M^{(5)} + \delta q_M^{(5)}$ would then be attributed to the function g. If this discrepancy is small, then the economist can rightly claim that he understands the butter price fluctuations pretty well.

A typical offhand approach that many economists take to indicate that the relationship is imperfect is to write the model as

$$p_B = f(q_B, p_M, q_M) + u,$$

where u is a "disturbance" term which is usually assumed to be a random variable whose distribution is normal with mean zero. This is the rug under which much incomplete understanding of economic phenomena is swept. The precise specification and interpretation of this offhand model, though, depends on which of the three aforementioned arguments the economist uses to justify the imperfection of the relationship.

The concepts of functional and structural relationship introduced in chapter III are useful bits of terminology here. If indeed the relationship $p_B = f(q_B, p_M, q_M)$ is a functional relationship, then the economist should write

$$p_B^* = p_B + \boldsymbol{u} = f(q_B, p_M, q_M) + \boldsymbol{u},$$

and treat his observed dependent variables as random variables. This model is the simplest of the "errors-in-variables" models and corresponds to the first answer the economist above might give.

The model corresponding to the second answer is that in actuality the functional relationship is

$$\begin{aligned} p_B &= h(q_B, p_M, q_M) \\ &= f(q_B, p_M, q_M) + u(q_B, p_M, q_M), \end{aligned}$$

where u is an error term (in the error-of-approximation sense). Use of least squares in this case is justified not on the statistical grounds of minimum variance estimation but on the mathematical grounds of being the means of finding the best linear approximation of f given p_B, q_B, p_M, and q_M.

Similarly, if the relationship is a structural relationship $\boldsymbol{p}_B = f(\boldsymbol{q}_B, \boldsymbol{p}_M, \boldsymbol{q}_M)$ then the economist should write

$$\boldsymbol{p}_B^* = \boldsymbol{p}_B + \boldsymbol{u} = f(\boldsymbol{q}_B, \boldsymbol{p}_M, \boldsymbol{q}_M) + \boldsymbol{u},$$

as his model to account for the imprecision of his determination of $p_B^{*(5)}$ as $f(q_B^{(5)}, p_M^{(5)}, q_M^{(5)})$. If we condition the structural relationship model on the values p_B, q_B, p_M, q_M, of the random variables $\boldsymbol{p}_B$, $\boldsymbol{q}_B$, $\boldsymbol{p}_M$, $\boldsymbol{q}_M$, we can in this case also introduce $u(q_B, p_M, p_B)$ as in the functional relation case, and interpret the imprecision as an error of approximation.

Finally, we can arrive at a variant of this same model via a regression approach. Assuming that $\boldsymbol{p}_B$, $\boldsymbol{q}_B$, $\boldsymbol{p}_M$, and $\boldsymbol{q}_M$ are random variables, we can interpret $f(\boldsymbol{q}_B, \boldsymbol{p}_M, \boldsymbol{q}_M)$ not as a mathematical function relating the values of the random variables $\boldsymbol{p}_B$, $\boldsymbol{q}_B$, $\boldsymbol{p}_M$, and $\boldsymbol{q}_M$, but as the conditional expected value of $\boldsymbol{p}_B$ given $(\boldsymbol{q}_B, \boldsymbol{p}_M, \boldsymbol{q}_M) = (q_B, p_M, q_M)$. Thus, the discrepancy between any value of $\boldsymbol{p}_B$ and the concomitant value of $f(q_B, p_M, q_M)$ is due to sampling variability about $f(q_B, p_M, q_M)$. By a change of variable we can write

$$\boldsymbol{p}_B = f(q_B, p_M, q_M) + \boldsymbol{u},$$

where it is $\boldsymbol{p}_B$ and not $\boldsymbol{p}_B^*$ on the left-hand side of the relation.

If the economist has not identified all the factors but writes

$$p_B = f(q_B, p_M, q_M) + g(\text{all other factors}),$$

then, whether we interpret f as specifying a functional or structural relation, we still have the problem that our observed p_B is not equal to

$f(q_B, p_M, q_M)$. When g is explicitly a function of other factors, i.e., when we admit that the total relationship is not embodied in the function f, then we say that we have an "errors-in-equations" model. Once again we replace the term g(all other factors) by that portmanteau u and either call u an error of approximation or make some "distributional" assumption about u. In the latter case we are slipping away from our goal of determining mathematical relationships and are replacing genuine lack of knowledge with apparent statistical scatter. The variable u is usually called a "shock" or "disturbance" variable (to distinguish it from an "error" variable in the case where the relationship is deemed perfectly correct except for observational error), and is treated as a random variable in econometric modeling. This is done not because its origin is some stochastic process nor because it is in truth a random variable, but rather because it is a modeling convenience to do so. The "shock" model thus becomes a replica in form of the "error-in-variable" model described earlier.

2. Causality in economic models

In any mathematical relation in which $y = f(x_1, \ldots, x_n)$ it may be possible, depending on the nature of f, to express any x_i as $x_i = f_i(x_1, \ldots, x_{i-1}, x_{i+1}, \ldots, x_n, y)$. (It may be that one cannot find a closed-form function f_i to exhibit this expression explicitly for a given f.) This symmetric treatment of the variables $y, x_1, \ldots, x_n$, in mathematical relations is at variance with the roles of y and the x_i in economic models. Typically in these models y is to be predicted from the x_i, and so any mathematically equivalent formulations of the model in which y is an independent variable are not very useful to the economist. Moreover, the relation is usually functional, or, if structural, treated conditionally on the values of the independent variables, and the dependent variable (and none of the independent variables) is assumed to be measured with error. Thus, we would not naturally think of inverting the relation and expressing an x_i as a function of y and the remaining x's.

In the regression model, though, a kind of symmetry does prevail. Given a vector $(y, x_1, \ldots, x_n)$ we can ask for the conditional expected value of any one of the components of the vector given values of the rest of them. We would have $n+1$ functions,

$$\mathscr{E}\boldsymbol{y}|x_1, \ldots, x_n = f(x_1, \ldots, x_n)$$
$$\mathscr{E}\boldsymbol{x}_i|x_1, \ldots, x_{i-1}, x_{i+1}, \ldots, x_n, y = f(x_1, \ldots, x_{i-1}, x_{i+1}, \ldots, x_n),$$
$$i = 1, \ldots, n,$$

which could be rewritten, by making appropriate transformations of variables, as

$$\boldsymbol{y}^* = f(x_1, \ldots, x_n) + \boldsymbol{u},$$
$$\boldsymbol{x}_i^* = f_i(x_1, \ldots, x_{i-1}, x_{i+1}, \ldots, x_n, y) + \boldsymbol{v}_i.$$

But here f and f_i are not a pair of inverse mathematical functions, as they would be in a functional or structural relation model.

So far, though, we have merely looked at the "reversibility" of these models, without regard to the economic interpretations of the model in its original form and any of the inverse models. A basic use of a model is to predict a value of a dependent variable from values of the independent variables in the model. In the structural or functional relations, the model and any of the inverse models can be used to predict the actual value of the dependent variable. Only the choice of variable to be predicted, its designation as the dependent variable, and the mathematical existence of a function relating this dependent variable to the remaining set of variables, determine the prediction relation. In the regression relation, each regression function separately can be used to predict the expected value of the dependent variable.

The notion of causality enters when we impart causal (and not merely predictive) power to the independent variables. This notion is the subject of great philosophical deliberation and is difficult to define precisely. The lexical definition of a "cause", namely the uniform antecedent of a phenomenon, is of small value. It can help us, though, in listing some properties that a causal model should exhibit, namely (1) *predictability*: the relation should specify how the dependent variables changes for given changes in the independent variables, and (2) *manipulatability*: the independent variables must be changeable by outside agents.

That not all mathematically equivalent formulations of a functional or structural relation have causality associated with the selected independent variables is illustrated by the following example. Consider Boyle's law, $PV = \alpha T$, where P is pressure, V is volume, and T is temperature. Then

$$P = \alpha T/V, \qquad V = \alpha T/P,$$

and both these relations exhibit causality, in that for fixed T a manipulated change in V caused a change in P and vice versa. But $T = PV/\alpha$ does not exhibit causality, for, despite the fact that knowing P and V of a gas we can predict its T, we cannot arrange an experiment with a given gas in which P or V (or both) can be altered to effect the value of T. The temperature of a gas is not "caused" by the gas's pressure and volume.

There are many useful predictive models which are not causal models. All regression models are of this variety, since they are not functional or structural relations but are merely designed to predict the expected value (and not the value) of a dependent variable. Unfortunately, introduction of an error term in a relation beclouds the determination of whether the relation is caused or merely predictive. When the dependent variable is observed with error and one looks at the relation conditional on the independent variables, the three types of relation–regression, structural, and functional–look alike.

A standard warning in elementary statistics courses is: "correlation does not always imply causation". The usual implication of this dictum is that "sometimes correlation does imply causation". Our contention is contrary to this. Certainly correlation implies association in a bivariate distribution. Son's heights are associated with father's heights . . . but not caused by them. We save "causality" for use as a descriptor of a characteristic of a functional or structural relation.

3. Simultaneous equation model types

We introduced the simultaneous equation model as an offshoot of the "general linear hypothesis" or "vector regression" model in which the ith observed vector $\boldsymbol{Y}$ has expected values $\mathscr{E}\boldsymbol{Y}_i = X_i\Pi'$, namely this model with constraints on Π in terms of other parameters B and Γ. Our approach was not that associated with a causal model. In analogy with the similarity in form of the single-equation regression model and functional and structural relation with error in the dependent variable, one can reinterpret the reduced form of the simultaneous equation model as a structural relation with errors in the dependent variables. That model can be written, disregarding the normalization constraint, as

$$\boldsymbol{Y}_i = X_i\Pi' + \boldsymbol{V}_i, \quad i = 1, \ldots, N,$$
$$\Pi = -B^{-1}\Gamma.$$

The associated relation without error is

$$Y_i = X_i\Pi', \qquad i = 1, \ldots, N,$$
$$\Pi = -B^{-1}\Gamma,$$

or, in regression form,

$$y_{ji} = Y_{(j).i}B'_{*(j)} + X_{j.i}\Gamma'_{*j}, \qquad i = 1, \ldots, N, \quad j = 1, \ldots, n.$$

(The reader should forgive our inconsistency in using $\mathbf{Y}_i$ as $Y_i + \mathbf{V}_i$ instead of our usual $\mathbf{Y}_i^* = \mathbf{Y}_i + \mathbf{V}_i$.) If the variables in the model satisfy the requirements for a causal model set forth above, this model is called a *causal chain model.*

As was pointed out in section 3 of chapter IV, occasionally the exogenous variables are really random lagged values of the endogenous variables. Such a model is in violation of the basic assumptions of the general linear hypothesis, but is nevertheless also referred to as a simultaneous equation model. Such a model, without errors-in-variables, is the general case of the structural relation counterpart of the functional relation given above, namely,

$$\mathbf{y}_{ji} = \mathbf{Y}_{(j).i}B'_{*(j)} + \mathbf{X}_{j.i}\Gamma'_{*j}, \qquad i = 1, \ldots, N, \quad j = 1, \ldots, n.$$

Taking into account the error in the dependent variables of the reduced form, and, for the moment, assuming that $X_{j.i}$ is non-random, we have the *general interdependent model* (GEID),

$$\mathbf{y}_{ji} = \mathbf{Y}_{(j).i}B'_{*(j)} + X_{j.i}\Gamma'_{*j} - \mathbf{u}_{ji}, \qquad i = 1, \ldots, N, \quad j = 1, \ldots, n.$$

Though the GEID model's antecedent may have been a causal chain model, it is not, in that one of the variables on the right-hand side of the relation, $\mathbf{u}_{ji}$, is unobservable and not manipulatable.

The treatment presented in section 5 of chapter IV, in which we introduced the use of instrumental variables in estimating parameters of simultaneous equations, rested on replacing $\mathbf{Y}_*(j)$ with some "true value" $\bar{Y}_{*(j)}$ plus an error. This model is sometimes referred to as the *reformulated interdependent model* (REID). If all the $\mathbf{y}$'s, including $\mathbf{Y}_{j.}$ are replaced by their "true values", i.e., their expected values plus an error term, this model would be equivalent to a change of variable in the general linear hypothesis. In the extent that this is done selectively, and only $Y_{*(j)}$ is so expressed, to that extent do problems of interpretation arise. For if some elements of $Y_{*(j)}$ are left-hand side elements of the kth equation, i.e., elements of $Y_{k.}$, then by replacing these elements in $Y_{*(j)}$ but not in $Y_{k.}$ by their expected values one is not merely transforming the model mathematically. One is in fact creating a different model, not equivalent to the GEID model (except perhaps in the probability limit as the sample size gets large), wherein even the predictability of the model is doubtful.

One special model in which the REID is equivalent to a transformation on the GEID is a *recursive model.* This is a model in which B is a triangular matrix, i.e., where the equations are so ordered that the ith endogenous variable does not appear in equations $i = 1, \ldots, n$. Its interpretation (if the error term is disregarded) is that variable 1 depends on variables $2, \ldots, n$, variable 2 depends on variables $3, \ldots, n$, etc., so that a causal order relation between endogenous variables can be established (if the model passes the test for being a causal chain model). A generalization of this notion is the *block-recursive* model, wherein the endogenous variables can be grouped into s sets and the equations reordered so that no endogenous variables in set i appears in sets $i+1, \ldots, s$.

We have until now been taxonomic, describing some theoretical issues involved in modeling. Practically, though, how does one construct an econometric model of an economic phenomenon? There are two approaches, the "theory-driven" and the "variable-driven" approach. In the "theory-driven" approach one has a theory which is expressible mathematically and whose parameters are estimated from the necessary data. In the "variable-driven" approach, one begins by listing the set of relevant variables. Next one checks for interrelationships in the form of identities between variables. These are clearly structural or functional relationships, depending on the vector of the variables. Finally, one conjectures other relations between subsets of variables, and, using Taylor's theorem, linearizes them to get an additional set of approximate structural or functional relationships.

In either case, one gathers data and estimates the parameters of the model. Since all estimation procedures produce numbers, the issue of which procedure to use hinges on the robustness of the procedure to violation of its underlying assumptions and on the discrepancy from these assumptions. For example, LIML requires normality and a general linear hypothesis model, not typically the case for models developed as described above. Yet it may be very robust and give good results for structural relations with errors-in-variables.

The direction of my bias is clear. I prefer to see models clear in their assumptions, rather than models in which error terms are tacked on as a rug under which to sweep who-knows-what. Too much specification error is a consequence of this latter style of modeling. Econometric modeling is not a substitute for economic theory. Instead of using it to "fish" for a theory, the economist should use it properly to confirm deductions developed from economic theory.

4. References

Though the ideas expressed in this chapter are mine, they have been heavily influenced by reading the works of Wold, a recent reference being:

Wold, H. O. and E. J. Mosbaek, 1970, Interdependent systems (North-Holland, Amsterdam).

One should also read the material on errors and causality in the papers of J. Marshak, "Economic measurements for policy and prediction", and H. A. Simon, "Causal ordering and identifiability", respectively, both papers appearing in:

Hood, W. C. and T. C. Koopmans, 1953, Studies in econometric method (Wiley, New York).

An example of the "variable-driven" approach to modeling is the aggregative model in:

Klein, L. R., 1953, A textbook of econometrics (Row, Peterson and Co., Evanston).

Good examples of the "theory-driven" approach to modeling are given in:

Christ, C. F., 1966, Econometric models and methods (Wiley, New York).

Index